the
Vandals

The Peoples of Europe

General Editors
James Campbell and Barry Cunliffe

This series is about the European tribes and peoples from their origins in prehistory to the present day. Drawing upon a wide range of archaeological and historical evidence, each volume presents a fresh and absorbing account of a group's culture, society, and usually turbulent history.

Already published

The Etruscans
Graeme Barker and Thomas Rasmussen

The Byzantines
Averil Cameron

The Normans
Marjorie Chibnall

The Norsemen in the Viking Age
Eric Christiansen

The Lombards
Neil Christie

The Serbs
Sima Ćirković

The Basques*
Roger Collins

The English
Geoffrey Elton

The Gypsies
Second edition
Angus Fraser

The Bretons
Patrick Galliou and Michael Jones

The Goths
Peter Heather

The Franks*
Edward James

The Romans in the Age of Augustus
Andrew Lintott

The Vandals
Andy Merrills and Richard Miles

The Russians
Robin Milner-Gulland

The Mongols
Second edition
David Morgan

The Armenians
A. E. Redgate

The Britons
Christopher A. Snyder

The Huns
E. A. Thompson

The Early Germans
Second edition
Malcolm Todd

The Illyrians
John Wilkes

The Irish
Michael Herity

In preparation

The Spanish
Roger Collins

The Picts
Benjamin Hudson

The Angles and Saxons
Helena Hamerow

The Celts
John Koch

* Denotes title now out of print

the Vandals

Andy Merrills and
Richard Miles

WILEY Blackwell

This paperback edition first published 2014

Edition history: Blackwell Publishing Ltd (hardback, 2010)

Registered Office
John Wiley & Sons Ltd, The Atrium, Southern Gate, Chichester, West Sussex, PO19 8SQ, UK

Editorial Offices
350 Main Street, Malden, MA 02148-5020, USA
9600 Garsington Road, Oxford, OX4 2DQ, UK
The Atrium, Southern Gate, Chichester, West Sussex, PO19 8SQ, UK

For details of our global editorial offices, for customer services, and for information about how to apply for permission to reuse the copyright material in this book please see our website at www.wiley.com/wiley-blackwell.

Library of Congress Cataloging-in-Publication Data

Merrills, A. H. (Andrew H.), 1975–
The Vandals / Andy Merrills and Richard Miles.
p. cm. – (The peoples of Europe)
Includes bibliographical references and index.
ISBN 978-1-4051-6068-1 (hardcover : alk. paper) ISBN 978-1-118-78509-6 (pbk. : alk. paper)
1. Vandals. 2. Vandals–Africa, North–History. 3. Africa, North–History–To 647. 4. Mediterranean Region–History–To 476. 5. Mediterranean Region–History–476-1517. I. Miles, Richard, 1969– II. Title.
D139.M47 2010
939′.703–dc22 2009027226

A catalogue record for this book is available from the British Library.

Cover image: 'Wandalus', an imagined reconstruction of a Vandal by the Dutch printmaker Cornelius Visscher. Originally published in Peplus Gothorum, Herulum . . . by Pieter Soutmann (Harlem, 1650). © The Trustees of the British Museum.
Cover design by Nicki Averill

Set in 10/12pt Sabon by Graphicraft Limited, Hong Kong

1 2014

For Dick Whittaker

Contents

Illustrations

Preface

> They were inured to hardship and coarse diet, which with nourishing liquors and constant exercise, greatly contributed to their bodily strength. Their spirits were not exhausted by speculative studies, nor were they enervated by early debaucheries, but entirely employed in manly exercise.
>
> Thomas Nugent, *The History of Vandalia*, p. 50 (London, 1761)

The Vandals have not been treated kindly by history, or by historians. For almost a hundred years, the group exerted a massive influence over the crumbling Roman world. From AD 439 when the Vandals first occupied Carthage, they created a strikingly precocious kingdom in the shadow of the old empire. For half a century they dominated the politics of the Mediterranean, and for a further 50 years ruled a state which flourished both economically and culturally. But the end – when it came – was swift. In 534 the kingdom of Carthage was swept aside by the resurgent forces of Justinian's Byzantium, and the Vandals vanished forever.

In the twenty-first century, the Vandals are remembered primarily as a metaphor for violent and uncultured destruction – the linguistic creation of an imaginative priest who wrote in the aftermath of the French Revolution. Their cause has not been helped by a peculiar neglect among professional historians. Some dedicated histories of the group have been written – including some remarkable works of scholarship – but they have been thin on the ground. The study that follows is the first dedicated history of the group to be written in English. It draws upon much recent scholarship from North Africa, Europe, and the United States, but seeks to present an original and provocative account of this much-neglected group.

This book is a collaborative project, and the different perspectives of the two authors may occasionally be glimpsed in the chapters that follow. Chapters 1–6 were written by AHM, chapters 7–9 by RTM, but all have benefited from joint criticism and discussion. It is hoped that this collaborative approach will result in a more wide-ranging assessment of the Vandals than would have been possible for one author writing alone.

ACKNOWLEDGEMENTS

(AHM) Much of the research for this project was completed with the support of an RCUK Fellowship at the School of Archaeology and Ancient History at the University of Leicester. It also benefited from two long and pleasurable summers as a Margo Tytus Fellow in the Blegen Classics Library at the University of Cincinnati. I am particularly grateful to Getzel Cohen, Jacqueline Riley, and Mike Braunlin for their help there.

Many individuals helped enormously by reading individual chapters, and for suggesting many improvements. In particular Simon Loseby, Christina Pössel, Jen Baird, Lesley McFadyen, Neil Christie, Anna Leone, Guido Berndt, and Jeremy Taylor. David Mattingly and Dave Edwards also listened to many less structured ramblings on matters North African and shaped my thinking greatly. Bruce Hitchner, Rob Wanner, Dan Stewart, David Stone, Roland Steinacher, François Furstenberg, Mark Handley, Julia Farley, and Mark Gillings also helped with many specific points. Parts of chapters 1, 4, and 5 were presented in front of audiences in the universities of Birmingham, Nottingham, Manchester, Leicester, and Palermo, and I am grateful to all participants in those discussions for their suggestions, especially Doug Lee, David Langslow, Andy Morrison, Eric Blaum, Wolf Liebeschuetz, Robert Markus, and Roey Sweet.

(RTM) The majority of the research for the later chapters in this book was undertaken whilst I held a Friedrich Solmsen Fellowship at the Institute of Research into the Humanities at the University of Wisconsin-Madison. I would like to thank the Director, Professor Susan Stanford Friedman, and the Fellows of the Institute, as well as the extraordinary Loretta Freiling for creating such a hospitable and intellectually stimulating environment in which to work. A number of the ideas that appear in this book were first aired at seminars at the universities of Cambridge, Chicago, Wisconsin-Madison, Princeton, St Andrews, and the Society of Antiquaries of London. I would like to extend particular thanks to Peter Brown, Heimo Dolenz, Peter Garnsey, Christophe Goddard, Jill Harries, Walter Kaegi, David Morgan, Brent Shaw, and Claire Sotinel for their hospitality and invaluable feedback.

We are grateful to the British Museum for permission to reproduce Cornelius Visscher's 1650 print of a Vandal from their Prints and Drawings Collection, which provides the front cover of this book. The image of the Bord Djedid Mosaic and the selection of Vandal coins come from the same institution. We would also like to thank David Mattingly for his kind permission to reproduce the photographs at pp. 87, 155, 157, 207, 209, and 254, and Heimo Dolenz and Sue Stevens for permission to reproduce the images of the Byzantine churches in chapter 9.

In many ways, the genesis of this study can be attributed to Mike Clover who has provided invaluable support and encouragement to both of its authors. The book, however, is dedicated to the memory of Dick Whittaker, who passed away as it was being finished. Dick fought long battles on the Roman frontiers, recast Roman social and economic systems in important new ways, and was an individual who was well aware of the power of North Africa to challenge assumptions and preconceptions; the Vandals would have appreciated him.

Abbreviations

AE (date)	*L'Année épigraphique*
AJA	*American Journal of Archaeology*
AL R	*Anthologia Latina*, A. Riese (ed.), Teubner (Leipzig, 1894), partially tr. in Kay (2006) and Rosenblum (1961)
ALS	*Anthologia Latina* D. R. Shackleton Bailey (ed.), Teubner (Stuttgart, 1982), partially tr. in Kay (2006) and Rosenblum (1961)
ANSMN	*American Numismatic Society Museum Notes*
Ant. af.	*Antiquités africaines*
ARTB	*Art Bulletin*
AT	Albertini Tablets
BCTH	*Bulletin Archéologique de Comité des Travaux Historiques et Scientifiques*
Budé	Collection des Universités de France publiée sous le patronage de l'Association Guillaume Budé
BZ	*Byzantinischer Zeitschrift*
CEDAC	*Centre d'Etudes et de documentation Archéologique de la Conservation de Carthage*
CIL VIII	G. Willmans, T. Mommsen, R. Cagnal and J. Schmidt, *Corpus Inscriptionum Latinarum, VIII, Inscriptiones Latinae Africae* (Berlin, 1881)
Cod. Iust.	*Codicis Justiniani*, D. Albertus (ed.), *Corpus Juris Civilis*, vol. 2 (Leipzig, 1843)
CP	*Classical Philology*
CRAI	*Comptes-rendus des séances de l'Académie des inscriptions et belles-lettres*
CCL	*Corpus Christianorum Series Latina*
CSEL	Corpus Scriptorum Ecclesiasticorum Latinorum
CCSL	Corpus Christianorum Series Latina

C.Th.	*Codex Theodosianus*, T. Mommsen and P. Meyer (eds.), 3 vols. (Berlin, 1905); tr. C. Parr, *The Theodosian Code, Novels and Sirmondian Constitutions* (New York, 1950)
EME	*Early Medieval Europe*
FC	Fathers of the Church
FHG	*Fragmenta Historicorum Graecorum*
GCS	Griechische Christliche Schriftsteller der ersten drei Jahrhunderte
ILC	E. Diehl (ed.) *Inscriptiones Latinae Christianae Veteres* (Berlin, 1925–31)
ILT	A. Merlin (ed.) *Inscriptions Latines de la Tunisie* (Paris, 1944)
JECS	*Journal of Early Christian Studies*
JRA	*Journal of Roman Archaeology*
JRS	*Journal of Roman Studies*
JTS	*Journal of Theological Studies*
LCL	Loeb Classical Library
MEFRA	*Mélanges d'Archéologie et d'Histoire de l'École Française de Rome, Antiquité*
MGH	Monumenta Germaniae Historica
AA	Auctores Antiquissimi
Ep.	Epistolae
SRL	Scriptores Rerum Langobardicarum et Italicarum saec. VI–IX
SRM	Scriptores Rerum Merowingicarum
Not. Prov.	*Notitia provinciarum et civitatum Africae*, M. Petchenig (ed.), CSEL, 7 (Vienna, 1881), 118–134; S. Lancel (ed. and tr.), Budé (Paris, 2002)
Nov. Just.	Justinian I, *Novellae*, R. Schoell and W. Kroll (eds.), *Corpus Iuris Civilis*, III, 15th edn. (Berlin, 1970)
Nov. Theod.	*Theodosius II, Novellae*, in C.Th. vol. 2, pp. 1–68
Nov. Val.	*Valentinian III, Novellae*, in C.Th. vol. 2, pp. 69–154
NPNF	Nicene and Post-Nicene Fathers. Second series
OCT	Oxford Classical Texts
PBSR	*Proceedings of the British School at Rome*
PCBEA	Mandouze (ed.), *Prosopographie Chrétienne du Bas-Empire. 1. Prosopographie de l'Afrique chrétienne (303–533)* (Paris, 1982)
PG	*Patrologia Graeca*, ed. J.-P. Migne (Paris)
PL	*Patrologia Latina*, ed. J.-P. Migne (Paris)

PLRE II	J. R. Martindale, *The Prosopography of the Later Roman Empire. Vol. II.* AD *395–527* (Cambridge, 1980)
PLRE III	J. R. Martindale, *The Prosopography of the Later Roman Empire. Vol. III.* AD *527–641*. 2 vols. (Cambridge, 1992)
Procopius, *BV*	*De bello vandalico*, H. B. Dewing (ed. and tr.), LCL (Cambridge MA, 1914)
SC	Sources Chrétiennes
SCNC	Sources Chrétiennes. Sér Annexe de textes non chrétiens
SEG	*Supplementum Epigraphicum Graecum* (Leiden, 1923–)
TA (number)	Albertini Tablets, in C. Courtois, L. Leschi, C. Perrat and C. Saumagne (eds.), *Tablettes Albertini: actes privés de l'epoque vandale (fin du Ve siècle)*, 2 vols. (Paris, 1952)
TAPA	*Transactions of the American Philological Society*
Teubner	Bibliotheca scriptorum Graecorum et Romanorum Teubneriana
TRHS	*Transactions of the Royal Historical Society*
TTH	Translated Texts for Historians
Vict. Vit., *HP*	*Historia persecutionis*, M. Petchenig (ed.), CSEL, 7 (Vienna, 1881); S. Lancel (ed. and tr.), Budé (Paris, 2002); tr. J. Moorhead, *Victor of Vita: History of the Vandal Persecution*, Translated Texts for Historians, 10 (Liverpool, 1992)

1

The Vandals in History

The fifth century was a period of chaos within the Mediterranean world. As the political authority of the western Roman empire crumbled, powerful new groups rose to prominence in the provinces.[1] Among the most important were the Vandals. Under Geiseric, their most famous king, they invaded the rich Roman provinces of North Africa and captured the grand commercial city of Carthage in AD 439. For the next century, the Vandals prospered at the very heart of the dying empire. In AD 455, Geiseric unleashed a cataclysmic sack of the City of Rome, and Vandal piracy remained a constant plague on Mediterranean shipping for decades thereafter. Within North Africa itself, the century of Vandal rule was a period of extremes. Remembered by many for their heretical beliefs, and their vicious persecution of orthodox 'Nicene' Christians, the Vandals were also sensitive patrons of learning. Grand building projects continued, schools flourished and North Africa fostered many of the most innovative writers and natural scientists of the late Latin West.

The successes of the Vandals were intimately bound up in the prosperous kingdom which they inherited. At the height of the Roman period, North Africa had been a jewel in the imperial crown.[2] The wealth of the African cities, the rich grain fields of Zeugitana and Numidia, and the extensive olive groves of Byzacena and the Mauretanias had become almost proverbial by the early fifth century. An anonymous merchant of the fourth century described Africa as 'exceptional and admirable'; to Martianus Capella, a scholar of the fifth century, it was 'awesome in its prosperity'.[3] For two and a half centuries the African provinces had produced a massive agricultural surplus to be shipped to Rome as tax. Any grain, olive oil, wine and fish which were not appropriated by a hungry state had been sold, either within North Africa itself or in cities scattered around the Mediterranean. Not everyone in late Roman Africa was rich, but the region was certainly prosperous: its cities were ornamented with public buildings, baths, theatres and amphitheatres; olive oil burned

Figure 1.1 North Africa in the Vandal period

prodigiously in lamps throughout the region and farms continued to flourish in the countryside. Culturally, too, Roman North Africa was unusually vibrant. Christianity had been brought to the region during the second century AD, and thereafter the faith flourished there with particular strength. The African Church was defined by its saints and martyrs, but was shaped by its great theologians: Tertullian was prominent in the second century, Cyprian and Arnobius in the third, and Lactantius in the fourth. This tradition reached its peak with Saint Augustine, who was educated in the Carthage of the late fourth century, provided leadership as the bishop of the city of Hippo Regius in the early fifth, and eventually died in AD 430, as the Vandals lay siege to his adopted home.

Yet the Vandal kingdom proved to be short-lived. In AD 534, a little less than a century after they occupied Carthage, the Vandals lost the city, this time to the resurgent eastern Roman Empire of Justinian and his general Belisarius. Less than two centuries after that, this restored imperial authority was itself swept away by the expansion of the Islamic powers from the east. As a result, North Africa was dramatically severed from Europe, and a region which had once nestled at the very heart of the classical world was all but forgotten by the successor kingdoms of the west. The Vandals, too, drifted into obscurity. When the historians of these expanding Christian nations tried to make sense of the great decline of the Roman west, and developed heroic traditions around the Goths, Franks, Angles and Alemans, the Vandals were frequently cast aside as curious anomalies. With no historian to preserve 'their' side of the story, the Vandals were presented as cruel persecutors and violent savages, but also as once-proud barbarians who collapsed into moral degradation and lost themselves in the decadent excesses of the later Roman Empire, a pattern which dominated scholarship from the medieval period to the nineteenth century. Today, if the Vandals are remembered at all, it is through the negative associations of the term 'vandalism' – a censorious term for the wanton destruction of art and architecture that is shared by all of the major western European languages. Yet even here, the legacy of the group is uncertain. What was once a vivid metaphor for this destruction – Vandalism – has since lost its capital 'V', and with it its historical specificity. Even the popularity of this most chauvinistic of caricatures has not managed to save the Vandals from obscurity.

The present book is an attempt to re-assess the Vandals from the perspective of the twenty-first century. It adopts a critical new assessment of the textual sources available to us – these are many and varied, including the lives and writings of saints, formal histories, chronicles, letters, poems and estates records – and combines this with a detailed discussion of recent archaeological evidence. For the most part, then, it is a history of North Africa and the Mediterranean world in the fifth and sixth centuries AD. But the history of the Vandals did not simply end with the destruction of their kingdom. If the Vandals have slipped from the popular imagination in recent years, if images of fur-clad barbarians have been supplanted by graffiti artists or protesters as symbols of social instability, this in itself is an interesting legacy and deserves some attention.

This chapter will introduce the Vandals through the accounts of later writers – historians, novelists, playwrights and politicians, amongst others. These are arranged into three groups. The first considers the Romantic image of the Vandals, that is to say the more or less fictionalized use of the group within idealized accounts of prehistory or the medieval world. The second discusses the stereotype of the destructive Vandals, and the notion that the group was particularly violent, even by the standards of the time. The third examines the peculiar 'pan-Germanic' discourse which presented the Vandals as a specifically *German* people, and which sought to associate their portentous name with the ruling aristocracies of different Scandinavian and German territories in the early modern period. These sections are primarily concerned with later medieval and early modern accounts – down to the end of the eighteenth century. Although images of 'Romantic', 'destructive' and (especially) 'Germanic' Vandals continued to circulate in the nineteenth and twentieth centuries (and indeed remain in popular currency), important changes in the writing of history from the end of the eighteenth century transformed scholarship on the group. The final section of the introduction discusses the emergence of modern historiography on the Vandals down to the present day, and explains the ambitions for the current book within this context.

'The Romantic Vandals'

Within a generation of the fall of Carthage in AD 534, historians began to manipulate Vandal history to their own ends. The Vandals, after all, had risen from relative obscurity to a position of extraordinary authority within the Mediterranean in a remarkably short time, and then just as quickly had disappeared from view. Such a bizarre trajectory proved irresistible to historians who were anxious to identify moral exempla in a changing world.

One of the first of these writers was the historian Jordanes, a minor civil servant who wrote his *History of the Goths* (commonly known as the *Getica*) in Constantinople in the mid 550s.[4] The *Getica* is an important source for Byzantine history at the time of Justinian's reconquest, and will be used frequently in the study that follows, but the chauvinism of his treatment of the Vandals is apparent throughout. Within the *Getica*, the Goths are the obvious heroes – Jordanes himself claimed to be of Gothic stock, and his history was composed in part as a celebration of Justinian's achievement in overcoming the Ostrogothic kingdom in Italy. The Vandals, by contrast, appear in consistently negative terms. Jordanes shows a grudging respect for their great king Geiseric (and his thumbnail sketch of the stocky, limping ruler is our only description of this key figure), but his followers are cast as weak-kneed cowards. The first movement of the Vandals into the empire is presented as the consequence of a massive defeat at the hands of the Goths; the invasion of Africa is similarly regarded as an example of Vandal cowardice in the face of the recent arrival of a Gothic army in Spain, and the complex diplomatic manoeuvrings of the early sixth century are predictably presented in terms which favour the Goths over their long-standing enemies.[5] Persuasive as Jordanes' narrative details can be, it is the striking consistency of this view of animosity between the two peoples (and the one-sided nature of their conflicts) which suggest that the historian was simply using the Vandals as a useful device for highlighting the strengths of the Goths. As a once-powerful group, the Vandals made worthwhile antagonists for Jordanes' heroes, as a group who had vanished from the political map at the time of his writing, they were a perfect – and uncomplaining – foil.

Jordanes' contemporary Procopius projected a rather different image of Vandal decline in his Greek *Histories of the Wars*. Like Jordanes, Procopius wrote during Justinian's western campaigns, and was himself directly involved in Belisarius' conquest of North Africa and Italy.[6] Where Jordanes remains positive about these long wars, however, Procopius is palpably more cynical, and his regard for the eastern empire seems to have cooled substantially as the reconquest wore on. Consequently it is not surprising that Procopius puts forward a more positive image of the Vandals than Jordanes did. For him, the collapse of the kingdom was not due to the inherent cowardice of the group, but rather to a tragic susceptibility to the temptations of the Mediterranean world:

> For the Vandals, since the time when they gained possession of Libya, used to indulge in baths, all of them, every day and enjoyed a table abounding in all things, the sweetest and best that the earth and sea produce. And they wore gold very generally, and clothed themselves in the Medic garments,

> which now they call 'seric' and passed their time, thus dressed, in theatres and hippodromes and in other pleasurable pursuits, and in all else in hunting. . . . and they had a great number of banquets and all manner of sexual pleasures were in great vogue among them.[7]

Procopius is not just talking about the Vandals here, of course: he is using the tragic decline of the kingdom of Carthage as a moral lesson for his readers. Later in the same passage, the historian goes on to talk about the Moors – the barbarians of the African mountains and pre-desert who continued to resist the Byzantine conquest. By contrast, the Vandals had lost their own barbaric vigour through their extended contact with the enervating luxuries of Carthage: a clear moral message to readers who had been brought up in just such an environment of theatres, hippodromes and fine dining.

Other historians of the early middle ages also found the Vandals to be useful illustrations for their more complex arguments. Isidore of Seville, who composed a bewildering variety of works in Visigothic Spain in the early seventh century, included an epilogue on the History of the Vandals to his long (and carefully crafted) *History of the Goths*.[8] Like Jordanes, Isidore sought to contrast the fate of the Goths and the Vandals, but while the earlier historian had depicted two peoples in more or less permanent opposition, the Spanish historian presented the narratives of the two kingdoms side-by-side. For Isidore, the decline of the kingdom of Carthage could be explained by the refusal of the Vandal kings to convert from the Arian heresy to Nicene Catholicism and by their failure to move beyond the internecine squabbling of their troubled early history. The Goths, by contrast, had converted to the historian's own faith, and had established a strong monarchy. Again, the Vandals provided a useful moral and political counterpoint for the historians of other groups.

Historians of the Lombards, another barbarian group, followed the lead set by Jordanes in their treatment of the Vandals. In the seventh century the anonymous author of the *Origo gentis Langobardorum* (Origin of the Lombard People) suggested that the Lombards had defeated the mighty Vandals at a formative stage of their prehistory. The account, in which the twins Ibor and Aio use some quick-witted hairdressing tricks to defeat the Vandal heroes Ambri and Assi before the benevolent gaze of the god Wodan, and hence earn their name 'Long-beards', must have been a recently coined myth, rather than a long-standing historical tradition.[9] The same narrative was then taken up in modified form in the eighth-century *History of the Lombards* by Paul the Deacon.[10] For the *Origo* author and for Paul, it was victory over the proud Vandals which won the Lombards the support of the gods – a triumph which was meaningful largely because of the later prominence (and decline) of the kingdom of Carthage. Here, the Vandals are little more than ahistorical monsters, lent a particular impact by the obvious resonance of their name.

The Vandals also had a role in the ecclesiastical histories and saints' lives of the medieval period. Gregory of Tours, a Gallic writer of the late sixth century, presents a garbled image of Vandal Africa as a violent, dysfunctional and heretical kingdom in his long history of early Merovingian Frankia. The Vandal kings of his account are more or less recognizable early medieval rulers, and may well have been drawn from a lost African source, but bear the obvious marks of caricature.[11] This is still clearer in Agnellus of Ravenna's eighth-century *Book of the Pontiffs of the Church of Ravenna*, in which an unnamed Vandal king is said to have wished to plunder a rich church of the city, some 20 years after the final defeat of the group.[12] Similar traditions abound in Italian and French hagiography, and the mysterious African barbarians proved to be a popular ingredient in countless exotic religious traditions.[13]

The Vandals were peripheral in the chivalric myths of the later middle ages. No members of the group appear in the *Nibelungenlied*, the Arthurian cycle, or the poems of the Cid, all of which helped to secure the position of the earlier medieval period in the romantic imagination. There is a brief allusion to the Vandals in *Don Quixote*, Cervantes' great pastiche of the chivalric tradition. A brief episode in the second book describes Don Quixote's meeting with the Knight of the Mirrors, heart-sick for the beautiful Casildea de Vandalia.[14] This imagined land of Vandalia is a mythologized rendering of al-Andalus, (or Andalusia) in the south of Spain, a place-name which had long been associated with the Vandals, for obvious reasons, but which had no direct historical connection with the group.[15] Cervantes' allusion does not amount to much in itself, but it does show that the Vandals retained some positive associations (albeit of a rather peripheral kind).

But the Vandals were not forgotten entirely. The group are included briefly in the sprawling early seventeenth-century novel sequence *L'Astrée*, originally written by Honoré D'Urfé from 1607, and completed by Balthasar Baro after D'Urfé's death in 1625.[16] For much of its length, *L'Astrée* is a bucolic romp through fifth-century Gaul, in which the grim realities of late Roman society are replaced with an idealized image of Merovingian and Gallo-Roman chivalry. A similar tone is maintained in a substantial passage in Balthasar Baro's fifth book, when the action briefly switches to Vandal Carthage.[17] In a plot loosely based upon the Vandal sack of Rome in AD 455 and the kidnap of the imperial women (a historical episode discussed more fully in chapter 4, below), Baro traces a complex web of courtship and love. Two Roman knights, Olimbre and Ursace, are smitten with the imperial women and seek to win their freedom. Obstructing them are the ambitions of the Vandal king Génseric (Geiseric) and the rather more wholesome love of his son Trasimond (Thrasamund). The plot takes several turns, including a North African beach scene and a substantial palace fire lifted almost directly from the pages of the *Aeneid*, but all turns out well in the end – the heart of the king is softened, and the various couples are allowed to attend to their nuptials in freedom.

This short episode was revisited twice over the course of the seventeenth century, in two plays inspired by the text. The first of these was *Eudoxe* (1641), a tragi-comedy by Georges de Scudéry, written in a period which saw several plays and poems on a late Roman theme.[18] The second was a rather bloodier (and rather more successful) tragedy, *Genseric*, composed by Mme Deshoulières for the Hôtel de Bourgogne in 1680.[19] Both plays largely kept the structure of Baro's text, but by the final version, the optimistic and bucolic tone had been entirely erased. In Deshoulières' *Genseric*, the Roman knights are entirely absent, and are replaced with a tragic African princess, Sophronia. By the end of the play Sophronia, Trasimond and the imperial princess Placidia lie as corpses on the floor of the stage and the two remaining principals – Genseric and the empress Eudocia – are left to live out a life of mutual hatred together.

The Vandals never dominated in popular narratives of the fall of Rome, but they did appear in some surprising contexts in the seventeenth and eighteenth centuries. Nicholas Brady's 1692 play *The Rape Or the Innocent Imposters* was a tragi-comedy about a star-crossed (and cross-dressing) royal couple at the court of the Vandal king Gunderic. In its heady mixture of extraordinary violence and sexual ambivalence, it neatly encapsulates one popular view of the tyrannical and corrupt Vandals.[20] A year later Johann Georg Conradi's opera *Geiseric: The Great King of the African Vandals* was performed for the first time in Hamburg.[21] This was one of the earliest operas with a 'barbarian' theme – a motif explored more fully by Jomelli and Handel during the eighteenth century, and by Richard Wagner in the nineteenth. Incidentally, its revival in the 1720s was the first opera to be reviewed in Matthesen's influential periodical *Critica Musica*.[22]

The Vandals were not central figures in this imaginative tradition, but they were familiar enough as supporting players. Much the same was true of the genealogical associations which developed around the group.

From the early sixteenth century, the Swedish and Danish royal families and the Dukes of Mecklenburg (later Mecklenburg-Strelitz) on the Baltic coast of Germany all claimed that they were descended from the Vandals, among other barbarian peoples.[23] Among the Swedes and Danes this was simply one claim among many – a point illustrated particularly clearly in the Swedish royal title *Svecorum Gothorum Vandalorumque rex* ('King of the Swedes, Goths and Vandals'), and in the three crowns of the Swedish royal standard. In Mecklenburg-Strelitz the claim to Vandal heritage was taken more seriously, and was based in part upon a convenient conflation of the Vandals who were supposed to have originated in the area, with the Slavic Wends, who settled there in the eighth century AD. These claims to Vandal royal heritage crossed the channel into Britain through the marriage of Charlotte of Mecklenburg-Strelitz to George III in 1761, and from there (perhaps surprisingly) migrated still further west to the American colonies.

In the early 1770s, the Grand (or 'Great') Ohio Company proposed to establish a new colony in the lands of the Ohio River Valley to the west of the Alleghenies: roughly the area that is now West Virginia and north-eastern Kentucky.[24] Among the names proposed for this putative colony (which won support from Ben Franklin, among others), was 'Vandalia', in honour of the Queen consort.[25] Despite a decade of wrangling, the proposal was not taken up, and both the proposed colony and its name were quietly shelved after the American Revolution. In spite of this, the dim traces of the 'Romantic' image of the Vandals may still occasionally be discerned in the United States today. A handful of settlements in the Midwest still bear the name Vandalia, including a city in Illinois, which was briefly the state capital. Still further west, the sports teams of the University of Idaho are collectively known as 'The Vandals' – a last idealized memory of the barbarian group.

'The Destructive Vandals'

This idealization of the Vandals lasted from Procopius to Franklin, but was not to survive in popular currency much longer. In 1794, less than two decades after the abandonment of the planned 'Vandalia' colony, the French Bishop Grégoire de Blois coined the phrase 'Vandalisme' to refer to the widespread destruction of works of art in the aftermath of the French Revolution.[26] Within months, the term had been adopted by journalists throughout Europe, by 1798 it had been enshrined in the *Dictionnaire de l'Académie Française*, and by the early years of the nineteenth century the term was a commonplace in all of the major European languages. From then on, the Vandals were no longer remembered simply as one barbarian group among many, but as particularly powerful agents of destruction. 'Vandalisme', 'vandalismo', 'Vandalismus' and 'vandalism' increasingly came to define the way in which the barbarian kings of Carthage were remembered.

Bishop Grégoire himself (or the Abbé Grégoire, as he is most commonly known) was a prominent Revolutionary and a devout French Catholic. Best remembered now for his agitation against racial discrimination within the Revolutionary state, his putative formulation of a national policy on heritage was a relatively minor feature of an impressive curriculum vitae. In his *Rapports sur le vandalisme* (Reports on Vandalism), issued in the summer of 1794, Grégoire advocated a national policy of protection for the arts. In doing so, he drew upon an existing stereotype of the Vandals. Whilst many historians, poets and playwrights regarded the group relatively fondly, the collapse of the western Roman empire was still viewed with a sort of awed horror, and the Vandals were among the barbarians felt to have been responsible. Consequently, the group had long been viewed as agents of destruction, even as they appeared in Romantic novels and elaborate genealogies. In a letter to Pope Leo X in 1517 for example, the artist Raphael condemned the builders of modern Rome, who plundered ancient ruins to beautify their own houses as 'Goths and Vandals'.[27] Rather closer to Grégoire in time, and feasibly a direct influence upon him, was the English poet William Cowper. In circumstances strikingly similar to those faced by the French Abbé, Cowper lamented the destruction of the library of Lord Mansfield during the Gordon riots of 1780:

> So then – the Vandals of our isle, | Sworn foes to sense and law, | Have burnt to dust a nobler pile | Than ever Roman saw![28]

Other references abound. Alexander Pope referred to the decadent Catholic Church as 'these Holy Vandals' in his vitriolic *Essay on Criticism* in 1711; in 1734, John Theophilus Desaguliers happily condemned Descartes and all opponents of Isaac Newton as 'this army of Goths and Vandals in the philosophical world'.[29]

Grégoire, then, drew upon a well-established tradition in invoking the barbarians of the dark ages to express his horror at contemporary events. Prior to Grégoire, however, that it was the Goths, rather than the Vandals, who were the most common emblems of barbarian destruction. While the Vandals do feature occasionally in these jeremiads, the Goths appear with almost monotonous regularity. Indeed, the negative associations of the group were so strong that Gibbon remarked in the tenth chapter of his *The Decline and Fall of the Roman Empire*:

> So memorable was the part which they acted in the subversion of the Western empire that the name GOTHS is frequently but improperly used as an appellation of rude and warlike barbarism.[30]

Two decades after Gibbon had published this observations, Grégoire's coinage had made it redundant. From 1794 on, it was the Vandals who stood as symbols for the violent destruction in the Age of Revolutions. Grégoire's motives in making the Vandals as the point of his metaphor are not clear. 'Vandalisme' certainly has a pleasing phonic quality, and trips off the tongue more readily than 'Gothicism' or (say) 'Langobardisme', and it is likely that this influenced the initial coinage of the term, and would certainly have helped its later popularity. While the Goths were familiar characters in the popular imagination, moreover, and had lent their name to styles of medieval architecture and an embryonic form of literature, the Vandals had few such associations: in invoking the Vandals, therefore, Grégoire did not have to compete with other contrasting usages. Finally (and perhaps most importantly), the short Vandal occupation of Gaul in AD 406–9 had become a subject of considerable interest to French historians of the seventeenth and eighteenth centuries as a particularly vivid episode in the great narrative of Roman decline. While many of these historians shared the idealized view of fifth-century history propounded by poets like D'Urfé and Baro, they regarded the Vandals as violent interlopers within this world, and were scathing in their criticism of the group.[31] Grégoire knew his history (and particularly his French history), and may well have been drawn by these traditions in his condemnation of the most zealous revolutionaries. Probably influenced by all of these factors, and apparently indifferent to the more positive associations that the group enjoyed at the time of writing, Grégoire cheerfully determined that the Vandals would forever be remembered as the agents of destruction.

'The German(ic) Vandals'

Grégoire's calumniation of the Vandals was met with horror from some quarters. The bishop himself acknowledged this controversy in his *Mémoires*:

> Those respected scholars, born in that part of Germany, whence the Vandals had once come, claimed that the meaning which I gave to the term 'vandalisme' was an insult to their ancestors, who were warriors, and not destroyers.[32]

These critics actually went rather further than Grégoire was willing to admit. Influenced by the historian August Ludwig von Schlözer, the scholar and travel writer Friedrich Meyer attacked Grégoire's chauvinism in his *Fragments sur Paris*, published in 1798. His argument includes the improbable defence that Geiseric's thorough despoliation of Rome in AD 455 indicates that the Vandals were connoisseurs of art, and not mindless barbarians, and ends with a passionate plea to his French audience to end the unjust denigration of a proud and free 'German' people.[33] This plea fell on deaf ears, of course, and most contemporaries probably shared Grégoire's view that the hurt feelings of a few German scholars were largely immaterial in the face of more pressing social concerns, but the objection highlights a third view of the Vandals within early modern society.

The complaints of von Schlözer and Friedrich Meyer demonstrate that the historical Vandals of the fifth century had not been entirely forgotten amid the romanticism and hostility of the seventeenth and eighteenth. Their insistence upon a direct connection between the Vandals of the early medieval period and the inhabitants of the modern Germany also highlights a central theme within much of the historical scholarship of this period. For many historians and antiquarians of the Enlightenment, the study of prehistory and the migration period was not simply an academic pursuit, it was the search for national origins.

During the sixteenth and seventeenth centuries the first reliable editions of texts relating to the history of the Vandals became available. It was the rediscovery of Tacitus' *Germania* during the fifteenth century which had the greatest effect upon the study of all 'barbarian' groups, including the Vandals.[34] The *Germania* was written in the late first century AD, and is largely concerned with the detailed description of the politics and social practices of the inhabitants of the lands beyond the Rhine and the Danube, chiefly as a contrast to what Tacitus perceived to be the moral failings of the contemporary Roman world.[35] The first printed edition was published in 1470, and the text attained particularly wide readership through the scholarly edition of Justus Lipsius in 1575.[36] To the Northern European humanists of the sixteenth century, the *Germania* promised a revolution in the understanding of the distant past. Tacitus seemed to offer a perfect taxonomy of ancient Germanic culture to a scholarly world increasingly captivated by the order and patterns they felt to be inherent in nature. At the centre of their reading of Tacitus was the notion of the Germani as a distinct biological group – proud, martial and morally superior to the peoples around them. Tacitus' statement that the Germani were divided into smaller subgroups, including the Marsi, Gambrivii, Suebi and (crucially) the Vandilii, could then be used as the starting point for the investigation of specific Germanic 'peoples', linked by blood and culture to their neighbours, but each worthy of historical study in its own right. Passing references in other classical sources – like the Elder Pliny's *Natural History*, or Ptolemy's *Geography* – could then be stitched together in a more or less coherent composite image of a thriving German 'golden age'. When coupled with early medieval texts, like Jordanes' *Getica* and Paul's *History of the Lombards*, which described the fourth- and fifth-century migrations of groups with the same names, the armature for coherent histories of these 'tribes' or 'peoples' came into focus. As shall be discussed, attitudes to ethnicity, particularly of the 'Germanic' barbarians, have been utterly transformed over the last two generations, but the notion of distinct, identifiable 'peoples' as worthy subjects of history was a dominant theme of antiquarian scholarship from the sixteenth and seventeenth centuries down to the middle of the twentieth.

Other texts were also examined critically by these manuscript scholars, and began to circulate in ever-improving scholarly editions. The *Historia Persecutionis* of Victor of Vita was perhaps the most important of these, and remains a text of central importance to the understanding of the Vandals. Originally written in the late 480s by a vicious critic of the Vandal kingdom, and largely concerned with the sufferings of the Catholics under their rule, the *Historia* widely circulated in manuscript form during the medieval period. From the late fifteenth century the *Historia* appeared in print, and several different translations into modern languages were known in the sixteenth and seventeenth, including one (now lost) Italian translation by Niccolo Machiavelli.[37] Most important was the edition with extensive notes produced by Thierry Ruinart in 1694, which provided a platform for all subsequent scholarship on the text. Procopius' Greek *History of the Wars* is the other crucial text for the study of Vandal history.[38] The African sections provide a detailed account of the fall of the Vandal kingdom, as well as some discussion on the background of the group. Like Victor, Procopius had long been known to scholars and his text had circulated for centuries in a variety of Latin translations. Surprisingly, printed Latin translations of the work were published only relatively late, and those relating to the Vandals were the last to appear. The text became known widely to western European scholars through Hugo Grotius' compilation *Historia Gotthorum, Vandalorum et Langobardorum* in 1655, and later in a similar compilation of Lenain de Tillemont in the early eighteenth century.[39]

This interest in the critical compilation of classical and medieval histories coincided with a growing fascination with the physical remains of the European past, as well as with the gradual rise to prominence of confident new early modern monarchies, particularly in the north of the continent. The result was the efflorescence of a variety of new 'national' histories from the early sixteenth century. Drawn by the wealth of newly uncovered historical material, scholars turned again to the twilight years of the Roman empire and the early centuries of the medieval period in the search for their national origins. François Hotman suggested that the political systems of contemporary France were to be found in the peculiar fusion of Gallic and Frankish identities from the sixth century in his *Franco-Gallia* (1573) – a lead that was widely followed over the course of the following century.[40] Scholars like Olaus and Johannes Magnus, and Drouet de Mauperty traced the origins of the Swedish monarchy to the heroic Gothic past, in the direct hope of winning royal favour.[41] Robert Sheringham's *De Anglorum gentis* in 1670 identified the origins of the English among the Angles, just as Johann Jacob Mascov's, *Geschichte der Teutschen* (1726–37) traced modern German identity to the Germani known to Tacitus.[42] Politically infused as these histories certainly were, all demonstrated a fascination with the minutiae of human history that reflected the scholarly spirit of the age.

The Vandals were generally shunned by these scholars for two reasons. First (and most obvious) was the fact that the Vandals established their kingdom in North Africa – a region that was later to be occupied during the Arab conquests of the later seventh century and consequently absorbed within the broader cultural milieu of Islam. When the scholars of seventeenth- and eighteenth-century Europe came to write the histories of 'their' nations, then, few had any particular interest in a long-forgotten group on the Barbary coast. Second was the fact that no major 'Vandal' history, written by the group itself survived from antiquity. While captivating narratives like the *Getica* or the *History of the Lombards* were not the only means by which the early modern scholars could investigate the medieval past, they did provide inspiring heroic stories and clear, coherent narratives to make sense of the jumbled world of the fifth and sixth centuries. Consequently, the absence of a similar 'Vandal' history deprived later historians of an obvious narrative scaffold against which to construct their own histories.

As we have seen, however, Baltic royalty and their court historians were not above claiming descent from the Vandals when this would add an extra crown to their coat of arms, and this proved to be a major catalyst to serious academic scholarship. To accomplish this, scholars concentrated upon the supposed prehistory of the Vandals within the north, and regarded their successes in North Africa as tangential to an essentially *European* history.[43] One of the earliest writers to attempt to compose a dedicated Vandal history was Albert Krantz, a professor at the University of Rostock, who composed his *Wandalia* in 1517 in honour of the Duke Magnus von Mecklenburg.[44] Krantz was not interested in telling the history of the Vandal state in Africa (although a brief narrative of the history of the kingdom of Carthage is included in his opening chapters). Instead, his concern was to locate the Vandals within the modern political map of Europe, and the approach which he adopted goes some way toward explaining the peculiar claims of the Baltic aristocracy to Vandal heritage. At the centre of Krantz's argument was the assumption that the Hanseatic towns of Lübeck, Rostock, Stralsrund, Greifswald, Elbingen, Konigsberg, Wismar and Lueneburg could trace their origins to a Vandal past. In fact, the towns were commonly assumed to have Slavic origins, but in certain medieval traditions the name 'Wenden' (or 'Wends') was frequently employed to refer to the Slavs of this region, and the towns were collectively known by the Latin term *vandalicae urbes* ('Vandal' or 'Wendish' towns – the ambiguity is important). By systematically conflating ancient references to the 'Vandals' with medieval references to the 'Slavs' or 'Wends', Krantz was able to provide these towns with a proud antiquity that was at least the equal of others' pretensions to Gothic ancestry. This confusion of the Wends and the Vandals did not withstand scholarly scrutiny for long, but proved to be so convenient politically that it took a long time to disappear entirely. In 1555, the Polish scholar Martin Cromer convincingly refuted Krantz's argument, only to see the *Wandalia* reprinted in 1575. Thereafter, a succession of Swedish and Finnish antiquarians returned to the issue throughout the seventeenth and eighteenth centuries.[45]

Two further studies of the Vandals were written during the later eighteenth century. The first of these, Thomas Nugent's *The History of Vandalia*, comprises a detailed history of Duchy of Mecklenburg from the Roman period to the later Middle Ages and was inspired by the marriage of George III to Charlotte of Mecklenburg-Strelitz in 1761.[46] As might be expected, Nugent followed German practice in focusing upon the supposed homeland of the barbarians, rather than their excursions in the empire, but an opening section does briefly consider the kingdom established by Geiseric in Carthage. Far more impressive from a scholarly point of view, and less immediately compromised by issues of royal genealogy, was Konrad Mannert's *Geschichte der Vandalen*, arguably the first narrative history of the Vandals worthy of the name. In striking contrast to Krantz and his successors, Mannert focused primarily upon the history of the Vandals within the empire, and argued that the Slavic occupation of the Vandals' original homeland had effectively ended their history as a 'German' people.[47] Mannert passes over the prehistory of the group relatively quickly, and closes his account with the Byzantine occupation of Carthage in 534. This was an approach which was to prove popular among the great German scholars of the nineteenth century, but was unusual among the continental historians of the eighteenth.

By the end of the eighteenth century, the basic outlines of Vandal history were clear. Although the confusion between the Vandals and the Wends had generally been resolved, the history of the Vandals remained an essentially northern European history. For scholars like Krantz or Nugent, the Vandals' occupation of North Africa was a largely peripheral episode to a proud European history. These historians regarded the passing references in Pliny, Tacitus and Ptolemy as proof positive that the Vandals had originated in the German territories, and most probably in the lands around the mouth of the Vistula. This approach was based more on tradition and scholarly consensus than on anything else. By contrast, the history of the group within North Africa – the period of Vandal history for which we have by far the greatest body of evidence – was relatively neglected, and came to be represented by a small handful of illustrative episodes.

The Vandals in the Nineteenth and Twentieth Centuries

After the publication of Gibbon's colossal *The Decline and Fall of the Roman Empire* in the 1770s and 1780s, the study of the *Völkerwanderungzeit* or 'migration period' was dominated by scholars in Germany and France. Throughout the nineteenth century, considerable methodological advances in scholarship, including the development of major research institutions and the application of new standards of source criticism, were coupled with a burgeoning romantic nationalism. It proved to be a heady combination. The concoction was at its most potent among scholars in the German provinces where the Germanic family of languages was increasingly regarded as a defining feature of social and cultural identity among prehistoric groups. Vandals, Goths,

Alemans and Franks were thus lumped together as different tribes drawn from the same 'German' stock. The scholarly foundations for these assumptions were impressive. From the early nineteenth century, the *Monumenta Germaniae Historica* set about the colossal task of collating and editing all texts from Late Antiquity and the Middle Ages which bore any relationship to the history of these 'Germanic peoples' (a remit that was very broadly defined).[48] Simultaneously, antiquarian research throughout the German provinces was bolstered by the foundation of a number of archaeological societies and the institutionalization of this study in the major universities. The same patterns were evident throughout western Europe, but it was the remarkable industrialization of the German historical tradition which had a particular effect upon the study of Vandal history.

This had a catalytic effect upon synthetic scholarship, and several new histories of the Vandals were written. Of these, the most important were Felix Papencordt's *Geschichte der vandalischen Herrschaft in Afrika* (History of Vandal Rule in Africa), published in 1837 and Louis Marcus' *Histoire des Vandales* (History of the Vandals), published in 1838. Other works included Carl Meinicke's short study of early Vandal history *Versuch einer Geschichte der Vandalen bis zu ihrem Einfall in Afrika* (Towards a History of the Vandals up to the Invasion of Africa) (1830), and Ferdinand Wrede's later examination of the Vandalic language *Über die Sprache der Wandalen* (Regarding the Language of the Vandals) (1884). Most important of all was the *Geschichte der Wandalen* of Ludwig Schmidt, first published in 1901, reissued in 1942, and later published in a French translation in the early 1950s. Schmidt was one of the central scholars of the *Völkerwanderungzeit* within Germany, and his studies remain standard works of reference for the modern historian.

What is striking about all of these histories is their application of the rigorous new scholarly practices of the nineteenth century with several long-standing assumptions about the nature of Vandal identity. Papencordt, Marcus and Schmidt all benefited greatly from the improved editions of texts available to them, and placed particular emphasis upon hitherto neglected sources like the *Historia Persecutionis* of Victor of Vita. But they were also concerned to tell the story of the Vandals as an essentially *German* history. Despite the almost total absence of textual evidence concerning the supposed 'homeland' of the Vandals, the historians of the nineteenth century placed particular emphasis upon the northern origins of the group, on the understanding that their political, social and cultural institutions were essentially unchanged from their earliest prehistory.

New methods of archaeological research accentuated this emphasis upon the Vandals' prehistory, and provided dubious scientific support for these assumptions. Within Northern and Central Europe during the nineteenth and early twentieth centuries, the archaeologists of prehistory were concerned primarily with the identification of different ethnic groups within the material record.[49] Gustav Kossinna was the most famous proponent of this approach, and was among the most influential archaeologists of his age, despite only once directing an excavation in person.[50] Kossinna's most lasting contribution to scholarship was his argument that certain recognizable 'material cultures' could be identified in the settlement and (especially) funerary archaeology of northern Europe. He then proposed that these cultures could be identified with the named peoples listed in the classical geographies of Tacitus, Pliny and Ptolemy. Kossinna concluded from these accounts that the Vandili were located around the Vistula basin during the first century AD, and deduced that the material culture found in the region was typical of the group. From here, Kossinna and his supporters argued that whole movements of peoples could be inferred from the changing distribution of certain typological artefacts, and hence wider patterns of migration could be traced through the archaeological record. Kossinna's arguments were widely accepted, first that the classical geographers were essentially trustworthy in their locations of 'Germanic' peoples, and second that the Vandals had probably originated in the Jutland peninsula or the Baltic littoral before moving south to Poland.[51] These findings were supported in contemporary studies of place-names, which saw in toponyms like Vendyssel in Jutland the indelible traces of prehistoric Vandal occupation.

The Vandals were of rather less interest to the historians and archaeologists working in North Africa in the same period. The French occupation of Algeria and Tunisia in the 1830s did trigger a concerted programme of research into ancient North Africa, under the Académie Royale des Inscriptions. Significantly, both Louis Marcus and Felix Papencordt drew upon this work in their histories of the Vandal kingdom. But the archaeologists working in the region had little interest in the Vandal or Byzantine past, and preferred to bash through the remains that they had left in the search for the splendours of the Roman period. Many of these excavators were officers in the colonial army, and recognized in the physical traces of Roman rule the antecedents to their own pretensions to pacify and civilize the continent.[52] The Vandals, as latecomers and unsuccessful colonists, who bore an unhealthy association with Germany, were largely irrelevant to this discussion, and consequently were rarely studied in detail.

Similar assumptions underlay contemporary French histories of North Africa, which relied upon textual sources. François Martroye's *Genséric: La conquéte Vandale en Afrique et la destruction de l'empire d'occident* (Geiseric: The Vandal Conquest in Africa and the Destruction of the Western Empire) (1907) and Emile Gautier's *Genséric, Roi des Vandales* (Geiseric: King of the Vandals) (1932) are both impressive historical studies, but both focus primarily on the Vandal conquests, rather than the functioning of the North African state which followed. More striking still are the historical and archaeological surveys of the middle years of the century. The second quarter of the twentieth century was an unusually fertile one within French historical scholarship, and the history of North Africa was a particular beneficiary of this efflorescence. Grand projects like Stephane Gsell's *Atlas Archéologique de l'Algérie* (Archaeological Atlas of Algeria) (1911), Pierre Monceaux's *Histoire littéraire de l'Afrique Chrétienne* (Literary History of Early Christian Africa) (1905–27) and C.-A. Julien's *Histoire de l'Afrique du Nord* (1931, rev. edn. 1951) all promised to set Roman North Africa within its historical context, and have proved enormously influential among later scholars, but again, all tended to peter out before the Vandals took occupation of Carthage.

To simplify only slightly, the Vandals of the late nineteenth and early twentieth centuries continued to be viewed primarily within a Germanic (and German) context. It was assumed that the central social institutions of the group, including language, law and patterns of government, had evolved fully in prehistory, and were exported as fixed traditions to the south during the fifth century. Although the theme was rarely addressed directly, most scholars assumed that these authentic 'Vandal' or 'Germanic' traditions disappeared in North Africa, in the face of cultural and military forces that the group was no longer able to withstand. Like Procopius, a millennium and a half earlier, these modern historians implicitly regarded Vandal history as a gradual narrative of Germanic virility and triumph, followed by cultural decay.

Unsurprisingly, this caricature – or at least the first half of it – was taken up with alacrity in popular historical works of the same period. Geiseric is held up as a quintessentially 'German' hero in John H. Haaren's *Famous Men of the Middle Ages* – an American school-text of 1904. Here, the history of the Vandals is traced from 'the shores of the Baltic' to Africa, but only down to the death of Geiseric in AD 477, when the African kingdom was at its height.[53] What we see, in other words, is a triumphant narrative of Vandal (and hence *German*) success, with little attention paid to the kingdom that Geiseric founded, or its fate after his death. As might be expected, this view proved popular in Nazi Germany during the 1930s.[54] Richard Theiss and Hans Friedrich Blunck both wrote solemn biographies of *Geiserich* which begin with the hero as a wide- (blue-) eyed German youth and end with his death at the head of a vast Mediterranean kingdom.[55] Most notable of all is the account of the king presented in Poultney Bigelow's eccentric *Genseric: The First Prussian Kaiser* (1917). Bigelow was a prominent American historian of Prussia whose formerly close relationship to the German royal family soured during the First World War. His peculiar work systematically compares Geiseric with Kaiser Wilhelm II, including amongst other things the striking (and completely unsubstantiated) suggestion that Geiseric's birthplace was exactly the location where the palace of Potsdam would later be built.[56]

The most important study of the Vandals to be written in the twentieth century was unquestionably Christian Courtois' *Les Vandales et L'Afrique* (1955). Courtois taught at the University of Algiers, where he had previously published a critical study of Victor of Vita, and had been involved in a collaborative publication of the Albertini Tablets – a collection of wooden estate records discovered in southern Tunisia and dating from the late fifth century.[57] By any standards, *Les Vandales et L'Afrique* is an exemplary scholarly study, and firmly placed the Vandals within their *African* context. Yet even this work was deeply influenced by the long-standing assumptions regarding the Vandals as a group. In a long opening section which he terms 'L'epopée Vandale' ('the Vandal Epic' is perhaps the best translation), Courtois describes the supposed origins of the group in Eastern Germania, and traces what he imagines to be their long migration south.[58] A second preface to the study proper is then provided through his substantial description of Roman Africa down to the time of the Vandal occupation. As a result, it is only on page 155 that Courtois' treatment of 'The Vandal State' begins in earnest. Conspicuously, this too is heavily influenced by the later colonial context in which the study was produced. As several later critics of the study have pointed out, the opposition between the 'changeless' semi-transhumant 'Moorish' populations of North Africa and the progressive Roman and Vandal colonizing powers forms a central explanatory device within the work.[59] This is not to dismiss the importance of the work – and Courtois' study remains a magnificent example of French scholarship of the Annaliste tradition at its finest – simply to note that all histories of the Vandals have been profoundly shaped by those that came before.

In the half-century that followed the publication of *Les Vandales et L'Afrique*, the Vandals suffered somewhat from scholarly neglect. In part, no doubt, this was because of the status of the book itself: Courtois' treatment of the topic seemed so thorough as to preclude any serious attempt to supplant it. But his study could scarcely claim to be definitive. The latter half of the twentieth century witnessed a massive expansion of archaeological research which promised to support or challenge many of Courtois' conclusions. This has helped uncover the urban fabric of late Roman, Vandal and Byzantine Africa through prestigious excavations like the UNESCO project at Carthage and major research projects at Leptiminus and Lepcis Magna, and has enabled the study of patterns of rural exploitation through extensive field surveys like those in Caesarea, the Segermes Valley and the region around Kasserine.[60] The development of new pottery typologies and an increasing concern for the study of Late Antiquity have ensured that modern scholars have far more information at their disposal than was available to Courtois or his predecessors.

Changes in political perspective have had a still greater effect upon our view of Vandal history. In many ways, Courtois was the last great voice of French colonialist scholarship on classical North Africa.[61] Following the Algerian Wars of Independence, the ancient North African past became a crucial intellectual battleground for the post-colonial writers both in France and the *maghreb*. Philosophers like Marcel Benabou in his *Le resistance africaine à la romanisation* (The African Resistance to Romanization) (1976) saw the notion of 'Roman' Africa itself as a problematic construct to be challenged, and replaced by a history which emphasized demographic, institutional and cultural continuity through successive imperial occupations.[62] While the ideological foundations of Benabou's scholarship have themselves been challenged – the image of 'continuous' African history which he propounds is just as simplistic as the model of straightforward 'Romanization' which he rejects – post-colonial approaches have revolutionized the understanding of North Africa during the first millennium.[63] The Vandal period itself rarely features within these debates and discussions, but its study is equally implicated within them.[64] Histories and archaeologies which increasingly talk about social and economic integration, and of cultural 'creolization', provide important models for the appreciation of the nuances of Vandal society.[65] The explosion of interest in the archaeology and history of the Moorish polities which developed during the same period has a still more obvious importance to the student of the Hasding state in Carthage.

Understanding of ethnicity has also changed profoundly over the last half-century, and this too has had a dramatic effect upon the study of the late Roman and early medieval period. Here again, recent political history has had a direct impact upon this scholarship. The horrific events of the 1930s and 1940s, and the hateful philosophies propounded at the time, prompted German and Austrian scholars in the generations that followed to examine critically notions of ethnicity within the migration period. Scholars like Reinhard Wenskus and his pupil Herwig Wolfram argued strongly that the 'tribes' of the *Völkerwanderung* were not immutable biological entities, which remained pure and unsullied throughout their history, but rather should be viewed as constantly shifting political communities, which were only solidified at a relatively late stage in their history.[66] These views have proved enormously influential in Europe and the United States, and later historians, notably Walter Pohl and Patrick Geary have done much to refine and further complicate this study of 'ethnogenesis'.[67] Since 1992, in particular, when contemporary notions of what it meant to be 'English', 'French' or 'Austrian' were brought into the limelight by the signing of the Maastricht treaty, 'identity' has become a major theme in early medieval scholarship.[68] The approach has also won its critics, often vitriolic, who have questioned some of the methodologies employed in this work, and have challenged the tendency to view very different barbarian groups through the same 'Germanic' lens.[69] But even in provoking this debate, the impact upon modern studies of the period has been profound. In numerous individual works of scholarship and in grand collective projects like the international *Transformation of the Roman World* project, the study of changing 'identities' in Late Antiquity found a place alongside such traditional historical subjects as political, economic and military history.

Over the course of the last decade, there has been something of a resurgence in studies of Vandal North Africa. A number of scholarly conferences have attempted to reintegrate the Vandal period into the wider currents of classical African and early medieval history. No less important have been some important recent editions and translations of the major texts, the publication of a number of crucial survey and site reports and the production of several important books from different parts of the EU. María Elvira Gil Egea's *Africa en tiempos de los Vándalos* (Africa in the Time of the Vandals) (1998) and Guido M. Berndt's *Konflict und Anpassung: Studien zu Migration und Ethnogenese der Vandalen* (Conflict and Accommodation: Studies on the Migration and Ethnogenesis of the Vandals) (2007) focus respectively on the African kingdom of the group, and their slow migration across Europe and early successes under Geiseric. Other books and articles have examined the development of Vandal political institutions, literary activity within Africa under the group and (at some length) the religious politics of the fifth century.

Against this long tradition of scholarship, the problems associated with attempting to write a history of the Vandals in the early twenty-first century stand out clearly. Can we really talk about *the* Vandals in a post-colonial world? If we accept the view that ethnic affiliations and identities are always in a constant process of change – as surely we must – is it possible to write a single history of a single 'people' like the Vandals? How should our approach to such a history change when we go from the writing an account of a small mercenary warband, fighting its way across a collapsing empire from 406–429, and gaining and losing members over the course of this long struggle, to the more complex narrative of a developing kingdom in North Africa? How can we integrate this with the problematic archaeological evidence for the prehistoric origins of the group? Or with the abundant evidence which demonstrates that the 'Roman' inhabitants of Africa readily integrated with the Vandals as their kingdom developed?[70] Does a 'Vandal' history demand that attention be paid to all citizens of the kingdom of Carthage: those who resisted, those who collaborated, and those who continued their lives more or less uninterrupted? And what of the varied outliers who bore the Vandal name? The *Notitia Dignitatum* – a puzzling Roman military list of the early fifth century – lists a unit of Vandal cavalrymen in imperial service in Egypt[71]: should these men be in our history? The western Generalissimo Stilicho and the usurper John, who briefly claimed the western throne in the 420s, were both occasionally condemned for their 'Vandal' heritage, but had little direct contact with the warbands who terrorized Gaul and Spain during the same period. Both figures should appear in a history of the early fifth century, but should they assume a central role in a history of the Vandals?

Faced with this army of anxieties, the authors of the present book have adopted an approach that is both conservative and radical. The principal focus of this book will be on the Vandal kingdom of North Africa between the arrival of Geiseric and his followers in 429, and the final defeat and deposition of Gelimer, the last of the Hasding kings in AD 534. As such, the discussion of the social and political history, religion, culture and economy of the region will not be limited to the contributions of the 'Vandals', but will also discuss the role played by the other groups within the kingdom, whether 'Roman', 'African', 'Moorish' (or indeed 'Alan', 'Sueve' or 'Hasding'). Precisely what each of these terms meant during the period of the Vandal occupation, the extent to which different ethnic affiliations changed and the capacity of individuals to identify with more than one group, will be discussed in some detail in chapter 4. But for the most part, this will be a study of North Africa in the Vandal period, not a prosopography of the Vandals in Late Antique history.

The rise and fall of the North African kingdom provide the clearest chronological parameters for this book, but they are not observed with absolute fidelity. A substantial epilogue discusses the fate of North Africa in the years which followed the Byzantine conquest, not least because the crises of this period reveal a great deal about the final years of the Vandal kingdom. For similar reasons the present history opens, not with the crossing to Africa in 429, or with the capture of Carthage ten years later, but with the first appearance of groups of 'Vandals' (in fact 'Hasdings') on the Roman Danubian frontier in the middle of the second century AD. Chapter 2 provides a brief narrative overview of the events which saw a variety of different 'Vandal' groups in action along the imperial frontier, and eventually witnessed the long expedition into Gaul and Spain during the first decades of the fifth century. The origins and composition of these warbands are poorly understood, but the relation of Geiseric's heterogeneous band of fortune hunters to the 'Vandal people' which eventually dominated Carthage and the Western Mediterranean remains a crucial question. As a result, the murky origins of the Vandals within this context are explored in some detail.

The decision to begin this study of the Vandals in the second century, and not to trace the history of the group still further back deserves some brief explanation.[72] As we have seen, modern histories of the Vandals have conventionally begun in what is now Northern Poland, either by discussing the appearance of the Vandals in the origin myths of the Goths and the Lombards, or (increasingly) through the discussion of the archaeology of this region and its relation to the classical ethnographies of Tacitus and Pliny. Both of these writers refer to a group called the Vandili somewhere in the murky regions of *barbaricum*.[73] It has been argued that these texts place the group around the Lower Vistula, at the heart of what modern archaeologists have identified as the 'Przeworsk' culture: a more or less coherent area which is defined by recognizable forms of coarse cooking wares, as well as some decorative metalwork and certain burial practices.[74] While few scholars would now claim that the settlement of the Vandals could be mapped precisely onto the extent of the Przeworsk culture – indeed most would argue vigorously against such assumptions – the association between the prehistoric 'people' and their supposed material culture remains close in much scholarship. The apparent spread of the Przeworsk culture into the Carpathian basin from the third century AD has often been read as evidence for the gradual migration of the Vandals south, and would appear to tally neatly with the earliest appearances of the group on the Roman frontier. If a relationship can be assumed between the Vandili of Tacitus and Pliny and the Przeworsk material culture, if these peoples were connected to the groups who later appeared on the Danube and the Rhine, and eventually conquered Carthage, then the Vandals quite clearly had an impressive prehistory.

Regrettably, such assumptions cannot be sustained, and it is for this reason that the present volume begins its Vandal history where it does.[75] Both Tacitus and Pliny do refer to groups of Vandili, but neither does so with any geographical precision. We can assume that groups of 'Vandals' did exist somewhere in the barbarian territories (or at least that Roman authors believed that these 'Vandals' existed), but we cannot say precisely where they were. Consequently, the link to the Przeworsk culture area is far from clear, and the subsequent assumption that the expansion of this region reflected either the migration or the expanding cultural influence of the Vandals and their neighbours cannot be sustained. Without this link, and the crucial assumption that the spread of this culture into the Carpathians represented a genuine migration, there is no link between the Vandili confederacies mentioned by our first-century ethnographic sources, and the 'Hasdings' and 'Vandals' who appear in historical texts of the later period. The historians and geographers of the later Roman empire commonly employed archaic names to refer to new groups who came to their attention on the frontier. Consequently, the fact that the warbands of the third- and fourth-century frontier bore the same name as the tribal confederations mentioned by Tacitus and Pliny several centuries earlier need not be taken as evidence for a direct connection.

This observation has some important implications for our understanding of the earliest stages of Vandal history. The association with the Przeworsk culture worked on the assumption that the Vandals of prehistory were a large and influential group, and itself helped to sustain this impression. When we look at conventional archaeological maps which depict north-eastern Europe in the later iron age, the Vandals seem to occupy an impressive chunk of territory beyond the Roman frontier. This, in turn, helps to foster the illusion that the later movement of the Vandals into the Roman empire had a devastating historical momentum, and provides a satisfying explanation for the group's eventual conquest of North Africa. This is not the narrative that appears in the contemporary sources. The Vandals who first appeared on the Roman frontier in the second and third centuries do not appear to be the representatives of a vast barbarian confederacy, but a rather small and mobile group of soldiers. Nor were the Vandals who moved through Gaul and Spain an irresistible military force, destined for great things in the rich provinces of North Africa. Instead, they were a small and unprepossessing military group. They developed in the shadow of larger military powers, and their movement through the western provinces took the form of a series of haphazard and stuttering steps through an empire collapsing in upon itself. They rose to power in North Africa not because of their long and proud heritage, but in spite of a history that was both short and undistinguished. But their history – and their brief moment in the Mediterranean sun – is all the more fascinating for that.

2

From the Danube to Africa

In AD 171 a barbarian group called the Astingi entered the Roman province of Dacia. They were led by two kings, named Raus and Raptus, and arrived in the empire in search of alliance, not plunder. This was a difficult period for the Roman empire of Marcus Aurelius; for five years the emperor had been campaigning along the Middle Danube frontier against the Marcomanni and Quadi, but from AD 170 these wars threatened to spill over into the provinces downriver.[1] In Dacia, the one Roman province beyond the Danube, the governor Cornelius Clemens was faced with the problem of balancing the interests of several barbarian peoples – the Lacringi, the Costoboci and now the Astingi. According to the historian Cassius Dio, our principal source on these events, Clemens encouraged the Astingi to attack the Costoboci, but then stood aside as the Astingi were attacked in turn by the Lacringi. Suitably chastened, the Astingi formally submitted to the emperor and proved themselves to be useful allies thereafter.[2]

In its frustrating mixture of detail and ambiguity, this brief episode is typical of the earliest fragments of Vandal history. It is generally assumed that the Astingi were Vandals – the name was later adopted by the royal family of the Vandals between the early fifth century and the collapse of the African kingdom in the 530s – but we cannot say much more than this. We do not know what linked this group to other 'Vandals' in the Danube region, if indeed there were any at this time. We are unable to say why this group of barbarians were ruled by two kings, and what the relationship between them might have been. Equally frustratingly, we have very little sense of what happened next to the Astingi within Roman Dacia. The *History* of Peter the Patrician states that the Astiggoi and the Lacringi were among Marcus Aurelius' allies in this period, and Eutropius lists the Vandals among those peoples defeated by the emperor.[3] Dio himself goes on to note that the next emperor Commodus made a treaty with the Marcomanni which forbad them from waging war with the Iazyges, Buri or the Vandals and later states that, in around AD 212 or 213, Fabricius Luscinus provoked the Vandals and the Marcomanni into making war on one another, as a way of strengthening his own hand in the imperial borderlands.[4] But these are tiny fragments of information within the huge military and political upheaval of the Danube frontier.

The textual sources for the early history of the Vandals in this region are notoriously problematic. We know of two texts which addressed the military and political chaos of the Roman Balkans – one of these is Dio's *Roman History*, the other the *Skythica* of Dexippus – and only fragments of these works survive.[5] Later historians provide a rather fuller narrative, but create more problems than they solve. The *Historia Augusta*, for example, consists of a number of colourful biographies of second- and third-century emperors, many of whom campaigned along the northern frontier. But these lives were written in the fourth century, and many of their more informative passages were evidently fabricated by later authors with particular axes to grind.[6] Much the same is true of Jordanes' *History of the Goths* (commonly known as the *Getica*), written by a minor civil servant in Constantinople during the 550s. Jordanes vividly evokes the political *danse macabre* on the fourth-century Danube, and has provided crucial support to many modern reconstructions of these events, but his perspective was resolutely that of a sixth-century historian with a particular interest in celebrating the ancient glories of the Goths. The *Getica* describes a large Vandal kingdom to the north of the Danube, which was crushed in the early fourth century by the Goths of King Geberich, and dissipated as the defeated Vandals fled across the Roman frontier.[7] Tempting as it would be to follow Jordanes' narrative of the power-politics on the edge of the empire, this is clearly his own invention. The description of the phantom Vandal kingdom is entirely typical of Jordanes' geographical rhetoric and could not have been drawn from earlier sources.[8] No other historical text makes any reference to this kingdom, or to the large number of refugees said to have been settled in the empire.[9] The archaeological evidence from the Middle Danube also argues against the idea that the Vandals of this period were gathered into a coherent political community. The Goths and the Vandals were bitter enemies, but this was in the fifth and sixth centuries, not in the third and fourth. Rather than engage with the hopelessly confused political situation of the late Roman frontier wars, Jordanes simply retrojected recent historical patterns onto the more distant past.[10]

When we assemble the disparate fragments of historical and archaeological evidence which relate to the Middle Danube region between the

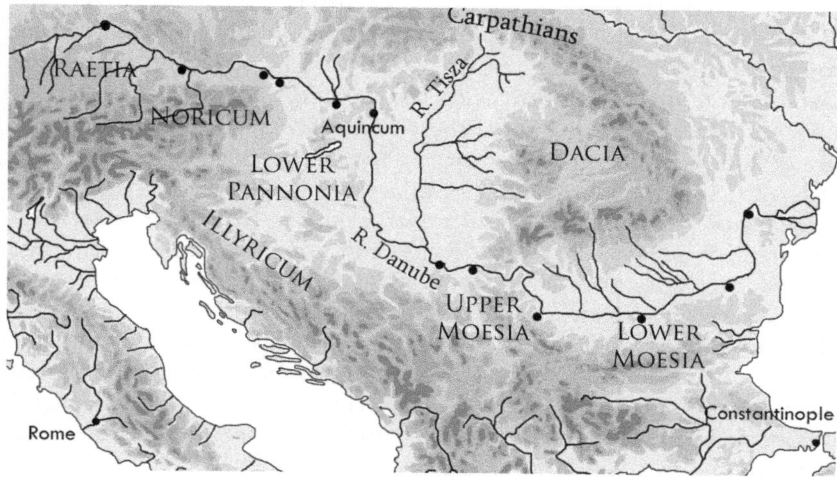

Figure 2.1 The Danube frontier at the time of the Marcomannic wars

mid-second century and the end of the fourth, it is clear that the Vandals were only very small characters in a grand – and tremendously complicated – drama. If all of the texts are considered together, we could draw up a list of around 50 different barbarian groups of different sizes who were active on the frontier in this period. Some were undoubtedly important: the Marcomanni and Quadi were a constant concern to the commanders on the frontier and the Goths were to rise to an unprecedented prominence over the course of this period. Other groups appear only once or twice before fading into obscurity. The Vandals were not quite in this last group, but they were far from being a major influence along the frontier: they do not appear on the famous fourth-century 'Verona List' of Rome's barbarian neighbours, and clearly were not among the major concerns of commanders on the frontier. Conventionally, modern studies have either overlooked this relative obscurity, or have explained the absence of the Vandals in Greek and Roman sources by stating that the centre of the group's influence lay far from the frontier of the empire. Unfortunately, there is no positive evidence to support this argument. The Vandals were to rise to extraordinary prominence during the fifth and sixth centuries, but we should not follow Jordanes in assuming that they were always so important. On the contrary, the texts and archaeological evidence suggest that their earliest history was far from auspicious.

We have to wait almost a century after the Dacian expedition of Raus and Raptus for the next appearance of the Vandals in our textual sources. In the late summer of AD 270, a Vandal warband crossed the Danube into imperial territory near Aquincum, near the modern city of Budapest.[11] The band harassed the countryside of northern Pannonia, but did not pose a significant threat to the towns; the emperor Aurelian ordered that livestock and crops be taken into fortified settlements in the expectation that this would preserve them from the attackers. Apparently weakened by this strategy, and perhaps unable to scavenge sufficient food for themselves as the winter drew in, the Vandals were then decisively defeated by the emperor. A fragment of Dexippus' *History* summarizes the treaty which followed this defeat, and explains that the Vandals were forced back over the frontier, having surrendered their booty and pledged 2,000 cavalrymen to the Roman army.[12] Dexippus further relates that some Vandals sought to renege on the terms of the treaty, but were easily suppressed by Aurelian while he supervised the retreat. Within the wider context of Roman imperial troubles on the Danube, this short raid was of little significance. Throughout the 250s and 260s groups of Alamanni and Marcomanni had repeatedly tested the weakening Roman military presence around the Rhine-Danube re-entrant, and had twice penetrated into Italy.[13] Further east, the pressure on Dacia was such that Roman control of the province was eventually formally relinquished. Aurelian's reign was a period of particular military crisis, but the Vandals could claim only a very small responsibility for this.[14]

The Byzantine historian Zosimus refers to a third engagement in which the Vandals were involved some ten years later.[15] Again, the group were very much the supporting cast within a wider drama, this time as a third act in the emperor Probus' campaigns against various German tribes and Frankish groups on the Rhine. According to Zosimus, Probus engaged a mixed force of Burgundians and Vandals along a river – probably the Lech in the western Bavarian Alps. Zosimus' narrative of the battle is not clear, but Probus seems to have been victorious, despite being outnumbered. Zosimus then states that the barbarians were attacked again for refusing to surrender their plunder and prisoners.

The Archaeology of the Vandals on the Frontier

Modest as it is, this historical information at least provides some broad geographical stage for the earliest acts of Vandal history. To judge from the scatter of references to the Vandals across the Middle Danube region, several different groups may well have borne the name. The presence of 'Vandal' raids into Dacia and Noricum, and their evident friction with the Marcomanni, suggests that the settlement of these groups was probably concentrated in the northern parts of the Alföld or the Great Hungarian Plain.[16] Archaeological investigation helps to narrow this down rather further, although not with the precision that was once believed. Detailed field surveys and piecemeal excavation reveal that the woody wetlands of the Upper Tisza Valley were relatively well populated during the later Roman period, and this is probably the region where the Vandals were settled. The region is generously watered and fertile, and also straddles a communications crossroads, marking as it does the principal routes of access between the Transylvanian plateau in the east, the Carpathian range in the north and the Hungarian plain to the south. Due west of the region, moreover, is the Great Bend of the Danube and the major crossing point at Aquincum. If we are to place the Vandals of the second and third centuries anywhere, it should be in the hamlets and agricultural settlements of the Upper Tisza.

Conventionally, a handful of warrior graves on the Upper Tisza have been labelled as specifically 'Vandal', in contrast to 'Sarmatian', 'Quadic' and 'Dacian' graves and settlements elsewhere in the plain.[17] Unfortunately, there is little to sustain this identification – our texts are silent on the precise location of Vandal settlement, and archaeology in itself is a notoriously unstable platform for ethnographic labelling. The supposed association of the material culture of the Tisza graves with the so-called Przeworsk culture of central Poland is hardly a basis for confident identification, as was discussed in the previous chapter. If we turn to the textual sources for assistance, the picture becomes still murkier. Ancient historians tell us about a displaced 'Dacian' or 'Getic' population in the area to the south of the Carpathians, along with Sarmatians and Iazyges who are said to have arrived from the east in the first century.[18] Inscriptions similarly refer to Carpi, Sarmatians, Taifali, Peuki, Zorani, Bastarnae and several different Gothic groups.[19] None of these peoples can be identified firmly on the ground, and there is no reason to suppose that the Vandals would be any easier to find.[20] But if we should be cautious in trying to distinguish 'Vandals' from 'Sarmatians', 'Dacians' or 'Iazyges' in the archaeological record, we can at least be confident in assessing the social, political and cultural environment in which all of these groups are likely to have interacted.

The archaeology of the Tisza basin provides the only means to investigate the cultural setting in which the Vandals (and their neighbours) developed in the second, third and fourth centuries. Two overarching trends are particularly clear.[21] The first of these might broadly be described as the gradual spread of 'Roman' influence throughout these groups. From the second century onwards, Roman jewellery began to appear in high status graves in the region, often combining with traditional forms of personal adornment to create a startling hybrid effect. Local ceramic manufacture, too, was influenced by an increased circulation of imported pottery, and began to adopt increasingly 'Mediterranean' forms. And even settlement location was shaped by cultural and economic forces from elsewhere. While detailed study of settlement in the Tisza Valley has revealed a strong adherence to established settlement patterns (and often closely respects features of the landscape like ancestral tombs), Roman military forts and watchtowers also acted as powerful economic magnets, drawing clusters of settlement on both sides of the frontier.[22]

Perhaps paradoxically, the other noticeable pattern in the archaeological record is a distinct level of continuity in many aspects of social and economic life. Regionally specific luxuries circulated alongside imported Roman goods, and foodstuffs continued to be transported (and eaten) in local containers as well as Mediterranean vessels.[23] The point is most clearly demonstrated by patterns of settlement within the Upper Tisza Valley. Here, despite an apparent growth in population, and an increased emphasis upon settlement near the Roman frontiers, occupation patterns retained a strongly conservative dimension. Many settlements remained in continuous occupation, and even those which grew during this period frequently respected the prominent features of the prehistoric landscape, which suggests a strong continuity in sacral behaviour.

This continuity and change occurred against a background of considerable political upheaval within the region as a whole. The establishment of the Roman military presence on the Danube and in Dacia during the first and second centuries, the conflict of the Marcomannic Wars in the mid-second, and the eventual abandonment of Dacia by the empire in the 270s all had massive repercussions in the political sphere. On a less dramatic level, prolonged contact with the extensive frontier zone of the empire also created an unstable political stage. The few glimpses that we have had of Vandal activity in this period illustrate vividly the enormous influence of the empire on the political balance of the frontier zone. We have seen the Vandals and the Astingi as the allies of the empire, used as a tool to attack other barbarian groups; as enemies who were themselves the victims of aggressive imperial diplomacy and as a manpower reserve which could supply auxiliary troops for the Roman army.

Diplomatic relations of this kind had a catalytic effect upon the social and political development of communities on the frontiers. This process has been particularly well-studied for the Franks on the Rhine frontier and the Alamanni in the Rhine-Danube re-entrant, but is perhaps best known with respect to the Goths on the Lower Danube, from the middle of the third century.[24] Here, prolonged contact with the Roman empire saw the Tervingi and Greuthungi – two hitherto obscure warbands – emerge as major political players north of the frontier. This increase in political power may be charted in the spread of an increasingly homogeneous material culture throughout the northern and eastern Carpathians, and eventually to the creation of a genuine new threat to the Roman empire in the east. When the Goths started to flex their political muscles, the barbarian and Roman worlds took notice.

From what we can gather, no group became dominant in the same way within the Tisza basin. Extensive textual references would suggest that the Sarmatians were the principal recipients of Roman support within the Alföld, and it seems likely that the vast earthworks which still scar the plain represent a systematic programme of Roman military aid during the early fourth century.[25] The Vandals, by contrast, did not rise to particular prominence along the Danube frontier. The strong patterns of continuity evident in the material record, and the relative paucity of references to the Vandals in the textual accounts, all suggest that the group remained relatively insignificant in a geo-political sense. As a small handful of groups bullied their way to prominence in the frontier zone, the relatively underdeveloped Vandals – along with many of their neighbours – were jostled along in their wake. While the Goths rapidly seem to have grown into something like a coherent political entity during the third century, and the Sarmatians found their own niche under the benevolent aegis of the empire, the Vandals remained a small and insignificant warband. This was to change over the course of the fifth century, and to change dramatically. But the Vandal 'coming of age' took place a long way from the Danube.

In the last quarter of the fourth century, the balance of power on the Middle Danube began to teeter precariously. The settlement in Thrace of a substantial number of Gothic refugees in AD 376 is conventionally regarded as the crucial turning point. The abuse of the group by the Roman provincial authorities, the subsequent revolt of the Goths and their crushing defeat of the imperial army in the environs of Constantinople in 378 created a semi-autonomous new military power in the Balkans, even after the peace settlement of 382.[26] Elsewhere tensions continued to run high. In a letter of 396 to the bishop of Altinum,

Jerome laments two decades of suffering across 'Scythia, Thrace, Macedonia, Dardania, Dacia, Thessaly, Achaia, Epirus, Dalmatia, the Pannonias' at the hands of assorted 'Goths and Sarmatians, Quadi and Alans, Huns and Vandals and Marcomanni'.[27] The Vandals again feature only among the supporting cast, but within a drama that was rapidly reaching its climax.

Matters came to a head in the first decade of the fifth century, when the deep political currents swirling around northern Italy saw the Vandals and their fellow bit-players wash up on the frontiers of Gaul. The initial catalyst for this was Radagaisus, an independent Gothic king who led a massive army, perhaps including some groups of Vandals, from the Danube across Raetia and into Italy in AD 405.[28] His campaign was devastating, and was recalled with horror by later Christian commentators, but was ultimately unsuccessful.[29] In 406, on the verge of securing Florence, Radagaisus was driven back by the forces of the *magister militum* Stilicho, who arrived on the scene with a mixed force of Romans and allied barbarians. Radagaisus was forced into flight, and eventually starved into surrender at the heights of Fiesole. There he was executed, many of his troops apparently allied themselves with Stilicho, and others scattered to seek their fortunes elsewhere.

The standard military narrative of this period now turns to a second Gothic soldier, Alaric in Illyricum. Since the turn of the fifth century, Alaric had been involved in a complex power struggle with Stilicho. This had temporarily subsided at the time of Radagaisus' invasion, but erupted again in the years that followed. In 407, Alaric marched on Italy, setting in chain a series of events which led to Stilicho's execution in 408 and – ultimately – to the Gothic sack of Rome in 410.[30] But as the attentions of contemporaries and historians turned to the unfolding power struggle between a Roman generalissimo and a Gothic king with powerful friends in Constantinople, the frontier did not remain silent. The successive threats posed by Radagaisus and Alaric forced Stilicho to withdraw many troops away from the frontiers and to keep them in northern Italy, leaving the protection of Roman interests in the frontier regions to a number of federated Frankish and Alaman troops.[31] This changing balance of power in the northern militarized zone had dramatic consequences in the long term.

Even as Radagaisus crashed into Italy in AD 405, other groups appear to have been moving within the frontier region.[32] These changes went largely unobserved by contemporaries more focused on the unfolding drama in the cockpit of northern Italy, but groups of Vandals and their allies were increasingly prominent on the Rhine frontier. Two independent sources describe a major conflict in the Rhineland, probably between Frankish federates and a Vandal army. Renatus Frigeridus, in a passage preserved in the *Histories* of Gregory of Tours, states that a Vandal army was badly mauled by the Franks, losing their king in combat, and avoiding total annihilation only by the timely intervention of their Alan allies.[33] Orosius' *History* of c. 417 does not support this exactly, but it does describe a major Frankish defeat in the Rhineland, which left the frontier region open to the barbarians.[34] The impact of this disaster for the empire was compounded by the dispersal of Radagaisus' followers following the defeat at Fiesole in 406. Some of these troops, including perhaps some Vandals, headed north to seek their fortune in the frontier zone; others crossed the Alps into eastern Gaul, where their presence sent shivers throughout the western provinces.[35]

This had ominous implications for the Roman provinces of Gaul, where stability was further threatened by the prospect of military rebellion across the channel in Britain.[36] The appearance of barbarian troops in eastern Gaul in the summer of 406 caused panic among the legions in Britain. The army there mutinied and in successive coups proclaimed three of their officers as emperor during the autumn and winter of 406/407.[37] The last of these was the usurper Constantine, who had apparently risen from the ranks before being elevated to the purple in February 407 on the strength of his auspicious name. Almost immediately his attention turned to the mounting crisis on the continent. In the last days of 406 – on New Year's Eve of that year according to our only source – a mixed group of Alans, Vandals and Sueves had crossed into Gaul, and were threatening the crucial supply port of Bononia. The security of the empire was threatened, Constantine departed for Gaul, and the Vandals had started on the next phase of their history.

406 and All That

Given the iconic position of the Rhine crossing of 406 in modern accounts of the 'decline and fall of the Roman Empire', it is sobering to realize just how little we know about the event itself. Prosper of Aquitaine – the only near-contemporary source to refer specifically to the event – states little more than that the crossing took place on New Year's Eve 406, a date that one recent scholar has suggested may be exactly a year too late.[38] The statement that the Rhine was frozen on the day of the invasion appears in almost every modern historical narrative of these events, but has no support in any of the ancient texts, and seems to have

Figure 2.2 Gaul AD 406–411

originated with Edward Gibbon.[39] Admittedly, a frozen river would have been easier for a warband of barbarians to cross, but rivers are not insurmountable obstacles to an army on the move, even in the dead of winter. Finally, it is unknown precisely where the crossing took place. A spurious eighth-century history identifies Mainz as the crossing point, but hardly on the firmest historical grounds.[40] Most modern scholars have been content to assume that the barbarians entered Gaul at an unidentified point (or points) between the cities of Mainz and Worms, both of which seem to have been attacked in the course of the invasion.[41]

The Vandals, Alans and Sueves crossed into Gaul in midwinter 405/6 or (more probably) 406/7, at an unspecified point along the Rhine frontier, and for reasons that are far from certain. Sadly, things scarcely get any clearer from there. The extant sources relating to Gaul in the troubled period from 406–411 are rich and varied, including a variety of historical narratives, chronicles, letters, isolated hagiography and occasional poetry. Conspicuously, however, very little of this material relates directly to the Vandals or their allies. Despite their penetration into the lands of the empire, the barbarians remained on the periphery of the political stage, a position they were to occupy for at least another decade and a half. The main reason for this was that Constantine's usurpation, and the invasion of his troops from Britain, was perceived to be a far greater threat to the stability of the empire than the activity of some barbarians in the north. The western emperor Honorius was candid in his ambition to deal with usurpers before bandits or barbarians, and Constantine likewise regarded his rivals for imperial power as a more pressing problem than the sundry warbands shuttling around the fringes of Gaul.[42] The historians of the time shared this concern, and devoted far greater energies to the discussion of the civil war than they did to barbarian activity, but the precise narrative of Constantine's usurpation remains confused. Our principal sources agree on the major events of the revolt, but in spite of this the relative timings of its different phases have been the matter of considerable dispute among historians.[43]

Constantine's first move seems to have been the consolidation of this authority within the Gallic provinces, and he initially held a strong hand. He probably met little or no resistance to his usurpation from within Gaul and rapidly established his shadow empire in Lyons, probably in mid-407.[44] In the summer of the same year, Stilicho responded vigorously to this threat and sent a federated Gothic army to Gaul under the command of one Sarus in the hope of removing the British pretender before he had the chance to establish his power. Sarus was initially successful: Constantine's two generals Nebiogast (who was probably a Frank) and Justinian were defeated in short order, but were rapidly replaced by the usurper. Faced down by reinforcements under the formidable British general Gerontius, Sarus had little choice but to return to Italy. He retreated in disarray, and was eventually reduced to the indignity of buying his safe passage through the Maritime Alps from the bandits who controlled the passes.[45] Shortly thereafter, Constantine sent his own troops to fortify the mountains and to secure the routes of communication between Italy and his own domains in Gaul.

Thereafter, Constantine's chief preoccupations seem to have been to consolidate his position in the western provinces of the empire, while negotiating his position with the Emperor Honorius in Ravenna. In late 408, Constantine sent his son Constans to Spain to shore up support in the peninsula, where a number of prominent local aristocrats and units of the imperial army remained loyal to the Theodosian house. Constans' troops, under the command of Gerontius, were victorious over the loyalists in two battles, one in the north of the peninsula, the other probably near Mérida in Lusitania. The rebel prince established his position in Caesaraugusta, and his father turned his attentions to Italy.

The invaders of 406 were little more than interested spectators to all of this frantic activity. Our sources hint that Constantine used a combination of military force and diplomatic finesse to dealt with the Vandals, Alans and Sueves, and he evidently regarded them as a minimal threat. Zosimus states that a barbarian army was decisively defeated at around this time, leading to major political reorganization, but whether these were the Vandals and their allies, or a different group within Gaul is not clear.[46] Orosius provides a more hostile view of Constantine's response to the threat, and his allusion to the 'uncertain treaties' with the barbarians probably indicates that negotiation was a necessary part of the new emperor's strategy.[47] At the very least, we know that Constantine refortified the Rhine frontiers, either through the despatch of his own troops or (more probably) through the revival of agreements with the federated barbarians there, and also refortified the Alps.[48] But Constantine's greatest attentions – and those of our sources – were on the struggle for the empire, not on the actions of a disparate group of barbarian stragglers in the forgotten provinces of the north.

Between 406 and the summer of 409, the barbarians were restricted to the northern provinces of Gaul. One chronicle source states precisely this, noting that the barbarians devastated one part of Gaul, but Constantine was able to occupy the remainder.[49] Further evidence is provided by the careful scrutiny of one of the most evocative sources from the period, the letter of Saint Jerome to the widow Ageruchia, which was probably written in the spring or summer of 408. By this stage in his life, Jerome was at the centre of an epistolary web that spread throughout the world from his monastery in Bethlehem, and he evidently took great pride in demonstrating his impressive grasp of current affairs to his correspondents. He often illustrated his meditations on the transient nature of human life or the sufferings of the Christian soul with apposite references to recent barbarian atrocities, whether the Huns in the Caucasus, the Goths in Pannonia and Italy, or the Vandals in Northern Gaul:

> Savage tribes in countless numbers have overrun all parts of Gaul. The whole country between the Alps and the Pyrenees, between the Rhine and the Ocean, has been laid waste by hordes of Quadi, Vandals, Sarmatians, Alans, Gepids, Herules, Saxons, Burgundians, Alemanni and – alas! for the commonwealth! – even Pannonians. For 'Assur also is joined with them'. The once noble city of *Moguntiacus* [Mainz] has been captured and destroyed. In its church many thousands have been massacred. The *Vangiones* [inhabitants of Worms] after withstanding a long siege have been extirpated. The powerful city of the *Remi* [Reims], the *Ambiani* [Amiens], the *Altrebatae* [Arras], the *Morini* on the edges of the world [Thérouanne], *Tornacus* [Tournai], *Nemetae* [Speyer], and *Argentorate* [Strasbourg] have been surrendered to Germania: while the provinces of Aquitaine and of the *novempopuli*, of *Lugdunensis* [Lyon] and of *Narbonensis* [Narbonne] are – with the exception of a few cities – one universal scene of desolation. And those which the sword spares without, famine ravages within. I cannot speak without tears of *Tolosa* [Toulouse] which has been kept from failing hitherto by the merits of its reverend bishop Exuperius. Even the provinces of *Hispania* are on the brink of ruin and tremble daily as they recall the invasion of the Cymbricae; and, while others suffer misfortunes once in actual fact, they suffer them continually in anticipation.[50]

Jerome's letter seems to imply that the Vandals and their allies ran amok throughout Gaul in AD 407 and 408, and has generally been read as such by modern historians. Yet careful scrutiny suggests something rather different. Conspicuously, the cities Jerome claims to have been attacked by the barbarians – from Reims to Strasbourg – were all located in the northern parts of Roman Gaul.[51] The peculiar specificity of Jerome's account here suggests that he may have been drawing on local sources. While archaeological investigation has yet to find destruction layers which may be identified conclusively with these attacks, we may assume that all suffered during the chaotic first decade of the fifth century.

The Vandals were not responsible for all of the suffering that Jerome describes in southern Gaul and Spain. At the time the letter was written, the barbarians had not yet entered Spain; clearly Jerome conflated the effects of Constantine's usurpation with those of the invasion in his lament for the state of the contemporary world. More striking still is his reference to the heroism of St Exuperius of Toulouse. While generations of historians have been happy to salute Exuperius' courage in the face of barbarian pressure, Jerome never explains the nature of the bishop's protection of his diocese.[52] In fact, as a later letter makes clear, Exuperius' accomplishment was not the physical defence of his city, but the provision of foodstuffs during a period of intense famine.[53] The barbarians added to the miseries of early fifth-century Gaul, then, but were not the sole cause of it, and all available evidence would suggest that their impact was felt most strongly only in the northern provinces.

Conspicuously, when the Vandals, Alans and Sueves finally did head south into Aquitaine and Spain, it was the civil war which set them in motion. In the spring or summer of 409, the foundations of Constantine's usurpation began to crumble. His attempts to gain formal recognition from Honorius, while initially successful, were hampered by the death of one Allobichus, the Master of the Imperial Horse and Constantine's chief sympathiser in the imperial court. Allobichus was replaced by Constantius, altogether less accommodating to the usurper and destined to become the dominant military power in the western provinces for the next decade and a half. Equally serious was the deterioration of Constantine's position in Spain. At some point in 409, Gerontius rebelled against his former master and sought to establish his own position within Spain. Subsequently, and perhaps as late as summer 410, Gerontius proclaimed Maximus, a member of his own household, as Augustus. Thereafter, Constantine's usurpation disintegrated. Gerontius invaded from Spain, as Constantius approached from Italy. Constantine was defeated and killed, and his former protégé Gerontius was subsequently eliminated as Constantius restored Gaul to imperial control.

Amidst this chaos, in mid-409, the Vandals, Alans and Sueves marched into Aquitaine and towards the Pyrenees. The fighting in the south meant that no-one was in any position to prevent this movement, in fact, a demand for troops among the different factions of the civil war probably encouraged it. Gerontius may have attempted to incite the barbarians into attacking Constantine, and it seems likely that Constantine himself regarded the warbands in the north as a resource that might be worth exploiting.[54] In the event, these overtures came to nothing. As the imperial presence in Northern Gaul collapsed, and the inhabitants of Armorica and southern Britain gave up on the empire for the last time, the barbarians moved towards the unguarded lands of the south.[55]

The barbarian attacks on southern Gaul were long remembered, even within this scarred landscape. As the poet Orientus put it in his *Commonitorium* ('Reminder'): 'All Gaul was filled with the smoke of a single funeral pyre'. For other poets of the period, the chaos under Gerontius and Constantine, and the later occupation of the Visigoths in the 410s all blurred together into a gruesome tableau. But the role of the Vandals was not forgotten. The true horror of the barbarian assaults, and the hopelessness of attempting to recover in a world of sin is illustrated best in an evocative modern translation of the *Epigramma Paulini*

(The Sayings of Paulinus). Here, the actions of the barbarians are merely the setting for a cruel inner struggle in the hearts of the Christians themselves:

> Turn to the inner plague, the war of fears
> Which numbs us with its thickening cloud of spears.
> That foe's the worst, who fights unseen of all.
> Yet, while Sarmatians waste and Vandals brawl
> And Alans ravish, we have set our will
> With hopes ambiguous and sick efforts still
> On building ruins to a world we've lost.[56]

Into Spain

The most important repercussion of the new phase of barbarian movement was the sudden invasion of Spain, which occurred either on September 28th or (less probably) on October 13th 409.[57] While the crossing of the Pyrenees would have required some effort, the mountains themselves were scarcely an insurmountable obstacle. Since the early fourth century, the overland supply routes, which stretched from the grain fields of southern Spain through the mineral rich north-west and up towards the Rhineland frontier, had been fortified, but the city walls and Pyrenean fortresses were primarily intended to see off local bandits, not to protect against a concerted invasion attempt.[58] This changed somewhat during the civil wars of the early 400s, when two local aristocrats undertook the defence of the mountains from the usurper Constantine. According to Orosius, Gerontius' defeat of these Theodosian loyalists led to a reorganization of the mountain defences and the replacement of local troops with a unit of barbarians known as the Honoriaci in the service of Constans – variously identified as British, 'Germanic' or Suevic federates by modern scholars.[59] He goes on to state that the barbarians plundered the *campi Pallentini* (presumably the agricultural region around the Roman city of Palentia) and later joined the Vandals and Alans in their wide-ranging devastation of Spain. Both Orosius and the Greek historian Sozomen declare that it was their dereliction of duty which allowed the barbarians free passage into the country.[60]

Either way, the Vandals and other barbarians crossed the Pyrenees. Some were certainly left in Gaul: we know of groups of Alans operating more or less autonomously both in Aquitaine in the 410s and in Armorica in the middle of the century.[61] Others very probably returned to Gaul with the army of Gerontius early in 410, and a famous historical tradition reminds us that the general's closest personal companion at the time of his defeat was himself an Alan.[62] Still others may have fought for Constantine or another power-broker in Gaul. But the focus of the history of the Vandals as a group thereafter moved southwards to the Iberian peninsula.

The two years which followed the crossing of the Pyrenees in autumn 409 were bleak for those living in the Spanish provinces. Three independent sources discuss the destruction caused by the barbarians in the region, and this suffering was compounded by the famine which swept through the region at the same time. Just as Jerome and the poets form the background to the activities of the Vandals in Gaul, so the Spanish chronicler Hydatius took up the narrative in Spain:

> As the barbarians ran wild through Spain and the deadly pestilence continued on its savage course, the wealth and goods stored in the cities were plundered by the tyrannical tax collector and consumed by the soldiers. A famine ran riot, so dire that driven by hunger human beings devoured human flesh; mothers too feasted upon the bodies of their own children whom they had killed and cooked with their own hands; wild beasts, habituated to feeding on the bodies of those slain by the sword, famine or pestilence, killed all the braver individuals and feasting on their flesh everywhere became brutally set upon the destruction of the human race. And thus with the four plagues of sword, famine, pestilence and wild beasts raging everywhere throughout the world, the annunciations foretold by the Lord through his prophets came to fulfilment.[63]

This is an apocalyptic combination of famine, pestilence and barbarian warmongering. But amidst the horrors a number of details are worth noting. Hydatius implies that the towns of the peninsula were largely spared the worst ravages of the barbarian assault, a happy result perhaps of the fortifications which had been erected over the previous century. While he then states that their escape from death simply resulted in heavier taxes, this itself is significant. Continuity of taxation implied an administrative continuity, too.[64] Destructive as the Vandals, Alans and Sueves may have been, the superstructure of Roman rule seems to have weathered the combined ravages of barbarian attack and famine. Conspicuously, after the barbarian depravations finally came to a halt two or three years later, the peninsula enjoyed a half-decade or so of relative prosperity.

By 411 or 412 the immediate crisis had passed. The new Roman generalissimo Constantius had successfully put down the last of the rebellions in Gaul. As if intimidated by this influential new policeman on

Figure 2.3 Hispania AD 409–422

the beat, the barbarians in Spain brought their ravaging to an end and sought peaceful settlement within the peninsula. The partition of Spain that followed is one of the stranger episodes in the early history of the Vandals. Hydatius, again, is our best source:

> They then apportioned to themselves by lot areas of the provinces for settlement: the Vandals took possession of Gallaecia and the Sueves that part of Gallaecia which is situated on the very western edge of the Ocean. The Alans were allotted the provinces of Lusitania and Carthaginiensis, and the Siling Vandals Baetica. The Spaniards in the cities and forts who had survived the disasters surrendered themselves to servitude under the barbarians who held sway throughout the provinces.[65]

Of the five provinces of mainland Spain, four were claimed by different barbarian groups, and the fifth – the Roman political centre of Tarraconensis – remained under the government of the usurper

Maximus. Of the division itself little can be said beyond the obvious fact that the Alans took by far the largest portion and the Hasding Vandals and Sueves shared the smallest.[66] Evidently, this was not a random distribution: the division probably represented the relative strengths of the different barbarian groups at the time.[67] The Alans were clearly the largest and most important group, and Hydatius later alludes to the fact that the Alan King Addax had enjoyed a hegemony of some sort over both the Sueves and the Hasding Vandals.[68] Quite how formal this division was is unknown. Hydatius states that the dividing up of the provinces was accomplished by the barbarians themselves, and was probably not ratified by the imperial court at Tarraco or Rome.[69] In 415, the barbarians in Spain approached the imperial authorities for a formal recognition of their status, a move which would not have been necessary had their initial settlement been officially ratified.[70]

In 415, however, the balance of power in the imperial province of Tarraconensis changed. The position of the usurper Maximus had collapsed after the suicide of Gerontius in 411, and his own Gallic troops drove him into exile among the barbarians.[71] Four years later, the hub of Roman authority on the Spanish Mediterranean coast was occupied by the Goths under King Athaulf.[72] The brother-in-law and designated successor of Alaric, Athaulf had overseen the movement of the Goths through Italy and into southern Gaul, where the group enjoyed an ambivalent relationship with the imperial court at Ravenna.[73] In Orosius' rather optimistic opinion, Athaulf had pledged himself to the defence of Roman civilization with Gothic arms, and he initially proved to be a valuable ally for the empire in its struggles against the new usurpation of Jovinus in northern Gaul.[74] Yet a more or less autonomous army was a dangerous prospect in the Mediterranean provinces, and Athaulf's position was further bolstered by his capture of, and marriage to, the imperial princess Galla Placidia at the time of the sack of Rome. Threatened by this, the Roman generalissimo Constantius did his best to smother Gothic independence. In 415, Athaulf was driven from his base in Narbonne by a combination of military and economic pressure. In flight from Constantius, and apparently desperate for food, Athaulf brought his Goths to Tarraco and Barcino.[75]

Matters did not improve for the Goths once they entered Spain. Suffocating under the continued economic blockade, the Goths underwent a series of political convulsions. Athaulf was assassinated in the summer of 415, apparently by his own men, and his successor Segeric was also killed shortly afterwards.[76] Meanwhile the Vandals mocked the Goths in their suffering, even as they sold them grain at prohibitive prices.[77] In an effort to break this stranglehold, a small number of Goths attempted to cross into Mauretania but this, too, ended in ignominious failure, and the new Gothic king Wallia was forced to try to consolidate his position.[78] The result seems to have been a shuffling of the political deck within Spain. All of the barbarian groups took this opportunity to open lines of negotiation with Constantius, either to offer themselves to the service of the court, or to pre-empt imperial action in their own corners of the Iberian Peninsula.[79]

Ultimately, it was Wallia who was nominated as agent of the empire, and in AD 417–18 he commanded a devastating campaign against the other barbarian groups within Spain.[80] The Siling Vandals in Baetica and the Alans in Lusitania were decisively defeated in a campaign that was presumably intended to re-establish imperial control over the city of Mérida and the rich grain-producing lands of southern Spain.[81] Hydatius states firmly that the Silings were entirely destroyed, and although this is certainly an exaggeration, nothing more is heard of them.[82] King Addax of the Alans was killed during the same campaign, and his followers turned to Gunderic of the Vandals for refuge.[83] Significantly, Wallia never marched into Gallaecia, and both the Hasding Vandals and the Sueves escaped from his systematic conquest unscathed. This was probably simply a reflection of the strategic irrelevance of Gallaecia, and the relative unimportance of the Sueves and Vandals settled there.[84] Constantius may also have regarded the barbarians as a potential source of military manpower, which he wished to keep available.[85] At the very least, neither group would seem to have been regarded as a major military threat, and Wallia was removed from Spain and resettled in Aquitaine in 418.[86]

The Hasdings – now apparently reinforced by the last remnants of the Lusitanian Alans – then came into conflict with their Suevic neighbours in Gallaecia, probably in around 420. This conflict was most likely caused by the re-emergence from obscurity of the imperial pretender Maximus, who had once been Gerontius' puppet in Spain. We know from several sources that Maximus found refuge with the barbarians after he had been deposed by his own troops, and a Gallic chronicle reports that a usurper of the same name rose to prominence in Gallaecia in 420.[87] In the same year an imperial army under the *comes Hispaniarum* Asterius arrived in Gallaecia. Hydatius' cursory account of these events tells us only that Asterius relieved the Sueves, who were under siege by the Vandals at the time, and then inflicted a minor defeat upon the Hasdings, which forced them to retreat towards Baetica.[88]

With hindsight, Asterius' campaign was a strategic disaster. As a direct result of his intervention, the Vandals were bumped from a peripheral province at the edge of the empire into the rich lands of southern Spain, whence they set about establishing themselves as a major power within the peninsula. But at the time the expedition was viewed as a success. Asterius was declared a patrician shortly after his recall from Spain – a social rank that seems to have been reserved for particular imperial favourites in this period.[89] We can conclude from this that his campaign in Gallaecia was never intended to be a major action against the Vandals, but was rather an attempt to crush Maximus' embryonic usurpation before it gained momentum.[90] This was certainly the impression of one Consentius, who wrote to Augustine from the Balearic islands in 420, and who probably reflects the assumptions of the Hispano-Roman establishment at this time.[91] To the mind of the imperial establishment at Ravenna, Maximus simply posed a greater threat to the empire than either the Vandals or the Sueves. The suppression of the usurpation was a success. Maximus was captured – perhaps in the battle in which the Vandals were defeated – and was taken to Ravenna with his companion Jovinus. There, the two of them were executed at a public games held in honour of the tricennalia of Honorius.[92]

Within two years, however, this smug triumphalism began to look distinctly short-sighted. Far from evaporating in the warm air of Baetica, the Vandals revealed themselves to be a major threat to imperial interests in the south. Shortly after Asterius' promotion, the *comes domesticorum* Castinus was charged with clearing up the mess that his predecessor had left.[93] Allied with the *magister militum* Boniface – the 'golden boy' of the western military, following his victories over usurpers in Gaul – and aided further by the presence of a substantial number of Gothic federates, Castinus moved to engage the barbarians. Despite quarrels with Boniface, and the latter's petulant departure for Africa in a sulk, Castinus was initially successful against the Vandals and was only deprived of a substantial victory by his desire for something more decisive.[94] No doubt buoyed by the reflection that the Vandals had engaged in only two (or perhaps three) fixed battles over the previous 15 years, and had lost all of them, Castinus resolved to engage his opponents in the open field. But the Roman general was betrayed by his Gothic federates and suffered a humiliating defeat.[95]

Castinus' defeat might justly be regarded as one of the most significant battles in the history of the western Roman empire, yet we know remarkably little about it. Hydatius implies that it was a siege of some description, but whether this represents the defence of a hill-top or (less probably) that of a town is unclear.[96] The result, however, was not. At one stroke, the Hasding Vandals were transformed in the most unlikely fashion from a fugitive group, simply awaiting their coup de grâce, to undisputed masters of southern Spain. Modern scholarship has tended to underplay the significance of this victory, largely because the Vandals were assumed to have been a formidable group at the time of the battle. In fact, the defeat of Castinus represented the first certain military victory in Vandal history, and it signalled the start of their great consolidation of power – first in southern Spain and Mauretania, and then in the provinces around Hippo and Carthage.

Vandal Identity at the Time of the Invasion

From their first appearance on the Danube frontier in the second century to the defeat of Consentius in 422, the Vandals appear only fleetingly within our written sources and leave little or no mark on the archaeological record. As a result, little can be said with confidence about their social and political organization during this period, and it is likely that both changed substantially over the course of 250 years. What does seem likely is that great changes occurred even in the decade or so that followed the Rhine crossing, and close investigation of the events of this period seem to indicate a multitude of smaller Vandal groupings, rather than a single coherent entity.[97] This is manifested most clearly in Hydatius' careful distinction between 'Hasding' and 'Siling' Vandals during the partition of Spain in 411 or 412. The modern consensus seems to be that the Hasdings and Silings were separated very early in their prehistory, and that their reunion was only effected with the invasion of Gaul.[98] This interpretation rests on assumptions of a long-standing and coherent 'Vandal' identity that both predated contact with the Roman frontier and remained intact through the long period of interaction with the empire. As has already been discussed, neither of these positions is tenable. It is rather more likely that the 'Vandal' invaders of 405/6 were never a coherent political group, and had been further fragmented by their defeat at the hands of the Franks in the battle of 405 and the possible death of a Vandal king in this battle. At some point between the Rhine crossing and the Spanish settlement, the Vandals assembled into two associated factions which nevertheless chose to occupy different parts of the peninsula. There is no particular reason to assume that the separation between 'Hasdings' and 'Silings' was more than a few years old at the time of the Spanish settlement.

The Alans provide a useful point of comparison here. We know of multiple examples of division and subdivision within the group, even during the brief occupation of Gaul. Frigeridus notes, for example, that there were two Alanic kings at the time of the battle with the Franks – Respendial who remained loyal to the invaders, and Goar who cast in his lot with the imperial administration. At the time of the crossing of the Pyrenees in 409, some Alans pillaged the countryside of Spain, others remained in Gaul, and still others joined in alliance with Gerontius.[99] Just as the Alans never comprised a coherent political whole, it is likely that that the same was true of the Vandals down to the defeat of the Silings in 417. Our sources support this impression. Both Zosimus and Orosius allude to the frequent periods of reinforcement and reorganization among the barbarian groups.[100] Even over such a short period of time, the form of the Vandal group within the empire was in a constant state of flux.

No less serious is our ignorance of the size and nature of these different Vandal groups. Conventionally, historians have presented the Vandals as a more or less coherent migrating 'people'. This is based primarily upon the assumption that the group numbered 80,000 at the time of the crossing into Africa. This figure is based upon several confused and contradictory references in Victor of Vita and two of Procopius' works, and has been shown to be largely fictitious.[101] Procopius is the fuller of the two sources and strongly implies that the figure of 80,000 was a misleading total created by Geiseric's military reorganization at some point after the establishment of the Vandal kingdom in 442, and that the actual Vandal population was much lower.[102] Small warbands seem to have been the norm in the confused military politics of the later empire. Even within the short military narrative laid out above we see several groups of Franks, Goths, Burgundians and Saxons operating within the Gallic and Italian theatres and many more barbarians of different hues fighting in the more or less 'imperial' armies of Stilicho, Constantius, Constantine and Gerontius. In several cases, moreover, the numbers involved seem to have been extraordinarily small. One Gothic leader, who fought Constantine III on behalf of Stilicho, and later flirted with the idea of joining Jovinus' uprising, is said to have employed a troop of only 300 horsemen.[103] Another commander fought against Alaric with a similar number of Huns.[104] While it should be remembered that excessively small numbers are no more trustworthy than very large figures in the historiography of the period, they do provide a valuable reminder that groups in the hundreds or low thousands could make a substantial military and political impact in the later Roman state, particularly in relatively unmilitarized provinces like southern Gaul or Spain. Such groups would be much more mobile than large groups of migrating people, would not require organized settlement and might be deployed at relatively short notice. All of this is circumstantial, of course, but the silence of our sources regarding the nature of the Vandal, Alan and Suevic threat encourages the suspicion that it was similar to that posed by other contemporary groups. The narrative of Vandal movement through Gaul and Spain would certainly fit more closely to a flexible group of mercenaries than it would to a substantial number of migrating peoples.

This is not to suggest that the history of the Vandals in this period can only have been the history of a tiny group of fighting men. Numbers of women and children are also likely to have been drawn along in the wake of the different barbarian groups. We know from contemporary Roman practice that military society was mixed, even within the field armies, and more than one later Roman emperor was brought up almost exclusively in camps and on campaign.[105] Gerontius apparently took his wife on campaign when he rose in revolt against Constantine.[106] Paulinus of Pella similarly alludes to Alan women fighting alongside their husbands during the siege of Beziers in 414, and at least some of these unions may have been made before the crossing of the Rhine.[107] The Vandals, Alans and Sueves were an army on the move, and presumably brought women and children along with them. It might have been a small army, and it might have been better at plundering than it was at fighting, but for the early years of the fifth century at least, the Vandals were defined primarily by their military character.

Vandal kingship and the likely succession of the kings themselves during the early decades of the fifth century deserves some brief discussion. That kings were central figures for the cohesion and military effectiveness of barbarian groups seems clear, and several kings were probably in command during the crossing of 405/6. Yet specific details remain elusive. In total we know the names of only three Hasding kings in this period.[108] Godigisel was certainly king immediately before the crossing of the Rhine in 405, and may still have been so at the time of the passage into Spain in 409. Frigeridus states that Godigisel was killed in the great battle with the Franks, discussed above, but other sources would suggest that he died peacefully, having survived the battle.[109] Gunderic was Godigisel's legitimate son and is said to have been his direct successor. He probably died in southern Spain in 428, shortly before the crossing into Africa, and Hydatius is explicit that this came about after his desecration of the cathedral in Seville.[110] Geiseric was Gunderic's half-brother, and may well have been the elder of the two.[111] According to some, Geiseric was illegitimate, but his succession to Gunderic appears to have been unchallenged, and he may well have been influential at court long before his formal accession.

Into Africa

Following the surprising defeat of Castinus in 422, the Vandals found themselves in a strong position in southern Spain. Victory not only removed an immediate threat to the group, it also strengthened their forces and Castinus' Roman and Gothic troops probably rallied to the Hasding standard, as the Alans and Silings had five years earlier. For the next half decade, the Vandals took advantage of this unexpected fortune and solidified their position within southern Spain. Prominent cities were besieged, presumably in an effort to suppress lingering resistance, and the Vandal kings increasingly looked beyond the fertile fields of Baetica to the rich pickings of the Balearic Islands and northern regions of Mauretania.

Hydatius' *Chronicle* provides the only record of this consolidation of Vandal power. His account is impressionistic, and several separate stages of growth are lumped together into just two short entries:

> 425 The Vandals pillaged the Balearic Islands and when they had sacked Carthago Spartaria and Hispalis, and pillaged Spain, they invaded Mauretania.[112]

> 428 Gunderic, the king of the Vandals, captured Hispalis, but soon after, when with overwhelming impiety he tried to lay hands on the church of that very city, by the will of god he was seized by a demon and died.[113]

Late Roman Baetica was a rich province in its own right but was also closely bound by economic and social ties to the maritime regions of Mauretania and the Balearic Islands. During the classical and early medieval period, the fishing regions of the Mauretanian coasts and the grain fields of the Guadalquivir Valley were part of the same broader cultural and economic system.[114] Texts and religious ideas happily spread from Spain to Africa and back again throughout Late Antiquity, and continued to do so for decades after the disappearance of the Vandal kingdom.[115] Economically, Baetica and Tingitania had long been bound together by the shared exploitation of the Atlantic coast and the western Mediterranean, and display a strikingly consistent material culture. Even politically, the two regions had been linked in the provincial reorganization under Diocletian, a change that was perhaps motivated by a desire to keep the few frontier troops of the Atlas Mountains fed from the bread-basket of Baetica.[116]

Hydatius implies that the Vandals were the happy beneficiaries of this unity, and extended their authority into Hispalis (Seville) and the coastal regions beyond. The occupation of Carthago Spartaria and other ports on the south coast provided the Vandals with control over the shipping with which they could extend their authority into Mauretania and the Balearics. Hydatius' language suggests that the Mediterranean islands were pillaged, while the north coast of Africa was settled more permanently, but whether we should read too much into the semantics of such a late source is not clear. What seems certain, however, is that by the middle or end of the 420s, the Vandals had established a relatively secure position in southern Spain and probably also along the coast of Mauretania Tingitania. The archaeology from southern Spain in this period can tell us little about the Vandals themselves – indeed one scholar has stated succinctly that the group left no 'footprint' within the rich soil of the Iberian Peninsula – but it does demonstrate the prosperity of the region in this period.[117] Field surveys have revealed a thriving rural landscape, and archaeological excavation a strong continuity in urban occupation throughout the region.[118]

Modern scholars have almost universally presented the Vandal move to the sea as a moment of almost cataclysmic significance within the history of the later Roman empire. It is true of course that Geiseric was later to enjoy his greatest political and military influence as the master of both Carthage and her shipping, but it should not be assumed that either the Vandals or their contemporaries viewed the passage to Africa Proconsularis as an inevitable final stage to their movement southwards. Nor did the spread of Vandal influence into Mauretania Tingitania necessarily send ripples of panic through the Roman administration in Carthage.[119] There is little to suggest that Vandal ambitions immediately turned to the rich lands of Africa Proconsularis and Sicily. The Vandals had recently proved themselves through the defeat of Castinus, but most observers of the time probably continued to see the group as lightweights on the world stage. In holding Baetica, the Vandals were already in possession of some of the richest cereal lands in the western empire, and the expeditions to the Balearics and Mauretania are best read as a consolidation of this southern Spanish kingdom rather than as a preparation for a still more ambitious campaign. To contemporaries – including perhaps the Vandals themselves – the movement into Africa was scarcely an obvious next step.

AD 429: The Crossing

By the late 420s, the political map of the western Mediterranean was changing. In Spain, the Goths and Sueves consolidated their power, and increasingly came into conflict with the Vandals in Lusitania and the south.[120] Further east, in the central Mediterranean, three Roman commanders competed for influence over the young western emperor Valentinian III and his mother and regent Galla Placidia. It was these political disputes between the senior western *magister militum* Constantius Felix, the count and junior *magister militum* Aetius and the African *comes* Boniface which provided the Vandals with an unexpected opportunity to move from Spain towards the city of Carthage.[121]

North Africa held two great attractions for the Vandals. It was tremendously wealthy, of course – a quality which Geiseric must have inferred from the African merchantmen in Spanish ports – but it was also relatively lightly militarized.[122] While a number of different barbarian armies jostled for position within Spain, North Africa was unusually vulnerable by the later 420s. The origins of this lay in AD 422 or 423 with the arrival of Boniface from Spain and his appointment as *comes Africae* (Count of Africa). By all accounts, Boniface was a fabulously popular ruler. Stories of his good government circulated long after his death, and he remained on good terms with Augustine of Hippo, in spite of the general's marriage to an Arian Christian and the baptism of his child in the rites of the same heresy.[123] Boniface's military reputation had been forged in struggles within Gaul against the usurper Jovinus, and he had further brightened his escutcheon with a series of successful campaigns against Moors on the African frontier.[124] In 425, his successes earned him promotion to the rank of *comes domesticorum et Africae* (Count of the Households and of Africa), but ironically, this success proved fatal to imperial interests in North Africa. As Boniface flourished, Felix and Aetius grew wary of his popularity and sought to curb his power. Consequently, the energies of the imperial military were once more directed inwards, and the barbarian warbands within the empire found themselves with plenty of room to manoeuvre.

Procopius provides us with the fullest and most fanciful account of the deterioration in relations between the three rivals in power, and even claims that it was this conflict which led to the Vandal invasion of Africa.[125] His account states that in an attempt to distance Boniface from the court in Ravenna, Aetius spread the rumour that his rival was plotting rebellion, and ensured that this news reached the ears of the regent Galla Placidia. Simultaneously, Aetius wrote to Boniface in the guise of friendship, and warned him that interested parties were attempting to entrap him upon his return to court. Just as Aetius intended, Galla Placidia summoned the suspected general to Ravenna, and Boniface duly ignored the summons, thus finding himself in a revolt which was not of his own making. Thereafter, a chronicle source tells us that an imperial force was sent to Africa in 427 under Mavortius, Gallio and Sanoeces, in order to suppress this revolt.[126] Boniface defeated this expedition with little difficulty, but was more receptive to a diplomatic mission sent the following year under Comes Sigisvultus – himself an able military commander – and the Arian bishop Maximinus. Over the next 12 months Sigisvultus and Maximinus entered wholeheartedly into the complex military and episcopal politics of Northern Africa.[127] In 429 a third imperial mission was sent to Africa under one Darius.[128] This mission finally negotiated peace with Boniface, and may also have received a rather warmer welcome in Hippo. Nominally at least, the Romano-African house within North Africa was in order.

Yet by 429, this house also had some unwelcome visitors. The coincidence of the Vandal invasion with the revolt of Boniface is notable, Procopius was anxious to make the link explicit:

> Boniface accordingly sent to Spain those who were his most intimate friends and gained the adherence of each of the sons of Godigisclus on terms of complete equality, it being agreed that each one of the three, holding a third part of Libya, should rule over his own subjects; but if a foe should come against any one of them to make war, they should in common ward off the aggressors. On the basis of this agreement, the Vandals crossed the strait of Gadira and came into Libya, and the Visigoths in later times settled in Spain.[129]

Several eastern historians recounted this tradition in the sixth century.[130] In their eyes, the cataclysmic loss of North Africa to the empire could at least be rendered comprehensible if blame for the disaster was laid at the feet of a Roman general. It is certainly true that a limited alliance with the Vandals would have made sense for Boniface (or his rivals): after all Geiseric could either have secured the western reaches of North Africa from counter-attack, or have provided allied troops for an ambitious generalissimo. But there is no contemporary evidence to support this accusation, and the likelihood remains that the Vandals simply benefited from this internecine fighting and invaded North Africa when the attentions of the world were elsewhere.

Geiseric committed his full forces to the invasion of North Africa in AD 428 or (more probably) 429: the chronicle sources are uncertain on this point.[131] The decision had momentous historical significance, but may not have seemed particularly portentous at the time. The transportation of the Vandals and their allies across the Straits of Gibraltar need not have been accomplished in a single operation, although generations of modern scholars have been fascinated by the imagined prospect of a vast barbarian flotilla heading into Africa.[132] Given that Geiseric had foothold in Mauretania Tingitania for around five years at the time of his 'invasion', the decision to move east need not have been a major logistical issue, and the fact that his following was certainly far smaller than the throng of 80,000 claimed by Victor also argues against the popular image of a carefully planned armada. Several historians have argued that the invasion fleet probably landed around the modern city of Oran for military reasons, but the lack of any corroborative contemporary evidence urges caution.[133] It seems perfectly feasible that Geiseric simply led his troops east from Mauretania Tingitania, with or without logistical support from the sea.[134] Regardless of the route taken, the move into Africa was a political gamble; in marching towards Carthage, Geiseric effectively surrendered his holdings in Baetica. Diplomatic links were retained with both the Visigoths and the Sueves, but after 429 the history of the Vandals was to be to the south of the Mediterranean.[135]

Movement within North Africa

The presence of a substantial Vandal army within North Africa threatened the stability of the Roman empire. By 429, Boniface had been formally restored with imperial favour, although personal reconciliation would have to wait. As *comes domesticorum et Africae* and the principal representative of imperial power, Boniface moved into action: first he attempted to parlay with the Vandals, and then met them in battle after these motions towards federation were rebuffed.[136] The battle did not go well for the African governor, however, and Boniface was forced to seek refuge in the fortified city of Hippo.

The progress of the Vandals through North Africa was violent and bloody. As the barbarians marched east towards the capital, terrified bishops wrote to Augustine, their spiritual leader, for guidance on what course of action to take – to stay with their flocks and risk death, or to retreat and preserve the word of God in exile.[137] Nor were these fears without foundation. Papal rescripts shortly after the invasion make it clear that the fate of those who chose to remain was often horrific, and one ruling alludes to the status of consecrated virgins who had been raped during the occupation.[138] Those aristocrats and professionals who could afford to fled from North Africa, and many sympathetic individuals spent the next decade or so taking care of these refugees.[139] Later historians list with mournful relish the brutality of the barbarians, particularly towards Nicene Christians. We read of persecutions throughout Mauretania Caesariensis, Numidia and the proconsular province, which reached a climax in 430 in the siege of Hippo, an assault upon the spiritual heart of Roman North Africa.[140]

Yet the Vandal invasion did not sweep all before it, and the worst of its furies eventually calmed. After 14 months, the Vandals abandoned the siege of Hippo.[141] Thereafter, they continued to ravage Numidia and probably moved still further east into Africa Proconsularis and Byzacena. At around this time, imperial reinforcements arrived under the command of one Aspar and, combined with Boniface's now revived Hippo garrison, undertook a second field campaign against the Vandals. Procopius' account tell us only that this second campaign was again defeated, and that its two commanders left Africa, Boniface to patch up his differences with Galla Placidia (an attempt which led ultimately to his murder by order of Aetius), and Aspar back to Byzantium and a lifetime of avoiding further conflict with the Vandals.[142]

Before his departure, Aspar negotiated a peace treaty of sorts with Geiseric. In a peculiar passage, Procopius describes Geiseric's encounter with a young Roman officer named Marcian who was later to become the eastern emperor, and the personal arrangement which the two men reached. Marcian, the historian claims, was freed on the understanding that he would never wage war against the Vandal kingdom.[143] Procopius' passage is best read as a pre-emptive explanation for Marcian's later failure to retaliate to Geiseric's sack of Rome in 455 – a hesitation which seems to have been met with some hostility at the time. But the diplomatic negotiations that provide the setting for this fable are likely to have been real enough. In any event, peace followed immediately afterwards, first through the cessation of hostilities, and then through the signing of the peace treaty of 435 with Valentinian III. The Vandals were acknowledged in their possession of Hippo Regius and the surrounding territory. Carthage lay just one short step away.

The final stage of the Vandal conquest came in 439 with the occupation of Carthage. With hindsight, this seems to have been inevitable after the contrived settlement of AD 435, and it provided the foundations for the consolidation of Vandal power in North Africa and the western Mediterranean. From a wider chronological perspective, however, the capture of Carthage is much more surprising, and seems a remarkable climax to a series of campaigns which began so inauspiciously around 35 years earlier. Having benefited – indirectly more than directly – from the political chaos of the early fifth-century west, the Vandals found themselves transformed from understudies to major players on the political stage.

3

Ruling the Vandal Kingdom AD 435–534

The Vandal kingdom of Carthage was not born fully formed. The Vandals came not as colonizers, nor as imperialists. The movement of the group through Europe, and perhaps even into Africa, had been determined by the wider strategic initiatives of a succession of Roman generals, generalissimos and usurpers. Vandal culture, such as it was, had been moulded by a full generation of military activity (and inactivity) within the western empire, and their political systems similarly were created from the immediate needs of this peripatetic mercenary lifestyle. In purely demographic terms, the Vandals, numbering only in the low tens of thousands at the most, were little more than a conspicuous minority within a North African population of between one and three million inhabitants.

The political history of the Vandal state in North Africa is one of perpetual negotiation between different groups: between the Vandal king and his family members, between the Hasding clan and the Vandal aristocracy, and between the Vandal minority and the Roman majority. This drama was played out on a number of different stages, not only in the entourage of the king, and among the various courts which surrounded other members of his family, but also in the governmental palaces and provincial courts, in the debating chamber and in poetry recitals, and (ultimately) on the foreign battlefields of the western Mediterranean. The results were dramatic, and led to the foundation of a politically stable and economically flourishing state that lasted for almost a century, and the gradual recognition of what it meant to be 'Vandal', 'Roman' or 'African' within this kingdom. Effectively, the Vandal state was always a work in progress; this was a project in which all members of the kingdom – invader and invaded alike – had a role to play.

A Gallery of Kings

The study of Vandal Africa is to a large degree the study of its kings. Far more is known about the Hasding monarchs than almost any other individual from the kingdom, and their characters and foibles are often sketched in vivid terms by contemporary sources. In part, this clarity can be misleading, and the proclivities of writers like Victor of Vita and Ferrandus mean that the kings themselves often seem caricatures rather than rulers. Thus, the figure of the cunning Geiseric, the evil Huneric, the benevolent scholar Thrasamund and the weak-willed Hilderic are all products of the violently contrasting sources which have survived from each reign. But some general overview of the monarchs is necessary before we examine the development and organization of the Vandal kingdom in more detail.

Geiseric (428–477) was certainly the most important of the Vandal kings, and indeed was among the most influential figures of the fifth-century Mediterranean world. It was under his watch that the Vandals crossed into Africa, and secured the two imperial treaties of settlement in 435 and 442. He established the position of the Vandals as a major naval power by commandeering the Carthaginian merchant marine, and was able to spread Vandal authority into Sicily, Corsica, Sardinia and the Balearic Islands. The climax of Geiseric's foreign policy came with the prolonged sack of Rome in 455, but this was simply one stage in a complex diplomatic choreography which witnessed the betrothal and eventual marriage of his son Huneric to the imperial princess Eudocia, the support of at least one pretender to the imperial throne, and the

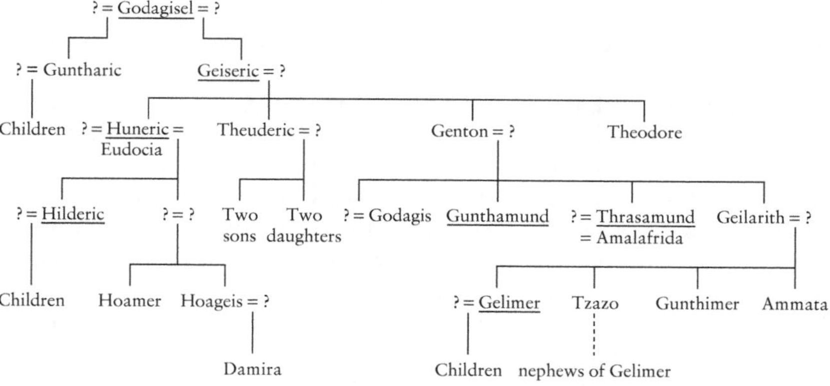

Figure 3.1 The genealogy of the Hasding family

successful resistance to two separate (and substantial) Byzantine campaigns against his kingdom. Geiseric was also responsible for the integration of the Vandals within what were still thriving North African provinces. His domestic policies were often brutal and Victor's *History* ensures that he is best remembered now for his anti-Nicene persecutions, yet he laid the foundations for a strong and largely successful state. The mid-sixth-century historian Jordanes sketches the king in evocative terms, from his stocky build to his slight limp, and emphasizes the ambition and strategic brilliance which underlay his success.[1]

Geiseric's son Huneric (477–484) is known to us largely through Victor of Vita's caustic account, and the brutal persecutions of 483–4 do tend to define his reign. Probably around 50 at the time of his accession, Huneric lacked his father's vigour in foreign affairs, and moved his kingdom back from the centre of world events. Thanks to the nature of the extant sources, it is easy to present Huneric's rule as a narrative of unremitting cruelty, even away from the religious sphere. Many of Geiseric's advisors found themselves out of favour at the time of Huneric's accession, and several other prominent state functionaries, including members of the royal family, were killed following the suppression of a plot in around 481. But his reign was not one of unremitting devastation, and Huneric seems to have instituted some financial reforms, and was probably a patron of the arts (albeit perhaps in a limited sense).[2] As the husband of a Roman princess, moreover, Huneric was closely integrated into the circles of Mediterranean power. In keeping with this status, his reign witnessed the testing of the limits of royal authority, as was most obvious in his attempt to redefine Geiseric's complex law of succession in favour of his own son Hilderic. Variously said to have died at his toilet, or to have been eaten from within by worms, Huneric's death – like his reign – was viewed with fascinated horror by contemporaries and later historians.[3]

Gunthamund (484–496) succeeded Huneric. The elder son of Huneric's younger brother Genton, Gunthamund was the eldest male Hasding at the time of the death of his uncle and succeeded by right of seniority. Huneric's attempt to subvert this system created some bad blood among the surviving members of the royal house (and led to some bloody deaths for the remainder), but was ultimately unsuccessful. There is some suggestion that Gunthamund instituted a purge of some of Huneric's advisors at the time of his succession, just as his predecessor had done.[4] Beyond this, however, very little is known of Gunthamund's reign. Procopius implies that religious persecution practically stopped under the king, but that some military conflict with the Moors continued, even if few other historical sources refer directly to the reign. The chance survival of both the Bir Trouch *ostraka* and the Albertini Tablets from this period may imply that the king instituted a major economic reform programme during the 490s, and his minting programme was certainly more ambitious than that of any of his predecessors, but the evidence available to us is far from conclusive.

Thrasamund (496–523) is far better known than his elder brother, thanks to his close relationship to the renowned Fulgentius of Ruspe. The *Life* of Fulgentius, probably written by his disciple Ferrandus shortly after the saint's death, provides the fullest account of religious life in Vandal Africa after Victor's *Historia*. Within the work, Thrasamund appears as a persecutor, but one unusually concerned with the intellectual context for his actions and anxious to debate the niceties of theology with the eponymous saint. This popular image of a barbarian 'scholar king' would seem to be supported by a number of poems written in Thrasamund's honour which survive in the sixth-century *Latin Anthology*.[5] While these poems remain important sources for the evolution of Vandal kingship, and the developing interdependence of the different populations of early sixth-century Africa, Thrasamund was perhaps not so different from his predecessors as these chance survivals might suggest. One thing that is clear is that Thrasamund's reign witnessed a substantial change in the diplomatic position of the Vandal *regnum*. In AD 500, the king married the Ostrogothic princess Amalafrida, and thereby established a strong alliance between the kingdoms of Italy and North Africa. Despite some periods of difficulty, this alliance was to last throughout Thrasamund's reign and was only to be jeopardized by the imprisonment and later execution of the Gothic queen under his successor Hilderic.[6]

Hilderic came to the throne in 523, fully 40 years after the succession envisaged by his father, Huneric. Variously castigated at the time of his reign as an ineffectual and indecisive old man, Hilderic nevertheless oversaw some major changes within the Vandal kingdom, including the official conversion of the state to Nicene Catholicism and the axial shift of Hasding foreign policy away from alliance with the Ostrogoths and towards the Byzantines.[7] The son of Eudocia, and hence the grandson of the former western emperor Valentinian III, Hilderic was keen to accentuate his own imperial status. Yet his successes appear to have been more ideological than military, and his reign witnessed a number of losses against the resurgent Moorish polities of the south. Either because of these defeats or because of an attempt to privilege the succession of his favoured nephews Hoamer and Hoageis to the Vandal throne, Hilderic won the enmity of his legal heir Gelimer who rose in revolt in 530 and proved to be the only successful usurper within the century of the Vandal kingdom.[8]

Gelimer's success was limited, however. After claiming the kingship and ridding himself of his principal rivals in power, a series of revolts in Sardinia and in Tripolitana forced Gelimer into crisis management. With the bulk of his army committed in Sardinia, Gelimer could not resist the Byzantine reconquest under Belisarius and the Vandal *regnum* folded with embarrassing rapidity. Apparently stoical in the face of these turns of fortune, Gelimer was treated with respect in Byzantium after his defeat, and became something of a folk favourite among the writers and painters of modern Europe.[9] Refusing the rank of patrician, for which he would have had to abjure his Arian faith, Gelimer was nevertheless invited by Justinian to retire to an estate in Greece – rather a subdued end for the last of the Vandal kings.

The Growth of the Vandal Kingdom

The Vandal kingdom took time to develop into its final form. Growth and change continued throughout the century in which the group ruled Carthage, but the main features of the new state emerged during the first decade and a half in North Africa. Within this period, Geiseric was presented with a number of challenges: to consolidate the position of his followers within the rich lands of the region; to secure the state against external enemies; and to confirm his own position (and that of his family) at the heart of the newly created Vandal state. The solutions which he adopted established the foundations of his kingdom, but also had a profound effect upon the lives of his subjects. Identities solidified, social structures were clarified, and Geiseric was able to create a new Vandal monarchy, suited to the rich lands in which his people had found themselves. As a starting point for a new kingdom, the grand experiment of the period from 435–445 was a resounding success.

The treaty of 435

The first formal treaty between the Vandals and the western empire was signed on 11 February 435 and bought a temporary peace to the region.[10] Augustine's former diocese at Hippo Regius became Geiseric's first capital, and the lands ceded for the settlement of the Vandals were probably restricted to northern Numidia and perhaps parts of Africa Proconsularis or Mauretania Sitifiensis. Treaties of this kind were common in the western empire, and indeed had long formed part of the imperial strategy for accommodating groups of federate barbarians. The Vandals themselves had requested a similar treaty following their occupation of Spain in the 410s, and may conceivably have been bribed by a *foedus* of some description during the negotiations with Boniface in the late 420s. Typically, treaties like these offered land, subsidies and some practical autonomy to the barbarian group in question, but placed them in a subordinate position to the western empire, and demanded military service in return.[11]

Geiseric rapidly outgrew his status as a junior federate. Shortly after settling in Hippo, the king expelled three prominent bishops from their sees – Possidius of Calama, Novatus of Sitifis, and Severianus, probably the bishop of Mila.[12] At around the same time, the king instituted a purge of his court and removed four prominent Hispano-Roman courtiers as well as some minor functionaries from his entourage, ostensibly for their refusal to convert to Arianism.[13] While these actions – particularly those against the church – probably overstepped the terms of his treaty, Geiseric's apparent indifference to the military responsibilities that came with federate status had far more serious implications. As early as 437, pirates became increasingly active within the Mediterranean, and these may well have been Vandals, operating with the king's tacit support.[14]

The most serious blow came two years later: on 19 October 439, with Aetius otherwise engaged in Gaul, and the imperial garrison in Carthage apparently unaware of the impending danger, Geiseric occupied the city.[15] The psychological impact of the fall of Carthage was considerable. As contemporary sources attest, the arrival of the Vandals was met with widespread panic and flight among the local population.[16] Christian sermons of the period and Victor's *Historia* all suggest that the occupation was a violent one, but this does not seem to have been the case. Portable goods, both secular and ecclesiastical, were certainly plundered, and some Catholic churches were handed over to the Arians or closed within a few months of the occupation, but as yet there is little archaeological evidence for extensive structural damage at the moment of the immediate aftermath of the occupation.[17]

442. The birth of the Vandal state

The treaty of 442 and the subsequent divisions of the African spoils were the point at which the Vandal *regnum* truly came into being.[18] Stunned

Figure 3.2 The Vandal kingdom after the treaty of AD 435

by the loss of Carthage, and chilled by the recent Vandal attacks on Sicily and Southern Italy, the emperor Valentinian in Italy was forced to compromise with Geiseric for a second time. In his *Chronicle*, Prosper states explicitly that 'peace was confirmed with Geiseric and the emperor Valentinian and Africa was divided between the two into distinct territories'.[19] This form of agreement was new. Whereas previous treaties, including that of 435, had granted land to barbarian groups for settlement, but had retained nominal sovereignty in the name of the empire, Prosper's forceful language suggests that there was a genuine division of land in 442. No longer simply federates of the empire, it seems that the Vandals were being given lands of their own. Other aspects of the treaty confirm this impression. According to Procopius, Geiseric's eldest son Huneric was sent as a hostage to the imperial court – indeed a number of poems composed in Ravenna at that time seem to refer to the young prince.[20] It was probably in this period, or shortly afterwards, that Huneric was betrothed to the imperial princess Eudocia, a dynastic union that was to play a central role in Geiseric's foreign policy over the decades that followed. No less important was the annual tribute (*dasmos*) to be paid from Carthage to the western emperor, which Procopius states was an important part of the agreement.[21] Crucially, payment flowed from the barbarians to the empire, and not the other way around, as was the case in all previous settlement treaties. The Vandals, in other words, were no longer paid employees of the Roman state.

The new Vandal kingdom was substantial. Victor of Vita's account of the treaty gives some impression of the division between the 'two distinct territories' of Roman and Vandal jurisdiction:

> [Geiseric] also made an arrangement concerning the individual provinces: Byzacena, Abaritana and Gaetulia, and part of Numidia he kept for himself. Zeugitana and the Proconsular province he divided up as 'heritable lots' for his army; and he allowed Valentinian, who was still emperor, to take for himself the remaining, and now devastated provinces.[22]

On the face of it, the division seems clear enough: the Vandals took for their own the rich grain-producing lands of Zeugitana (Africa Proconsularis) and eastern Numidia;[23] in addition, the treaty granted Geiseric jurisdiction over the Roman province of Byzacena (or Byzacium), incorporating the rich cereal lands in the hinterland of Hadrumetum and the eastern coastal plain, as far as the mountains and pre-desert of what is now western Tunisia and the Algerian border. Abaritana and Gaetulia are more difficult to identify, and may well have been new administrative divisions, introduced by the Vandal government

Figure 3.3 The Vandal kingdom after the treaty of AD 442

around the time of the treaty.[24] While their identification is not certain, Abaritana has been plausibly associated with the Aures massif, in the south-east of Numidia, and Gaetulia with the region immediately to the north.[25] Although Victor does not mention it, the Vandals also probably took control of the coastal strip of western Tripolitana.[26] For his part, Valentinian evidently retained control over the three Mauretanian provinces (Tingitania, Caesariensis and Sitifiensis), as well as the easternmost part of Numidia.

This territorial division was observed down to Valentinian's death in 455. From the imperial perspective, the great virtue of the treaty was that it ended the Vandal attacks, and firmly asserted Valentinian's control over the Mauretanias and western Numidia. A spate of imperial legislation from the 440s and early 450s demonstrates that the government in Ravenna took their responsibilities over these regions seriously. Within these proclamations (*novellae*), Valentinian remitted taxes for those landholders who had suffered in the recent wars, supervised the imperial estates and occasionally granted portions of them to those who had seen their own lands confiscated by the Vandals, and he did his best to manage the chaotic military situation at the Numidian frontiers.[27] These laws read as sensible, pragmatic responses to a dramatically changed situation in North Africa, and as a realistic attempt at damage limitation.

Having said that, Valentinian clearly had not given up hope of reclaiming the provinces lost to the Vandals. The legislation which he passed relating to African refugees within Italy, and to those individuals who had lost lands or business interests with the fall of Carthage, repeatedly hints at the possibility of Africa returning to the imperial fold.[28] Although Valentinian acknowledged Vandal autonomy in 442, he did not regard the rich lands of Africa as permanently lost to the barbarians.

These hopes were to prove unfounded. Although the treaty won some 13 years of peace, Valentinian's death in AD 455 precipitated a further wave of Vandal violence. From the spring of that year, attacks resumed on imperial territories across the Mediterranean, and many of the African territories which bordered on the Vandal kingdom were also absorbed within the expanding state.[29] This had a dramatic effect upon the foreign relations of the Vandal kingdom, as will be discussed elsewhere, but the effect within North Africa itself is rather harder to trace, and it is not always easy to identify the expansion of Vandal authority on the ground. In AD 463 an inscription employing a distinctively 'Vandal' dating system was erected in Cuicul on the provincial border between Numidia and Mauretania Sitifiensis.[30] This may well indicate that an area which lay well within the imperial 'zone' in 442 had been taken by the Vandals 21 years later. Perhaps more telling is the evidence provided by the so-called *Notitia Provinciarum* – a list of the bishops of Africa and the western Mediterranean islands who attended the Council of Carthage convened by Huneric in 483. According to this document, and the corroborative evidence of Marcellinus Comes, between 334 and 338 bishops were expelled from their dioceses during the great persecution of 483–4.[31] Yet the *Notitia Provinciarum* states that the combined number of bishops in office in Zeugitana, Byzacena, Tripolitana and Numidia (that is the 'original' Vandal kingdom as it stood in 442) was only a little over 260 at that time. The most obvious explanation for this discrepancy is that Vandal authority had expanded substantially from the frontiers established in 442, and by the early 480s their kingdom (and hence the region that Huneric could persecute) included not only the whole of Numidia, but also Mauretania Sitifiensis, and perhaps parts of Mauretania Caesariensis as well.

The Vandals do not seem to have ruled this expanded kingdom for very long. In the Aurés Mountains, for example, Vandal authority was partial at best. Inscriptions and *ostraka* bearing Vandal dating systems are known from the northern foothills of the massif from the end of the fifth century, and may indicate that these regions remained under the control of Carthage. But the highlands beyond seem to have been effectively autonomous within a few years of Geiseric's death.[32] Control over Numidia and the Mauretanias is less certain, and these regions, too, may well have been absorbed into the Moorish states developing at this time. It seems likely that a Vandal military presence was maintained at Tipasa close to the old provincial border between the Proconsular province and Numidia. Victor refers to the mutilation of Catholics in the town square of Tipasa by a military contingent – a firm assertion of Vandal authority over the surrounding region. But by the 490s, the area may well have become more of a frontier.[33] One inscription of 495 refers to a Catholic exile buried in the city who was killed in a 'Moorish War'.[34] By the end of the fifth century, then, the Vandal hold even on the towns of eastern Numidia appears to have been weakening. By the early sixth century, all that can be said is that the Vandals continued to dominate Africa Proconsularis and Byzacena, and maintained a strong presence in certain strategic ports further along the coast.

The *Sortes Vandalorum* and the Settlement of a New State

The treaty of AD 442 officially recognized Vandal authority in Africa, but Geiseric was still faced with the problem of creating a stable kingdom. His power depended upon his military strength, a tremendous advantage in the fifth-century world, to be sure, but the king nevertheless relied upon existing administrative structures to exploit the territories which he now ruled. Equally seriously, Geiseric's own military position cannot have been completely secure. While his fortuitous alliance of Vandals, Alans, Sueves and the rest could be fearsome when combined together, Geiseric's magnified authority was heavily dependent upon their continued loyalty. The settlement of AD 442 brought all of these issues to a head, since Geiseric needed to find a system in which the loyalty of his followers was rewarded, and his own position was solidified further. No less importantly, he needed to avoid substantial disruption to the productivity of their new homeland. Precisely what form the settlement of the group took has been the matter of considerable scholarly dispute in recent years, and remains a controversial issue.[35]

Central to the Vandal occupation of North Africa was the confiscation of lands which had previously been occupied and farmed by Romano-African landholders.[36] Not all Romano-African estate owners were affected by this procedure, but many of the richest lands would certainly have been abandoned or surrendered to the newcomers. It is likely that lands taken from the vast imperial *latifundia* (literally 'great estates') formed a large proportion of the confiscated territories, and the invaders no doubt also divided up the estates which were either owned by Italian senators or had been abandoned by the African aristocrats who had fled in the face of the occupation.[37] The emperor and these senators would have lamented the loss of prime estates, but it was those who remained in Africa who felt the Vandal confiscations most keenly. Procopius naturally refers to large numbers of Romano-Africans who lost everything at the time of the occupation, and countless claims were made for the restitution of lost family lands at the time of the Byzantine invasion in 534.[38]

The mechanics of the Vandal occupation are poorly understood, but it was clearly an orderly process. In the passage cited above, Victor of Vita states specifically that Geiseric was responsible for the redistribution of lands, and notes further the distinction between the 'Royal' lands of Byzacena, Arbitana, Gaetulia and Numidia and the territory of Africa Proconsularis which he 'divided up as "heritable lots" for his army'.[39] In his account, Procopius confirms the separation of 'Royal' and 'Vandal' lands, and also notes the fate of some Romano-African landowners:

> [He enslaved the African nobility and handed them over] together with their estates and all their money, to his sons Huneric and Genton. For Theodorus, the youngest son, had died already, being altogether without offspring, male or female. And he robbed the rest of the Libyans of their estates, which were both very numerous and excellent, and distributed them among the nation of the Vandals, and as a result of these, the lands have been called 'Vandals' estates' up to the present time. And it fell to the lot of those who had formerly possessed these lands to be in extreme poverty and to be at the same time free men; and they had the privilege of going away wherever they wished. And Geiseric commanded that all the lands which he had given over to his sons should not be subject to any kind of taxation. But as much of the land as did not seem to him good he allowed to remain in the hands of the former owners, but assessed so large a sum to be paid on this land for taxes to the government that nothing whatever remained to those who retained their farms.[40]

This settlement created two essential pillars for the Vandal state. First, the lands distributed among the Vandals provided the territorial heartland of the new kingdom. According to both of our principal textual sources, these lands were restricted to the province of Africa Proconsularis. Procopius terms these lands the *kleroi Bandilon*, which probably represents a Greek approximation of Victor's *sortes Vandalorum* (or '[Lands] allotted to the Vandals'), a term which later appears in royal documentation.[41] Victor terms the land divided among the Vandals in AD 442 as the *funicul[um] hereditatis* ('the inheritable allotment'). The estates within this area were exempt from taxation, and (as the name suggests) were passed on by hereditary right.[42] Naturally, individual holdings would have changed over time, as individuals' estates expanded or declined, and it is certainly possible that other lands passed from Roman to Vandal ownership over the decades that followed, although there was no recorded period of systematic confiscation after 442.[43]

This *funiculum hereditatis* seems to have been regarded as a coherent block of territory, and over the following decade this view of the 'Vandal lands' seems to have changed.[44] Over time, its meaning expanded to encompass not simply the individual estates of the Vandals, but the whole of Zeugitana – the heartland, in other words, of the Vandal kingdom. Both Geiseric and Huneric passed legislation restricting the religious freedoms of the Catholics within the *sortes Vandalorum*.[45] It seems likely that this included not only the confiscated lands, but also the territories in Zeugitana which were retained by their original owners. From the middle of the fifth century, the Proconsular province was administered as a 'Vandal Pale', and it was here that Hasding authority was imposed most firmly.

Royal lands

The *sortes Vandalorum* only represented a proportion of the lands that were confiscated by Geiseric. Equally significant were the huge tracts that the king claimed for himself and for his sons. These royal lands included agricultural estates in Africa Proconsularis, Byzacena and eastern Numidia, as well as vineyards, mines, lakes, urban palaces and rural villas throughout the kingdom.[46] Significantly, the royal princes Huneric, Theoderic and Genton all received estates along with the king, as well as the administrative machinery for governing them.[47]

What is important here is not simply that Geiseric took many prime lands for himself, but that the estates of the king and his sons were clearly distinguished from those of the lower-ranked Vandal landowners. This provided each of the Hasding princes with his own individual authority – an issue that was to have bloody repercussions later – and also underscored the social and economic separation of the ruling family of the Vandals from their subjects. The lands which Geiseric himself divided among his followers and family provided an economic platform for, and a symbolic attestation of, this superiority.

It is difficult to overstate the significance of this settlement to the history of the Vandals. At the time of the first invasion of North Africa, the social stratification of Geiseric's retinue can only have been based on military hierarchy, and the *ad hoc* organization developed during the occupation of Spain. Social distinctions developed along the Danube cannot have survived the long campaign across the empire, and the systematic formation and re-formation of the 'Hasding', 'Siling' and 'Vandal' groups after defeats and victories can only have further muddied the waters. Thus, when Geiseric distributed the African estates in 442, he introduced a clear new social and political stratigraphy among his followers. While military service still provided a channel for advancement for ambitious Vandal aristocrats, land was to be a crucial status symbol within the new kingdom. As the power responsible for the division of the spoils, Geiseric had tremendous influence over the shape which his kingdom was to take.

We know very little about the precise mechanics of the land settlement; if we knew more, a great deal of early Vandal history would be much clearer. Frustratingly, our general understanding of the history of North Africa in the 440s is not very much better. The sources hint at social upheaval and political unrest, but the details of these events are hard to assess. When viewed together, however, these fragments evoke a period of political turmoil and aristocratic resistance, created by Geiseric's forceful redefinition of the power structures of his new kingdom.

Typical of these royal initiatives was the re-organization of the army. Again, the details of this programme can only be partially known. Procopius states that Geiseric placed the army under the command of 80 'chiliarchs', a strategy which had the side-effect of making the Vandal army seem rather larger than it was.[48] We are not told when this re-organization took place, but the position in Procopius' narrative would seem to favour a date at some time in the early 440s.[49] 'Chiliarch' itself is a Greek term, which probably represents Procopius' rough translation of the Latin *millenarius*, that is an individual in (nominal) command of a thousand men.[50] Victor describes one Vandal landholder as a *millenarius*, but for the most part the title seems to have had only a military significance within North Africa.[51] With more information we might say a great deal more about the significance of this change, but the very fact that Geiseric re-organized his army shortly after the establishment of the Vandal kingdom is surely significant. The investiture of this new rank must represent a redefinition, or at the very least a formalization of the king's power over his army.

If any group stood to lose from Geiseric's careful social engineering, it would have been those Vandals who were not members of the king's immediate family, but had nevertheless been prominent at the time of the invasion of North Africa. These powerful aristocrats would have found themselves excluded from the distribution of the 'royal' lands and may perhaps have witnessed the erosion of their military authority as a result of the reorganization of the army. Our sources do not allow us to examine this group in detail, but we do hear of one major political uprising in 442, which originated among Vandals of precisely this kind:

> Some of Geiseric's magnates conspired against him because he was proud, even among his own people, due to the successful outcome of events. But when the undertaking was discovered, they were subjected to many tortures and killed by him. Whenever others seemed to venture the same thing, the king's mistrust seemed to destroy so many that he lost more men by this anxiety of his than if he had been overthrown in war.[52]

Little else is known of this putative uprising. It is possible that it was linked to changes in Geiseric's foreign policy; at around this time a Visigothic princess was expelled from the Hasding court following an accusation that she attempted to poison the king.[53] But it is far more likely that the Vandal magnates revolted in protest at their exclusion from the new channels of political power that the king was establishing. Even in outline, the outbreak and suppression of the nobles' revolt confirms the radical political upheaval of the period. The year 442 was one in which the future of the Vandal kingdom hung in the balance. The Hasdings shored up their military authority through their ambitious appropriation of land, and Geiseric's diplomatic activities moved him yet further away from his mercenary background towards the high table of Mediterranean politics. The king viciously suppressed the one major rebellion of his reign, and perhaps reorganized his army in an attempt to prevent further challenges to his power. The Vandal kingdom – and the Vandal King – began to assume an air of permanence.

New Kingship for a New Kingdom

North Africa offered Geiseric a blank canvas upon which to create his own image of Vandal rule. According to Jordanes, writing in the 550s, Geiseric was the true progenitor of the Hasding monarchy, 'the father and lord' (*pater et dominus*) of the ruling house.[54] Some 300 years later, the Byzantine chronicler Theophanes describes how Geiseric 'proclaimed himself *basileos* after gaining control of the land, the sea, and many islands.'[55] Geiseric established the platform for a monarchy based on Roman, African and Christian (as well as 'barbarian') precedent, and successive ideological layers were barnacled on by the kings who followed him.

Geiseric and his successors were heavily influenced by imperial precedent in the forms of rule that they adopted. Jordanes notes the importance of divine support behind Geiseric's rule, stating that he claimed to receive his authority 'from God himself', a typical conceit of the later Roman emperors.[56] Procopius implies that a similar sense of divine support propelled Geiseric's foreign policy.[57] More directly, religious policies also drew upon this imperial tradition of Christian pastoral responsibility. Bitterly ironic as it may have seemed to Catholic observers who suffered during the persecutions, the Hasdings regarded their promotion of Arianism as God's work.[58] The Vandal kings were confident that religious action was among the duties expected of a ruler. By the time Huneric came to the throne, religion had become a major point of political contention within the kingdom. Nevertheless, Huneric explicitly followed imperial precedent in his legal actions against the Nicenes, and attempted to establish himself as a protector of the Arian faith throughout the world.[59] Victor himself accepted that the persecution of the Manichaeans fell within Huneric's remit as a religious ruler, even as he lamented the same king's actions against the Catholic Church.[60] Few seem to have questioned the right of Huneric and later Thrasamund to convene councils of the African Church. In their discussions of the monarchy, Dracontius and Fulgentius both stress the need for Christian responsibility in the person of the king, regardless of his denomination.[61]

The appropriation of imperial precedent was also apparent in the Vandals' attitude towards the Moorish powers which were developing to the south and west.[62] During the imperial period, the elites of the African frontier had frequently derived their authority from the imperial power in Rome or Carthage; in some cases the kings or dukes of the region had been formally invested by the empire, in others less rigid forms of recognition nevertheless helped to formalize social hierarchies within these groups and secure their relation to the centre. Although many different Moorish polities arose within the political vacuum left by the empire, and their relations with Carthage certainly differed, the Hasdings provided a legitimating agent for these elites in some cases. Procopius famously describes a Moorish embassy to Belisarius shortly after the Byzantine capture of Carthage which highlights the long-standing relationship between the groups:

> For all those who ruled over the Moors in Mauretania and Numidia and Byzacium sent envoys to Belisarius saying that they were slaves of the emperor and promised to fight with him. There were some also who furnished their children as hostages and requested that symbols of office be sent them from him according to the ancient custom. For it was a law among the Moors that no-one should be a ruler over them, even if he was hostile to the Romans, until the emperor of the Romans should give him the tokens of office. And though they had already received them from the Vandals, they did not consider that the Vandals held office securely.[63]

This passage highlights an important political symbiosis which probably continued throughout the Vandal period.[64] Not only did alliance with Carthage help to secure the power of the Moorish princes who received their regalia from the city, the very act of political legitimation also underscored the Hasdings' claim to imperial authority within their own kingdom. The Hasdings acted like emperors, to the benefit of all.

As the Vandal kingdom matured, the Hasdings appropriated other imperial ideologies for their own use. Huneric was a conspicuous innovator, a trait which he may have developed during his stay at the western imperial court or as a result of his marriage to Eudocia. It was Huneric who adopted the unmistakably imperial conceit of renaming an African city in his own honour (Hadrumetum was known as Unericopolis for the duration of his reign), and adopted the portentous honorific *dominus* ('Lord').[65] From Gunthamund's reign on, title *dominus* began to appear on silver coin issues, itself an important ideological declaration. Huneric, Gunthamund and Thrasamund all had panegyrics composed in their honour, in the best imperial tradition, and it is from one of these texts (the meretricious panegyric by Florentinus) that we hear of the annual oaths of loyalty, apparently introduced by Thrasamund.[66] Under Hilderic, these pretensions grew still more pronounced. As the son of the princess Eudocia, Hilderic could claim direct descent from Valentinian III and the Theodosian house, and a poem dating from his reign suggests that he celebrated this lineage in the wall paintings of his new palace complex in the Carthaginian suburb of Anclae.[67] Hilderic's successor Gelimer is often presented as the sober proponent of 'traditional' Vandal values, yet he too embraced many of the pretensions of his family. Procopius' account of the Vandal triumph of Belisarius clothes the deposed king in pseudo-imperial purple and states that Hasding queens commonly rode around in imperial carriages.[68] Even if Procopius is exaggerating for effect, this was clearly a form of rule that had developed substantially from the early years under Geiseric.

Geiseric and his successors were not simply insipid mimics of imperial rule. The Vandal kings displayed an unusual sensitivity to the opportunities offered by North Africa itself in the justification of their rule. Shortly after the conquest of Carthage, Geiseric recalibrated the state calendar, declaring the occupation of the city in 439 to be the 'year of Carthage' – i.e. 'year one' of his reign, and of the kingdom as a whole.[69] The evidence for this shift is disparate but striking. Apparently first used in 'official' inscriptions and coins, the earliest use of the dating may well be in a series of coins from the 440s. By the 450s and 460s, examples are known from inscriptions scattered throughout the kingdom, including one from the grave of a religious exile in Maduros. Later kings refined this system, preferring to see coins, inscriptions and official documentation dated according to the length of their own reigns, rather than to the year of Carthage. Neither system was adopted universally, but each was widely practised. Other methods of chronological reckoning continued to be used throughout Africa, but even the most resolute enemies of the Hasding regime, and even those living some distance from the Vandal capital at Carthage, found themselves falling into step with the royal calibration of time.

Florentinus' panegyrics to Thrasamund reflect the close association that had developed between Hasding rule and Carthage by the early sixth century. In the poet's words, Carthage – and not Rome or the distant settlements of Northern Europe – was truly 'mother city to the Hasdingi'. The Vandals encouraged this association, and employed traditional Punic motifs in their copper coin issues, while evoking a glorious Carthaginian past in their diplomacy. Other poets in the *Latin Anthology* drew upon famous Carthaginian traditions, and may well have been encouraged in this by the court. When the Latin *literati* of Carthage sought to flatter their Vandal rulers, they did so through reference to their successes as the masters of Africa and the glories of the Punic heritage, not through accounts of the long-forgotten Vandal past. Both literally and figuratively, Geiseric regarded the occupation of Carthage as the true beginning of Vandal history.

All of these innovations were important in establishing the Hasding kings as respectable authorities on the wider Mediterranean stage. Indeed, in this sense, their adoption of the grammar of late Roman power was simply a reflection of their desire to communicate with their Roman, barbarian and Moorish neighbours, and to present themselves as legitimate new rulers. But these were not the only stages on which the Hasding kings performed. Equally crucial to Geiseric and his successors was the establishment of Hasding authority among the Vandals themselves, and this was by no means a straightforward process.

The Hasding Family and the Vandal Succession

The element which bound all of the Vandal kings together, and which distinguished them most clearly from the great mass of their subjects, was the Hasding lineage itself. In contrast to many of the other barbarian rulers of the fifth and sixth centuries, the Hasdings seem to have set little store by the propagation of improbable claims to ancient ancestry. But even if the circulation of fabulous genealogies and spurious histories held few fascinations for the Vandal elite, Geiseric became king because his father (and brother) had ruled before him. Geiseric and his 'Hasding' family may not have been the latest in a long chain of Vandal kings but they did recognize the importance of the familial name to their power.[70]

Geiseric was determined to ensure the continued power of his family. The favourable distribution of lands in 442 provided an economic grounding for this, but the king also took more direct action. The first of these was the vigorous pruning of his own family tree, in an attempt to limit succession disputes in the future. Rumours abounded that Geiseric was responsible for the death of his brother Gunderic, and that he had also killed his sister-in-law and nephews, for fear of the political threat that they posed.[71] Brutal as these actions may have been, they appear to have been effective, since the king endured few challenges to his authority during his reign and none from Hasding pretenders. Anxious to pass these benefits along to his descendents, Geiseric adopted a further innovation, namely the implementation of agnatic seniority as the system of royal succession within the kingdom.[72] According to this system, power passed to the eldest member of the Hasding family upon the death of the ruling monarch. The system had obvious advantages. While succession by primogeniture could often lead to the succession of a minor or a dispute between rival claimants, and partible inheritance often resulted in the division of a kingdom into warring parts, the system adopted by the Vandals would keep the *regnum* intact.[73]

On the face of it, this innovation was a resounding success. Geiseric's eldest son, Huneric succeeded him, followed by Gunthamund, the son of Huneric's brother Theoderic and the oldest living Hasding in 484. Gunthamund was succeeded by his younger brother, Thrasamund in 496, who was then followed in turn by Hilderic, Huneric's eldest son and the eldest male member of the family. If the succession had been governed by the laws of primogeniture, Hilderic would have succeeded Huneric in 484, and would have come to the throne as a youth. Instead, he was crowned as an old man in 523 after the death of his cousin. Conventionally, the system is only thought to have broken down in 530 when Gelimer, himself the heir apparent to the kingdom through his descent from Thrasamund's brother Geilarith, became impatient with Hilderic's ineffectual rule and Byzantine sympathies and pre-empted the law of succession to seize power for himself.

In fact, two major political crises suggest that Geiseric's law of succession only enjoyed inviolable 'constitutional' status when it was in everyone's interest for it to do so. In 480 or 481, Huneric instituted a major purge of the Hasding family and some of its more prominent advisors.[74] In a frenzy of persecution, the king exiled his brother Theoderic, killed Theoderic's wife and son and publicly executed a number of important figures associated with them, including a prominent Arian bishop and some of Geiseric's old advisors. According to Victor, Huneric suspected that a plot was developing around his ambitious sister-in-law and her (unnamed) son, an upstanding member of the royal family who had been educated in the classical Roman manner. Although Victor claims that Huneric's suspicions were unfounded, it is clear from the king's actions that he was responding to a political threat that he regarded as genuine. Theoderic's son and his immediate entourage were all killed, and other prominent Vandals summarily exiled from the kingdom. Given the importance of Geiseric to the establishment of the Vandal kingdom, it does not seem surprising that his death put the courts of his sons in conflict with one another. Huneric's indecisive foreign policy and confused religious ideologies doubtless increased these tensions, and a well-educated Hasding prince (as Theoderic's son is described by Victor) might well have provided an obvious rallying point for dissatisfied factions. Arian church leaders and Geiseric's advisors could have acted as power-brokers in such a situation, and Huneric's purges of both groups may thus be placed in context.

It is within this context that Huneric's attempt to overthrow his father's law of succession needs to be viewed. According to Victor, Huneric assembled a number of prominent Nicene churchmen at the site of the Temple of Memoria in Carthage, and hinted that they might be afforded freedom of worship if they would support Hilderic's succession to the throne.[75] The bishops rejected these overtures, and there the matter rested; when Huneric died, he was succeeded in due course by Gunthamund, as the eldest living Hasding, and not by his son. But the timing of Huneric's scheme remains interesting. Conventionally, the dramatic purges of AD 480/481 have been interpreted as the precursor of Huneric's attempted elevation of his son, and this is certainly the impression which Victor would wish to give. But it seems more just to Huneric to regard the reformulation of the law of succession as a response to the earlier plot; the proposed elevation of Hilderic may have resulted as much from a desire to secure his own position from further revolt as from a genuine dynastic ambition.

Hilderic was the victim of the second major succession crisis. In 530, little more than seven years after coming to the throne, Hilderic was deposed by a coup under the Hasding prince Gelimer.[76] This coup was later exploited by Justinian as a justification for Byzantine intervention, and led to the collapse of the Vandal kingdom. But the rebellion was more than a futile gesture in the face of fate, and there is more to this political struggle than meets the eye. According to Geiseric's law of succession, Gelimer stood to inherit the crown upon the death of Hilderic, his first cousin once removed. Given Hilderic's likely age at the time of the coup (at least 59 and perhaps as old as 75 in 530), the impatience of the rebel seems extraordinary.[77] Why did he not simply wait for his aged cousin to die, and avoid the need for a bloody revolt? The most likely explanation is that Hilderic himself had precipitated the rising by excluding his distant relative Gelimer from the succession. The evidence for this is circumstantial, but telling. A handful of references in the *Latin Anthology* indicate that Hilderic was particularly proud of his Roman imperial lineage, and sought to re-invent the Vandal royal house as a fusion of the Hasding and Theodosian families.[78] It was in this light that the wall-paintings of the Anclae palace noted above were to be viewed. This heritage reflected not only on Hilderic, but also on his two nephews Hoamer and Hoageis, both of whom enjoyed some minor celebrity in late Vandal Carthage as military leaders and princes of the royal blood.[79] Significantly, Gelimer, as the son of prince Geilarith and the grandson of Genton, could claim no such descent from the imperial house, and may well have regarded Hoamer and Hoageis as likely usurpers of his title. It is conspicuous that the brothers were targeted when the revolution came. Hoageis was killed outright, but Hoamer was blinded – a common punishment for defeated usurpers in both Byzantine and Persian politics.[80]

Neither of the Vandal succession crises is narrated particularly clearly within our sources. Victor does his best to obscure the political context in which Huneric's purges took place. Gelimer's rising is known only from the Byzantine accounts, and these, too, were anxious to present a complex succession crisis in morally straightforward terms as the background to Justinian's 'regime change'. But a close analysis of these episodes reveals the cracks within the façade of Hasding rule. Geiseric's law of succession often smoothed over difficult periods of political transition, but it did not form an inviolable political constitution. As the succession crises reveal, Hasding kingship was in a constant process of evolution, and in periods of crisis those in power adopted a variety of strategies for remaining there.

Networks of Power in the Vandal Kingdom

The structures of state power in the Vandal kingdom were not limited to the person of the king and his family. A complex administration had developed in the later Roman empire to maintain the military and bureaucratic commitments of the state, and the Vandals came into possession of much of this governmental infrastructure. It is impossible to gauge the scale of the administration in place during the Vandal century, but details from the Justinianic reconstruction are instructive. When he created a new Praetorian Prefecture for Africa after the conquest, Justinian envisaged a central administrative staff of around 400, working for the Praetorian Prefect, together with a smaller office of around 50 bureaucrats for each of the constituent provinces of the region.[81] While these numbers reflect the norms of early Byzantine government, rather than those of the Vandal administration, they do provide an order of magnitude for the scale of government in this period. The Vandal administration may not have been as extensive as later Roman or Byzantine rule, but North Africa could not be ruled without a government of some kind.

The royal court

The king and his immediate entourage were at the heart of the Vandal kingdom. It is tempting, but misguided, to imagine the Hasding court as a barbarian feasting hall, familiar from *Beowulf* or Tacitus' *Germania*. The court culture at Carthage was very much a product of its wider Mediterranean setting.[82] The movement of individuals between Ravenna, Constantinople and the households of the barbarian kings led to a cultural homogenization. At different times the Vandal court entertained a future eastern emperor, a Visigothic princess, the imperial widow Eudoxia and her two daughters, a number of prominent aristocratic hostages including (perhaps) a future western emperor, an Ostrogothic queen and her substantial entourage, and an exiled Visigothic pretender.[83] Huneric was a guest of Valentinian III in Ravenna and Hilderic may well have been a familiar figure in Constantinople.[84] Geiseric's advisors included the far-travelled Count Sebastian, who had previously spent time in Constantinople, and the Visigothic court of Toulouse, as well as a strikingly cosmopolitan array of advisors.

Alongside these well-known figures, we must consider the large population of envoys, who shuttled more or less constantly between the different Mediterranean capitals, and the episcopal and secular aristocracies who provided further links between Carthage and the world beyond.

This 'imperial' context was exemplified by the physical setting of Hasding power. The principal Vandal court was located in the old proconsular palace on Byrsa Hill in Carthage, and this structure remained in use down to the Justinianic conquest: indeed, it was in this building that Belisarius established the provisional Byzantine government in 534.[85] But smaller royal centres also remained important: Geiseric, Thrasamund, Hilderic and Gelimer all maintained royal estates away from Carthage, and conducted royal business upon them.[86] While the Vandal kings never adopted the peripatetic rule of their Frankish or Visigothic contemporaries, they were not tied to Carthage and, when they did move, the political focus of the kingdom moved with them. Rather less prominent, but still politically significant, were the smaller courts of the minor members of the Hasding family. It was at such courts that the revolt of 481 seems to have been hatched, and the rising of 531 developed. The king provided the principal focus of government within the Vandal kingdom, but this did not preclude the emergence of other centres of royal power.

Personal Contacts

The daily politics of the Vandal court involved the constant struggle of individuals and interest groups beneath the penetrating gaze of the king – or so Victor and our other written sources would have us believe. The *Historia Persecutionis* is densely populated with court figures, from the hostile Arian episcopate and scheming counts to the Catholic court functionaries who fell from power when forced to choose between their political responsibilities and their faith. It is from Victor that we know of the *praepositus regni* – apparently the most senior position within the Vandal court, and held successively by one Heldica (under Geiseric) and Obadus (under Huneric).[87] The rank is unknown outside Vandal Africa, but was evidently of very high status. The *Latin Anthology* refers to a *referendarius* under Thrasamund who supervised the reconstruction of a basilica, and an exalted senator called Victorinianus, who held the rank of *primiscriniarius*.[88] Again, the titles sound impressive, and the fact that poets drew particular attention to them probably indicates that they were, but we cannot tell precisely what each entailed. Victor also refers to various *comites* (counts), both named and unnamed, who formed an advisory panel for the king, acted as his military and naval commanders, and frequently undertook diplomatic missions on his behalf. Procopius, similarly, depicts various Vandal kings surrounded by sundry hoary elders and *aristoi*, all offering their advice in the best tradition of the Tacitean *concilium*.[89] Regardless of the truth behind these stories (and many seem to owe more to Procopius' peculiar sense of what a barbarian council *should* be like than to his direct experience of Vandal rule), prominent figures in the kingdom – both Vandal and Roman – could certainly expect to have the ear of the king.

Prominent as these personal intrigues may have been, the court also formed the bureaucratic centre of the Vandal kingdom. Our sources for the day-to-day operations of government are far from perfect, but some general outlines may be traced. We know, for example, that the court issued writs and promulgated official edicts, indeed, several are preserved verbatim in the *Historia Persecutionis*. In all likelihood, these were the responsibility of a more or less fixed royal notariate, which had probably been inherited from the old administrative system of Roman Africa, and was perhaps incorporated into the royal chancellery. The relatively rapid spread of Vandal dating systems throughout the kingdom was probably helped by a formal documentary office of this kind.[90] The individuals likely to have staffed these offices are recorded in various ways. Victor refers collectively to *homines in aula* ('men in court')[91] and *qui . . . domus nostrae occupati militia* ('those who serve in our [the royal] household',[92] with respect to Huneric's royal entourage and to the *diversa ministeria* ('various offices') in the courts of Geiseric and the Vandal princes. Victor also refers to the upkeep and salary (*annona* and *solita*) provided for courtiers, which could be suspended for those who refused to convert to Arianism. Several authors refer to the royal *domestici* (literally 'householders') – a term which could have radically different meanings.[93] The *domesticus* might be a high status companion – the future emperor Marcian, for example, had been a *domesticus* to Aspar at the time of his capture by Geiseric.[94] Used collectively, however, the term might refer to anything from the court as a whole to the immediate household servants of the King.

Power beyond the court: provincial administration

The Hasding court was the true political heart of Vandal North Africa. Foreign dignitaries made the royal audience chamber their first port of call, and it was from here that the bloody edicts of persecution dripped down to the wider territories of Catholic Africa. Yet Vandal North Africa was far from being a centralized state. The Vandals represented a tiny minority of the fifth-century population, and their settlement was heavily concentrated into one small part of their kingdom. Within such a context, the articulation of direct, intensive rule from the court would have been impossible. Counts and other court appointees could implement royal policies throughout the Proconsular province and beyond, and individuals could be despatched to problem areas in times of crisis, but in the day-to-day government of Africa the Vandal kings depended upon existing networks of power.

The most important of these were the institutionalized administrative systems of the later Roman empire, organized around the provinces and the towns.[95] These systems were doubtless disrupted by the political disputes of the 420s and the widespread upheaval of the 430s and 440s. The flight of prominent office holders is well attested in the historical sources, but so too is the readiness of those left behind to ingratiate themselves with the barbarians. From his exile in Italy, the Bishop Quodvultdeus lamented the eagerness with which some of his countrymen offered their support to the new rulers of Africa.[96] A generation later, Victor condemned those who looked past the barbarism of the Vandals to the opportunities for social and political advancement beyond.[97] We should resist the temptation to view the politics of this period as one of intractable opposition between collaboration and resistance. It is likely that political pragmatism, rather than the carefully defined oppositions of Victor and other Catholic writers, was the norm for many Romano-Africans living under Vandal rule, whatever their religious denomination.

The most important individuals in the civic administration of later Roman North Africa had been the Proconsul and the Vicar of Africa.[98] The former was responsible for government within Carthage and for Africa Proconsularis, the latter for the administration of the other North African provinces, and seemingly, control of the organization of the collection and shipment of the *annona*. For much of the Roman period, these positions were typically filled by Italian senatorial aristocrats, who may or may not have had their own landholdings in the region.[99] By the fourth and early fifth centuries, an increase in the number of Romano-Africans who held the rank may be detected, but governors with local roots remained the exception, rather than the rule. During the later Roman period, then, the opportunities for local advancement were generally limited to provincial or municipal appointments, at least for those Africans who did not choose to seek their fortunes elsewhere in the empire. Under the Vandals, of course, this changed and the political separation of the

North African provinces from Italy and the empire may have opened up new opportunities for local aristocracies within their own system.

The evidence for the survival of traditional provincial government is scanty but telling. The African proconsuls may have lost their palace to the Vandal kings, but the position remained important and we know of two individuals who held the rank during the mid-fifth century. Pacideius was the patron of Dracontius and the dedicatee of some of his poems, and served as proconsul either in the latter years of Geiseric's reign, or under Huneric.[100] Victorinianus of Hadrumetum attained the same position under Huneric and was apparently among the most trusted individuals within the kingdom, as well as one of the wealthiest.[101] According to Victor, Victorinianus lost his position for refusing to abjure his Catholicism, but other political disagreements may have underlain this dispute. At the very least, the fact that African Catholics could attain important positions at court, despite their unfashionable sectarian beliefs, demonstrates a strong level of institutional continuity.

Outside Zeugitana, administrative authority was divided between provincial, municipal and episcopal aristocracies. At the provincial level, this was in the hands of *Iudices* (literally 'judges'), who are probably best regarded as provincial governors, with both political and legal responsibilities.[102] Lower down on the political ladder, social ranks and responsibilities can only be surmised. Huneric's edict instituted incremental fines for *illustres*, *spectabiles*, senators, 'leading men' (*principales*), decurions and common people (*plebes*), all terms which might signify strong continuity, but the form of the legislation was taken directly from an earlier Roman law and it is not clear whether the neatly defined social ranks retained any meaning in the Africa of the 480s.[103] We do hear of prominent *ordines* and municipal councils, and we know that the traditional markers of civic status continued to have a resonance – most obviously in the widespread continuity of the institution of the *flamines perpetui*.[104] At the very least what we see here are local aristocracies for whom Roman patterns of identity continued to mean something rather important. The institution represented a strong centripetal force, and something which worked to the advantage of the Vandal state, even if the precise ideological statement made by the cults was ambiguous.

General Conclusions

Within North Africa, the consequences of the Vandal occupation were at once dramatic and surprisingly short lived. Our literary sources testify to the sheer terror that the invaders inspired, and many former inhabitants of the region were scattered to the distant shores of the Mediterranean. The heart of the African political system was also transplanted, as Vandal kings replaced imperial proconsuls in their own palace. Royal authority evolved anew, and the Hasding monarchs drew upon Vandal, Roman and even Punic ideologies in creating a form of rulership in their own image. Court society emerges only imperfectly from the textual and archaeological sources available to us, but its outlines are clear.

But many networks of power remained in place. The Vandal occupation was largely limited to the fertile valleys around Carthage, and the presence in Byzacena and Numidia was probably largely limited to military garrisons and estates held in the name of the Hasding family. In these regions, still rich agricultural and pastoral lands, the change of government in Carthage meant relatively little. Provincial government remained in the hands of the senatorial aristocracy (at least of those who had not flown at the coming of the barbarians), and municipal government, too, remained active. Where change came in these regions it was not from the Vandals, but from the emergence of new – rival – centres of political activity on the periphery of the Vandal kingdom. Moorish rulers provided local aristocracies with new channels for political and economic development.

Among these changes, the inhabitants of North Africa continued to live alongside one another in (relative) peace and (general) prosperity. The political systems functioned, educational and legal structures remained strong. These relations did occasionally descend into violence and persecution, as is well known, but the fault lines within this society did not run simply along the ethnic boundary between 'Vandal' and 'Roman'. Geiseric and Huneric victimized Vandals as well as Romans, Arians as well as Catholics. Romano-Africans could earn promotion within the Vandal court and municipal aristocracy, just as Vandals could find themselves ostracised for political, religious or personal reasons. But the overall impression of the kingdom of Vandal Carthage is of integration under a strong – and evolving – form of kingship.

4

Identity and Ethnicity in the Vandal Kingdom

At some point in the middle of the fifth century, an aristocrat called Arifridos died and was buried in the choir of a church in the African city of Thuburbo Maius. In 1917, archaeologists uncovered the remains of his tomb, and found nail fragments from a wooden coffin, a limestone plinth upon which the body had been placed, and the remains of Arifridos' strikingly rich costume. A large, gold buckle ornamented his belt, and smaller fastenings decorated his shoes. A brooch of striped agate in a gold setting was also found with the body, and had probably originally held a large cloak. The splendour of this clothing was reflected in the prominence of the tomb itself. His burial was surely public, and was formally commemorated through a large funerary mosaic in the floor of the church which recorded his name.[1]

Arifridos' grave highlights how complex personal identity could be within the Vandal kingdom. His name, which is certainly Germanic in origin, suggests that Arifridos would have regarded himself as a member of the ruling military elite within the African kingdom.[2] Yet the means by which he asserted his status were remarkably conservative. Arifridos was buried within the choir of his church – a particular privilege reserved for few late Roman Christians. The use of a Latin funerary epitaph was also typical of North African practice, although again few would have been rich enough to enjoy such commemoration.[3] Even Arifridos' clothing is typical of the late Roman aristocracy. Although the prominent buckle and decorated shoes might have seemed out of place in the streets of Thuburbo Maius during the first or second century AD, by the fourth or fifth, the chic dressers among the Mediterranean aristocracy typically adopted such pseudo-military garb for everything from hunting to swaggering around town. Arifridos was a Vandal who dressed very much like a late Roman dandy.[4]

Arifridos is an individual who would be forgotten were it not for the chance survival of his epitaph and his surprising funeral dress, and this brings us back to the question of identity and ethnicity within the Vandal kingdom. This is an issue which was discussed briefly in the opening chapter, and which has lurked in the background throughout our discussion since: namely what made a 'Vandal' a 'Vandal' in the Hasding kingdom of North Africa? At first glance, this might seem like a straightforward question, and indeed it was rarely asked by historians until the scholars of the later twentieth century turned their attention to the complex identity politics of the early Middle Ages. Their work has demonstrated that political, social and ethnic affiliations were in a constant process of flux.

It is clear from our textual sources that the warband that followed Geiseric into North Africa in AD 429 was a mixed bunch; the group was heterogeneous and probably included Alans, Sueves, Hispano-Romans and Goths, as well as Vandals, among the king's followers.[5] Geiseric's army was a peripatetic collection of soldiers and their entourage, which numbered in the low tens of thousands, and had come together as a more or less unified group only within the 420s. Yet within a few years of the crossing into Africa, the textual sources are agreed that this disparate band had become a coherent 'Vandal' group. As Procopius saw it:

> . . . by their natural increase among themselves and by associating other barbarians with them they came to be an exceedingly numerous people. But the names of the Alans and all the other barbarians, except the Moors, were united in the name of the Vandals.[6]

The 'Alans and other barbarians' may not have lost their own distinct sense of separateness, but they were increasingly included within a broader 'Vandal' ethnicity. This identity was not set in stone, then, but proved to be a broad church in which many different groups could gather. But how did this come about?

Equally significant were the relations between the evolving Vandal people and the different groups already resident in North Africa. The Vandals were, after all, a relatively small group, and came into a region with a total population somewhere between two and three million.[7] Subsumed within this world, the circumstances in which the Vandals lived, and the means by which they distinguished themselves can only have changed over time, particularly during the second and third generation of settlement. At the time of their first arrival it was probably easy enough to distinguish the hostile barbarians who spoke a strange language from the rest of the population, but these rough edges would be smoothed off soon enough. As the barbarians settled, interacted politically and economically with their neighbours, and as they slowly transformed from the motley barbarians of AD 429 into the 'Vandals' identified by Procopius, the manner in which they marked out their identity, or how they put such needs to one side, must have changed. Diet, dress, social and sexual behaviour and even speech are likely to have changed, perhaps substantially, during the century of Vandal occupation in North Africa, as the epitaph of Arifridos reminds us. When viewed within such a context, the politics of identity within the Vandal kingdom were clearly a complex business.

The present chapter seeks to examine closely what it was to be 'Vandal' within the North African kingdom, and argues that this cannot be understood without an appreciation of the other forms of social identity within North Africa at that time. It suggests that 'Vandalness' is best viewed as an ethnic identifier which lent meaning and significance to Geiseric's military aristocracy. It was often articulated in ways which were strikingly different from the familiar forms of identity in the late Roman world, but in many cases it drew heavily upon social categories which had developed in the region long before the arrival of the Vandals. Vandalness was profoundly shaped by late Roman notions of masculinity and political status.

Ethnicity and Identity in Late Antiquity

Modern understanding of ethnicity and identity has drawn heavily upon the work of the Swedish sociologist Friedrich Barth.[8] Barth's great breakthrough was to recognize that ethnicity was essentially a social construct, rather than an entity which existed independently of human action. He observed that an ethnic group was not defined by the objective biological kinship of its members, by shared language or by similarities in physical appearance as had often been assumed. All of these characteristics were strategies by which groups might identify themselves, or might be distinguished by others, but it was precisely this recognition – this acknowledgement of similarity and difference – which created ethnic identity. If the members of a group had a sense of their own unity, and if outside observers appreciated this, they could be said to have shared an ethnic identity. Signs of this group cohesion could thus be employed, consciously or otherwise, to mark this difference, whether through physical attributes, language or cultural choices. But it was the ideology of the group which defined its ethnic cohesion, not its visible symbols.

Barth and his successors also recognized that ethnicity was never fixed. The ethnic identity of groups could emerge, develop and fade in response to wider political and economic stimuli, in the manner that Procopius recognized in the Vandals.[9] The symbols by which these identities were expressed also fluctuated in response to differing circumstances. If an ethnic group found itself in a precarious political position, or indeed enjoyed unprecedented power, the means by which it positioned itself with respect to other groups would inevitably change. Barth's paradigm stressed that communal ethnic identities were in a constant process of change, and also revealed how individuals could employ different ethnic affiliations at different times. If we return to Arifridos, and speculate on his possible background, we can illustrate the principles behind these observations. If we assume from his name that Arifridos would have regarded himself as a 'Vandal', this would clearly have provided an important expression of his personal identity within post-Roman Thuburbo Maius. But this 'Vandal' identity would have meant different things when Arifridos engaged with other Vandals, with other members of the urban aristocracy or with the poorer sections of society. If we went further and suggested that Arifridos was one of those Sueves or Goths who came over with Geiseric in AD 429, and later assumed a 'Vandal' identity in the manner described by Procopius (there is no direct evidence for this, but his name does not exclude the possibility), the ambiguity of his ethnic identity becomes still more apparent. Among other 'Vandals', Arifridos would perhaps have accentuated his Suevic (or Gothic) identity; when among Romans, he would simply be a 'Vandal'; among women, slaves or the lower classes he could have been any of these things but was also a male aristocrat. As a final point we might add that a rich female burial was found relatively close to Arifridos' in the same church in 1912.[10] Like Arifridos, this woman was buried in the gaudy jewellery popular among the late Roman and post-Roman aristocracy, which included an impressive gold necklace, a pair of gold brooches, and two earrings with inset stones. We do not know her name, and nothing apart from the general proximity of the two burials can connect her with Arifridos, but further speculation again reveals complexities inherent in the understanding of early medieval identity. If Arifridos was a 'Vandal', and had been married to this unknown woman since before the crossing, what might this imply about her identity? How would this have changed if she was a native of Thuburbo and had married the glamorous military aristocrat who had recently arrived in town? Or if Arifridos was the

Figure 4.1 Arifridos' church: The Christian church constructed in the Temple of Ceres, Thuburbo Maius. Reproduced by permission of Professor David Mattingly

native African and had married one of the women who had come over with the invaders? We cannot know, of course. There remains a possibility that neither of the two individuals buried in the church at Thuburbo Maius would have seen themselves as a Vandal, and a strong probability that the two were not related to one another, but the possibilities help to highlight the depth of our ignorance about the precise workings of Late Antique identity.

Studies of Late Antique and early medieval ethnicity have blossomed over the past generation and have become a major point of intellectual dispute among scholars in several disciplines, and across a wide geographical stage.[11] These disputes have focused primarily upon the different means by which ethnicity might be articulated within the period, and particular attention has been paid to the importance of a sense of shared history to the evolution of group identities, as well as to the political function which new ethnic identities might have within the emergent successor kingdoms.[12] The Vandals have rarely been at the centre of this debate, but the ambiguities inherent in their emerging identities make them a particularly interesting case study.[13] Ethnic unity was not something that Geiseric and his followers were simply born into, but a system of social signs and behaviours which developed over time and became recognized as something quintessentially 'Vandalic'.

Being 'Roman' in Roman North Africa

To understand the formation of identities in post-Roman North Africa, it is best to start with a brief discussion of the situation as it stood in the later Roman period. This is partly because we simply know more about the nature of Roman provincial identity than we do about the ideological origins of the successor states, but also because the fifth-century Vandals were heavily influenced by the post-Roman environment in which their shared sense of identity developed. As we shall see, being Vandal was as much about being a man and being an aristocrat as it was about anything else, and to understand these ideals we need to understand what defined these roles within the Roman world.

Roman identity was hardly a straightforward ethnic affiliation, and was based primarily upon political and legal definitions, and upon shared social and cultural practices.[14] 'Roman' identity itself was never based upon a fiction of shared biological descent among members of a specific group. In an empire which spanned the Mediterranean, different categories of social belonging were needed to create an illusion of cultural cohesion. As recent studies have demonstrated, Roman ethnicity and the expression of *Romanitas* ('Romanness' provides a clumsy approximation) was essentially performed, rather than innate, and was overwhelmingly based upon certain notions of appropriate male behaviour.[15] An individual might show himself to be Roman through the manifestation of a number of personal virtues, including courage, dignity and social decorum; he might display his *Romanitas* through the wearing of certain clothes, undertaking public service and benefaction, spending his leisure time in appropriate fashion and so on. It was such attributes that made a man a Roman, made him an appropriate husband, father, general and politician, and which distinguished him from a woman, child, barbarian or slave. The specific symbols through which this Roman ideal of masculinity was expressed varied in both time and space, and *Romanitas* is better regarded as an orchestra of different – and constantly changing – variations on a cultural, political and social theme, than as a normative cultural ideal. Roman ethnicity, moreover, did not exclude the maintenance of other ethnic affiliations; indeed contrasting regional identities could affect the form in which *Romanitas* was expressed in different places and in different circumstances.[16] In North Africa, for example, regional identities retained a profound influence throughout the Roman period and beyond.[17]

This is illustrated by the different ways in which *Romanitas* was expressed in late Roman Africa. The rapid spread of Christianity within the region had a profound effect upon local and regional identities. Martyr cults increasingly dominated expressions of civic affiliation, and bishops (many of whom came from the old aristocracies) were happy to harness these new loyalties. Christian – and African – identities were also combined in the recognizable name-stock from which Romans within the region drew.[18] The spread of the church also threatened to redefine the cultural ideals of the aristocracy. Augustine of Hippo, the ecclesiastical aristocrat *par excellence* in North Africa illustrated this clearly through his constant criticism of traditional forms of secular evergetism and public activity, whether the observance of long-standing civic rituals, or through the provision of games for the public.[19] In spite of this criticism, these traditional modes of cultural display remained. Secular and civic notions of *Romanitas* survived into the Vandal period, as we shall see, but the conflict that Augustine stirred up recalls the different media through which cultural identity might be expressed in the later fourth and early fifth century.

The emergence of the military aristocracy as a prominent social group was a further significant change within late Roman society.[20] From the early fourth century, the increasing frequency with which the emperors were drawn from the Roman army, and the gradual implementation of a service aristocracy structured along more or less military lines, led to dramatic changes in the symbolic display of the Roman aristocracy more generally. Whilst the senatorial toga remained an important symbol of political status, pseudo-military uniform and hunting garb became common among the upper classes.[21] By the end of the century, Honorius and Theodosius were issuing laws to insist that senators in the Roman forum adopt their traditional garb, rather than donning the fashionable trousers and tunics of the new elite.[22]

This militarization of *Romanitas* was less pronounced within the North African provinces than it was elsewhere in the empire. Africa had never been intensively militarized, and did not experience the same social and political upheaval that had such an effect upon the northern frontier zones within this period. Yet in spite of this insulation, the African aristocracy were aware of the changing world around them. As we have seen, the later fourth century and the first decades of the fifth saw some military activity within the region, as powerful local figures ceded from the empire, or sought to use military authority to make their mark on the centre.[23] These social changes had an effect upon the ideal of *Romanitas*.

The famous hunting mosaics discovered at Bord Djedid in Carthage illustrate the point particularly well.[24] These mosaics were excavated in the mid-nineteenth century from a rich villa on the edge of the city, and three fragments of the largest mosaic are now on display in the British Museum. Each of these sections depicts a rider in trousers, tunic and cloak, one lifting his hand in salutation, another in the act of lassoing a deer, and a third following a hunting dog. For a long time, these hunters were assumed to be Vandals on the strength of their strikingly 'un-Roman' dress, but recent research suggests precisely the opposite. By the end of the fourth century and the beginning of the fifth, clothing of this kind was precisely the means by which *Romanitas* could be expressed.

Vandal Ethnicity within North Africa

The barbarian conquest of AD 429 thrust a powerful new group into the society of Roman North Africa. Relatively rapidly, these barbarians became the *de facto* military aristocracy of the emerging kingdom, and it was this institutional position which provided the framework in which a distinct 'Vandal' identity could develop.[25] These newly minted Vandals were distinct from both the ruling household (the royal Hasdings, who were careful to cultivate their own separate identity in the aftermath of the conquest), and from the 'Roman' secular aristocracy which already existed within North Africa, and which continued to cultivate its *Romanitas* throughout this period.[26] The means by which the Vandals could be recognized were varied, and our textual and archaeological sources can only provide an imperfect impression of the complex social semiotics of the period. Some of these markers of identity – like language – stand out clearly within the post-classical society of North Africa, while others were certainly assumed after years or even decades of interaction with indigenous elites. The result was an unambiguously 'North African' creation: the 'Vandals' of 535 would have looked very different from the group of barbarians who invaded in 429, and much of this change would have been inspired by the African setting in which they lived.

Vandal identity was a gradual creation, and was shaped by a variety of different impulses, but was no less real for that. Individuals regarded themselves as Vandals, and were recognized as such by others. When Procopius described the Byzantine reconquest of North Africa, he was confident that a visible distinction existed between 'Vandals' and 'Romans' within the kingdom.[27] It might occasionally be difficult to distinguish between the two groups, as Belisarius learned to his peril, but the ethnic categories were meaningful at the time of the conquest. It was for this reason that Justinian could order the unilateral removal of all 'Vandals' from the region, and expect this to be accomplished with few problems. This is not to suggest that these ethnic boundaries were absolute, or that notions of 'Vandal' or 'Roman' identities should be regarded as absolutely inseparable. Although our sources are not explicit on the subject, it seems likely that individuals could adopt different identities over their lifetimes, and members of the same family might certainly change their principal affiliations over generations.[28] No less significantly, we know of individuals who temporarily assumed certain symbols of ethnic identification that were not their own, by dressing in 'barbarian' clothing, for example.[29] But this should not obscure the existence of the distinct and meaningful identities. A Roman could not become a Vandal simply by dressing up as one, nor could a Vandal shed his own identity by impulse of will alone. Crucially, 'Vandal' ethnicity meant something important to the inhabitants of Hasding Carthage, and continued to mean something down to the Byzantine conquest, even if it can seem like an artificial construct to modern observers.

The examination of these ethnicities is complicated by a number of factors. Chief among these is the problem of setting 'Vandal' identity within its wider social context. As we have seen, a crucial function of ethnic identity – indeed of identity of any kind – was to distinguish members of a group from non-members. In many studies it has simply been assumed that the principal cultural distinction within the successor kingdoms of the fifth and sixth centuries – the opposition which emergent ethnic identities were intended to underscore – was between 'Romans' and 'barbarians'. That is, when Vandals (or Goths or Franks) articulated their own sense of community, a chief concern was to separate themselves from the Roman inhabitants of the regions in which they lived.[30] This perspective is partly a function of our source material, of course, the vast majority of which was written by 'Roman' authors, and frequently presents a chauvinistic account of non-Roman groups. When writers like Victor of Vita insist vociferously on the difference between Romans and Barbarians, we tend to take notice. It is easy to assume that such distinctions were of equal importance to all members of society, and that this binary ethnic opposition between 'us' and 'them' was the primary conceptual distinction in the period.

For the Vandals themselves, however (and indeed for Victor and his 'Romans'), there were other distinctions which were equally important, and this is crucial to the understanding of identity within their kingdom. A 'Vandal' was not only defined by being a non-Roman (although this was important), he was also a non-Jew, a non-Greek and a non-Moor; he was free (not a slave), an adult and, crucially, a man. The Vandals were not set apart from the complex hierarchies and gender distinctions of post-Roman African society, they were embedded deep within them. Vandal identity was not articulated in straightforward opposition to 'Roman' identity, then, but developed alongside and within a whole series of different forms of identity which were already in operation within the Roman and post-Roman world. Crucially, this meant that the symbols by which the Vandals defined themselves were often similar or even identical to Roman aristocratic norms. The Vandals adopted the trappings of African elite lifestyles, not because they wanted to be Romans, but because they wanted to be elites; this offered them a means of establishing their own identity in a meaningful form in the post-Roman world. Through careful scrutiny we can identify some of the ways in which the members of this group distinguished themselves from other 'Roman' aristocrats, but we should not lose track of the other forms of social distinction at work within this politics of identity.

In order to explore the complex politics of identity within the Vandal kingdom we will discuss first the political foundations of Vandal identity, as they were established under Geiseric and developed under his successors. This will also consider the most obvious symbols by which the Vandals distinguished themselves from their Roman neighbours, including legal privileges, language and some sense of their own shared heritage. But this only tells one side of the story. The next section will consider the complex interdependence of the relationship between 'Vandal' and 'Roman' identity within this period, and will argue that the new military aristocracy readily assumed many of the elements of *Romanitas* as a means of purely social distinction. The chapter will then consider the importance of gender to the formulation of ethnic identity in North Africa in this period, and will argue that 'Vandalness' was an essentially masculine form of identity. This is not to say that women should be excluded from the study of the Vandals, or that only a 'masculine' reading is appropriate to the study of this period – indeed gender issues are central to understanding the operation of the states – simply that ethnicity can only be understood as the product of specifically male forms of behaviour.

Vandals and Romans

Several key factors distinguished the newcomers from their Romano-African neighbours, and hence laid the foundations for a recognizable

'Vandal' identity. The first of these was economic. The settlement of AD 442, by which the lands of Africa Proconsularis were divided up amongst Geiseric, his family and his followers, had a crucial practical role in distinguishing the barbarian invaders from their new neighbours.[31] The precise mechanics of this distribution are poorly understood, as we have seen, but in purely ideological terms this is not especially important. At the very least, it seems likely that specific estates were granted to the invaders which were rent free, which normally passed on by inheritance. Victor refers to these lands as *funicula hereditatis* ('heritable plots') at the time of the settlement, but by Huneric's reign they were conventionally referred to as the *sortes Vandalorum* (or 'Vandal shares').[32] This terminology was so widespread that the Byzantine occupiers of the 530s referred to the same lands as *klēroi Bandilōn* – a simple Greek translation of the same phrase.[33] It was rent from these estates which supported Geiseric's military followers economically, and the status that these landholdings afforded which justified their pretensions to being a genuine landed aristocracy. The important point to note here is the extent to which the estates helped to ground the emerging identity of the Vandals. When Geiseric made the land settlement of 442, he distributed the lands among his followers; by the time his son came to the throne (if not before) possession of these 'Vandal shares' helped to define who was included within this ruling elite. One of the fundamental markers of Vandal identity, in other words, may have been the legal and economic privileges associated with the *sortes Vandalorum*. Vandals came to be identified as the people who lived on 'Vandal estates'.

Language provided a further means by which the Vandals could be distinguished.[34] Vandalic itself was a dialect of Gothic, and Roman contemporaries may have regarded the two languages as indistinguishable in their coarse incomprehensibility. In an epigram from the *Latin Anthology*, a poet laments the barbarous sounds of the foreign language:

> Amongst the Gothic 'cheers!' [*eils*] and 'eat and drink!' [*scapia matzia ia drincan*], No one ventures to write decent poetry.[35]

Eils and *scapia matzia ia drincan* are either Gothic or Vandalic, a dialect of the same language group.[36] But the image of a Latin writer, adrift in a sea of barbarity, is powerful enough and was a popular one in this period; a similar sentiment may be found in the fifth-century writing of the Gallic bishop Sidonius Apollinaris.[37] For these writers, complaints about the barbaric languages of the invaders provided a means to express their own impeccable *Romanitas*, but need not be read as evidence for an implacable hostility. The anonymous poet of the *Latin Anthology* understood the barbarian language well enough to incorporate it within his work, and apparently expected his audience to have understood the allusion. Indeed, the incorporation of the Vandals within the gentle mockery of this poetic epigram rather suggests that the different social groups of North Africa were comfortable with one another.

The Vandalic quotation in the *Latin Anthology* suggests that the language was still used at some level down to the fall of Carthage in AD 534. Vandalic liturgy was probably employed in Arian church services, and this may have helped to keep the language alive.[38] Huneric's insistence in his negotiations with Leo that the Arians of the Balkans be allowed to celebrate in the vernacular certainly implies that this was normal practice in North Africa.[39] Famously, the Arian patriarch Cyrila also attempted to debate with the Nicene bishops in Vandalic, although his opponents rejected the gambit on the strength that his Latin was perfectly adequate to be understood.[40] It is likely that the majority of Vandals within Africa would have been at home with Latin, but their language provided a strong bond of association.

This is also evident in the naming conventions among the Vandals. Arifridos, as we have seen, sported an unmistakably 'Vandalic' name, and many other examples are known from inscriptions and the textual sources. Victor refers to Armogas, Dagila, Gamuth, Heldica, Maioricus, Marivadus, Muritta, Obadus and Vitarit, as well as Cyrila and the familiar names of the Hasding family.[41] In each of these cases, distinctively 'barbarian' names provided a means by which members of the group could identify themselves, but these were not infallible markers of ethnic identity. The name 'Maioricus', for example, is a combination of the familiar Latin prefix '*Maior*' with the Germanic suffix '*-rikus*' ('powerful').[42] The cosmopolitan origins of this name may well reflect Maioricus' background; Victor tells us that this young Nicene martyr had a mother called Dionysia and an aunt called Dativa, a classical Greek name and a Christian Latin name respectively.[43] Strikingly, even Cyrila's name would seem to be a hybrid of sorts, which combined the Greek 'Cyril' with a common Germanic suffix.[44] Names, then, were often labels of ethnic identity, but we need to be careful when we attempt to interpret them.[45]

Vandal identity may also have been facilitated by the sense of a shared history among members of the group, which has always been a common feature of ethnic affiliation. This is rather a controversial issue. Many historians have expressed surprise that the Vandals never produced (or patronized) a historian who celebrated their origins in the manner of

Cassiodorus and Jordanes for the Ostrogoths, Isidore of Seville for the Visigoths or Paul the Deacon for the Lombards.[46] It might be concluded from this that such matters were of little importance to the self-identity of the muscle-headed warriors of Carthage. While it is true that no secular narrative history has survived from the kingdom, several allusions in Procopius may imply that some historical traditions did circulate within the group.[47] Admittedly, these did not go back very far, and seem to have been tremendously confused: Procopius' own garbled narrative of the Vandal occupation of Spain is said to have drawn upon these sources. But such imperfect recollections are precisely what we might expect from genuine communal memories. If Procopius did draw upon existing Vandal traditions in writing his account, their existence testifies to the development of a shared sense of heritage among the group by the last days of the Vandal kingdom.

Vandals, Alans and Sueves

It is possible that individuals who were regarded as Vandals by the historians and poets of Roman North Africa continued to maintain secondary ethnic affiliations. In other words, those Sueves and Alans whom Procopius claimed had disappeared among the greater body of Vandals may well have maintained their own distinct identities. The evidence for this, however, is rather less substantial than many commentators have assumed. There is little to suggest, for example, that the Alans had their own distinct military organization, or maintained distinctive naming practices. The most striking evidence in favour of a continued ethnic identity comes from official documentation. After the Byzantine conquest, Justinian claimed the victory title *Alanus Vandalicus Africanus* (Alan-, Vandal- and Africa-Conqueror).[48] Of more direct relevance is the legislation of Huneric which was issued in the name of *Rex Hunirix wandalorum et alanorum* (Huneric, king of the Vandals and the Alans).[49] Some 50 years later, the last of the Hasding kings was celebrated as *Geilamir rex Vandalorum et Alanorum* in an inscription on a magnificent silver basin, probably sent to the Ostrogothic court as a diplomatic gift.[50] This dual claim to authority may have been a hangover from the peculiar alliance of the Alans and the Hasdings after Wallia's campaigns in 416, or might simply reflect the pretensions of Huneric and Gelimer, who felt that their authority might be bolstered by an anachronistic claim to rule over an obsolescent group.[51] Given the fact that no other Hasding king claimed authority over the group

(Gunthamund and Thrasamund are both *Rex Vandalorum* in the few cases when their titulature includes an ethnonym), and most Hasding titulature simply employs *rex* or *dominus*, it seems unlikely that the Alans existed as a meaningful political entity within North Africa after the first generation of occupation.[52] Nevertheless, a small handful of apparently 'Alanic' names are known from North Africa in the Vandal period, and individuals may well have maintained some sense of ethnic independence from the great mass of Vandals.[53]

An epitaph discovered in the Grand Basilica in Hippo in 1951 provides our other possible evidence for the survival of significant sub-groups within the Vandal population. This inscription was erected in AD 474 to commemorate the death of a woman called Ermengon, who was survived by her husband Ingomar.[54] From the epitaph that he erected, we know that Ermengon was 35 at the time of her death, and that she was regarded by her husband as a *Suava* or Sueve. It may well be that this couple were not natives of the Vandal kingdom, and that Ingomar was actually an ambassador or merchant from the Suevic kingdom who had died abroad, although the presence of his wife in Hippo would argue against this. If both were subjects of Geiseric, however, the epitaph would indicate that individuals born at around the time of the fall of Carthage could maintain their Suevic identity throughout their life. This need not have excluded Ermengon and Ingomar from assuming a Vandal identity too – they may have been viewed as part of a Suevic community among the Vandals – but it does indicate how complex the politics of identity formation could be in this period.

Vandals and Romans: Case Studies

The Vandal aristocracy of fifth-century Africa was quite unlike anything the inhabitants of the region had seen before, but it was still an aristocracy which had adopted more or less recognizable form. While the Vandals kept their distinctive naming patterns, may well have commonly spoken a strange language and perhaps cultivated a sense of shared heritage, they were also acutely aware of the social expectations thrust upon them as a new ruling caste within a Roman province. The most striking feature of our textual sources on Vandal identity is the extent to which it was shaped by existing notions of *Romanitas*, and particularly by ideals of Roman masculinity. As shall be discussed, this can frequently look like acculturation or the 'Romanization' of the Vandals, but this would be a simplification. We can state confidently that the Vandals did not become 'Romanized', simply because their own identity developed within a profoundly Roman milieu. 'Vandal' identity, as it was understood by Victor and Procopius (and probably by the individuals who professed it) had always assumed strong elements of Roman culture. This is best demonstrated with a series of specific illustrations, which relate either to individuals who are explicitly labelled as 'Vandals' by our sources, or who bear recognizably 'Germanic' names and might tentatively be regarded as members of the group.

Victor provides us with a first case study, an unnamed individual who is explicitly identified as a Vandal:

> There were, at that time, some slaves who belonged to a certain Vandal, one of the Vandals called 'millenarii', Martinianus, Saturianus and their true brothers as well as a slave, a noteworthy handmaiden of Christ called Maxima, who was beautiful in both body and heart. And because Martinianus was the one who made his weapons, and was always held in high regard by his lord, while Maxima was mistress over the entire household, the Vandal thought that he would unite Martinianus and Maxima in marriage, in order to make these members of his household more faithful to himself.[55]

The Vandal's matchmaking was not a success, and Victor goes on to describe the resistance of the two slaves, their torture at the hands of their master and the eventual death of the persecutor along with most of his family.[56] Victor's principal concern, of course, is to relate the story of the confessors, and consequently he provides relatively little information on the Vandal himself, but what he does provide is telling. First, the social status of the Vandal is evident and is a defining feature of Victor's account: Victor specifies his rank, which must have been common knowledge. The fact that he was a *millenarius* probably implies that the Vandal was in the army, and his particular affection for his armourer may also suggest that weapons provided a further mark of social status for him.[57] The unfolding story of the persecution reveals that the Vandal lived on his own estate, along with a houseful of family and slaves, above whom he held absolute authority. His only legal deference seems to have been to the king, who supported him in his right to pass authority over his slaves. Following the death of the Vandal and his children, his wife inherited the estate, presumably in keeping with the laws of AD 442.

A second illustration is provided by Fridamal, the recipient of a poem by the Latin writer Luxorius, probably in the 510s or 520s.[58] To judge from his name, Fridamal was a Vandal nobleman, and he had recently commissioned a painting of a hunting trip for the decoration of his rural estate:

> But, although things that give pleasure have been enclosed in such splendour, and although the beautiful rooms are resplendent with varied artistry, yet must be admired the picture of your brave deed, Fridamal, and the great and glorious feat of slaying a wild boar. Excited by love of your characteristic courage, you set your mind upon picturing your exploits in a worthy setting. Here, drawing back and aiming the spear from behind your back, you are striking the foaming boar straight on its forehead and two-nostrilled face.[59]

Here we see the Vandal aristocrat in the familiar cultural register of the later empire. His taste for hunting, and his desire to be commemorated in the act of the kill, reflects a pastime which had been common within North Africa long before the arrival of the Vandals. The fact that he chose to have his painting celebrated in Latin elegy simply underlines the classical context in which he was acting. Indeed, in many ways, Fridamal's layered self-presentation recalls nothing so much as the pre-Vandal hunting mosaics of the villa at Bord Djedid in Carthage. Here, strikingly, we see a Vandal assuming the guise of the Roman aristocracy.

A further illustration of the Vandal aristocratic ideal may be found in two letters, preserved in a sixteenth-century manuscript from Monte Cassino, one a letter from the *comes* Sigisteus to the *presbyter* Parthemius, the other Parthemius' reply.[60] Sigisteus' ethnic identity can inferred from his Germanic name, and the fact that his rank of *comes* suggests employment in administration or the military, although neither of these assumptions can be made with complete confidence.[61] Sigisteus revealed himself to be a generous, if somewhat over-enthusiastic, correspondent: at one point he declares Parthemius to be the equal of the pope in his spiritual stature. Parthemius returned the compliment in terms evidently intended to appeal to the Vandal:

> Learned Greece has not produced such a man, nor has great Larissa given birth to such an Achilles, as you, whom Africa, warlike and productive of harvests, has exalted to the stars.[62]

Evidently this was a popular form of flattery in the North African kingdom: Procopius reports that the Hasding prince Hoamer was also known as the 'Achilles of the Vandals' on the strength of his military successes against the Moors.[63] Here we see a conflation of ideals, at once classical and militaristic. Sigisteus is a military champion, but in the mould of Achilles, he was a noble warrior who is African, and not barbarian by birth.

These three different perspectives seem to provide contradictory impressions of Vandal identity. Victor's unnamed Vandal is a violent, persecuting thug, Luxorius' Fridamal is a slightly rough-edged nobleman with aspirations to the finer things, and Parthemius' Sigisteus seems like an enthusiastic patron of the church. This apparent shift in Vandal behaviour over the course of the fifth and early sixth century has frequently been explained in terms of acculturation or 'Romanization'.[64] It is assumed that, as the Vandals spent more time rubbing shoulders with wealthy Romano-Africans in the flesh-pots of Carthage, and less time plundering along the Mediterranean coast, they lost their essentially 'Vandal' identity, and started to assume many of the trappings of the late Roman aristocracy. Ethnic affiliations were eroded, in other words, in the warm air of Carthage.

This is to misrepresent the way in which the Vandals viewed themselves and were viewed by others. Fridamal and Sigisteus would not have accepted that their behaviour was unbefitting for a Vandal, and may not have regarded themselves as being so very different from the unnamed barbarian of Victor's account. Victor's anonymous barbarian derived his status primarily from his military function; we may assume that the same was true of the *comes* Sigisteus, and Fridamal's interest in hunting would seem to indicate something similar. Significantly, Fridamal, Sigisteus and the anonymous barbarian all behaved like Vandals, whether fighting, hunting or writing, it is just that Vandal behaviour was often very similar to 'Roman' behaviour. If we assume that 'Vandal' identity had been thoroughly imbued with the cultural and social associations of *Romanitas* from its very inception in North Africa, the apparent contradictions between these three noblemen disappear. Roman aristocrats had long marked themselves out by their authority over the household, their literary tastes and (more recently) their patronage of the church, and Vandals were evidently keen to follow this lead. Social standing was a central part of what made a Vandal; what we see here are individuals expressing just that.

This is not to suggest that notions of Vandal identity did not change over the course of the occupation of Carthage. Each generation born within the kingdom would have inherited traditions of ethnic affiliation in different ways; the changing behaviour of the Hasding kings may provide a rough index of this transformation.[65] The crucial point is that the appropriation of new forms of cultural expression, or the more widespread appreciation of different manifestations of 'Vandalic' behaviour did not represent a compromise or a contradiction. Vandal and Roman aristocracies may well have looked very alike by the end of the reign of Gelimer, but this does not mean that the groups were identical, or that the signs by which they distinguished themselves were unimportant.

The extent to which Vandalic identity was dependent upon Roman norms for its definition is illustrated particularly well by one of the most famous passages relating to the group. Procopius' explanation for the gradual decay of the Vandals has already appeared once within this book, but it deserves to be repeated in full:

> For the Vandals, since the time when they gained possession of Libya, used to indulge in baths, all of them, every day and enjoyed a table abounding in all things, the sweetest and best that the earth and sea produce. And they wore gold very generally, and clothed themselves in the Medic garments, which now they call 'seric' and passed their time, thus dressed, in theatres and hippodromes and in other pleasurable pursuits, and in all else in hunting. . . . and they had a great number of banquets and all manner of sexual pleasures were in great vogue among them.[66]

Procopius includes this passage as an explanation for the rapid demise of the Vandal kingdom in the face of the Byzantine conquest, a point which he develops by stressing the proud resistance of the still-barbaric Moors. The passage itself has been widely cited as an illustration of the widespread 'Romanization' of the Vandals, indeed it is almost always interpreted in these terms.[67] But Procopius' intention was not to demonstrate that the Vandals had become more 'Roman' during their occupation of North Africa, but rather that they had become *less* 'Vandal'. To Procopius, the Vandals had lost an essential part of their identity which had kept their kingdom intact. In order to understand this passage we need to appreciate that lamentations of this kind had been commonplace throughout classical antiquity. Inhabitants of the Mediterranean world had been upbraided for their sexual and sensual excesses, the triviality of their behaviour and their adoption of foreign 'oriental' traits since the classical Greek period. In the more recent past, Christian writers like Augustine, Salvian and Quodvultdeus had condemned Roman North African society in precisely these terms, for losing themselves in a sea of delights when moral and physical perils lurked around the corner.[68] The luxuries listed by Procopius, in other words, were important not as symbols of *Romanitas* to which the Vandals aspired, but as markers of inappropriate behaviour which threatened any well-ordered society, whether Vandal or Roman.

A certain school of nineteenth-century scholarship regarded the history of the Vandals as essentially a narrative of decline and decay, of a gradual 'Romanization' of a pure Vandal identity.[69] The idea that there was ever such a thing as a 'pure' Vandal identity has since been universally dismissed, but the concept of Vandal 'Romanization' should also be rejected. Roman cultural traits did not in themselves represent a significant challenge to the coherence of Vandal identity, simply because 'Vandalness' was not solely expressed in opposition to notions of *Romanitas*. Indeed, as we have seen, a substantial proportion of the means by which Vandals identified themselves would seem to have been shared with traditional notions of Roman ethnicity. If many prominent Vandals spent a large amount of their time hunting, dining or reciting Latin poetry, this need not have implied a deterioration of their Vandal identity, it simply shows that what it meant to be 'Vandal' was strongly imbued with classical ideals.

Procopius' use of a familiar literary conceit to explain the demise of the Vandals and the survival of the Moors means that the passage cannot be used as evidence for the gradual acculturation of the barbarians. But it is striking that Procopius felt able to explain Vandal decadence in terms which had traditionally been reserved for the societies of the classical Mediterranean. Emasculation of the kind the historian describes would have been abhorrent according to Roman ideals of masculinity, just as much as the Vandal. In seeking to explain how the Vandals had lost their essential 'Vandalness' during the fifth and sixth centuries, Procopius vividly highlights the strongly 'Roman' ideals around which their identity had been built, and the essentially masculine identity which underpinned all of these social constructions.

'Men and Women in Barbarian Clothes'

The nature of the integration of the Vandals into Roman African society is illustrated particularly clearly by a further passage in Victor's *History of the Vandal Persecutions*.[70] Towards the beginning of his second book, relating events which probably took place in the early 480s, Victor describes how the bishops of the Arians were incensed at the piety and popularity of Eugenius, the bishop of Carthage, and lobbied for a response from the king:

> They made a proposal to the king concerning [Eugenius], that he should on no account preside from his throne and preach to the people of God as usual; and then, that he should forbid the entry of any men or women in barbarian clothes who were seen going into the church. That man replied as was right, 'The House of God is open to all, and no-one should turn away people going in'. This was especially so because a huge number of our Catholics who served in the royal household used to go in dressed like Vandals. . . .[71]

> When the king received this answer from the man of God, he ordered that torturers were to be stationed at the entrances to the church; when they saw a woman or man who looked like one of their race going there, they were straightaway to thrust tooth-edged stakes at that person's head and gather all the hair in them. Pulling tightly, they took off all the skin from that person's head, as well as the hair.[72]

Victor's account implies clearly that individuals wearing barbarian dress (*de habitu barbaro*) would be recognizable enough, both for the Arian bishops and their henchmen and (presumably) for the audience of the *Historia* itself. He does not state what these clothes were. Several modern scholars have made their own suggestions, but Victor's only hint is in his reference to the persecutors scalping their victims: long hair may well have been a conspicuous feature of a typically 'barbarian' appearance in this period.[73] In itself, this passage suggests simply that the 'barbarians' within Carthage had a recognizable and distinct visual signature of their own, without saying what this might have been.

But the passage says rather more, of course. Crucially, Victor also states that this *habitus barbarus* was also worn by a large number of individuals who were not Arians, and were not barbarians. His statement that these were individuals who served in the royal household (*domus regiae*) might imply that these fashionistas were members of the Romano-African aristocracy who affected the dress of the barbarians in order to curry favour with the king, but this seems unlikely. After all, the same individuals continued to wear their court clothing to worship in Nicene churches in contravention of a royal decree, and at great peril to themselves. It is rather more likely that the type of clothing referred to as *habitus barbarus* was the common designation of the typical dress of the Hasding court, which could be worn by Arian and Nicene, Roman and barbarian alike. 'Barbarian' dress, then, was not limited to the Vandals: it was adopted by all of those inhabitants of post-Roman Africa whose social or political position made the adoption of such dress appropriate. 'Barbarian' might thus be read as a synonym for 'those who appear in court' in this context.

The end of this episode is also important, and highlights the symbolic significance of 'barbarian' clothing as a marker of social, as well as ethnic, identity:

> After this punishment the women, their heads stripped of skin, were paraded through the streets with heralds going before them, so that the whole town could see.[74]

What is crucial here is not that Huneric and his bishops were persecuting Romano-Africans for wearing 'barbarian' clothing, or Vandals for attending church but rather that they were punishing courtiers for attending Nicene services when in court dress. If the chronology of Victor's account may be trusted, this was followed shortly afterwards by a series of further actions against Nicenes at court, including the suspension of their pay, expulsion from Carthage and loss of social status.[75] From this perspective, the public humiliation of women who had transgressed this law took a grimly appropriate form: where once their clothing and hair had marked them out as members of court, they were now stripped of both before the eyes of the public.

Victor describes punishments of this kind in loving detail throughout his *Historia*. He talks at length of the humiliation of bishops and laity of high social standing who were forced to travel beyond their endurance or to wallow for days in their own filth.[76] He notes that the aged were abandoned, that aristocratic women were forced into union with uneducated farmers and describes repeatedly how high-born Nicenes were cast out from their positions of influence in the city to take demeaning jobs elsewhere.[77] In so doing, Victor wished to show how the Vandals wished to turn African society 'upside-down'.[78] But it is conspicuous how frequently clothing appears as a status symbol in Victor's account. On several occasions he notes the nakedness of those expelled from Carthage, or those martyred in public:

> They did not spare people of any age or either sex, except those who had submitted to their will. Some were tortured by being beaten, others by being hung, and others by the fire; contrary to the laws of nature, women, especially the noble, were tortured entirely naked and in full view of the public.[79]

This nakedness had a sexual dimension, of course, and Victor describes the Vandals' particular fascination with the violation of Nicene chastity more than once, but it is the social dimension which is most relevant here.[80] Victor's note that it was 'especially the noble' women who suffered this degradation provides a further clue to the meaning of this action. Clothes represented a specific marker of social status within society of the period. When the Vandals confiscated the clothing of their noble victims, they also removed one of the signifiers of their nobility. Humiliation of this kind was particularly pointed when women were persecuted, but Victor includes several other examples. During the persecutions of Geiseric, Quodvultdeus and a great throng of clergy were stripped and forced into exile.[81] In the same period, other bishops and 'noble laity' were driven to flight when completely naked.[82] Individuals of all social classes could be humiliated, of course, but Victor only associates the punishment of public nakedness with the victims from the highest social ranks.

Crucially, Victor was equally aware that Vandals and Arians had a place upon the same social hierarchy. In his account of Huneric's reign, Victor makes particular reference to the punishments of Gamuth, the brother of Heldica and one of the former advisors of Geiseric, who had fallen foul of his son's political purges:

> Afterwards, [Huneric] condemned them to dig ditches to be used for the planting of vines, in the company of a certain goatherd and a country fellow. In addition, he had them set about with harsh whips times a year, that is on a monthly basis, and they were scarcely allowed a drink of water or bread to eat.[83]

Gamuth was an Arian, not a Catholic, and Victor is at pains to stress that his forbearance would have meant much more had he adhered to the true faith. What is significant, however, is that the historian could still recognize the social humiliation inflicted upon an Arian Vandal who had once been a prominent advisor to the king, and might expect his audience to do the same. Victor implicitly acknowledged that Gamuth had enjoyed a significant status within the Vandal kingdom, and that its loss was worthy of note.

This context casts important light upon the persecution of those who wore 'barbarian clothing' to a Nicene church. Just as bishops and senators could be punished by having their marks of office forcibly removed, so too could the courtiers of Carthage. Victor's account clearly implies that 'barbarian clothing' was a badge of status which was appreciated not only by the king and his Arian advisors, but by Nicene Africans and even by the historian himself. Had he not recognized the social importance of individuals at court – both Arian and Nicene – his description of their punishment, and the form that this punishment took would have been meaningless. As it stands, his account describes a world in which 'barbarian' court clothing was primarily a mark of social, rather than ethnic status. The individuals who wore it did not do so in pursuit of an ethnic identity.

Victor's response to the Vandals, then, was by no means straightforward. The strength of his own Nicene faith, his hostility to the Arians and the generic demands of the martyrological form in which he wrote all demanded that he represent the barbarians as a hostile – and homogeneous – force, external to the society of Catholic North Africa. Yet he was fully aware that this was an impossible simplification; towards the end of the *Historia* he harangues those Romans whom he regarded as collaborators with the ungodly barbarians:

> Those of you who love barbarians and sometimes praise them, in a way worthy of condemnation, give thought to their name and understand their ways. Surely there is no name by which they could be called other than 'barbarian', a fitting word connoting savageness cruelty and terror? However many may be the gifts with which you befriend them and however many the acts of compliance with which you placate them, they can think of nothing other than looking on the Romans with envy, and, to the extent that things turn out in according with their will, it is their constant desire to darken the nobility and brightness of the Roman name.[84]

As we have seen, many Africans had come to terms with the Vandals by the time Victor wrote, and many more were to do the same in the generations which followed. In the pragmatic world of North African politics, the Vandals and the Romans were clearly not implacably opposed. But it is the intensity of Victor's plea which is striking here, his desperate insistence that *barbarus* did not just mean 'courtier' or 'soldier', as seems to have been the case, but was a term of opprobrium for hostile outsiders. The nature of his tirade suggests that the *barbari* had a widely accepted social position within his homeland, and other passages in his own text confirm that this was the case. The 'Vandals' of the fifth and sixth centuries were very much the creation of North Africa; it was Roman 'acts of compliance' towards them, as well as their own emulation (or 'envy' – *invidia*) of the African aristocracy which defined their very identity, and not just their Arian faith or strange Germanic tongue. Victor may seem an unlikely witness to the extent of this integration, but his testimony is striking.

Women, Children and Barbarians

The discussion above suggests that 'Vandal' identity was largely restricted to the adult, male members of the military aristocracy and that it was underpinned by political and economic considerations which were largely restricted to men. But this naturally leads us to enquire about the women and children who were associated with this group. The invaders of AD 429 were a warband rather than a migrating 'people', but they would have brought a substantial entourage with them: Victor excludes women from his spurious calculation of the precise number of the invaders, whom he lists as 'old men, young men and children, slaves and masters', but they would certainly have been included in the group.[85] Within North Africa, we occasionally catch glimpses of women moving within 'Vandal' circles. Victor's discussion of 'barbarian dress' explicitly states women as well as men adopted this distinctive clothing (and that Roman as well as barbarian women chose to dress in this fashion). The literary and epigraphic record also indicates that female Germanic names were in common use within the kingdom; we hear of one Dagila, a female member of the royal household of both Geiseric and Huneric, Munifrida, a Christian woman buried in Carthage, and Damira, the daughter of the Hasding Oageis who died in childhood.[86]

The precise role played by these women in the articulation of Vandal identity, and the extent to which they could claim this ethnicity as their own, is unknown thanks to the relentlessly engendered image provided by our principal literary sources. Neither Procopius nor Victor ever unambiguously refers to a woman as a 'Vandal' in her own right; for the most part the historians pass over the female actors in their dramas remarkably quickly. Of the countless royal women associated with the Hasding line, we know of only five: the imperial princess Eudoxia, the Ostrogoth Amalafrida, an unnamed Visigoth, the anonymous wife of Theuderic who died in the purge of AD 481 and the infant Damira.[87] The epitaph to the female Suava Ermengon found in Hippo may indicate that women could be bearers of ethnic identity, but she provides an isolated example within the kingdom, and she was not a part of the dominant Vandal group.[88] For the writers of our textual sources, the most interesting features – one might say the definitive features – of Vandal identity were overwhelmingly masculine. 'Vandals' were primarily soldiers, administrators or landlords who held their land by right of (male) inheritance, who fought and governed on behalf of their Hasding kings and who assumed the engendered trappings of the late Roman military aristocracy.

The overwhelmingly engendered manner in which Victor and Procopius defined 'Vandalness' may simply reflect the historians' own predominantly political, military and religious concerns; these were all fields in which men were traditionally dominant in the later Roman empire. We may not hear of Vandal women, in other words, simply because our sources were not interested in them. But this in itself is telling. If ethnicity was constructed in Late Antiquity, that is to say if ethnicity was created by the sum total of spoken and unspoken assumptions about it, then texts like Victor's *History* and the poetry of the *Latin Anthology* were among the media which helped to define who the Vandals were.

This image of engendered Vandal identity is illustrated most clearly by an episode which would initially seem to be an exception to this rule. In the spring of AD 536, some months after Belisarius had shipped the last of the Vandal men off to fight on the eastern front, the women they had left behind started to stir up discontent among the Byzantine army. Procopius provides our only source:

> After the Vandals had been defeated in the battle, as I have told previously, the Roman soldiers took their daughters and wives and made them their own by lawful marriage. And each one of these women kept urging her husband to lay claim to the possession of the lands which she had owned previously, saying that it was not right or fitting that if, while living with the Vandals, they had enjoyed these lands, but after entering into marriage with the conquerors of the Vandals they were then to be deprived of their possessions.[89]

The land claim made by these women can only have been based upon their inheritance rights over the *sortes Vandalorum* or *kleroi Bandilon*.[90] We know from a single reference in Victor that widows did enjoy such rights among the Vandals, although sons presumably stood to inherit under normal circumstances.[91] What Procopius describes, then, are the exceptional circumstances in which women might assume certain aspects of an ethnic identity – that is the traditional claim to economic and land rights – in the absence of the Vandal men. With no male Vandals left, but with the issue of the 'Vandal allotments' still unresolved in the chaos after the conquest, the women who remained came to take on some characteristics of the wider group. Yet even here the ethnic identity of the women is ambiguous. Procopius does not say that the women were Vandals, indeed he rather implies that they were not. He notes that they had once lived with Vandals, and had enjoyed their rights by proxy. At best, the wives and daughters of the Vandals could claim to transmit certain ethnic privileges, but their own ethnic status remained ambiguous.

This is not to suggest that issues of gender were unimportant within the Vandal kingdom. It could easily be argued that gender identities were far more central to the concerns of North African society in this period than were issues of ethnic belonging. After all, the poets of the *Latin Anthology* had very little to say on ethnographic or even religious subjects, but returned repeatedly to the eunuchs, hermaphrodites, cuckolds, chaste and promiscuous women and prodigiously-endowed men of Carthaginian society.[92] Their interest in the human body was also profound: witness the dwarfs and hunchbacks of the epigrams, or repeated reference to unusually ugly or spectacularly beautiful individuals.[93] But these identities were rarely expressed in ethnographic terms. Vandal Africa was a society in which gender identities meant a great deal, and Vandal ethnicity was itself heavily engendered, but women themselves had only an uncertain ethnic status within the kingdom.

5

The Vandal Kingdom and the Wider World, AD 439–534

> Dwelling on the Sea-coast, and being a rapacious, cruel, violent and tyrannical People, void of all Industry or Application, neglecting all Culture and Improvement, it made them Thieves and Robbers, as naturally as Idleness makes Beggars: they disdain'd all Industry and Labour; but being bred up to Rapine and Spoil, when they were no longer able to ravage and plunder the fruitful plains of *Valentia, Granada* and *Andalusia*, they fell to roving upon the Sea; they built Ships, or rather took Ships from others, and ravag'd the Coasts, landing in the Night, surprising and carrying away the poor Country People out of their Beds into Slavery.
>
> Daniel Defoe, *A Plan of the English Commerce* (1728)

Vandal 'foreign policy' seems like a macabre oxymoron. The countless raids and *razzias* which were sent out from Carthage throughout the fifth century did as much to secure the fearsome reputation of the Vandals as the persecutions within Africa itself. Chronicles and hagiographies testify to a fear of Vandal attack from Gallaecia to Alexandria, and their plundering expeditions were the subject of respectful poetry. In a period in which diplomacy increasingly overshadowed military action as the principal medium for Roman imperialism, the Vandals were the target of three major military expeditions to limit their authority in the Mediterranean and to reconquer North Africa. Their thalassocracy posed a genuine threat to the established powers in Ravenna and Constantinople.

Yet Vandal relations with the wider world were not simply confrontational. The sea-borne raids launched from Carthage (and there were a lot of them), did not take place in a simple political vacuum. Several recent historical studies have highlighted the complex diplomatic network which spanned the Mediterranean and its outlying territories.[1] When viewed within the context of these 'international relations', Vandal actions, both military and otherwise, take on a different light. While Vandal attitudes to foreign relations were somewhat unusual, even by the standards of the fifth century, they were at least coherent, and they provide a vital clue to the understanding of the kingdom as a whole. Understanding what these policies were remains a challenge – none of our sources adopts even a remotely sympathetic position towards the Vandals, and the events of the fifth and sixth century have to be pieced together from the sherds and fragments of indifferent historical evidence and a lacunose archaeological record. But an assessment of what can be known allows some patterns in Vandal action to be detected.

Inevitably, Vandal policies changed over the lifetime of their kingdom. The world of 439 was very different from that of 533. The gradual eclipse and eventual disappearance of the western imperial court at Ravenna during the third quarter of the fifth century was counterbalanced by the emergence of Odoacer's kingdom and later the Ostrogothic state of Theoderic within Italy. The struggles of the Sueves and Visigoths and – from the later fifth century – the Franks similarly altered the political 'map' of Gaul and Spain substantially, and forced the Vandals, the Ostrogoths and the eastern empire into new diplomatic contortions. The eastern Roman empire also changed within the same period, not least through the altered circumstances in its perpetual stand-off with the Persian empire to the east. The period saw the Balkan military elites supplant traditional ruling houses in court, the emergence of new bureaucracies and – arguably – the transformation of the later 'Roman' empire into something more recognizably 'Byzantine' during the reign of Justinian.

Inevitably, attempting to define a coherent 'Vandal' or even 'Hasding' foreign policy within this world is virtually impossible, but broadly three periods of distinct interaction with neighbouring Mediterranean polities might be identified. The first covers the sudden emergence of the Vandals on the world stage and their dealings with the Emperor Valentinian III from AD 439–455. After an initial phase of conflict, this was largely a period of peaceful entente, during which Geiseric established his own position within the high politics of the empire, helped in no small measure by the constant threat of further violence. With the sack of Rome in AD 455, the political stage changed again, and the two decades that followed witnessed a period of almost constant conflict between the Vandals and the two empires, until the signing of the 'perpetual peace' in 476. Thereafter, the role of the Vandals changed once more. The coincidence of the death of the last 'official' Roman emperor, Romulus Augustulus in 476, and that of Geiseric in 477 simultaneously removed the greatest theatre for political intrigue within the western Mediterranean, and the Vandal king who most enjoyed acting upon its stage. Geiseric's successors proved less adept than their progenitor at playing the great game of western politics, and largely concerned themselves with domestic tensions, or with the rising power of the Moorish kingdoms. Yet Geiseric had left them with a powerful Mediterranean empire. The last 50 years of the Vandal kingdom, then, from the death of Geiseric to the invasion of Belisarius, are best viewed through these 'imperial' possessions – Sicily, Sardinia, Corsica and the smaller islands – and the extent to which they shaped relations with the newly emergent powers of Italy, Gaul, Spain and Byzantium.

439–455: The Phoney War

The capture of Carthage in AD 439 gave Geiseric access to the African merchant fleet and its shipyards, and he was quick to press home this advantage.[2] By the spring of 440 the first Vandal attacks struck Sicily, and the emperor in Ravenna grew anxious that an invasion of southern Italy would follow shortly afterwards.[3] By all accounts Valentinian III was right to be nervous. The city of Lilybaeum was besieged, and the Sicilian countryside was so devastated that Valentinian was later forced to grant substantial tax remissions to the farmers of the island, who took time to recover from the blow.[4] Panormus (Palermo) too was attacked by the Vandals, although the locals were said to have put up stiff resistance.[5]

The imperial response to the new threat posed by the Vandals was commendably swift and apparently successful. On June 24 440, shortly after receiving news of the departure of the Vandal fleet, Valentinian III ordered that the vulnerable coast of Calabria be protected from this threat: 'whose sudden excursion and fortuitous depredation must be feared by all shores', and offered protection to merchant shipping in the area.[6] The *magister militum* Sigisvult was charged with the organization of troops within the region, and the Patrician Aetius was recalled from Gaul, but Valentinian and his eastern colleague Theodosius encouraged the inhabitants of the region to do their part.[7] One individual who responded to this charge was the great-grandfather of the prominent sixth-century statesman Cassiodorus, who had helped organize the defence of the coasts of Sicily and Bruttii (the 'toe' of Italy) during a Vandal attack at around this time – an accomplishment which his descendent remembered with some pride.[8] This new defensive policy also left its physical mark on the landscape of southern Italy. The mid-fifth century witnessed a substantial period of urban fortification, both in the construction of new walls and the restoration of existing circuits. In Naples, an inscription of 449 AD commemorates the erection of new defences against unnamed threats from land and sea; the standing walls of Terracina further up the coast probably date from the same decade, and other fortifications in Calabria rose up in the years that followed.[9]

The response of the eastern emperor to this revived Vandal aggression took rather longer to organize. By spring 441, Theodosius II had organized an expeditionary force, formed of troops drawn from the Danube frontier and placed under the command of Areobindus, Ansilas, Inobindos, Arintheos and Germanus, and supposedly transported on 1,100 cargo ships.[10] Impressive as these figures sound (and they are certainly a grotesque exaggeration), the campaign was never to engage with the enemy. Interrupted in his second year of campaigning by rumours of this expedition, Geiseric made immediate pleas for peace – a pattern of last-ditch diplomacy that was to serve him well over the decades that followed.[11] But these overtures proved unnecessary. The expedition was delayed, and never got beyond Sicily.[12] As the task force lingered, the situation in the east deteriorated rapidly. The Persian emperor Yezdegerd II and the Huns under their new leaders Bleda and Attila took advantage of the distraction in Sicily and launched independent attacks upon Mesopotamia and Thracia.[13] A temporary peace with the Persians was bought through diplomacy, but the Hunnic attack on Thrace demanded the immediate recall of the eastern army.[14] Deprived of this support from the east, Valentinian III was forced to deal with Geiseric through diplomatic channels.

The result of this short stand-off was the signing of the second treaty of 442 – a more lasting diplomatic agreement than the treaty of 435 in which the federated position of the Vandals was redefined.[15] Precisely what this agreement entailed is something of a moot point; the treaty itself is lost to us (as are all of the formal diplomatic arrangements between the Vandals and their neighbours), and our major sources only hint at it in passing. It seems clear, moreover, that the relationship represented new ground in Romano-barbarian relations, so points of comparison are hard to find. The Vandals were recognized in their possession of Africa Proconsularis and its neighbouring provinces. A second feature of the treaty was the formal dynastic alliance of the Hasdings with the Theodosian house through the betrothal of the Vandal prince Huneric to Valentinian's elder daughter, Eudocia. Huneric was sent to Ravenna as a hostage, where he was to make an anonymous cameo appearance in several of the celebratory verses of the court poet Merobaudes.[16] Eudocia herself – who was only five at the time that the treaty was signed – was still some way short of her legal majority, but the very promise of a formal union with the imperial house proved to be a crucial diplomatic coup for Geiseric.

The betrothal between Eudocia and Huneric forced the Vandal king to sever other dynastic ties, and led to a major realignment within Vandal politics. According to Jordanes, Huneric was already married at the time of the betrothal, to the unnamed daughter of the Visigothic king Theoderic.[17] This union, which had probably taken place in the previous decade, would have provided a valuable bond between the new rulers of Carthage and the Visigoths – then the major political and military power in south-western Gaul – but clearly stood in the way of Geiseric's aspirations to associate with the imperial family. Geiseric's solution to this dilemma was swift and brutal. Accusing the princess of plotting to poison him, the king had her physically disfigured, and sent back to her father in disgrace. It is possible, of course, that the humiliated princess actually had been involved in a plot against her overbearing father-in-law, and was perhaps even involved in the minor aristocratic rebellion which Prosper dates to the same year.[18] In citing poisoning as grounds for divorce, Geiseric followed imperial legal precedent, but the suspicion remains that his primary motivation was to insult the Visigothic monarch and to destroy the value of a diplomatic playing piece for which he no longer had any use himself. The Hasdings certainly benefited from the imperial match – and it was to shape Geiseric's political actions for the next 13 years – but in making it they had aligned themselves against the Visigoths.[19]

The years which followed were relatively quiet within the Mediterranean. Procopius omits the period entirely within his discussion of Vandal history.[20] Priscus alludes to some unrest in the eastern Mediterranean in AD 447, which some scholars have associated with the Vandals, but this is far from conclusive.[21] The only major campaign known to have taken place in this period is a Vandal attack on Turonium in Gallaecia in 445.[22] Quite what prompted this show of force, however, is unclear. Hydatius states that the Suevic state had been in the ascendancy within the Iberian Peninsula since the a successful campaign in Baetica in 439. It is possible that Geiseric retained interests in southern Spain, and wished to fire a warning shot across the bows of his former neighbours.[23] Perhaps more likely is that Geiseric's coastal raid was connected to the imperial campaigns against the Sueves and Bacaudae of north-western Spain. Imperial expeditions were sent to the area in AD 442,

443 and 446, and Aetius may well have enlisted Vandal naval strength to support imperial authority in the area. It is possible, of course, that Hydatius wrongly attributed attacks on the coast to the Vandals, or it may be that this was simply the only one of many raids to have been recorded. At the very least, the reference demonstrates that fear of the Vandals had spread even to the Atlantic coast.

This, in itself, is an important point. The diplomatic leverage provided by Vandal sea-power throughout Geiseric's reign was based as much on the threat of action as it was on its execution. This was to become still more evident after 455, when raiding from Carthage became widespread throughout the Mediterranean, but the effects of this new strategy were felt even in the 440s. Hagiographic tropes of the time provide some indication of the extent to which the Vandals exerted a psychological hold over the wider world. Nestorius' *Book of Heraclides*, written in 451 and surviving only in Syriac translation, alludes to Vandal assaults on both Italy and Rhodes – a historical reference which would be more trustworthy if the text did not state elsewhere that the Vandals even attacked the area of the River Ganges.[24] A similar theme is evident in the anonymous *Life of Daniel the Stylite*, written towards the end of the fifth century. This *Life* describes how the inhabitants of Alexandria feared attacks from Carthage – an anxiety that would seem to have been very real, despite the fact that no Vandal actions are known to have taken place in Egypt.[25] Even Pope Gregory the Great reflects this fear in his *Dialogues* – a collection of Italian hagiographies in Socratic form from the late sixth century. At the opening of the third book, Gregory includes an impossible account of Paulinus of Nola's experience as a captive of (and sometime gardener for) a Vandal noble in North Africa, and discusses the saint's ransoming of hostages taken during the 455 campaign and his actions in converting his barbarian master.[26] In fact, Paulinus died some 14 years before the Vandal assault on Rome, but the environment in which he lived, and in which stories about his life later circulated, were thoroughly infused with the spectre of Vandal aggression, even when it occurred relatively rarely. In many ways, of course, traditions such as these are not unique to the Vandals – Goths and Franks also turn up in countless hagiographic traditions in more or less 'barbaric' guise – But this 'shock and awe' was a major tool in Vandal foreign policy, and it was this perceived power which provided them with the time to establish their position in the Mediterranean.

It was the Huns, not the Vandals, who posed the greatest threat to the western empire in the middle decades of the fifth century. Like Geiseric, Attila, the king of the Huns, gained much of his political leverage from a vigorous diplomacy based as much upon the threat of violence as upon violence itself. Aetius – who had himself been a hostage of the Huns early in his life, and had maintained close bonds with the group – was able to use their fearsome reputation in his dealings with other barbarian leaders within the western empire. In return, Attila was granted the honorific title of western *magister militum*, and happily exchanged embassies with both imperial courts.[27] By the late 440s, however, the alliance upon which Aetius had founded so much of his power was starting to crumble. In 449 or 450, Attila claimed his own title to the western throne on spurious grounds and in 451 launched his climactic invasion of Gaul.[28] This campaign fractured the fragile diplomatic peace of the western empire and led directly to the collapse of Aetius' power and, ultimately, to that of Valentinian III.

Geiseric remained an interested spectator to the dramatic events that unfolded in the north, but was not directly involved: the suggestion that the Hasding king was responsible for inviting the Huns to attack the west was almost certainly the invention of a later historian.[29] There was no place for the Vandals in the bench-clearing brawl which saw Aetius, Avitus, the Visigoths of Theuderic and sundry Gallic barbarians halt the advance of the Huns, Gepids, Rugi and Burgundians at the Battle of the Catalaunian Fields in AD 451. But the events which followed were crucial to Hasding interests. Attila was defeated in 451, of course, and while his invasion of Italy in the following year created further difficulties for the reeling western state, his death in 453 ended the long-standing threat from the north. The repercussions of the defeat were long lasting, particularly within the court at Ravenna. The estrangement between Aetius and Attila had deprived the Roman generalissimo of both a diplomatic tool and a military ally, and his own position became increasingly unstable.[30] In 454, in an effort to compensate for this loss of influence Aetius arranged the marriage of his son, Gaudentius, to Valentinian's younger daughter, Placidia.[31] While this arrangement was accepted at court, Valentinian and his advisors increasingly viewed Aetius' dynastic aspirations with suspicion. The Roman aristocrat Petronius Maximus and the court eunuch Heracleius organized the assassination of the patrician, and one tradition states that Valentinian himself struck the fatal blow.[32] Other members of Aetius' circle were murdered immediately afterwards, but the emperor did not long outlive his erstwhile lieutenant. Shortly afterwards Valentinian was killed on military exercises on the Campus Martius, presumably by federate troops who remained loyal to Aetius.[33] Valentinian's death created a power vacuum at the centre of the western empire that Petronius Maximus was only too happy to fill. He immediately sought to integrate himself with the populace through a programme of copious bribery, and with the ruling family through the by now familiar route of dynastic marriage. To this end, he married Eudoxia, the widow of Valentinian and also betrothed his son Palladius to her younger daughter, Placidia.[34]

The impact of these events was felt throughout the Mediterranean, but nowhere more acutely than in Carthage. As late as 454, the relations between the Vandals and the two imperial courts had been warm. Aetius' military difficulties had weakened one of Geiseric's major rivals for military authority within the western Mediterranean and, in a show of faith towards the Catholic emperors, the Vandal king had allowed the appointment of Deogratias as the Catholic bishop of Carthage, the first since the departure of Quodvultdeus in 439 or 440. Yet within little more than a year, the position changed irrevocably. The arranged union of Placidia and Gaudentius threatened to derail the careful dynastic plans which Geiseric had developed and Valentinian's death removed a figurehead who may well have been increasingly sympathetic towards the Vandal cause. Most seriously, Petronius Maximus' usurpation not only placed a hostile authority on the throne of Ravenna, his marriage to Eudoxia also trumped the yet unconsummated union of Huneric and Eudocia. With the emperor dead and his own dynastic pretensions suffocating, Geiseric's position was critical. His reaction was dramatic. Faced with the danger of seeing his careful dynastic strategy come to nothing, the Vandal king abandoned his policy of talking softly and carrying a big stick. The threat of action had underscored Vandal foreign relations for much of the previous decade and a half. From 455, the threats were to be carried out.

In the years that followed the sack of Rome in 455, a persistent rumour circulated throughout the Mediterranean world that the Vandal attack had been instigated by Eudoxia, who had turned to Geiseric for help against her tyrannical husband Maximus. Like Honoria before her, the imperial widow was said to have turned to a fearsome barbarian in an effort to retain her own authority. The fact that several of the sources who recount this tradition are explicit in their own scepticism about it tells its own story.[35] Eudoxia probably never called for help. But Geiseric came anyway.

455–474. The Sack of Rome and the Fourth Punic War

Geiseric's response to the imperial crisis of 455 was swift and devastating. Two months after the death of Valentinian III, an army of Vandals,

Alans and Moors, with the king at its head, landed at the mouth of the Tiber and moved inland towards the imperial city.[36] Maximus hurried from Rome, but was killed in flight, either by the slaves of the royal household, or by a popular mob.[37] The protection of the city was left to Pope Leo, who was said to have met the Hasding king at the gates of the city, as he was rumoured to have done with Attila three years earlier.[38] While these negotiations may have ensured that rights of sanctuary would be respected, they did not save the city, and for the next fortnight Geiseric's troops plundered Rome.

The sack of Rome represents the high- (or low-) point of true Vandal 'vandalism'. Even here, what we see is not simply mindless destruction, but a pointed and overwhelming show of force with a definite political agenda.[39] The scale of this plunder is hard to assess, but seems to have been impressive. When Procopius came to recount the plunder taken from Carthage at the time of Belisarius' defeat of the Vandal kingdom, he listed many objects taken from the western capital, including countless statues and the menorah originally looted from the Temple in Jerusalem at the time of Titus' sack of AD 70.[40] Attempts were made to take even the less obviously portable wealth; Procopius preserves a story that the Vandals stripped the gilded bronze roof from the ceiling of the temple of Jupiter Capitolinus.[41]

The most important spoils, however, were human. Eudoxia, Eudocia and Placidia were all taken from Rome and brought back to Carthage, as was the 15-year-old Gaudentius, along with many other hostages.[42] Eudocia was a crucial political figure for Geiseric, given the importance of her betrothal to Huneric, but even Placidia was a valuable pawn for the Hasdings. Shortly before the death of Valentinian, she seems to have been betrothed to Anicius Olybrius, a Roman senator who was in Constantinople at the time of the Vandal sack. Geiseric's willingness to honour this union, and to act as patron to a bemused Olybrius, was to provide the king with a further political strategy over the decade and a half which followed.[43] Other prominent figures among the 'many thousands' whom Prosper claims were taken hostage had their own value in financial and political terms.[44] The prospect of returning individuals from both the 455 attack and from later *razzias* was a constant issue in political treaties with the empire.

The Vandals returned to Carthage after their attack, but the new policy of aggression was only just beginning. According to the conventions of late imperial diplomacy, treaties functioned as personal agreements between individuals, rather than binding contracts between states.[45] Consequently, the death of Valentinian III had freed Geiseric from the obligations and restrictions posed by the treaty of 442. He was to make the most of this new political freedom. From 455 onwards, there are abundant references to Vandal raiding along the coast of Italy and the Mediterranean islands. Sidonius lent the conflict an epic dimension by describing it as a fourth 'Punic war', in a poem performed on New Year's Day 456. Two years later, the same poet bewailed 'a savage foe . . . roaming at his ease over an unguarded sea', and demanding the prompt actions of the emperor.[46] For Procopius, writing a century later, the destruction of this period was widespread and more or less arbitrary: 'enslaving some of the cities, razing others to the ground, and plundering everything'.[47] The same historian expressed the omnivorous rapacity of the Vandals in a famous vignette:

> And again he [Geiseric] went off to Sicily and Italy and kept plundering and pillaging all places in turn. And one day when he had embarked on his ship in the harbour of Carthage, and the sails were already being spread, the pilot asked him, they say, against what men in the world he bade them go. And he in reply said: 'Plainly against those with whom God is angry.' Thus without any cause he kept making invasions wherever chance might lead him.[48]

A close reading of other sources, however, suggests a political coherence to this raiding. Victor of Vita is clear that Geiseric occupied Sardinia, Sicily, Corsica and the Balearics after 455, as well as those strategically significant parts of Africa which had previously been in imperial hands.[49] In a more general account of Vandal raiding in the same period, he refers to attacks upon 'Spain, Italia, Dalmatia, Campania, Calabria, Apulia, Sicily, Sardinia, Bruttium, Lucania, Old Epirus and Greece'.[50] Impressive as this sonorous roll-call undoubtedly is, Vandal raiding was clearly concentrated in southern Italy and the Adriatic littoral. The same pattern is implied in Procopius, and even in Greek prophetic literature of the period.[51] While fear of these attacks may have spread far beyond the central Mediterranean, the Vandals themselves seem to have limited themselves to the imperial coastlines that lay closest to Carthage.

Neither imperial court was in any position to respond to these attacks. In the west, the new emperor Avitus had recently been elevated with the support of the Goths and the Gallic aristocracy, and was too recently established in the purple to adopt an aggressive policy towards Carthage immediately. In Constantinople, the Emperor Marcian had also recently been elevated, and was similarly reluctant to involve himself in an expensive western war. The result was a series of ineffectual embassies sent to Carthage from both courts, which bore hollow demands that Geiseric return the imperial princesses.[52] As the Vandal king pointedly rebuffed these advances, discontent in the imperial courts rose. Contemporary commentators evidently took a dim view of this, and rumours rapidly circulated that either Marcian or his advisor Aspar were long-standing allies of the Vandals and refrained from attacking Carthage for arcane reasons.[53]

It was the western empire which was the first to formulate a coherent response to the Vandal threat. This was largely thanks to the efforts of the *comes rei militaris* Ricimer, an officer of mixed Suevic-Gothic ancestry. Ricimer defeated the Vandals in a substantial engagement at Agrigentum in Sicily in 456, and used this success as a springboard to further influence.[54] Promoted to *magister militum* in the west by Avitus, Ricimer overthrew his patron in October 456 and installed as emperor a former companion in arms named Majorian.[55] After a brief but traumatic hiatus in the imperial succession in Ravenna, Constantinople formally recognized Ricimer's creature Majorian as the emperor of the west in early 457.[56] Ricimer himself was named Patrician and this new axis set about restoring the imperial house. Under Majorian, relations with the Goths in Gaul and Spain improved, with the result that the ports of the western Mediterranean again lay open to imperial shipping.[57] Equally significant was the reconciliation with the *comes* Marcellinus, a former ally of Aetius who had distanced himself from the imperial administration after the latter's death and had effectively carved out a semi-autonomous kingdom for himself along the Dalmatian coast.[58]

From this position of strength, Majorian began planning for a new offensive against Carthage in the summer of 458 – a campaign which he hoped would end the persistent threat of Vandal raids to the coasts of the empire and bring some of its richest provinces back into the fold.[59] At the heart of Majorian's strategy lay a major sea-borne campaign from Cartagena on the coast of Spain. In concert with this, Marcellinus was to command an expeditionary force which would take Sicily from the Vandals and hold the island against pressure from Carthage. While Marcellinus secured Sicily, Majorian's mixed task force of imperial troops and federated barbarians was to land in Mauretania and head east towards the Vandal capital. The plan had, however, been very public in its gestation and by the time Majorian had marshalled his allies and assembled his fleet in 460, Geiseric had had time to make diplomatic overtures to many of the emperor's allies as well as to plead for peace with the emperor himself.[60] When this failed, Geiseric was still able to put a 'scorched earth' policy into effect in Mauretania – scouring the land and poisoning the wells in advance of the planned imperial offensive – and to take his own fleet to the western Mediterranean to engage with Majorian directly.[61]

What happened next is unclear. The primary sources allude darkly to the betrayal of the expedition and, in light of the extensive trading links between Carthage and eastern Spain, the Vandals may well have had sympathetic supporters in or around the imperial fleet. It is reported that the Vandals captured a squadron of ships outside the port of Cartagena, possibly acting on inside information.[62] The remainder of the fleet was destroyed or scattered, and the proposed invasion came to nothing. Majorian was forced to limp back to Italy in disgrace, where he was decapitated by the disgusted Ricimer.[63] The one minor victory of the campaign had been the successful re-occupation of Sicily under Marcellinus, although whether this had involved the expulsion of a Vandal garrison or simply a defence of the island from counter-attack is not clear. Even this, however, proved to be short-lived. Uncertain of Marcellinus' loyalty, Ricimer deposed the count, after bribing the federated barbarians under his command to turn against him. Marcellinus returned to Dalmatia, fostering new resentments against the western administration, the Vandals cheerfully resumed their sporadic attacks on Sicily, and the western empire was back to where it had started two years earlier.[64]

In the aftermath of this disaster, Ravenna and Constantinople reverted to diplomacy in dealing with Geiseric, but this time with more success. In 461 or 462, the Vandals reached an accord with the new eastern emperor, Leo. Geiseric returned Eudoxia and Placidia to the custody of the imperial house, the legitimacy of Huneric's union with Eudocia was recognized and the much-delayed wedding took place.[65] The Vandal king also took the opportunity to register his family's claim on the estate of Valentinian III on the strength of Huneric's marriage to Eudocia. Whilst this was never formally accepted by the empire, it remained a feature of Vandal negotiations until Huneric formally renounced these claims in his own reign.[66]

The treaty of 461/2 marked Geiseric's entry into the labyrinthine world of high imperial politics. The Italian aristocrat Olybrius represented Geiseric's foot in the door: a member of the Theodosian house who was related to the Hasdings by virtue of his marriage with Placidia.[67] It seems likely that one clause of the treaty established that both Carthage and Constantinople would support his candidacy when the western throne next fell vacant.[68] Naturally, this did little to improve relations between the Vandals and the western court. Indeed, the Vandal truce with Byzantium may well have driven a wedge between the different halves of the empire.[69] In November 461, Ricimer snubbed eastern advice and established the obscure aristocrat Libius Severus as western emperor.[70] At the same time, Vandal attacks continued unabated on the unfortified coastal settlements of southern Italy and Sicily, and the eastern empire refused Ricimer's pleas for aid.[71]

In 464 the situation changed somewhat. Olybrius was nominated as consul at the beginning of the year, the eastern patrician Tatian was sent as a legate to Carthage on behalf of the western empire (but was rebuffed without an audience), and Ricimer had the ineffectual Libius Severus 'disappeared'.[72] By now, Geiseric's stubborn refusal to entertain lasting relations with Ravenna had exhausted the patience of both the eastern and the western courts. Libius Severus was succeeded by Marcian's son-in-law Anthemius to the western throne, and not by Olybrius, as Geiseric must have been expecting.[73] While Anthemius was greeted with some diffidence in Italy, as a Greek aristocrat very different from the emperors who had come before him, the marriage of his daughter Alypia to Ricimer provided an important façade of unity within the west. The result was a tightening of the bonds between the different halves of the empire, and once more Geiseric was excluded from the imperial political orbit. The Vandal king was curtly informed of Anthemius' elevation and instructed to cease his attacks on Italy and to abandon Sicily forthwith.[74] One result of this was an apparent intensification of Geiseric's contact with other powers in the west. In 465 he entered into negotiation with Aegidius, an alienated *magister militum* in Gaul who was in dispute with Ravenna, and in the following year he was directly engaged in the settlement of disputes between the Visigoths and Sueves in Spain.[75] Another result was the more open acknowledgement of the state of hostility that existed between the Vandals and the imperial powers. Hasding raiding on southern Italy continued unabated in this period, and fear of the Vandals extended as far as Alexandria.[76] In response, and in an effort to lend credence to his diplomatic threats, Leo turned to Marcellinus in Dalmatia, and set him loose upon the islands of the west.[77] In 466 or shortly thereafter, Marcellinus attacked Vandal Sardinia, and reclaimed it in the name of the eastern empire. But the greatest offensive was yet to come.[78]

AD 468 witnessed the most ambitious campaign ever launched against the Vandal state in Africa, which deserves admiration for its logistical brilliance, if not its eventual result. A massive naval operation, under the command of the emperor's brother-in-law Basiliscus, lay at the heart of this offensive, which was intended to strike directly at the Vandal capital. The statistics for this campaign given by sixth- and seventh-century historians are clearly grotesquely exaggerated, but even if we can reject Theophanes' assertion that the fleet numbered 100,000 ships or even John the Lydian's more modest (but still unlikely) figure of 10,000 ships, it is clear that the logistical operation was massive.[79] Marcian ordered the extensive requisition of merchant shipping in eastern ports, including considerable numbers of Carthaginian vessels.[80] Simultaneously, western troops were mustered under Anthemius or Ricimer, and Sicily was again taken by Marcellinus and his barbarian federates.[81]

The mobilization of this campaign startled the inhabitants of Carthage into action. The Suevic and Gothic envoys in the city fled, and Geiseric rapidly deployed his own legates in an attempt to make peace.[82] Quite what happened next is unclear, but Geiseric's overtures apparently had some effect. In the early stages of the campaign, the imperial forces enjoyed some success, and may even have defeated Vandal ships sent out to intercept them.[83] Crucially, however, Basiliscus delayed the crucial landing operations and kept his ships anchored at Mercurium off the African coast for five days. Various explanations for this delay circulated among later historians. Some suggested that Basiliscus had simply been bought off by Geiseric, others that Aspar had promised him the eastern throne if he agreed to sacrifice his fleet to the Vandal allies of the *magister militum*.[84] Whatever the cause, the delay proved to be fatal. After a long stand-off, a shift in the wind allowed Geiseric to launch a fire-ship raid on the becalmed fleet. The effects were devastating. Basiliscus' vast armada was scattered and the opportunity for a crippling blow at Carthage was lost.

As Basiliscus led his fleet towards the cataclysm of Mercurium, and Marcellinus occupied Sicily, a third front was opened up on the southern frontier of the Vandal kingdom. Drawing his army from the Byzantine troops and federates of Egypt, Heracleius led an expedition by sea against the Vandal coastal stronghold of Tripolis.[85] Heracleius occupied the city, and then followed an overland route towards Byzacena, with the intention of uniting with Basiliscus in the Proconsular province. This expedition would have represented a considerable threat to the Vandal kingdom, but it seems to have been halted by news of Basiliscus' defeat. Apparently demoralized, Heracleius led his army back to the relative safety of Tripolis. Tripolis remained in Byzantine hands until 470 when military pressures on the Balkan frontier, and political infighting at court, required that the troops in Africa be withdrawn.[86] A formal peace treaty was probably signed in the same year.[87]

The years which followed saw the final acts in the prolonged conflict between the Vandals and the two empires, but the frantic intensity of

Geiseric's political activity was starting to dissipate. Carthage itself was never threatened after 468 and the western imperial court was fading as a theatre for political ambition. In the aftermath of Basiliscus' defeat, the tensions between Anthemius and Ricimer lurched towards civil war.[88] Olybrius was sent to mediate between the two in 472, but was instead taken under Ricimer's wing and elevated to the imperial throne.[89] If Olybrius' long-standing connections to the Vandals made his elevation welcome in Carthage, his death after just sixth months of rule permanently ended Hasding speculation in the imperial succession. Chaos then returned. In 473, Glycerius was installed as a Burgundian puppet on the throne, and in 474 Nepos was elevated by the troops of Dalmatia.[90] Disillusioned at the meaningless gyrations of imperial politics, Geiseric concentrated his foreign relations upon the consolidation of his overseas territories.[91] Sardinia and Sicily were both reoccupied in this period, following their loss in the campaign of 468. There is some evidence for sporadic raiding in the eastern Mediterranean, and the period may also have witnessed some diplomatic contact with the emerging Ostrogothic groups of the Balkans, and perhaps with Euric's Visigoths in south-western Gaul.[92] After the scares of 468 and 470, Geiseric was slowly re-establishing his authority across the Mediterranean.

Geiseric's authority was formally acknowledged, and the long convulsions of war finally ended, in the so-called 'Perpetual' Peace Treaty of 476, which the king agreed with the new eastern emperor Zeno.[93] Geiseric made substantial religious concessions to the empire: he accepted the opening of some Catholic churches in Carthage and agreed to the return of some religious exiles.[94] Other details of the treaty are lost, but it seems to have been different in kind from the personal agreements that had come before it. For the first time, the Vandal *regnum* and the Byzantine empire dealt with one another as states, and established a treaty which would extend beyond the lifetimes of the signatories. Vandal authority was recognized in the African provinces and in the western Mediterranean islands, and Geiseric halted Vandal raids throughout the Mediterranean and apparently returned the remaining hostages. The points at issue were similar to those which had been debated over the previous 30 years, but the treaty of 476 was a success. Relations remained relatively good between the eastern empire and the Vandal kingdom until the campaign of Belisarius nearly 60 years later.

Yet the balance of power within the Mediterranean was in a constant state of flux. In 477, Geiseric died in Carthage, depriving the Vandals of their greatest presence on the imperial stage. A year earlier, in 476, the last 'Roman' emperor, Romulus Augustulus, died in exile on the

Neapolitan coast. Odoacer, his regent and the *de facto* successor to Ricimer as the principal military authority in the western empire, formally took power for himself as king of Italy in the same year. The Italian kingdoms, first of Odoacer and later of Theoderic the Ostrogoth, had less nominal authority than the former empire, but were less burdened with the ideals of empire. The result was a rival for control of the western Mediterranean which was to affect Vandal foreign relations fundamentally over the next half century.

477–533. The Vandal Empire in a Changing World

After the death of Geiseric in 477, the Vandals lost their central role on the Mediterranean stage. The cessation of widespread raiding after the peace settlement of 476 meant that the Vandals appeared rather less within the written sources. Odoacer's rise to power in the same year and the final disappearance of the western imperial court closed an important theatre for political intrigue, but Huneric's apparent distaste for the political posturing which had so served his father was also partly responsible for the eclipse of Vandal power. Shortly after his accession to the throne, Huneric sent an embassy to Constantinople which formally withdrew the last Vandal claims over the patrimony of Valentinian III, and accepted the appointment of a Catholic archbishop in Carthage.[95] Embassies continued to shuttle between Constantinople and the Vandal kingdom throughout the 470s and 480s, but the diplomatic brinksmanship of Geiseric was no more.[96] The historian Malchus argues that this diplomatic retreat was evidence of a gradual deterioration in the martial spirit of the Vandals – a concept that was to prove popular among later Byzantine historians.[97] But the Vandals had not become cowards overnight. With Geiseric's death and the political upheaval of the Italian peninsula came a profound reassessment of the Vandal role within the wider world. If the first half of the Vandal century had been marked by attempts to find a place within the collapsing political world of the fading western empire, the 50 years which followed Geiseric's death were defined by the defence of the Vandal kingdom at home, and the maintenance of the political position abroad.

The African frontier

From the 480s, the Vandals had to pursue an active external policy within Africa as well as in the wider world. The ominous emergence of several Moorish power blocs on the southern frontier of the kingdom restricted the freedom of the later Hasding kings to dominate the Mediterranean as Geiseric once had. Crucially, this threat was not created by the sudden appearance of new peoples on the African frontier, nor by the rampages of desert nomads attacking settled communities. Instead, these Moorish polities are best regarded as local responses to the political vacuum left by the gradual disintegration of imperial power in the frontier regions.[98] As the Roman empire progressively retreated from the African interior, from the early fourth century to the effective cessation of imperial authority in 455, local elites became increasingly powerful. Very similar processes took place among the local military aristocracies of the Basque country, Brittany or upland Britain, but the sheer size of the African frontier zone meant that the Moorish successor states were both many and varied. In some cases, as with the Garamantes in the Libyan desert, or the Arzuges in the south of Mauretania Caesariensis, these kingdoms developed with relatively little direct contact with the Hasding kingdom of Carthage. In the south of Byzacena and Numidia, however, and in the upland regions of the Aurès massif, these local military aristocracies represented a direct challenge to Vandal authority.

Geiseric managed this situation well, and effectively precluded any substantial challenge to Vandal authority in the south of his kingdom. He did this in part by establishing his own position as the principal arbiter of imperial authority to the south: where local elites had once relied upon Rome or Ravenna for the ranks and titles that legitimated their authority, they increasingly turned to Carthage.[99] In this, Geiseric was doubtless helped by the fact that his own vigorous military policies not only discouraged revolt, but also allowed his neighbours the opportunity for fruitful alliance with the Hasding regime.[100] Writers like Victor and Sidonius Apollinaris note the enthusiasm with which the Moors joined in the Vandal plundering expeditions throughout the Mediterranean, and this cannot all be put down to rhetorical embellishment.[101] The ideological pre-eminence of Carthage within Africa did not disappear entirely with Geiseric's death, and Procopius refers to formal Hasding patronage of some Moorish polities as late as the reign of Hilderic (and perhaps even Gelimer). But this authority was not what it had been in the early years of the Vandal kingdom. From the 480s onwards, the balance of power had begun to shift. Like the Hasding kingdom, the Moorish states grew and changed over time. When Huneric ascended to the throne in 477, therefore, he was not only acting without his father's enviable reputation, he was also dealing with

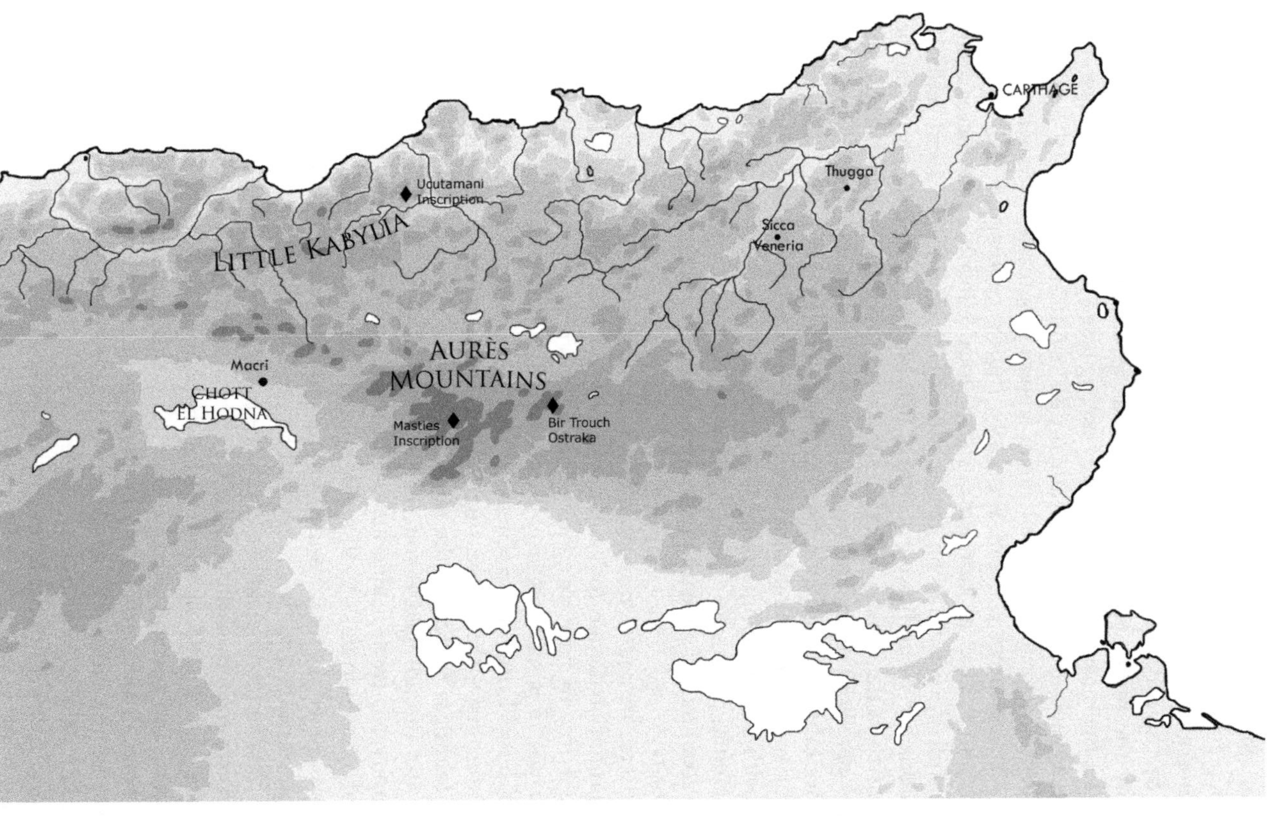

Figure 5.1 The Vandals and the Moors

Moorish polities which had benefited from an additional three or four decades of semi-autonomous development.

Procopius states that the first troubles occurred in the Aurès Mountains towards the end of Huneric's reign. This region had been a keystone of the frontier and like many regions of Africa had become thoroughly Christianized.[102] It seems to have passed under Vandal authority with the treaty of 442, but the reasons for its subsequent secession are not immediately clear.[103] Procopius simply states that Huneric lost control of the mountains towards the end of his reign, and that the Vandals never recovered them.[104] This is likely to have been true – certainly it would have taken a concerted campaign to bring the highlands themselves back into the kingdom, and we know of no such expedition. Nevertheless, the distinctive Vandal system of dating is employed on the Bir Trouch ostraka, which were found in the eastern foothills of the same range, and which date from the reign of Gunthamund. It seems likely, therefore, that while effective control may have been lost over the Aurès uplands, Vandal authority remained recognized in the lowlands, and this may have continued down to the Byzantine period.[105]

A Latin inscription found in the middle of the Aurès massif casts some light upon the changing political circumstances of the 470s and 480s. The text was erected in honour of the Moorish leader, Masties, probably in the late fifth century:

> I, Masties, duke [*dux*] for 67 years and emperor [*imperator*] for 10 years, never perjured myself nor broke faith with either the Romans or the Moors, and was prepared in both war and in peace, and my deeds were such that God supported me well.[106]

The inscription is undated, but the text does hint at a major political change that took place during Masties' lifetime.[107] Clearly, Masties was a *dux* for most of his adult life, a term which is best regarded as a Latin rendering of an indigenous political title. Masties, in other words, was the head of a group of Moors for more than half a century. Ten years before his death, however, he assumed the title of *imperator*, a bold claim of political authority which strongly implies that he recognized no other external power. It has recently been suggested that this sudden claim to power probably coincided with the Aurès revolt of AD 483–4. This would imply that Masties was first made *dux* in around 426 and died in 494, presumably in his eighties. The strong Christian overtones of the inscription hint that Masties' break from Vandal authority may well have been prompted by the onset of Huneric's persecution. Faced with these horrors, the formerly loyal lieutenant in the south of Numidia revolted from the Vandals and permanently removed his territory from the control of the Arian Hasdings.

The inscription was presented in the political language of the old empire, in a world where this clearly continued to mean something. Masties' had been a *dux* and an *imperator*, and his successor chose to celebrate this service in the very traditional form of a Latin inscription. But the sentiments of the epitaph are not wholly classical, and declarations of hybrid political authority are found on other Latin inscriptions elsewhere along the African frontier. Around the same time as Masties was honoured for his fidelity to both Romans and Moors (*Mauri*), an inscription in Altava, to the far west of North Africa, commemorated the construction of a fort in the kingdom of Masuna, the 'King of the Moors and the Romans'.[108] A fragmentary and undated inscription found at the eastern end of the Little Kabylia has obvious similarities. This text refers to the *rex gentis ucutaman[orum]* ('King of the Ucutamani Peoples'), and was set up as a Christian epitaph after the king's death.[109] Like the inhabitants of the Aurès, the Moors of Kabylie had experienced an uneasy relationship with Roman imperial power. Nevertheless, it is conspicuous that when this unnamed king was commemorated it was in Latin and in a formal inscription. The political and cultural environment in which all of these polities developed was not identical to that which nurtured the Vandals in Carthage, but nor was it so very different. In both cases, military power was celebrated and legitimated through traditional channels.

Huneric enjoyed rather better relations with the Moorish leaders who ruled along other stretches of his frontier. Victor of Vita describes how the first Nicene exiles of his reign were sent out from Carthage and were handed over to Moorish soldiers on the main road into Numidia, and were escorted into the distant reaches of that province.[110] These may well be the same exiles whom Victor of Tunnuna places in Tubunae, Macri and Nippis in the area around Chott El-Hodna.[111] Geiseric had adopted a similar policy in concert with the Moorish king Capsur, whose kingdom 'Caprapicta' has been variously located by scholars in the far south of Byzacena or on the southern frontier of Numidia and Mauretania Sitifiensis.[112] In each case, the involvement of the Moorish rulers in the punishment of the enemies of the Vandals testifies to the close relations between the different powers. The fact that this continued under Huneric highlights the complexity and delicacy of diplomacy at the frontier.

As the authority of the different Moorish rulers rose along the frontiers, so that of the Hasding kings fell. It is difficult to chart this process in detail, but occasional references in the textual sources testify to a level of unrest in the countryside. Procopius states that Gunthamund fought numerous campaigns against the Moors but does not elaborate.[113] The same writer provides a rather fuller narrative of Thrasamund's campaign against the Moorish ruler Cabaon in Tripolitana. Procopius' account suggests that the Moors went out of their way to win the support of the provincial Romans, which may testify to expansionist ambitions on the part of Cabaon, but the causes of the conflict are not made clear.[114] A general atmosphere of instability is further suggested by allusions to 'barbarian' violence in the *Life of Fulgentius*, although it is never clear where references to general rural banditry stop and where those to genuine political conflict begin.[115] Certainly, this conflict does not seem to have been sufficiently serious to interrupt production, and left little mark on the archaeological record before the third decade of the sixth century.

By the reign of Hilderic, however, this conflict escalated substantially. Procopius refers to extensive campaigning in Byzacena during the 520s, and Corippus alludes to a series of Moorish uprisings all along the frontier.[116] Certainly, the Hasding princes Hoamer and Gelimer both won their spurs in fighting against the Moors, and the Byzantine writers commonly assumed that the Vandal military resented Hilderic's poor performance on the battlefield.[117] Precisely what caused these new tensions is unclear. It is only following the Byzantine conquest – when the empire of the east found that the Moorish polities would not be so easily overcome as they had originally imagined – that the military history of this region can be written in any detail. Nevertheless, it seems clear that by the reigns of Hilderic and Gelimer, the African frontier had grown to dominate the external policies of the kings of Carthage.

Sicily

Sicily was the most important of the Vandal overseas territories, for economic and strategic reasons, and came to dominate Hasding Mediterranean policy in the last half-century of the kingdom. As with many other regions in the Mediterranean, Sicily changed dramatically in the fourth, fifth and sixth centuries, both in the towns and in the countryside. For much of the early imperial period, the island had been celebrated for its extraordinary fertility, but the comparable wealth of Africa and Egypt meant that it had rarely been intensively exploited.[118] The great senatorial landholders of Rome maintained villas there, but chiefly seem to have used them as places for retreat and pleasure, rather than as centres of production. With the foundation of Constantinople in the early fourth century, however, and the redirection of Egyptian grain to the new eastern

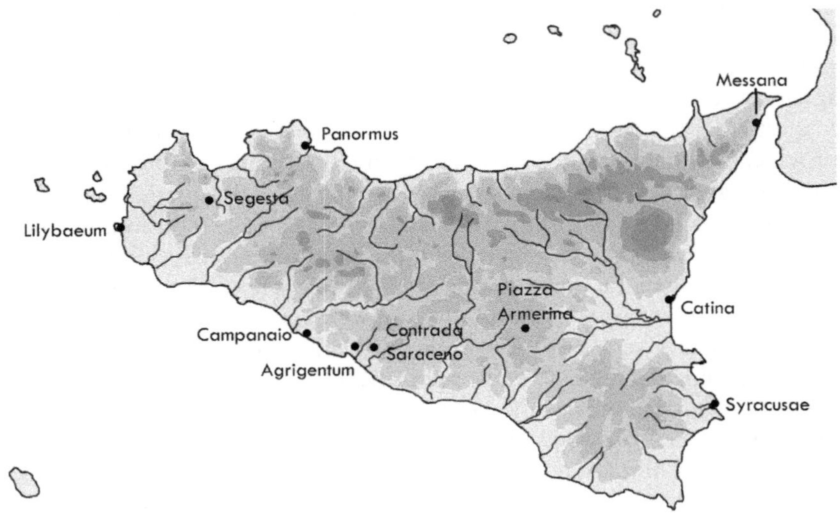

Figure 5.2 Vandal Sicily

capital, Sicily once more took up the burden of feeding Rome. As the rebellions of the fourth century made African supply routes less reliable than they had been previously, and particularly after the events of 439 took Carthage and its rich hinterlands permanently out of the hands of the western empire, Sicily became a crucial mainstay of the imperial economy.

The presence of this rich island so close to Africa inevitably drew the attention of the Vandal kings. As early as 437, barbarian pirates had harassed the coast of Sicily, and it was no surprise that one of Geiseric's first actions after the capture of Carthage was to attack Lilybaeum and Panormus.[119] But the Hasdings struggled to establish their authority over the island. In the treaty of 442, Sicily remained in imperial hands and, even after the invasion of 455, the Vandals were far from secure.[120] Ricimer defeated a Vandal fleet at Agrigentum in 456, and in 460 and 468 Count Marcellinus twice re-established Roman power in concert with the grand imperial campaigns against Carthage.

This period of conflict left less of a mark on the archaeology of Sicily than might be expected. The relative scarcity of well-excavated urban sites within Sicily makes generalization about the state of the island's towns difficult, but the fragmented image which does emerge is scarcely one of crisis, and was certainly not one of panic.[121] Few towns in the island seem to have been fortified, in striking contrast to southern Italy, and imperial investment in the defence of the island would appear to have been sparing. In Marsala, the ancient defences, erected during the Hellenistic period, never seem to have been repaired, despite abundant evidence for Vandal attacks between 440 and 475. At Agrigentum, such defences that were put up were only ever temporary. It is possible – even probable – that traces of 'Byzantine' defences in the other cities of the island have been misdated, and may have been erected in the fourth or fifth century, but it seems unlikely that there was a concerted programme of fortification in response to the Vandal threat.[122] At Catania, for example, the wall circuit was only restored during the Ostrogothic period, and even then as a local operation.[123] Yet despite this, Sicily seems to have survived this prolonged period of conflict relatively well. An imperial tax remission from the mid-440s suggests that productivity was interrupted by the earliest Vandal attacks, and several small settlements were destroyed or abandoned in the middle of the fifth century, but in the medium term Sicily seems to have remained surprisingly healthy.[124] The preserved estate records of one Lauricius from AD 445/6 attest to continuity of landholding even during a period of particular difficulty, and the literary sources all attest to the wealth of Sicily in this period, even after the Vandal attacks.[125]

We hear nothing else of Sicily in the historical record until 476, when the Vandals formally ceded their authority over the island. According to Victor, Geiseric reached an agreement with Odoacer in that year, which surrendered the island in return for an annual tribute:

> One of these islands, namely Sicily, [Geiseric] later conceded to Odovacer, the king of Italy, by tributary right. At fixed times, Odovacer paid tribute to the Vandals, as to his lords; nevertheless, they kept back some part of the island for themselves.[126]

The most convincing explanation for this peculiar agreement is that Geiseric sought to consolidate the position of the Vandal kingdom in the months before his death.[127] Sicily had long been a bone of contention between Carthage and the ruling powers in Italy, and the Vandal king may have wished to spare his successor such difficulties. Realising that Odoacer might later have been in a position to take the island by force, Geiseric may simply have decided to gain the best possible deal for a territory which the Vandals could not hope to hold in perpetuity. The treaty with Zeno would have reassured the Hasdings that the period of the great imperial expeditions against Carthage was probably in the past, but by retaining his claim over a part of the island Geiseric retained a strategic foothold. Victor does not state precisely where the Vandal *pars* of Sicily was located, but it can only have been the promontory of Lilybaeum – the closest point to the African mainland and a long-standing strategic objective of the Vandal state.[128]

The treaty of 476 did not end Vandal interest in Sicily. In 489, the *magister militum* Theoderic began his conquest of Italy and founded the Ostrogothic kingdom. While Theoderic and Odoacer were occupied in the north, Gunthamund turned his attention to Sicily. The only source for this campaign is an allusion in a contemporary African poem to recent Vandal 'triumphs of land and sea'. The poem names one 'Ansila' as among those present at the victory celebrations, and it is commonly assumed that he was an Ostrogothic general, defeated in an otherwise forgotten Sicilian campaign.[129] Cassiodorus' *Chronicle* states that the Vandals stopped their attacks on Sicily in AD 491, which implies both that attacks had been taking place before this date, and that a peace treaty was reached in that year.[130] The details of this treaty are unknown, but a fragmentary inscription (which has been lost) alludes to the boundary between the Vandals and the Goths and may indicate that a formal territorial division was invoked at this time.[131] Regardless of its form, the peace seems to have held until the end of the century.

In AD 500 the wedding of Thrasamund with the Ostrogothic princess Amalafrida formalized the diplomatic relations between the Vandals and the new rulers of Italy. Procopius is our principal source on the wedding, which was the second great dynastic union in Vandal history:

> wishing to establish his kingdom as securely as possible, he [Thrasamund] sent to Theoderic king of the Goths, asking him to give him his sister Amalafrida to wife, for her husband had just died. And Theoderic sent him not only his sister but also a thousand of the notable Goths as a bodyguard, who were followed by a host of attendants amounting to about five thousand fighting men. And Theoderic presented his sister with one of the promontories of Sicily, which are three in number – the one which they call Lilybaeum – and as a result of this Thrasamund was accounted the strongest and most powerful of all those who had ruled over the Vandals.[132]

The marriage was a momentous political event. In Ravenna, poets and courtiers boasted of the new Ostrogothic ascendancy. Ennodius celebrated the 'obedience' of the Vandals to Theoderic's rule in his famous panegyric of AD 507, and in the same year Cassiodorus implied that the great enemy of Italy had been brought to heel by Gothic diplomacy.[133]

Nor can the Vandals have missed the political posturing that accompanied the wedding. The granting of Lilybaeum as a wedding gift, in particular, offered a concession to the Vandals, but also asserted Ostrogothic suzerainty over the island as a whole: Lilybaeum, it was implied, was theirs to give.

The marriage of AD 500 was probably more of an alliance between equals than an assertion of Ostrogothic hegemony. Jordanes did not see the wedding as a triumph of Gothic power, despite his long-standing disdain for the Vandals, and Procopius states explicitly that Thrasamund's wedding made him the most powerful of all the Hasding kings.[134] In normal circumstances Amalafrida's huge Gothic escort might well have represented a pointed show of force, but Thrasamund was at war with several Moorish kingdoms at the time of the wedding, and Theoderic's troops may simply have been military aid for a fellow monarch – and now brother-in-law – who was in difficulty.[135] This is not to suggest that the provision of military support was entirely without political overtones, but Thrasamund, as an ally of the eastern court and the possessor of a large navy, was not quite ready to adopt the position of vassal king to the new ruler of Italy.[136]

For the remainder of his reign, Thrasamund proved inconsistent in his dealings with the Ostrogoths. The extant sources have rather more to say about Ostrogothic activities in this period than they do about the kingdom of Carthage. When the Vandals do drift into focus, it can be seen that Thrasamund clearly acted in his own self interest, rather than as a vassal or even as a warmly supportive ally. In AD 507 or 508, the Byzantine fleet attacked Italy by sea, just as the Vandals had once done.[137] If the Ostrogoths expected their allies to help, they were to be sorely disappointed, and the Hasding fleet remained in Carthage. In 510, Theoderic's interventionism in the Visigothic kingdom of Toulouse led to the disgrace and expulsion of the pretender Gesalic. In defiance of Theoderic's policies, Thrasamund offered sanctuary to the exile, and eventually surrendered him only after some delicate diplomatic negotiation from Ravenna and then only to prevent the escalation of the situation into a major incident.[138]

This uneasy peace was not to last. After the accession of Hilderic in 523, the Vandal kingdom was strongly linked to Constantinople, and the relationship with the Ostrogoths deteriorated seriously. Amalafrida survived her husband, but was imprisoned shortly after Thrasamund's death on suspicion of treason, along with the remaining Goths in her retinue.[139] By 526, she had been put to death.[140] In all likelihood, this provocative act simply reflected the general shift in Vandal diplomacy, away from the Gothic court at Ravenna and towards the Constantinople of Justin and Justinian. Indeed, from 523, the court atmosphere at both Carthage and Ravenna seems to have changed. In Carthage, the homecoming of prominent Catholics brought to prominence men like Fulgentius, who had spent their years in exile fostering valuable links with the clerics of Rome and Italy.[141] In Ravenna, Theoderic's domestic policy became increasingly intransigent towards Byzantine sympathizers, a trend which resulted most famously in the imprisonment and later execution of Symmachus and Boethius, but which also led to the increased marginalization of prominent Roman Catholics.[142] As Theoderic distanced himself from the imperial capital, Hilderic found himself forced into choosing sides between the Ostrogoths to the north and his own particular sympathizers in the eastern empire. If Amalafrida had kept Thrasamund more or less in the Ostrogothic party, no such ties bound his successor; Hilderic turned to Constantinople.

One peculiar result of this change in diplomatic allegiances was Theoderic's ambitious decision to assemble his own fleet in 525/6 AD, a project that may be traced through the various letters of Cassiodorus' *Variae*.[143] This represented a direct challenge to the naval mastery of Carthage and Constantinople, and a symbolic defence of Gothic interests at sea and along the coasts. As Theoderic himself put it: 'there is no reason for the Greek to fasten a quarrel upon us, or the African to insult us.'[144] Quite whether the assembly of the fleet was the prelude for a still bolder military operation is unclear, but Cassiodorus' letters do testify both to the enormous logistical capacity of the Gothic state, and to the king's anxiety that the fleet be ready, manned and paid for at Ravenna in June 526.[145] Quite what Theoderic might have accomplished with this fleet can only be speculated; he died on August 30 of the same year. Despite the late tensions between Theoderic and Hilderic, and Athalaric's later protests over the execution of Amalafrida, however, relations between the Ostrogoths and the Vandals were generally good. Sicily was at the heart of this *détente*.

Sardinia

Sardinia provides a different image of Vandal imperialism, but during the first 20 years of this period, its history closely paralleled that of Sicily.[146] Like Sicily, Sardinia only passed under the full authority of the Vandal crown towards the end of Geiseric's reign. Raids in the early 440s did not last, and the island remained an imperial possession after 442. The island was among the regions which were occupied in 455, but a defeat of the Vandal fleet off Corsica in the following year suggests that

Figure 5.3 Vandal Corsica and Sardinia

the western empire did its best to resist this expansion. Sardinia was recaptured by Marcellinus at some time between 466 and 468, but came back under Vandal control during the following decade, and must have been among the territories permanently ceded to Geiseric in the treaty of 476.

Like Sicily, Sardinia was celebrated in antiquity for its fertility. Palladius is emphatic in his praise of the island, and the rich plains in the hinterland of Neapolis are among the most fertile regions in the Mediterranean.[147] Documentary and archaeological evidence for the exploitation of the landscape is more sparing for Sardinia than it is for Sicily, but once again broad patterns of continuity throughout the Vandal period are evident. The towns of Caralis, Cornus, Turris Lisbonis and Neapolis all changed over the course of the fifth century, but these developments – typically the abandonment of some areas of occupation and the evolution of new centres of urban life – may be witnessed throughout the western Mediterranean in this period.[148] The material record also testifies to intensive mercantile contact between Sicily, Sardinia and North Africa, and if textual evidence occasionally hints at interruptions in shipping, these seem to have been the exception, rather than the rule.[149]

Where Sardinia differed from Sicily, however, was in its position as a more or less permanent Vandal territory.[150] Less politically contested than Sicily, Sardinia remained under the nominal rule of Carthage until the Byzantine reconquest of 533. Vandal rule of the island probably followed imperial precedent; certainly there is little evident that the Hasdings introduced substantial administrative changes. Late imperial power in Sardinia had been entrusted to a *praeses*, an official who combined military, judicial and civil governmental functions. The Vandals may have granted some degree of effective autonomy to the governors of Sardinia, if only for practical reasons, and it is not impossible that the ruler of the island was largely left to his own devices in return for an annual tribute to Carthage.[151] Whatever the arrangement, it seems likely that the *praeses* of the fifth century issued coins on his own authority.

The only Vandal governor about whom any information survives is Godas, a Gothic soldier and the last representative of Hasding rule within Sardinia, and his administration was exceptional.[152] Sent there by Gelimer following his usurpation in 530, Godas was charged with securing the loyalty of Sardinia and its troops, a responsibility that he shirked in spectacular fashion. Recognizing the imminent danger of Justinian's reconquest, Godas declared his intention to break from Vandal authority and requested military support for this coup from the eastern emperor. Justinian received this embassy warmly and offered military support, but rejected Godas' demand to be afforded royal status as the ruler of Sardinia in his own right. The emperor promised troops to the rebel, but proposed to send them under the command of a general loyal to Constantinople. In Carthage, Gelimer got wind of this plot and crushed the rebellion at source, sending Stotzas – a rather more trustworthy ally – to put down the revolt. In the event, Stotzas was successful, but the large expeditionary force within Sardinia critically weakened the defences of Africa itself.

Godas' period of office was unusual, but the episode does cast some light upon the nature of the Vandal administration of Sardinia. First, and most obvious, is the fact that the island was an important part of the kingdom, and yet apparently enjoyed some autonomy from Carthage by virtue of its geographical position. Gelimer felt it important enough to send Godas to establish his authority there, presumably in order to prevent rebellion. When Godas revolted in turn, Gelimer suppressed the rising with considerable force, even at the cost of losing the city of Tripolis, which was also in revolt, and ultimately Africa itself. Sardinia, then, was an important component of the Vandal 'empire'.

Godas' appointment and later rebellion also highlight the military nature of the Vandal presence in Sardinia. Although Godas' appeal to Constantinople suggests that the garrison in the island was relatively small, there clearly was a permanent military presence on the island. This might have been intended to defend Sardinia from other colonizing powers, but the island was rarely contested after the departure of Marcellinus in 468, and intensive Vandal occupation probably only took place after the major treaties with Zeno and Odoacer secured a lasting peace within the western Mediterranean. The garrison was probably intended to provide security from occasional banditry and unrest in the central highlands. The Roman occupation of the island had proved similarly troubled, and the Byzantines were later to suffer from the bandits and rebels they termed *barbaricini*. The Vandals probably faced very similar problems.[153]

Among the *barbaricini* who resisted Byzantine occupation in the 530s and 540s were a group of Moors, probably hidden in the mountains to the south-west of the island.[154] According to Procopius, these Moors had been sent into exile in Sardinia following a rebellion against the Vandals in Africa, but this scarcely seems credible. The Moors had been sent to settle Sardinia with their families, and apparently as a coherent group, both factors which suggest a conscious policy of garrisoning, rather than an ad hoc process of exile. Other Byzantine sources of the period confirm that the Moors were included among the Vandal army which occupied the island.[155] Given this, it seems likely that the rebels who resisted the Byzantine occupation had originally settled peacefully in the island, either as colonizers or as a military garrison, and had revolted, probably at the time of the invasion from Constantinople. It is impossible to say whether the Moors and Vandals had been settled as distinct groups within the island. One coin minted in the later fifth century bears a monogram that has been read as the mark of a *presidia Maurorum Sardiniae*, which would suggest both that the Moors were a consciously established part of the Sardinian garrison and that they may have been organized independently from their Vandal allies.[156]

The Vandal occupation of Sardinia had a dramatic effect upon the development of the church within the island. From around AD 482,

Sardinia became the principal place of exile for Catholic bishops and clerics, and thereafter the islands of the Mediterranean supplanted the Moorish kingdoms as the preferred destination for the turbulent priests of Africa.[157] From the early years of Thrasamund's reign, when the Catholic clergy were expelled from dioceses and parishes even beyond Zeugitana, the Sardinian capital of Cagliari became the focal point of the African Church in exile. Through the extensive correspondence, sermons and scriptural commentaries of Fulgentius of Ruspe, Ferrandus' *Life* of the Saint and the constantly expanding corpus of archaeological material, it is possible to appreciate the vibrancy of Christian life in the island at that time.[158]

The years of African exile represented the first great period of Christian evangelism within the Sardinia. The island had, of course, received missionaries before: bishops from Cagliari, Cornus, Forum Traiani, Sulci and Turris Libisonis had attended the African Church council convened by Huneric in February 484, and Sardinia retained metropolitan jurisdiction over the three dioceses in the Balearic Islands which were also represented in Carthage. Church foundations and Christian catacombs are also known from Sardinia from the fourth century. But the number, wealth and cosmopolitan connections of the African churchmen witnessed an extraordinary expansion in Christian building and had a galvanizing effect upon the church.[159] The monastic foundations of Fulgentius, the widespread adoption of Augustinian theology, the popularity of African martyr cults and liturgy and the systematic and precocious expansion of the church into the interior were all brought about by the religious refugees.[160] Sardinia created two popes during the Vandal period. Of these Hilarius, who held office from AD 461–468, largely succeeded in spite of the barbarian presence around his island, but his successor, Symmachus (AD 496–514), was doubtless helped by the sudden prominence of the Christian life in Sardinia.

This is a paradox that deserves some attention. As Huneric and Thrasamund sent Catholic bishops to Sardinia, so the church in the island flourished. No less importantly, a province of the Vandal realm chosen for its very isolation as a place of exile was drawn into the cultural and intellectual orbit of the wider Mediterranean world by this very programme of expulsion. There was constant communication between Cagliari and Carthage generated through the passage of secular and clerical exiles.[161] Fulgentius himself had made religious journeys to both Sicily and Sardinia long before his own exile from Byzacena, and such pilgrimages may not have been unusual.[162] The same bishop's correspondence testifies to the extensive contact between the bishops and their compatriots, both for spiritual and secular reasons. Simultaneously, the Sardinian exiles fostered increasingly close links with the papacy and the Catholic aristocracy of Rome, a cultural bond that may well have had fundamental implications for the balance of power in the Mediterranean when the clerics were eventually recalled.[163] Content as Fulgentius might have been to bewail his isolation in a forgotten corner of the Vandal kingdom, the bishop could make his voice heard by both the pope and the Vandal king when it was necessary.

Corsica and the Balearics

Like Sicily and Sardinia, Corsica and the Balearic Islands only came under Vandal control after 455. Frustratingly, these smaller islands are mentioned only very briefly in the textual sources. It may be that the Balearics were only occupied in 460, as a result of the Vandal expedition against Majorian, but this cannot be stated definitively. The scale of the Vandal occupation throughout the islands is entirely unknown, but in the absence of evidence to the contrary it seems likely that there was some level of administrative continuity in Corsica and the Balearics just as there was in Sardinia.[164] Where archaeology of secular settlement patterns exists – it is virtually absent in the Balearics and limited in this period of Corsican history to the inland rural site at Castellu in Haute Corse – there is strong evidence for continuity throughout the Vandal period and even down to the Lombard occupation of the later sixth century.[165] As was the case in Sardinia, the expansion of imperial authority over these islands had been slow. In Corsica, the Byzantine forces under Cyril met some resistance, although little is known of the form that this took.[166] Belisarius took no such chances with the Balearics and entrusted their control to Apollinarius, an Italian who had been a trusted functionary of Hilderic before Gelimer's coup led him to lend his support to the imperial reconquest. This precaution proved wise, and the islands were retaken by the empire without difficulty.[167]

Corsica comes into better focus when viewed through its Christian past. The island did not send any representatives to the Council of Carthage in 484, but some exiles are known to have been sent to the island before that date, and in the wake of the conference 46 more bishops joined them.[168] Where Fulgentius provides a positive voice for the exiles of Sardinia, however, the exiles of Corsica are represented only by two mournful poems of exile in the *Latin Anthology*:

No bread, no drawn water, no distant flame;
These two things alone: the exiled one and his exile.[169]

Yet the conventions of poetic lamentation should not disguise the vibrant Christian culture that the exiles brought to the island. Those who died in exile, including Appianu of Sagona and Firenzu, were venerated in the island.[170] Those who survived left their mark in other ways: the cults of the third-century African martyrs Julia and Restituta were introduced by those sent into exile by the Vandals, and remained even after their departure.

The impact of the Christian exiles is most visible in the Christian architecture of Corsica. The whole early Christian complex at Mariana, the church of S. Appianu at Sagona and that of S. Amanza at Bonifaziu all date from the late fifth or early sixth century, and the early Christian cult site of Pianottoli-Caldarellu was substantially reworked in the same period.[171] Christianity also appears for the first time in rural contexts during the Vandal occupation.[172] As was the case in Sardinia, the Vandal exiles drew Corsica back into the deeper currents of Mediterranean cultural life. And here too, the departure of the exiles in the early 520s seems to have led to an ossification of the local church. Gregory the Great found much to lament when he gazed upon the poorly Christianized towns and landscapes of Corsica, but it was to Africa that he turned in the hope of a solution.[173] The close ties that had been forged in the later fifth century still remained long after Vandal power itself had disappeared.

The Balearics – the islands of Mallorca, Minorca and Ibiza – offer little to compare. As has been discussed, the Vandals made raids on the islands as early as 425, but these were probably attacks in search of plunder, and by 449 the islands were back in imperial hands. Victor's account includes the archipelago among the regions which were occupied by the Vandals in 455, but most modern scholars have assumed that the effective occupation only occurred in 460, during the attack on Majorian's fleet at Cartagena.[174] Most have been content to assume that the islands were occupied for purely strategic reasons. The Balearics offered the Vandals a military foothold in the western Mediterranean, which would have seemed valuable in the light of imperial and Visigothic activity along the coast of Spain. Thereafter, the islands probably remained safely Vandal, and sent three bishops to the Council of 484. It is not clear, however, when the occupation ended.

6

The Economy of Vandal Africa

Writers of the fifth and sixth centuries were both entranced and appalled by the prodigious wealth of Vandal Carthage. Procopius repeatedly revisits the stuffed coffers of the Hasding capital: twice he describes the plunder brought back to the city following the sack of Rome in 455, and in one long passage he recounts the attempts by Gelimer to save the royal treasury from the Byzantine re-occupation. So rich was the kingdom, Procopius insists, that all of Belisarius' ingenuity was needed to prevent the imperial troops from stripping the rich countryside bare in their surprise and delight.[1] Victor of Vita exhibits a similar fascination, but his emphasis is on the greed that brought the Vandals such wealth – the occupation of estates, theft of senatorial riches, despoliation of Catholic churches, imposition of harsh taxation, collection of impossible ransoms and – of course – widespread piracy throughout the Mediterranean.[2] Accounts like these tend to stick in the memory; consequently the Vandals became closely associated with piracy and plunder – and with the material rewards that came with them.

The Vandals were rich, but most of their wealth came from the continued prosperity of their kingdom, and not from the ill-gotten gains of their campaigns and raids. North Africa was affluent in the fifth and sixth centuries, just as it had been under the Romans, and the Vandals benefited from this success. But the Mediterranean world was changing during Late Antiquity, and North Africa changed along with it. Long before the Vandals first set foot in region, its towns and rural estates had started to adopt unfamiliar forms. From the later fourth century, social and political developments, reforms of taxation and coinage and changes in patterns of land exploitation all had an effect upon the economic life of the Mediterranean. With the slow disintegration of the western empire in the middle decades of the fifth century, still greater transformations were set in motion. The whole of the ancient world was influenced in different ways by these changes, but Africa – as a central cog in the late imperial machine – was particularly affected.

The present chapter explores the effect of the Vandal occupation of Africa upon the economy of the region, and the importance of economic considerations to the development of the Hasding kingdom itself. To do this it will be necessary to change the focus of our investigation slightly, and to look in detail at the nature of the North African economy that the Hasdings inherited. This will involve a brief discussion of the position of North Africa within the later Roman Mediterranean, before looking at how these trading patterns changed during the fifth and sixth centuries. The chapter will then consider economic activity within North Africa itself, both in the cities and in the countryside.

Inevitably, the Vandals themselves will occasionally lurk only in the background to this survey. In some cases they have only a peripheral relevance to the topic under consideration, in other cases, general economic trends will be discussed which can only be approximately associated with the period of the Hasding occupation of Carthage. Changes in towns and in the countryside were rarely sudden, and still more rarely can they be dated with great confidence to a specific year or decade. After all, the Vandal occupation spanned a period of some considerable transformation which neither began nor ended with the conquest and eventual loss of Carthage. In the final section of the chapter, however, the Vandals will again occupy centre stage. This section will explore the fiscal and monetary policies of the Hasding kingdom: that is the taxation and other revenues from which Geiseric and his successors benefited, and the role which coins played within the economy of the period.

Exploring the Ancient Economy

The wealth of the Vandal kings has long been recognized by modern scholars, but the economic prosperity of their kingdom has rarely been studied in detail. In part, of course, this is simply a methodological issue. Attuned to the long, slow cadences of their subject – subtle shifts in trading patterns, gradual changes in production and exploitation – economic historians have conventionally toned down the sharp pizzicato of political and military change in their accounts. Catastrophic wars and invasions, along with earthquakes, plagues or other natural disasters, may frequently be cited as turning points in economic history, but they are rarely seen as causes for long-term change in themselves: an invading army may destroy a town, factory or farm, but only a settlement that is already in decline will fail to recover from the blow.[3] The archaeological record, similarly, brings gradual social change out more clearly than it does political cataclysm. Consequently, most studies of the late- and post-Roman economy tend to focus on long timescales, rather than ephemeral kingdoms and dynasties – on the history of the fifth, sixth and seventh centuries, not on the Vandal state and its kings. The Vandals themselves are all but invisible in the material record of North Africa, and it is this absence which has long defined their role in economic history.[4] If the new masters of Carthage did not directly destroy the systems of production and distribution upon which the ancient world relied, and made few changes to the firm foundations on which their kingdom developed (and there has been some dispute about this) it has been concluded that theirs was only ever a fleeting role within the economic life of their world. In many accounts, the Vandals are presented as interested (but uninteresting) spectators of the gradual transformation of the ancient economy.[5]

These assumptions have been supported by recent methodological advances. A massive growth in archaeological data has revolutionized modern understanding of the ancient economy, but its interpretation can create difficulties. From the early 1970s, systematic assessments of hundreds of tonnes of ceramics found throughout the Mediterranean promised a wholly new perspective on ancient trade routes which crossed the sea and the patterns of supply and demand which stimulated them.[6] With increased confidence, archaeologists could date and identify the provenance of amphorae, finewares and coarsewares and outline a complex web of economic interdependence, changing over the centuries but remaining more or less intact down to the Vandal period and beyond.[7] Other studies focused upon production centres within North Africa itself. Although detailed research excavations in rural areas were rare (and remain so), the implementation of a number of large scale archaeological surveys in the 1980s and early 1990s helped to uncover the landscapes of Roman and late Roman Africa.[8] Supported by the weighty testimony of thousands of sherds, and the visible remains of vast olive oil processing plants in Central Tunisia, Zeugitana and Tripolitana scholars emphasized the liquidity (in both senses of the word) of the Roman economy.[9] Crucially, the Vandal period was increasingly seen as a continuation of this prosperity, rather than marking a dramatic decline.

This confident appraisal has been muted somewhat in more recent scholarship. A proliferation of studies of late Roman ceramics has immeasurably improved understanding of many aspects of the African economy, but each new study challenges assumptions about the dating of certain vessel types and demands recalibrations of scholars' narratives.[10] Vessels once thought to have been produced in the late fifth century are now dated with confidence to the early Byzantine period; others traditionally regarded as later Roman now seem to date to the mid-fifth century.[11] This does not invalidate the view that economic life remained vibrant in the Vandal period, but does demand a more nuanced appreciation of the ebb and flow of post-Roman production.[12]

Equally significant has been an increasing interest in the varied agricultural production of Roman and Vandal Africa. Historians have always acknowledged that grain is likely to have been the principal export of the region and was probably the mainstay of the economy, but the fields in which it was grown, the hard-earth threshing floors on which it was processed, and the sacks in which it was transported have left little trace in the archaeological record. As a result, the details of its production and distribution are frequently obscure. Countless amphorae sherds, and well-studied remains of olive presses have created a contrasting problem in the study of olive-oil production. Recent analysis of African amphorae has noted that a substantial proportion of these vessels (perhaps around half) were lined internally with pitch.[13] This was probably common practice for the transportation of wine or fish-sauce, but would have spoiled olive oil. Consequently, an economy once thought to have rested heavily upon the olive is now being re-assessed. Oleiculture was still very important in Roman Africa – and continued to flourish under the Vandals – but viticulture and fish processing are increasingly recognized as crucial cash crops for the region.

Another major conceptual shift has been an emphasis upon non-commercial forms of economic exchange, particularly those related to the operation of the empire itself. One result of this has been to move the Vandals back towards the centre of the stage. Studies have highlighted the importance of taxation to the functioning of the complex Roman state and to the operation of a monetized and vibrant inter-provincial economy.[14] Once the ties of taxation had been loosened, the world system of the late empire began to unfold and regional economic structures began to predominate. This did not happen immediately, and its true effects are best discussed in terms of decades and centuries rather than years, but the crisis of the imperial fisc may be regarded as a crucial turning point in the economic history of the ancient world. So important were African taxes to the functioning of the later western empire, and so great were the implications of their decline, that the Vandals have plausibly been identified once more as the authors of its eventual collapse.[15]

Taxes, Trade and African Prosperity in the Late Roman Economy

Roman Africa was undoubtedly rich, but the single greatest boost to its economic growth came through the direct intervention of the Roman state. In the late second century, the emperor Septimius Severus formalized a massive state requisitioning programme whereby a substantial proportion of North Africa's land taxes were paid in the form of grain and olive oil. These goods (conventionally referred to as the *annona*) were shipped north through the harbours of Carthage in order to feed the populace of Rome and the thousands of soldiers, bureaucrats and state functionaries upon whom the empire depended.[16] Like the fertile islands of Sardinia and Sicily, Africa had long been a producer of agricultural surplus, but the demands of an omnivorous state saw these efforts multiplied. From the later second century until well into the fourth, much of the North African countryside witnessed an intensification of production, a process most visible to archaeologists in the olive-processing plants and urbanized production centres or 'agrovilles' of the Proconsular province and Byzacena. The redistribution of this grain and oil also hastened the development of a bureaucratic and physical infrastructure, which may well have included the enhancement and maintenance of harbours.[17] Some suggestion of the scale of this investment is provided by the circular harbour in Carthage, where excavations have revealed storage depots, administrative centres and (probably) warehouses, as well as a number of written records on ceramic *ostraka* that hint at a whole network of collection and redistribution nodes inland and along the coast.[18] The sophistication of the classical Mediterranean economy was at its peak in the fourth century, and North Africa had a central position within it.

This state redistribution certainly accounted for a substantial proportion of agricultural production in the third, fourth and early fifth centuries, but it also had a catalytic effect upon African commerce.[19] The transportation of the *annona* was undertaken by nominated shippers of the *corpus naviculariorum*, who enjoyed a variety of privileges, including exemption from tariffs for a whole sailing season once they had done their duty to the state.[20] As a result, these shippers found themselves at a huge commercial advantage over shippers from other regions, and eagerly crammed their holds with oil, grain, fish products and fineware for sale across the Mediterranean.[21] This 'piggy-backing' of goods also proved beneficial to producers; with few transport overheads to be borne, the landholders and entrepreneurs of North Africa found themselves in a

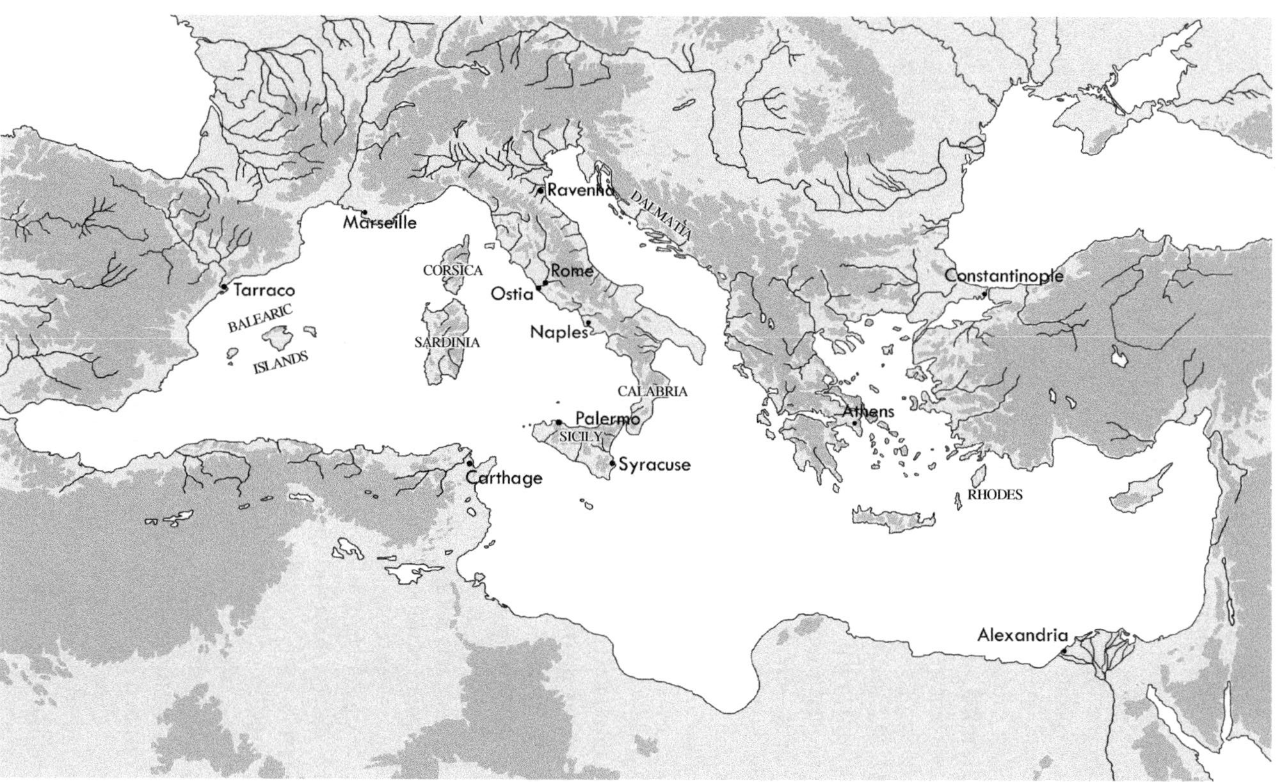

Figure 6.1 Economic life in the Mediterranean world

position to exploit a far wider array of extra-provincial markets than might otherwise have been the case. Anxious to exploit the commercial opportunities on offer, many of the estates of North Africa expanded and diversified. This is most clearly visible in the case of African *sigillata* or 'Red slipped ware' (ARS), the highly desirable tablewares produced on the estates of Africa Proconsularis and Byzacena. Most regions of the Mediterranean produced fine tablewares of their own, and continued to do so, but it was the African variety – or varieties – which came to monopolize the central Italian market by the mid-second century and was dominant elsewhere in the western empire by the mid-third. ARS was never officially transported as a part of the *annona*, but subsidized shipping provided a huge commercial benefit to African workshops, and continuous investment and diversification doubtless helped to press home this advantage.[22]

Olive oil, wine and fish-sauce production within Africa enjoyed similar advantages, and here economies of scale may also have played a part. This is most apparent from the evidence for oil processing and shipping throughout the region, but comparable patterns have also been assumed for viticulture and fish salting, neither of which has been studied in anything like the same detail.[23] Surveys in Central Tunisia have revealed the presence of vast oil-pressing centres, which could scarcely have developed without the constant demand represented by the *annona*, but which would have been well placed to exploit commercial opportunities once established.[24] Rather less is known about the sites on which wine was produced and fish processed, but the wide distribution of amphora sherds allows us to state with confidence that both were important until the Byzantine period at the earliest.

A change occurs

The connection between Carthage and Rome formed the backbone of the Mediterranean economy, but was put under severe strain during the political crises of the later fourth and early fifth century. The rebellion of the Numidian princeling Gildo in 397–8 temporarily halted the shipment of grain to Rome, provoking a spasm of imperial legislation in response, and later contributing to severe food shortages in the capital.[25] A decade later, the *comes Africae* Heraclian withheld supplies in an effort to unseat the Gothic puppet Attalus at Rome, and in AD 413 reverted to the same strategy in support of his own usurpation.[26] It was possibly fear of precisely this situation that led Aetius and Placidia to respond so forcefully to the threat of Boniface's rumoured rebellion in the mid-420s.

But it was the Vandal occupation which finally severed the umbilical connection between Africa and Italy. After October 439, when Carthage fell to Geiseric, the *annona* fleet would have ceased to be a regular sight along the quays of Portus and Ostia. It is possible that the treaty of 442 reinstated the limited shipment of grain as a formal tribute to the western empire, but this seems unlikely, and in any case the merchant fleet can scarcely have been subsidized to the same degree as had previously been the case.[27] Valentinian's legislation of the following years hints at a major fiscal crisis in Ravenna, and his concern to maximize revenues in the lands still under his control following the loss of the African tax base.[28] We know from the ceramic evidence that the merchant ships of Carthage continued to trade, but without the generous state subsidies this must have become a considerably more expensive business. The *annona* shipments had long provided a crutch for the Mediterranean economy, and once the Vandals had kicked it away, the system began to totter perceptibly. But when viewed from an African perspective, this narrative of economic collapse is rather more complex.

The implications of the change for Africa

To the farmers and merchants of North Africa, the collapse of the state redistribution system had a number of contrasting effects. On the one hand, the disappearance of the *annona* removed a stable and captive market for African oil and (especially) grain. Equally seriously, the ending of the state subsidies to African ship-owners removed a major commercial advantage to the farmers and merchants of this region: without a guaranteed market and preferential shipping rates, African producers were denied the safety net which had allowed their region to develop so quickly. On the other hand, the landowners of Africa now found themselves to be the producers of a large agricultural surplus which could be sold on the open market. Where Rome had once taken the bulk of the African harvest at a fixed price in the name of taxation, this grain and wine was now available to be sold. The presses, kilns and threshing floors which had been built at the height of imperial consumption remained in use, and while African *navicularii* may have lost their generous governmental grants, most of them retained their ships and the commercial contacts that they had developed in happier years.

All of the available evidence suggests that agricultural production continued with little interruption into the Vandal period. Procopius implies that African farms continued to produce, but the revenues simply went to Carthage, rather than to Rome or Ravenna:

> since the land [of the Vandals] was an especially good one, flourishing abundantly with the most useful crops, it came about that the revenue collected from the commodities produced there was not paid out to any other country in the purchase of food supply, but those who possessed the land always kept for themselves the income from it for the ninety-five years during which the Vandals ruled Libya.[29]

The majority of land in North Africa remained in the hands of its original owners, and the change of rulers in Carthage probably had little direct effect upon them. Even in Zeugitana, where the Vandals settled most intensively, there is little evidence for any substantial alteration in agricultural practice. Their estates continued to produce as they always had, and paid their surplus to their new landlords in the form of rent. Many landowners, whether Vandal or Romano-African, would have found themselves with surplus to sell, and would happily have availed themselves of the infrastructure to make this possible.

To judge from the ceramic record, African production did experience a slight recalibration during the middle of the fifth century, but this is best read as an illustration of the continued vibrancy of the region, rather than as a marker of decline.[30] Zeugitana – previously the heartland of African fineware manufacture – produced less pottery that it had done in the early years of the century and witnessed a stagnation in the development of new vessel types between c. 430 and c. 480.[31] At roughly the same time, Central Tunisian wares developed in sophistication and became relatively common throughout Mediterranean.[32] By the end of the fifth century or the beginning of the sixth, a balance between the two types of wares seems to have been restored and both were widely exported. It is hard to know whether this disjuncture in ceramic manufacture reflected a wider economic recession at the time of the Vandal conquest. Our other evidence suggests not: amphorae exports remained relatively high, and field surveys indicate strong continuity of occupation throughout Zeugitana. Instead it might be better to interpret the mid-fifth-century shift positively, as a reflection of the increased diversity of manufacture in Byzacena as landowners in that region sought to exploit the new opportunities open to them. If the producers of Zeugitana found themselves unable to compete with their near-neighbours in the brief hiatus after the Vandal invasion, the resumption of pottery production at the end of the century showed that this was only a temporary setback.

New markets in the Western Mediterranean

Merchants continued to ply the shipping lanes of the Mediterranean during the fifth century, but there were probably fewer of them than there had been at the height of late imperial trade. Merchants certainly remain a relatively constant presence in the literary sources throughout the Vandal century. Fulgentius of Ruspe readily found a berth on ships between Carthage, Sicily, Sardinia and Rome, and was confident of passage to Alexandria and beyond. The bishop was so closely associated with fifth-century maritime life that a sermon attributed to him compares the happy promise of the resurrection to the bustling of a port:

> How happy the port seems, when it is full with cargoes and bustling with merchants! Bundles of various goods are displayed about the ships, many rejoice in the joyfulness of the sailors' songs.[33]

Procopius, too, was aware of the continued commercial prosperity of the Vandal kingdom. The final preparations for Belisarius' campaign against Africa were made with the help of a merchant in Syracuse – one evidently familiar with the topography of the realm.[34] Procopius also describes the political influence of the merchants within Carthage, both before and after Belisarius' conquest.[35] His intended point may have been that the Byzantine occupation helped to revive African commerce, but it was scarcely moribund at the time of the invasion.

The disappearance of the great axial link between Carthage and Rome opened up a variety of new trading routes throughout the Mediterranean. No longer bound to Rome, African shippers increasingly turned elsewhere in their search for markets. Simultaneously, eastern merchants, no longer priced out of the region by the African monopoly, carried their goods further and further west. The principal evidence for these changes is provided by the distribution patterns of amphorae and ARS between the mid-fifth century and the early decades of the sixth.[36] Whilst these data need to be interpreted with some care, broad patterns may be traced with some confidence. The first and most obvious feature of the period is a perceptible shift of trade away from Portus, Ostia and central Italy, and towards the other regions of the Mediterranean. From around AD 450, finds of both African amphorae and ARS decline substantially along the Italian coast, and begin to disappear almost completely from inland sites.[37] This contrasts sharply with the evidence from sites along the eastern coast of Spain and in the Vandal-controlled islands of Sicily and Sardinia (and to a lesser extent Corsica and the

Balearics). Throughout these regions, African ceramic imports either remained at a relatively constant level, or increased in the second half of the fifth century.[38] The reasons for this seem clear: while African merchants had previously been constrained by their responsibilities to the state, the ending of *annona* allowed them a freer rein in the sale of their cargoes. In some cases, of course, the Italian market may well have remained attractive – the demand for foodstuffs in Rome, for example, is unlikely to have diminished substantially. But consumption of African goods elsewhere in Italy can only have reduced with the removal of the state subsidy.

Eastern merchants also turned their attention westwards in the fifth century. The ceramic record of the period in Carthage, Italy and southern Gaul includes an increasing proportion of imports of eastern origin.[39] In part, this probably reflects a resurgent eastern economy, which benefited from the political and financial eclipse of the western capital, and from the ending of the African monopoly: as the shippers of Carthage turned away from Italy, their Levantine colleagues swooped in. But eastern goods could also be transported in western ships, and it need not be assumed that this expansion was necessarily at the expense of African trade. In many cases, these Levantine ceramics may represent the cargoes brought back to Carthage by African shippers plying the profitable eastern trade routes, and distributed from there around the western Mediterranean. Like Rome, Constantinople was a hungry city, and much of the African grain surplus may have been shipped eastwards for sale. Frustratingly, the trade in grain leaves little trace in the archaeological record, but the wide distribution of ARS throughout the eastern Mediterranean in the Vandal period shows that African goods found a market in the region and perishable produce may well have done too. Wheat and barley could have been taken east in either African or Levantine ships, and eastern amphorae brought back in the empty holds. That the inhabitants of Africa enjoyed a fruitful (and by no means one-sided) commerce with the eastern empire is also demonstrated by the large quantity of eastern gold which circulated in the Vandal kingdom (as discussed more fully below).

Taken as a whole, the ceramic evidence suggests that the production capacity of North Africa suffered only a slight decline throughout the Vandal period. Patterns of distribution certainly changed over the course of the fifth century – the ending of the *annona* saw African oil, wine and tablewares (and presumably also African grain) sold far more widely throughout the Mediterranean, in both eastern and western markets – but the overall demand for African goods seems to have remained relatively high. This pattern of continuity with some slight recalibration may also be detected within North Africa itself.

Town and Country in Vandal Africa

The internal economy of North Africa remained robust under the Vandals. Changes certainly took place – as they always had – in the fabric of the cities and the exploitation of the land, but the historian or archaeologist would be hard-pressed to find any evidence of abrupt transformation or cataclysm with the arrival of the Vandals. The urban and rural landscapes of North Africa had undergone a constant series of changes over the centuries of Roman domination. New lands were brought under cultivation and others fell out of use; patterns of land-ownership and exploitation changed as emperors, senators and provincial aristocrats found new ways of exploiting their property holdings and as tenant farmers on the ground sought to improve their own lot. Patterns of urban life were also transformed in response to new social and economic needs; the prominent landmarks of many cities had begun to change in the later fourth century, and long-standing transformations were already well underway by the time of the Vandal occupation of Carthage in AD 439. The Vandal period of occupation, then, was just another chapter in this narrative.

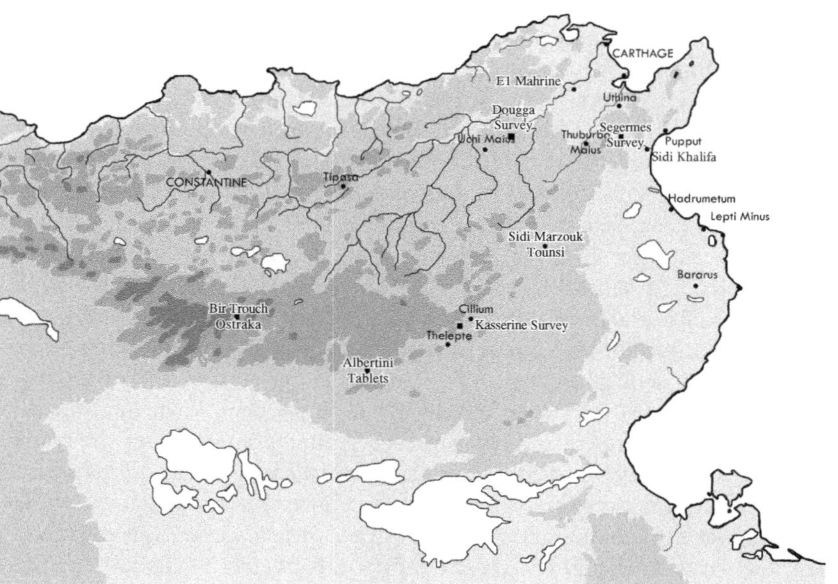

Figure 6.2 Economic life in North Africa under the Vandals

Towns and industry

Towns and cities had a crucial economic function in the Late Antique world, and this was certainly true in Vandal North Africa.[40] From the Roman period, towns (which could often be quite small) were scattered quite thickly across the African countryside. These urban centres acted as markets for the produce of the surrounding hinterland, and for other regional and inter-regional trade. Cities also had an important manufacturing role. Metalworking, pottery, and textile manufacture were common to all African towns and activities like fish processing and dyeing flourished in regions where this was possible. The available evidence suggests strongly that this manufacture continued with relatively few interruptions throughout the period of Vandal rule and into the Byzantine occupation. Inevitably, some towns – and some individual enterprises – proved to be more successful than others over the century or so of Vandal domination, and there are examples of once-flourishing towns which fell into abeyance before the Byzantine conquest. For the most part, however, North Africa remained a vibrant urban society throughout this period.

The availability of trustworthy evidence provides the major obstacle to the understanding of Vandal-period urbanism. Despite extensive recent excavation in Carthage, Caesarea and Leptiminus, the economic function of these settlements has only recently been analyzed. Markets are more difficult to assess in the material record than are churches or theatres: although the grand basilical buildings which commonly housed urban markets may be identified easily enough, the produce sold in these markets, their social importance and their relationship to the rural hinterland need to be considered with care. Urban light industry is rather more visible on the ground – through iron slag, pottery wasters, loom weights, murex shells and so on – but only when excavators are looking for it. Until relatively recently, urban excavation in Africa (as elsewhere) tended to focus upon the more glamorous cultural buildings and their gradual disappearance – a phenomenon which will be discussed more fully in a later chapter. In recent years, archaeologists have increasingly investigated the economic foundations which allowed these cities to thrive. The present chapter will discuss some of the major case studies.

Towns underwent a number of physical changes from the later fourth century, which could often be quite dramatic. A number of examples may be taken to illustrate the point. An inhabitant of Carthage, Uchi Maius or Bararus, who was born at the time of the Vandal occupation, or perhaps a little before, and who lived into old age, would have seen the familiar landmarks of her native city completely transformed over the course of her lifetime. In Carthage, the *Kardo Maximus* – once the grand boulevard of the classical city – was choked by the encroachment of shops and small houses over the course of the fifth century.[41] Traffic could still pass through it, but it was not the great public space it had once been. The *via Caelestis* (the 'Temple of Caelestis Road') was probably a similar concourse, which Victor of Vita accuses the Vandals of having 'destroyed' at the time of their occupation. Quite what this entailed is unclear, but there can be little doubt that the urban spaces of the city had changed, even within Victor's lifetime. The circus probably remained in use within the city, but the theatre, forum and several bath complexes were abandoned or turned to private housing by the Vandal period, if not before.

Comparable changes happened throughout North Africa, as buildings and public spaces which had lost their social or cultural significance were gradually turned over to private housing or light industry. In Uchi Maius, a small town in the Medjerda Valley, an oil press was constructed in the forum during the latter part of the fifth century and further production complexes sprang up in the northern and eastern parts of town.[42] Similar phenomena are apparent from throughout the kingdom. Inhabitants of Bararus in central Byzacena would also have seen their town square fall out of use, either after the earthquake of AD 365, or in the decades that followed. The fate of its forum was sealed during the fifth century when its paving slabs were robbed out for use elsewhere, and the discovery of two small cellars containing amphorae suggests the presence of a new oil-processing plant nearby. By the sixth century, the forum area as a whole was occupied with private housing.[43]

This industrialization of public space in North Africa had begun in the later Roman period, and was to intensify under the Byzantines, but the transformation continued under the Vandals. The re-occupation of bath houses was particularly common, thanks to the supply of water in such buildings, the substantial foundations upon which many were built and the ready adaptability of their marble basins for craft use. In Uthina, midway between Thuburbo Maius and Carthage, for example, a private bath complex that had been abandoned before the arrival of the Vandals was re-occupied as a small industrial centre in around AD 480. The discovery there of potters' tools, punches and moulds suggest that the complex had been turned over to the small-scale manufacture of fineware. That this was something of a local specialty is suggested by the identification of a second ceramic workshop on the outskirts of the city.[44]

Figure 6.3 An oil press erected near the forum in Thuburbo Maius. The press itself is visible at the bottom left of the picture. Reproduced by permission of Professor David Mattingly

Two dedicated light industrial zones are known from Carthage. Unlike the examples discussed above, these had not been adapted from other uses and retained their function throughout Late Antiquity. A number of craft centres have been found in the so-called Magon quarter, for example, in the north-eastern part of the city, close to the coast road.[45] More striking (and more fully excavated) are the city blocks immediately to the north of the circular harbour that had housed a mixed craft centre during the later Roman period, and included a focal formal building, perhaps a guildhall. The excavators of the complex tentatively identified it as an imperial *gynaceum* or textile manufacturing plant, but a variety of other craft and metalworking activities would also seem to have taken place on site. The complex did not survive unchanged through the fifth and sixth centuries, since the main 'guildhall' was subdivided into smaller rooms during this period, and the harbour-front porticoes seem to have been walled up in the sixth century. Importantly, these changes testify to continued use rather than abandonment, and craft working evidently continued on the site until the seventh century at least.[46]

Occupation and production in the North African countryside

Like the towns, the countryside of North Africa underwent a number of changes in Late Antiquity, few of which may be attributed directly to the Vandals. Roman patterns of land exploitation in North Africa had always been varied. Field survey, excavation and the fragmentary literary and epigraphic evidence are testament to nothing so much as the huge diversity of practices adopted.[47] The best-known forms of exploitation were the great imperial *latifundia* of Africa Proconsularis and Numidia, huge estates which were primarily farmed by the tenants who lived on them. But even here systems of tenantry seem to have varied, and certainly changed over time and between regions. These estates were typically owned by the imperial state or by aristocratic landowners (who may or may not have lived on their properties), and administered by local middlemen or *conductores*, who were typically appointed on a quinquennial basis and were responsible for the day-to-day running of the estate. Farming itself would have been the responsibility of tenants (*coloni*) who typically paid rent on their lands in kind, and may well have been required to work on the central demesne land of the estate.

The first and most obvious point to make is that the Vandal occupation would have made very little difference to this system as it operated on the ground. The majority of farmland outside Zeugitana remained in the hands of its original owners, and doubtless continued to be exploited as it always had been. Even within the *sortes Vandalorum*, where the land distributions between AD 439 and 442 saw estates pass into the hands of the Vandals, the disruption upon them may not have been particularly marked. The majority of the new Vandal estates were probably carved out of the large imperial and senatorial landholdings which had once dominated the landscape of Zeugitana. As such, their transfer to the new military aristocracy would have had little effect upon the practicalities of farming within the region. Few Vandals can have been anxious to change agricultural practices which were working well for them, and most were probably content to retain the services of the *conductores* and *coloni* who had always worked their land.

The evidence provided by the Segermes field survey supports this assumption and reveals a landscape which continued to flourish under the Vandals. Lying some 40 kilometres south of Carthage, and situated on the major trunk roads between Thuburbo Maius and the coast at Pupput and Hadrumetum, the Segermes Valley probably lay well within the limits of the *sortes Vandalorum*, and many of the surveyed lands may have been among those distributed to Geiseric's followers. Any Vandals

Figure 6.4 The arcades of a Vandal-period church in the Kasserine survey region. Reproduced by permission of Professor David Mattingly

who occupied the valley would have found a mixed agricultural region. At the start of the fifth century, the landscape was dominated by a small handful of relatively modest villas, as well as a number of working farms and agricultural villages. The staple crop was probably grain, but the evidence for widespread oil processing throughout the valley is impressive, and several sites had multiple presses, suggesting a high level of surplus production and export. Noticeably, patterns of occupation within the valley were little affected by the Vandal conquest; if anything, the density of settlements suggest a slight increase in population over the course of the fifth century.

The landscape of south-western Byzacena provides a further illustration of economic continuity (and even vibrancy) under the Vandals. A substantial field survey in the hinterland of the Roman towns of Cillium and Thelepte, in the Kasserine region, has revealed both the diversity of settlement types in the late Roman period, and the strong continuity of occupation through to at least the first decades of the Byzantine occupation.[48] This was far from the most intensively cultivated region of Byzacena in either the pre-Vandal or Vandal periods, and was of course a long way from the main area of Vandal settlement.[49] Nevertheless, the evidence of the survey is instructive. In many cases, the patterns of land occupation are familiar enough: in the upland landscape to the south of Kasserine, for example, were found the terraces, field walls and irrigation channels typical of agricultural practice from elsewhere in North Africa, where farmers struggled to exploit the seasonal (and often violent) wadi inundations.[50] But this was not solely a landscape of small farms: dotted around the landscape are a variety of larger production centres, including a small town at Ksar el Guellal to the north-east of Cillium. This complex may well have originated as a military outpost, but the presence of a massive pressing facility indicates that oleiculture dominated here from the third century. By the Vandal period, the settlement was also furnished with an aqueduct, a small bath complex, a Christian basilica and a circuit wall, but the prominence and size of the pressing facility suggests that this was an economic centre (or 'agroville' in the modish terminology of the surveying team), rather than a city in the traditional sense.[51] Ceramic evidence indicates that the town manufactured amphorae and finewares on a scale unrivalled elsewhere in the region. It continued throughout the Vandal period, with some indication of an expansion in ceramic production during the later fifth century.

Less substantial than the agroville at Ksar el Guellal, but perhaps more typical of the Vandal countryside as a whole, are several large farms throughout the survey area which were equipped with oil presses (often more than one), and which occasionally exhibit signs of ceramic manufacture or metalworking. Two larger oil-processing plants were discovered around 400 metres apart in the southern part of the survey area, which include large pressing rooms, as well as stock enclosures and perhaps the residential quarters for a slave labour force. The utilitarian architecture of these complexes would suggest that they were not the permanent residences of elites, but the villa at Henchir el Guellali may well have been. Equipped with its own bath, this structure was clearly an important cultural landmark, but the surrounding array of small farm buildings, which were used for olive processing, ceramic manufacture and perhaps metallurgy, testify to a considerable economic role.

Farm settlements of this kind were the mainstay of production in Roman North Africa and continued to be so under the Vandals, despite some considerable changes in their economic orientation. Some of these settlements fell out of use in the fifth and sixth centuries, but the dominant image provided by field surveys is one of general continuity of occupation with some economic diversification from the fifth century. At Sidi Marzouk Tounsi in northern Byzacena, and at several complexes in the Sahel, estate centres seem to have undertaken their own amphora manufacture.[52] From the mid-fifth century, in other words, olive oil and wine were no longer transported to the coast in skins, to be decanted at designated collection points, but were bottled at source. This transition was by no means uniform, and happened at different rates in different parts of Africa. As a result, it is very difficult to associate these changes with a conscious Vandal 'agricultural policy' – as some scholars have suggested.[53] Instead, these changes in practice, and the further diversification of estate production, are better regarded as localized responses to the decline of the *annona* system. Without a state bureaucracy to manage the collection of surplus, landowners may well have felt that their economic interests were best served by bottling and transporting their goods themselves. Naturally, landowners adapted more or less quickly to these challenges, and different regions of the Vandal kingdom changed more or less dramatically. But at the very least this variety testifies to a vibrant landscape and a class of land-owners anxious to respond to changing economic circumstances.[54]

Other estates diversified through the intensification of fineware production. Smaller research projects in the Vandal heartland of Zeugitana, including those in the hinterland of Carthage, the Dougga Valley and El Mahrine have detected a new economic impetus in many of these settlements.[55] Sidi Marzouk Tounsi again provides a good illustration: here, a particularly distinctive form of ARS was manufactured in some volume down to the beginning of the sixth century. While vessels manufactured at Sidi Marzouk are common in Central Italy, they are almost unknown in Africa itself: few examples are known from either the Kasserine Survey area or the Dougga Valley, despite the relative proximity of both. This suggests that the finewares produced on the site were made almost exclusively for an export market.[56] Inhabitants of the neighbouring regions largely dined on tableware of local manufacture, while the owners of estates like that at Sidi Marzouk Tounsi exploited the distant markets which remained open throughout the Vandal period.

The Albertini Tablets

The so-called 'Albertini Tablets' cast further light upon the functioning of the late fifth-century countryside.[57] This collection of 34 documents on 45 wooden panels (each roughly the size of an A5 piece of paper), was found in the early twentieth century in rather mysterious circumstances, buried in a small pot, at the foot of a wall in the Djebel Mrata, some 75 kilometres from the area covered by the Kasserine survey. These tablets reflect the economic activities of a group of tenant families, their *conductores* and landlords in the last years of the fifth century. The majority of the documents record land sales, or more precisely the sale of the right to farm small blocks of marginal land on the edges of a large estate called the *fundus Tuletianos*, owned by one Flavius Geminius Catullinus and managed on his behalf by three of his kinsmen or freedmen. These parcels of land were exchanged according to the *lex Manciana*, a first-century AD Roman law by which tenants could undertake to farm uncultivated marginal land.[58] Where this was successful, more land would be brought under cultivation. Where these initiatives failed, the Mancian law provided some financial protection for the cultivator, and determined that land-owners should 'buy back' such plots. The parcels of land in question are often rather small, and frequently contain fewer than ten trees – one records the transfer of a plot containing just two olive trees, which cannot have represented much more than a tiny terraced field.[59] The most frequently farmed crop on these lands was certainly the olive, although some documents also refer to fig and almond trees.

These tablets allow us to glimpse the lives of peasants in rural communities in a way which field surveys and excavations do not. They provide a rare – if brief – view of families who were clearly struggling to make ends meet. Several texts record the transactions of Processanus and Siddana, for example, an illiterate married couple who seem to have expanded ambitiously into the marginal regions of the *fundus Tuletianos* only to find themselves in difficulty. Documents from October 493 and November 494 record their disposal of several parcels of land which included fig trees as well as olives. At some point in the next two years, the couple also sold their olive press, again to their landlord. Within another two years, Processanus then passed away. According to Mancian law, rights over the cultivation of the remaining lands passed to Siddana and her sons Quodvultdeus and Fortunatianus, but their difficulties seem to have continued; in 496 a further six or seven plots were sold to Geminius Felix for the rather meagre sum of one gold *solidus*.[60]

Different accounts of frustrated ambition may be read in the other tablets of the collection, but this is neither the story of economic collapse, nor of a rapacious landlord exploiting the misfortune of his tenants. Processanus and Siddana certainly evoke sympathy, but their misfortune also illuminates a surprisingly vibrant agricultural world. The couple had their own olive press and a broad portfolio of lands which had been rendered partially cultivable through the addition of water channels and other irrigation systems. The Mancian law protected them from destitution when these initiatives failed, but more significant fact is that their attempts were made at all. Comparable attempts at upward mobility may also be found in other actions recorded on the tablets. Donatianus and Saturninus, two neighbours of Processanus and Siddana, sold a young slave by the name of Fortinus to Geminius Felix for a substantial fee in the summer of 494. While it is hard to say what particular duties Fortinus may have had, we may again glimpse a relatively economically active peasantry at work.[61] The prospects for Fortinus may have been bleak on the edge of the Vandal kingdom, but Donatianus and Saturninus (and even Siddana and her sons) would have enjoyed some legal support for attempting to better their lot.

On a different social scale, the documents hint at the mixed cultural identities of major landowners. Famously, all of the documents are dated by reference to the reign of Gunthamund in Carthage. The landlord Flavius Geminius Catullinus is repeatedly referred to as a *flamen perpetuus* (the priest of the imperial cult), an important position in Roman civic society.[62] But if the landlords of the *fundus Tuletianos* were scrupulous in their deference to Vandal political authority as well as anxious to parade their traditional credentials, their African roots also show through. The most famous document in the collection is a dowry for Ianuarilla of the Geminii, presumably the sister or daughter of the landowner. Alongside a lump sum of silver, Ianuarilla took a substantial and varied trousseau with her to the altar – a pure African *dalmatica* dress to the value of 2,000 *folles*, a veil or *mafors* worth 400 and a mysterious garment called a *colussa* worth a further 200. Taken together with an eclectic collection of 50 torques, bracelets and rings, a hundred bull skins, shells, earrings, slippers and a loom, these are not the conventional accoutrements of a Roman bride.[63] Roman in name and civic status, 'Moorish' (or 'African') in dress, and deferential to Vandal rule in Carthage, the Geminii nevertheless seem to have owned an estate that was governed on strictly imperial lines.

A slightly different image of estate management from the same period is provided by the agrarian accounts on the five 'Bir Trouch *ostraka*', found in the Wadi Mitta at the eastern end of the Aurès Massif.[64] Like the Albertini Tablets, the Bir Trouch *ostraka* are concerned with marginal land on the edge of the Vandal kingdom, and they too are formally dated by the regnal year of King Gunthamund. Where the *ostraka* differ from the Albertini Tablets, however, is in the transactions they describe. The documents themselves are rather formulaic and record the quantities of barley (and perhaps other crops) that the landowner Messiesa derived from his *pars dominica*: the 'lord's portion' of the estate.[65] The significance of this term is uncertain. The *pars dominica* may well be comparable to the medieval demesne, which was typically a small portion of an estate owned directly by the landholder, but farmed by his tenants through a certain number of days' labour each year. Alternatively, the 'lord's portion' may have been a region farmed on behalf of the landlord in return for wages, or perhaps simply a designated fraction of the rent from the estate. Regardless, the documents from Bir Trouch hint at an agricultural accounting system which is comparable in detail, if not in form, to that of the *fundus Tuletianos*.

Remarkable as these rare *ostraka* and wooden tablets are as historical documents, their most important feature may well be the sheer mundanity of the transactions that they record. Even if we cannot be sure of the circumstances of their production and deposition, it is at least clear that landowners and tenants in the far south of Byzacena and Numidia continued to exploit marginal land, and to cultivate estates, much as they always had. They did so using laws that seem to have been customary in Roman North Africa for generations, and even illiterate farmers took care to document their transactions. Their crops included olives, nuts, fruit and barley, and they apparently paid for their land-rights in coin (or at least calculated their debts in such terms). No other comparable documentary sources have survived from Vandal Africa, but scattered *ostraka* and tablets from the later Roman and Byzantine periods do suggest that records of this kind may have been the rule, rather than the exception.[66] If this system was the norm in the quieter backwaters of Vandal Numidia and Byzacena, and in the foothills of the Aurès Mountains, it seems reasonable to assume that similarly sophisticated transactions – and similar patterns of exploitation – were being carried out in similar lands throughout the kingdom.

Vandal Fiscal Organization

The archaeology of fifth- and sixth-century North Africa reveals the economic foundations of the Vandal kingdom, but can offer little indication of the actions of the Hasding kings themselves. In general, however, the continuities and changes in agricultural practice and manufacturing suggest that the occupation of Carthage forced a redefinition of Africa's position in the wider world, but that the settlement of the Vandals had little discernible effect upon the exploitation of its rich lands. To ascribe an economic agency to the Vandals – to see how Geiseric and his successors helped or hindered the prosperity of their region – we need instead to investigate the fiscal and monetary policies of their new government.

The financial structures of the Vandal kingdom are most visible to us in the legacy that they left. In 534, shortly after the Byzantine occupation of Africa, Justinian sent two officials named Tryphon and Eustratius to take a census of the new imperial provinces for tax purposes.[67] Procopius suggests that this undertaking was unpopular among local landowners, who were hardly anxious to pay new taxes, but necessary because the old census records had been destroyed by Geiseric at the time of the Vandal occupation. Much of the Byzantine legislation of the same period is concerned with the disentangling of the confused financial systems that had evolved since AD 439. The fifth century had not been a period in which Romano-Africans were spared from the attention of the taxman – ample literary evidence testifies to his continued activity under the Hasdings – but changed political circumstances had led to a much changed fiscal organization. It was that which caused the Byzantines such problems.

The basic principles behind this transformation are clear enough, even if the available evidence is not always as full as might be hoped. As we have seen, the Vandals inherited a rich province, which continued to flourish, and which remained geared towards the generation of tax revenue. What the Hasdings were spared, however, were many of the overheads of the later Roman state.[68] While public expenditure under the empire was minute in comparison to that of modern states, its fiscal commitments were still sizeable, and far greater than those of the early medieval kingdoms. The vast revenues committed to the imperial army in the fourth and early fifth century – estimated at around 50 per cent of fiscal expenditure – were slashed under the Hasdings, supported as they were by an army which gained its sustenance from the revenues of the land, rather than from salaries, and which could supplement this with the rich plunder they obtained on campaign and on raids.[69] The Vandal fisc still had to pay for the civil bureaucracy of the new state and two passing references in the historical literature demonstrate that the official government post or *cursus publicus* remained a drain on the treasury.[70] But in each case, the commitments of the Hasding monarchy can only have been a fraction of those of the later Roman state. In short, Vandal administration was probably a rather reduced version of that which had come before, with a concomitant reduction in cost.[71] Africa had always been one of the wealthiest provinces of the Roman world. With easy access to a more or less constant source of taxable wealth, but with few immediate financial commitments, the Vandals could not dispense with taxation entirely, yet they did not necessarily have to collect it with the same diligence as the later Roman (or, indeed, Byzantine) administrators.

Taxation and vandal fiscal policy

The Vandal kingdom, like the late empire, recognized a formal separation between the rent and profits from royal lands (*res privata*) and the state wealth generated primarily from taxation, which was the responsibility of the state treasury or *fiscus*. The former had an ideological as well as economic significance. It was through these landholdings that the Hasdings asserted their status amid a military aristocracy which increasingly enjoyed some economic autonomy. The royal possessions were diverse and impressive, and included mines and forests as well as agricultural land in Zeugitana and Byzacena. The *res privata* may also have been supplemented intermittently by the proceeds accruing from Geiseric's vigorous foreign policy; it is certainly likely, for example, that much of the wealth taken from Rome in 455 ended up in the king's private coffers, rather than in the state treasury.

The *fiscus* was central to the economy of the kingdom. Fiscal revenue was primarily drawn, as it always had been, from taxation on the land. During the later Roman period, responsibility for the assessment and collection of this taxation trickled down the bureaucratic hierarchy to pool at the feet of the *curiales* – the civic aristocracy. Since these *curiales* were afforded little financial responsibility after the Byzantine occupation, it has been suggested that effective municipal taxation came to an end during the Vandal period.[72] If this was the case, it took some time to die. Fulgentius of Ruspe, for example, held the curial rank of *procurator* in his early life.[73] While his precise duties are not outlined in the *Vita Fulgentii*, the fact that his biographer draws extensive parallels between Fulgentius' secular duties and those of Matthew the tax-collector in the New Testament probably tells its own story. Later in his life, moreover, Fulgentius was to encounter an *exactor* in Ruspe who used his political influence (and doubtless financial clout), in supporting his preferred candidate for the episcopate of the city.[74]

The detailed mechanics of Vandal taxation are rather less clear, but it is certain that landholdings continued to be taxed. Procopius tells us that the appropriated lands of the *sortes Vandalorum* were exempt from taxation in perpetuity, and this seems plausible.[75] But those estates which remained in the hands of their original owners did continue to be taxed: in other words the overwhelming majority of agricultural land within the kingdom, and a substantial proportion even in Zeugitana remained subject to assessment. Procopius insists that Romano-African landholdings were taxed particularly heavily in this period, but given the political circumstances in which he was writing, this seems unlikely.[76] More luridly, Victor alludes to the taxes and trickery of Huneric towards the beginning of his reign, and suggests that his calumny had become proverbial in Africa at that time.[77] Victor's accounts of Huneric's actions always pose difficulties of interpretation, but the accusation is unlikely to have been groundless.

Protests about taxation continued to the very end of the Vandal period. The poet Luxorius included two particularly caustic verses on the subject of one 'Eutychus', a royal *minister* who is depicted unlawfully seizing property with the mantra '*regis habenda*': 'All belongs to the king!'[78] Several scholars have pointed out that Luxorius' Eutychus may be identical to a royal minister under Gelimer by the name of Bonifatius. While both names are common enough in Late Antique Africa, Eutychus is a Greek rendering of the Latin Bonifatius – a linguistic ploy which Luxorius may have adopted for reasons of discretion, or simply to advertise his facility with Greek.[79] The chronicler Victor of Tunnuna states that Bonifatius acted as Gelimer's agent in the confiscation of property, perhaps in response to the military crises in Sardinia and Tripolis, or simply in an attempt to line his pockets after his recent usurpation.[80] Procopius' account is at once more intriguing and more dubious: he states that Bonifatius was given responsibility for the royal treasury at the time of the Byzantine occupation, and was charged with transporting it to Spain in the hope of buying Gelimer a bolt-hole in the kingdom of the Visigoth Theudis.[81] Frustrated by a series of contrary winds, Bonifatius was eventually forced to hand over the treasure to Belisarius, who was suitably impressed by both his diligence and the spectacular treasure under his charge.

Other references to taxation within the Vandal kingdom are rare, but reward patient research. The *Latin Anthology*, for example, contains two anonymous epigrams, on the subject of a man with genitals so prodigiously swollen as to resemble an amphora in size and finish:

> You sport a flask hanging down from your groin [. . .], which turns into a swollen amphora when the wind blows. You could have paid potters' tax to the fiscus, since you excel their product with such a smooth swelling![82]

The humour of this epigram depends in part upon the fact that *fiscus* (literally 'bag') can mean both 'tax office' and 'scrotum'.[83] This aside, the epigram remains the only extant reference to the potter's tax (*vectigal figulorum*) within Vandal Africa, although it was apparently a common duty in the late empire.[84] It is reasonable to assume that similar taxes were levied on metal-working, dyeing or fish processing, just as they had been in the later Roman period.[85] If the Hasdings continued to tax potters, there is no reason to assume that other craftsmen were spared.

Other forms of income also made their way into the Vandal coffers. The Mediterranean islands paid tribute to Carthage, presumably annually. It was Gelimer's concern to secure the payment of the Sardinian tribute that led him to send Godas to the island as governor, and then forced the expedition of Stotzas following Godas' own revolt. The treaty with Odoacer in AD 476 indicates that Geiseric had drawn a tribute from Sicily before ceding control of the island (and its annual duty) to the rulers of Italy.[86] No evidence exists from either Corsica or the Balearics, but it is reasonable to assume that a similar arrangement would have been in place in these islands.

Fines and extraordinary taxation also provided a source of revenue for the crown. Inevitably, religious fines are the best documented of these levies, but even here the mechanics of collection are not always clear. In the midst of Huneric's edict of persecution is a confusing passage regarding the fines which might be levied on the *procuratores* and *conductores* of royal estates if they remained intractable in their own Catholicism, or harboured others who refused to convert to Arianism:

> This was the punishment for leaseholders on the royal estates: by way of punishment, they would be forced to render to the *fiscus* as much as they paid to the royal household [*domus regiae*]. This, we determine, is to be observed in the case of all leaseholders and proprietors of land who believe that they should persist in the same superstition.[87]

Mutatis mutandis, this is a more or less direct borrowing from an edict of Honorius and Theodosius made to the proconsul of Africa in June 414 for the suppression of the Donatist sect.[88] As such, the law may reflect little more than Huneric's peculiar veneration of late imperial legalese. But if the law was intended to be implemented, its choice of language remains interesting. The implication is that a clear distinction existed between the *domus regiae*, which collected land rents, and the *fiscus*, which received fines.[89] Victor states elsewhere that it was the *fiscus* which confiscated the property of Catholic bishops upon their death, and which levied an inheritance tax of 500 *solidi* on the successor to the diocese.[90]

Little can be stated with confidence about Vandal taxation, but the fragmentary evidence we do have suggests that taxes and fines continued to be collected down to the Byzantine conquest. The traditional distinction between the *res privata* (or *domus regiae*) and the *fiscus* seems to have been maintained at least down to the reign of Huneric, but may well have disappeared over the following half century. Belisarius and his financial advisors certainly stumbled upon a confused situation when they tried to put their African house in order, but this was not simply because the Vandals had refused to tax. They had benefited from the wealth of North Africa, but did so in their own – typically idiosyncratic – way.

Payment of the military

The reduced expenditure of the Vandal state was a tremendous boon to the Hasding kings. Of central importance here was the army. The military commitments of the new kingdom were substantially less than those of the western empire had been; the Hasdings faced few direct challenges to their rule from usurpers and the shifting frontier with the Moorish polities to the south did not demand substantial military investment until the middle Vandal period at the earliest. But the most significant change was the shift from an army that was primarily paid by salary (which placed the responsibility for their upkeep onto the fisc), to one which was supported on the land. This change was not absolute – the late Roman state had experimented with similar approaches for some time, and elements of the Vandal army continued to be paid by the fisc – but the shift in emphasis was crucial.[91]

Virtually all commentators are agreed that the payment of the Vandal military came – directly or indirectly – from the *sortes Vandalorum*. If the settlement of 442 involved the distribution of actual land to Vandals and their families (as seems likely), this effectively represented a fundamental re-organization of the military system.[92] No longer directly dependent upon the state for support, members of the military aristocracy enjoyed some degree of financial (and hence also political) autonomy. Geiseric's attempts to control the problems this presented have already been outlined, but the economic benefits of a primarily landed army deserve some consideration. Where the later Roman state expended a substantial proportion of its revenue upon the army, the Hasding system had no such burden to carry. The army may also have been largely self-financing, particularly during Geiseric's reign. While it is possible to over-estimate the financial damage caused by Vandal raiding through the Mediterranean between 439–442 and 445–476, there can be little doubt that the plunder taken on these raids did much to ensure the continued satisfaction and loyalty of the Vandal nobility without the need for substantial additional outlay on the part of the Hasdings. As far as we can tell, the muscle-bound marines of Carthage never mutinied for food and pay.

The practicalities of campaigning overseas and maintaining the peace at home did entail some modest financial commitment on the part of the state. Procopius' confusing allusions to the Moorish units stationed in Sardinia suggest that there may have been an attempt to settle them on the island, and hence to instigate there the military system that existed in North Africa.[93] The survival of coins bearing the monogram of the *presidia Maurorum Sardiniae* ('garrison of the Moors of Sardinia') may reflect the donatives that were given to the occupying forces. Faint echoes of the same institution are found in an anonymous poem of the *Latin Anthology* on an immoral army officer; the poem notes that both the *fiscus* and the lot of the ordinary soldier are impoverished by the steady misappropriation of military provisions (*populi pastus*).[94]

Fulgentius also refers in passing to cash donatives to Vandal troops on garrison duty.[95] It seems likely that units stationed in towns were paid directly from the *fiscus*, rather than from their own landholdings, or the estates of their superior officers. One frequently cited example derives from the city of Tipasa, in Mauretania Caesariensis. This town lay far beyond the *sortes Vandalorum* proper, but was of some strategic importance, and evidently housed at least a nominal Vandal presence, to judge from Victor's accounts of persecution there, and from the coins found in two Vandal-period hoards from the Villa of the Frescoes in the city.[96] Although the majority were minted locally, and only one named Vandal coin was included among the finds – a *nummus* of King Thrasamund – a number of anonymous bronzes have cautiously been identified as Carthaginian issues of the Vandal period.[97] This in itself is significant: low-denomination Vandal coins were primarily minted for use in Carthage and its immediate hinterland – at least this is where most known examples have been found.[98] While the handful of Vandal bronzes from Tipasa may simply be a chance survival, the implications of this for the circulation of money in Vandal Africa are significant; military payment may then have been a stimulus for the circulation of money – at least in the African regions beyond Zeugitana.

Coins and Vandal Monetary Policy

The large number of coins that survive from the Vandal kingdom and surrounding regions provide an invaluable adjunct to the understanding of the post-Roman economy, but their interpretation is rarely straightforward.[99] On the one hand, numismatic evidence provides unrivalled access to the everyday world of commerce and exchange in the fifth and sixth centuries. The coins themselves are diverse and fascinating, and the patterns of their production and development (where these can be traced) provide a rare point of contact between the long rhythms of the North African economy and the short-term actions of the Hasding kings. The iconography on the coins also hints at the ideologies of the powers that produced them.[100] But the evidential base is far from perfect. The overwhelming majority of extant coins are known from stray finds either in the field or the auction house, or have only the most approximate archaeological context. Where coins were deposited in hoards, and where these hoards have been excavated and published, the numismatist is provided with a useful impression of the different coins likely to have been in circulation at the time of deposition. In many cases it is difficult to ascertain precisely when such hoards were deposited. Most of the coins in circulation in Vandal Africa were undated and anonymous issues, with little immediate clue to their point of origin; many were minted in deliberate emulation of existing imperial coins, with greater or lesser degrees of success; many clearly remained in circulation for decades – even centuries – after their original production. Rich as the numismatic evidence is, then, its interpretation can only be undertaken with some caution.

In the first decades of the Vandal kingdom, monetary exchange was carried out almost entirely through the medium of imperial coins which remained in circulation. In fiscal terms, the gold *solidus* was by far the most important form of currency, and it retained its significance (and solidity) throughout the Vandal century.[101] It was the *solidus* which had provided the foundation for the substantial bureaucratic reforms of the fourth century, and it remained a trustworthy 'gold standard' and currency of account into the Justinianic period and beyond. The Albertini Tablets employ the *solidus* as a unit of account for large values, although here it seems clear that payment was typically rendered in bronze *folles* of much lower value. For all of these transactions, the population of Vandal Africa used gold coins minted outside the kingdom, and their appetite for the yellow metal was impressive.[102] In the first half of the fifth century, gold coins came into Africa from both the western and eastern halves of the empire in roughly equal proportion. Thereafter, however, almost all of the *solidi* in use originated in the eastern mints, a pattern which closely parallels the increased circulation of eastern ceramics in the western Mediterranean discussed above.[103]

a. An African imitation of a Honorian silver issue, probably dating to the reign of Geiseric (BM Cat. Wroth I [Vandals] Gaiseric 6 [AR])

b. A bronze issue of 42 *nummi*, with a horse's head image on the reverse, probably dating to the reign of Gunthamund (BM Cat. Wroth I [Vandals] Gaiseric 10 [AE])

c. A bronze issue of 42 *nummi* with NXLII and wreath on reverse, probably dating to the reign of Gunthamund (BM Cat. Wroth I [Vandals] Huneric 3 [AE])

d. A bronze issue of 42 *nummi* with NXLII and wreath on reverse, probably dating to the reign of Gunthamund (BM Cat. Wroth I [Vandals] Huneric 8 [AE])

e. A bronze issue of 4 *nummi* with a bust on the obverse and the value on the reverse, probably dating to the reign of Gunthamund (BM Cat. Wroth I [Vandals] Huneric 18 [AE])

f. A silver issue of 100 *denarii*, dating from the reign of Gunthamund (BM Cat. Wroth I [Vandals] Gunthamund 2 [AR])

g. A silver issue of 50 *denarii*, dating from the reign of Gunthamund (BM Cat. Wroth I [Vandals] Gunthamund 3 [AR])

h. A silver issue of 50 *denarii*, dating from the reign of Thrasamund (BM Cat. Wroth I [Vandals] Trasamund 10 [AR])

i. A silver issue of 50 *denarii*, dating from the reign of Thrasamund (BM Cat. Wroth I [Vandals] Trasamund 11)

j. A silver issue of 50 *denarii*, with a personification of Carthage on the reverse, dating from the reign of Hilderic (BM Cat. Wroth I [Vandals] Hilderic 4 [AR])

k. A silver issue of 50 *denarii*, dating from the reign of Gelimer (BM Cat. Wroth I [Vandals] Gelimer 1 [AR])

Figure 6.5 Vandal coin issues. © The Trustees of the British Museum

a. An African imitation of a Honorian silver issue, probably dating to the reign of Geiseric (BM Cat. Wroth I [Vandals] Gaiseric 6 [AR])

b. A bronze issue of 42 *nummi*, with a horse's head image on the reverse, probably dating to the reign of Gunthamund (BM Cat. Wroth I [Vandals] Gaiseric 10 [AE])

c. A bronze issue of 42 *nummi* with NXLII and wreath on reverse, probably dating to the reign of Gunthamund (BM Cat. Wroth I [Vandals] Huneric 3 [AE])

d. A bronze issue of 42 *nummi* with NXLII and wreath on reverse, probably dating to the reign of Gunthamund (BM Cat. Wroth I [Vandals] Huneric 8 [AE])

e. A bronze issue of 4 *nummi* with a bust on the obverse and the value on the reverse, probably dating to the reign of Gunthamund (BM Cat. Wroth I [Vandals] Huneric 18 [AE])

f. A silver issue of 100 *denarii*, dating from the reign of Gunthamund (BM Cat. Wroth I [Vandals] Gunthamund 2 [AR])

g. A silver issue of 50 *denarii*, dating from the reign of Gunthamund (BM Cat. Wroth I [Vandals] Gunthamund 3 [AR])

h. A silver issue of 50 *denarii*, dating from the reign of Thrasamund (BM Cat. Wroth I [Vandals] Trasamund 10 [AR])

i. A silver issue of 50 *denarii*, dating from the reign of Thrasamund (BM Cat. Wroth I [Vandals] Trasamund 11)

j. A silver issue of 50 *denarii*, with a personification of Carthage on the reverse, dating from the reign of Hilderic (BM Cat. Wroth I [Vandals] Hilderic 4 [AR])

k. A silver issue of 50 *denarii*, dating from the reign of Gelimer (BM Cat. Wroth I [Vandals] Gelimer 1 [AR])

The failure of the Hasdings to strike gold coinage of their own may have an ideological significance, but precisely what this was has been much disputed. The apparent refusal of the Vandals to mint coins in gold when other barbarian kings readily did so has been variously explained as a reflection of their deference to imperial prerogative, a profound hatred of the empire, and the simple lack of economic necessity.[104] Of these explanations, the last seems the most likely: there was certainly enough imperial gold circulating in the region to save the Hasdings from the effort of minting their own. Imperial gold was trusted and, as long as African exports ensured its ready supply, there was little obvious need for the Vandals to mint gold coins in their own name.

The minting of lower denomination coinages was much more widespread. But evidence from hoards suggests that initially the majority of silver and bronze coins in circulation in Africa during the early years of the Vandal occupation had either been in circulation from before the conquest or were imported from outside.[105] Formal silver issues were relatively rare in the later Roman period, and lacked the authority of the gold *solidus*, but it was here that the Hasdings made their first tentative steps towards a meaningful monetary policy. The earliest coins which can be ascribed with confidence to the Vandals come from a series of imitation silver coins depicting the bust of the western emperor Honorius on the obverse, and the legend *VRBS ROMA* on the reverse.[106] These imitations have survived in relatively large numbers, most of which have been traced to a single hoard, which was probably deposited in around AD 480. There is some difficulty in establishing the date of these issues, but it seems likely that they were produced over a relatively long period, to judge from the deterioration of design and changing weights of extant specimens. These were probably produced during the reign of Geiseric, and were intended in part to fill a practical economic need for a high value quotidian coinage. It may also have reflected the sudden influx of bullion which came into Vandal hands at the time of the occupation of Carthage in AD 439 or (more probably) the sack of Rome in 455.

At some stage, these pseudo-imperial imitations were supplemented by a further series of Vandal issues, again based on imperial exemplars, but now marked with an image of the personified Carthage on the reverse, and countermarked clumsily with a recognizably 'Vandalic' dating system.[107] The handful of extant examples include only two distinct dates, *ANNO IIII K[arthago]* and *ANNO V K[arthago]*. Numismatists are agreed that these dates refer to the regnal years of a specific Vandal king, and have seen the inscription as a simple abbreviation of the dating formula *anno (N) Karthaginis domini nostri regis (X)*, also employed on the *ostraka* from Bir Trouch. There has been less agreement on the identity of the ruler concerned, but most scholars are content to regard them as the work of Huneric or Gunthamund. In all likelihood what we see here is the first direct Vandal intervention in the coinage of North Africa, broadly datable either to AD 480/1 (if the reign indicated is that of Huneric), or 488/9 (if we are to assume that it is Gunthamund), and thus an innovation of the mid-Vandal period.

Gunthamund was certainly responsible for the next major development in Vandal monetary policy. During his reign a series of silver coins were minted bearing the image of the king and the legend *DN Rex Gunthamundu* ('Our Lord, King Gunthamund').[108] On the reverse the values of the coins in the traditional silver unit of the denarius were prominently marked: 100, 50 and 25 *denarii*. The relative weights of these coins approximated their nominal values (so the 100 *denarius* coin weighed around twice as much as the 50, and so on). Gunthamund's successors followed his lead, and all minted coins under their own names, albeit with some fluctuation in weight and without the 100D denomination. Unremarkable as this might seem to modern commentators, the innovation was significant. The iconography of these new issues dispersed the image of the Vandal king and his rule throughout his territories. No less important was the reintroduction of silver as a medium of monetary exchange after a long period of abeyance, and, crucially, the introduction of an integrated coinage system in the name of the new king.

This last point only becomes fully apparent when parallel advances in the minting of base metal coinage are also taken into account. The vast majority of daily transactions in the Vandal kingdom took place, not in silver or gold, but in coins of copper or bronze. In the early decades of the Vandal occupation, these were typically older, sometimes centuries-old coins which remained in circulation, or had arrived in the kingdom having been minted elsewhere. The standard unit of this coinage was the *nummus*, although few of the thousands of extant coins may be ascribed specific monetary values with any confidence. According to a law of AD 445, the gold *solidus* was valued at 7,000 *nummi*, but rampant inflation (caused in part no doubt by the promiscuous minting of these small coins) had seen the rate of exchange rise to around 1:12,000, and perhaps beyond, by the last years of the fifth century.[109] Just as they did with the silver coinage, the Vandals authorized the production of imitation issues and a number of local ateliers also produced a bewildering array of different series to meet popular demand for local tokens for everyday transactions. Hoards from El Djem (dated to around AD 450), and Aïn Merane (deposited after 476) are testament to the variety of coin types in circulation, and include several examples inscribed *DOMINO NOSTRO* and *CARTAGINE P(er)P(etua)*, which may well have been produced under royal authority.[110] But again, it was only under Gunthamund that an attempt was made to bring order to this chaos of coinage through the denoting of specific values on the coins themselves.

By far the most common of Gunthamund's countermarked issues, and probably the most important, bore on its obverse a standing personification of Carthage, with an ear of grain in her hands. On the reverse was a prominent letter N, and beneath it the stylized figure XLII. Smaller coins from the same series are also known and bear the numbers NXXI, XII and IIII. A later series of these bronzes incorporates the legend *KARTHAGO*, along with a standing soldier in place of the personification, and a horse's head, along with the denominations (in the same values) on the reverse.[111] Minting coins with marked values of 42, 21, 12 and 4 *nummi* may seem eccentric at first sight, but there was an impressive method in this numerical madness. As several scholars have noted, figures of 42 and 21 make perfect sense within a duodecimal system of monetary reckoning, in which *nummi* were bound directly to larger denominations. We know that the standard unit of account in the fourth and fifth centuries was the gold *solidus*. The next denomination down, conventionally labelled the '*siliqua*' by modern numismatists, was valued at $^1/_{24}$ of a *solidus*. The named silver coins of Gunthamund almost certainly represent the *siliqua* and its fractions. If it is assumed that, by Gunthamund's reign, the value of the solidus was 12,000 *nummi*, the *siliqua* would therefore be worth 500 *nummi*. In the light of these ratios, the coins of 42 and 21 *nummi* may be recognized as representing $^1/_{12}$ and $^1/_{24}$ of a *siliqua* respectively (the precise figures are $41^2/_3$ and $20^5/_6$, but 42 and 21 represent the closest whole numbers). All this constitutes, in other words, an integrated exchange system between bronze, silver and (in principle) gold, with the respective values of each coin clearly marked upon them.

The date of this innovation is not clear, and the problem is complicated by the fact that similar developments were taking place in Italy at around the same time. Italian mints produced bronze coins to the value of 40 and 20 *nummi* under either Odoacer or Theoderic.[112] Because neither the Italian nor the African coins can be dated precisely, it is unclear whether the Hasdings followed an Italian innovation or vice versa; or indeed whether the new minting represented a joint innovation under the rulers of Africa and Italy together.[113] Most scholars have been content to assume that the issues can be dated to the 480s or 490s, and that they certainly anticipate the Byzantine monetary reform of 498 (which was itself influenced by this system). Regardless of its precise date, the programme seems to have been a success. Bronze coins (both marked and unmarked) circulated relatively freely between Italy, Africa and the western Mediterranean islands, and the Anastasian reforms of 498 and 512 both regularized the system and backed it with imperial authority.[114] Thirty years later, Justinian would embrace the monetary systems of his newly-conquered territories in Africa and Italy, and in Carthage remained an important mint throughout the sixth century.

Taken as a whole, the numismatic evidence hints at an impressively international monetary economy. The discovery of coins of African origin in the coastal regions of Italy and in the Vandal-held islands broadly corresponds to the trade patterns suggested by African finewares. Particular concentrations have also been found in south-eastern Spain, although there are fewer than might be expected along the southern Gallic coast.[115] The large number of foreign coins found within Africa testifies to the same phenomenon in reverse, and provides further confirmation of the eastward shift economic activity over the course of the fifth century.

The local distribution of Vandal coins within Africa is also illuminating. Gunthamund's named issues did not circulate far from Carthage, and bronzes of recognizably 'Vandal' origin are rarely found outside the heartland of the kingdom in Zeugitana, northern Byzacena and eastern Numidia.[116] Indeed, amid the profusion of local coinages produced during the fifth and sixth centuries, the named and marked currencies of the Vandal kings represented only a very small minority. This is not to suggest that the provinces beyond the *sortes Vandalorum* were unaffected by the monetary changes of the centre; the Albertini Tablets provide striking evidence for an active monetary economy within the pre-desert fringe, even if a close reading of the prices contained within these documents hint at an exchange rate somewhat different from that institutionalized in Hasding Carthage.[117] What is significant, though, is that the inhabitants of the *fundus Tuletianos* (and estates like it throughout North Africa) employed their own local currencies more or less tied to the economic conventions of the centre but probably minted relatively close at hand. Developments in Carthage remained important to the inhabitants of rural Africa, but many of their transactions took place within their own profoundly localized micro-economies.

Conclusions: The Economy of Vandal Africa

The Hasdings did have a role to play within the economic development of their kingdom, but the prosperity of the region, and the difficulties it faced, resulted from factors far beyond the control of the rulers in Carthage. Like other regions in the Late Antique Mediterranean, North Africa had started to undergo substantial changes from the fourth century, for social and political as well as economic reasons. This reached a tipping point in the western Mediterranean in the middle of the fifth century, when the collapse of the imperial taxation system removed one of the major supports for the economy of the empire. The Vandals can claim some responsibility for this change – it was, after all, the capture of Carthage which marked the end of the *annona*, and the sack of Rome in 455 certainly added to the woes of the western empire. But the full economic implications of these actions were revealed only slowly.

Within North Africa, the Vandals presided over something of an Indian summer for the ancient economy. Farms continued to produce and even diversified, many towns continued to flourish, and money which once flowed northwards to the imperial capital remained within Africa itself, to the benefit of its inhabitants. This was not a situation which could last forever: prosperity depends upon continued demand as well as supply, and there is every indication that this had begun to decline over the course of the fifth century. To the Hasdings' credit, however, they did not simply watch the great imperial economic machine unwind. The Vandal state continued to tax its inhabitants, and to provide some degree of public spending. Equally significantly, the Hasding kings followed an ambitious monetary policy, which further stimulated daily exchange within the kingdom and (more importantly) acted as a catalyst for international contact with both Italy and the eastern empire.

When Belisarius and Procopius entered Carthage, they found a fiscal system which they could barely understand; to be re-integrated into the new Roman empire, the region would have to undergo a complete financial re-appraisal. The effort which this took testifies to the changes which had taken place in the African economy (and in the economy of Constantinople) since 439, but should not be regarded as evidence for its failure. As Procopius testifies, the Vandals were extraordinarily rich at the time of the Byzantine conquest, but it seems likely that many of their Roman subjects were too.

7

Religion and the Vandal Kingdom

> A man such as he had to see cities overthrown and destroyed and within them their inhabitants and their buildings on their estates wiped out by a murderous enemy, and others put to flight and scattered. He saw churches denuded of priests and ministers, holy virgins and others vowed to chastity dispersed, some amongst them succumbing to tortures, others perishing by the sword.[1]

Such was the bleak account of the last days of Augustine of Hippo, Africa's greatest ecclesiastical figure, left by his biographer and protégé, Possidius, bishop of Calama. The 'murderous enemy', whose rampage through Africa in the 420s AD was so vividly described by Possidius, were the Vandals. Indeed, Augustine was said to have died whilst the Vandal army was actually besieging his episcopal see of Hippo Regius.[2]

From the existing accounts of the invasion, mostly supplied by partisan ecclesiastical writers, it would be easy to gain the impression that the violent eradication of the Nicene Church from Africa was high on the agenda of Geiseric, the Arian king of the Vandals.[3] Arianism had developed out of conflicting views within the Christian community over the exact relationship between God the Father, Jesus the Son, and the Holy Spirit. For the Alexandrian priest, Arius (250–336), and many others especially in the Eastern Church, the answer was that the Son had been created by God, His Father. Thus, God the Father as Unbegotten (always existing), was separate and superior to Jesus, the only begotten. The Holy Spirit, the last component of the Trinity, had been created by the Son under the auspices of the Father – and was therefore subservient to them both.

Arius' views, although accepted in some quarters, were strongly opposed by others in the church – particularly as they appeared to undermine the divinity of Jesus Christ. At the Council of Nicaea, convoked by the first Christian emperor Constantine in 325, Arius' theological opponents won a great victory. A new creed was formulated that defined the relationship between Father and Son as being one of consubstantiality (*Homoousios*) – of the same substance. In other words, God existed as three persons, the Father, Son and Holy Spirit but only as One Being. Arius and other hard-line supporters who refused to accept this ruling were subsequently exiled by the Roman emperor Constantine and their theological work was banned.

The controversy was by no means brought to a conclusion by Nicaea, however. In the following decades imperial intervention, which often sought to affect some kind of compromise between the main protagonists, had, in fact, had the opposite effect and saw the hardening of attitudes on both sides. Many eastern churchmen were unsatisfied with the Nicene solution, which seemed to be extra-scriptural, and to deny any difference between the Father and the Son. Consequently, the 'Homoean' school argued that a vision of the Son as 'like' the Father (*homoios*) did better justice to the scriptural evidence. It won official imperial support under Constantius II, and the backing of enough bishops to be enshrined as doctrine at the Councils of Seleucia and Rimini in AD 359. This new settlement was rejected following the death of Constantius in 361, but was revived by Valentinian I and Valens. Only after the Council of Constantinople in AD 381, when the emperor Theodosius threw his weight behind *homoousios*, was Nicene Christianity firmly established as the orthodoxy. Theodosius had then set about dismantling the Arian Church in Constantinople. Demphilus, the bishop of the imperial capital, was expelled and an imperial edict banned the heresy within the Roman Empire and handed over all of their churches and property to the Nicene establishment.[4]

Arianism returned to prominence during the military crises of the early fifth century. The Roman army was heavily Arian, and the rise to prominence of a new generation of generalissimos changed the religious landscape of the empire. This was the environment in which the barbarian warbands developed, and it is likely that the Arianism of the Goths and Vandals was shaped by their prolonged contact with the Roman military. Traditions certainly circulated about the Arian missions to the barbarians of the Danube, which had been sponsored by the emperor Valens in the mid-fourth century, but the majority of the barbarian groups had simply adopted the religious customs of the Roman army.[5] Others appear to have become Arian Christians later. The date of the Vandal conversion to Arianism is unknown and much disputed; it is commonly supposed that it was a result of coming into contact with the Arian Visigoths in either Gaul or Spain.[6]

Looking back on this period, Nicene ecclesiastical writers portrayed the Vandals as Arian fanatics who had persecuted the Homoousian Church since before their arrival in North Africa.[7] Once the Vandals had arrived in Africa, Quodvultdeus and other members of the Nicene ecclesiastical hierarchy represented the conversion of Homoousians as one of Geiseric's priorities. Prosper's account of the Vandal occupation is typical:

> Neither refraining from despoiling churches, which were deprived of both their sacred vessels and the administration of priests, nor from the places of the divine cult, he immediately ordered them to be his own dwellings. Savage towards every group of captive people, but especially hostile towards the noble and religious, he did not seem to be attacking men as much as he was attacking God.[8]

Other accounts emphasize the devastation suffered by the African Church in the first years of the occupation. Possidius, in particular, provides a moving account of the effects of the invasion: churches remained empty and for those who sought the divine sacraments, it became difficult to find anyone administer them. Clergy were reduced to hiding in caves and other remote places, or they were stripped of their assets and reduced to begging. According to Possidius only the churches of Carthage, Hippo Regius and Cirta survived the onslaught.[9]

Life certainly became far more difficult for the Nicene Church in North Africa after the invasion. The gradual Vandal encroachment across the region was a cause of great alarm within African ecclesiastical circles. This can be plainly seen in a letter sent by an African bishop, Honoratus, to Augustine asking whether or not clergy should flee from these barbarians:

> If it is important to remain in the churches, I do not see how we can benefit either ourselves or to our congregations, whilst before our eyes men are murdered, women raped and we are ourselves collapse under torture, whilst what we do not possess is demanded of us.[10]

In AD 431 Capreolus, bishop of Carthage, was compelled to write to the assembled Christian bishops at the Council of Ephesus explaining why none of their African episcopal colleagues would be in attendance:

> For the prompt ability of any that could travel is impeded by the excessive multitude of enemies and the huge devastation of the provinces everywhere

> which presents to eye-witnesses one place where all its inhabitants have been killed, another where they have been driven into flight, and a wretched vista of destruction spreading out far and wide and in every direction.[11]

Geiseric's reputation as an Arian zealot deepened shortly after the treaty of AD 435 had created a Vandal homeland around Hippo Regius. According to Prosper, the king attempted to destroy the power of the Nicene Church in his new territories by seizing the basilicas of three of the most intransigent bishops and expelling them from their cities.[12] After the capture of Carthage in 439, Geiseric transferred the episcopal seat to the Arians and shut down the other Nicene churches in the city. He then stripped Quodvultdeus and his clergy and loaded them onto a leaking ship with the intention that they should drown at sea.[13] This boat struggled to Naples, where the bishop settled for the remainder of his life until he died in sometime in the early 450s.[14] Geiseric was also said to have exiled many other North African bishops during his period.[15]

Although Arianism had never been strong in North Africa, Arian clergy had begun to appear there during the last decades of Roman rule, usually as members of the personal entourages of senior military officials. This was a development that had provoked a number of public confrontations with Nicene churchmen such as Augustine.[16] Quodvultdeus was quick to conflate the proselytizing activities of these Arian clergy with the Vandal takeover. In a sermon thought to have been delivered at the time of the fall of Carthage, the bishop argued that the Vandals were in fact the shock troops of Arianism and urged his congregation to resist:

> Why are you silent? Your enemies who detest you, they have said that you are inferior to God, they have humiliated you by re-baptising your members. . . . Therefore Lord Jesus Christ, our David, our King, take up your war baggage and go forward to fight against him who casts reproach upon the army of the living God.[17]

In another homily given in Carthage, Quodvultdeus warned catechumens about the Arian missionaries who would attempt to catch them at times of weakness and despair.

> Do not permit the Arian heretic to revile the Church. He is a wolf: recognise it. He is a serpent: smash his brains in. He flatters but he deceives. He promises much but defrauds. 'Come', he says, 'I will protect you. If you are in trouble, I will feed you; if stripped bare, I will clothe you. I will give you money; I will arrange it so that you receive a daily allowance.'[18]

However, an elision of the initial aims of Geiseric in North Africa and the Arian Church should be treated with some scepticism. Other accounts of Vandal Arianism suggest that the adoption of the faith was largely pragmatic. In the mid-sixth century Jordanes claimed that the Vandals had offered to convert if the emperor promised to help them against their enemies.[19] A rumour had also spread about that Geiseric had, in fact, only abandoned the Nicene faith for Arianism whilst in Spain, implying that he was something of an opportunist.[20] Although personal belief most probably did play some part in the adoption of Homoian Christianity by Geiseric, there were other motivations too. Christianity was the religion of the Roman Empire and, as we have seen, part of Geiseric's success was his ability to appropriate and adapt different aspects of Roman political, economic, military and cultural structures. As Peter Heather has suggested a particular attraction for the leader of a fairly recently integrated grouping was the position that Christian emperors had enjoyed as divinely appointed rulers. Thus:

> The Empire offered Geiseric both a model of an entwined Church and state, and Homoean theology an appropriate but different brand of Christianity with which to recreate the model for his own purposes.[21]

However, initially at least, Geiseric and the Vandals targeted the African Nicene Church because of its wealth, and not because of any particular religious fervour.[22] Some churches were handed over to the Arians but Nicene land and other assets were also kept by Geiseric and his family, or distributed amongst the Vandals.[23] Many of the accounts provided by Nicene ecclesiastical figures of the worst excesses of the occupation focussed on the confiscation rather than destruction of church property; this implies that economic opportunism rather than strongly held belief was the dominant motivation behind these actions.[24]

As his hold on Proconsularis became more secure, Geiseric would increasingly use religious affairs, and particularly the threat of the persecution of the Nicene Church in Africa, as a way of leveraging concessions out of the various claimants to Roman imperial authority in the west. The appointment of Deogratias as Nicene bishop of Carthage in 454 was almost certainly determined by diplomatic considerations, perhaps a desire to secure the marriage of Huneric to the emperor Valentinian III's daughter, Eudocia.[25] When that marriage alliance failed to secure him the status amongst the other power brokers in the western Mediterranean that he desired, Geiseric once more changed his domestic religious policy by not replacing Deogratias when he died in 457.[26]

Despite the somewhat resigned tenor of many of the descriptions of the Vandal invasion provided by the ecclesiastical community, it is clear that many of their accounts were intended to help defend the integrity and authority of their church from the Arians. For African Homoousians, their ace in the hole was Augustine of Hippo, who in death would prove himself to be as formidable opponent of heresy as when he was alive. Possidius' biography of Augustine, for example, was primarily written as a way of instructing African Nicene clerics how to respond to the Arian Vandals in what was a post-Augustinian world. In particular, the work placed a heavy emphasis on Augustine's diligence in respect to fulfilling his pastoral duties – travelling around Africa, writing letters, ministering to his people as both a priest and a judge.[27] This was a model that its author clearly considered that African Nicene clerics should follow themselves.[28] Moreover, a long letter from Augustine to Honoratus, bishop of Thiave, on how to face the Vandal challenge, that takes up nearly 20 per cent of the whole biography, was certainly included as part of this strategy.[29] In highlighting Augustine's commitment to the ascetic, and particularly, monastic life, Possidius was placing such practices at the centre of Nicene resistance to the Vandal Arian challenge, a development that would have important implications towards the end of the Vandal epoch.[30]

There were other Nicene responses to the difficult circumstances that now faced them. For much of the Vandal tenure in Africa, exile proved to be a cruel but effective weapon against the ecclesiastical leadership of the Nicene Church, but these churchmen did their best to overcome this obstacle. Quodvultdeus' writings suggest that his long sojourn in Naples had led to his increasing marginalization from contemporary affairs in Africa. His most significant work, the *Book of Promises and Predictions of God* (*Liber de Promissionum*), was written in Italy in the later 440s. In it, Quodvultdeus used scriptural testimonies to show his audience that they needed to put aside the pleasures of the world and to prepare themselves for the coming apocalypse. The exiled bishop insisted, through a multitude of biblical illustrations, that Arianism in Africa was the harbinger of the apocalypse, and that his audience needed to start paying attention to his warnings:

> And the apostle John says: 'You have heard that Antichrist is coming; now there are many antichrists' [1 John 2.18]. And he shows who these are: 'They went out from us', he says, 'but they were not of us. For if they had been of us, they would certainly have remained with us' [1 John 2.19]. He is exposing all heretics and especially the Arians whom we now see

> seducing many either with temporal power or with the industry of an evil genius or with a certain moderation of temperance or the deception of all sorts of signs.[31]

Quodvultdeus also hints at the concerns that lay behind these dire warnings. After providing a theological rebuttal of Arianism, the exiled bishop spelled out the mortal dangers of succumbing to the pressure of their missionaries. Conversion to Arianism would end in damnation in the eternal fire of the apocalypse.[32] The re-baptism that the Homoians insisted upon merely led to multiplication rather than the absolution of sins.[33] However for those who repented quickly salvation could still be attained:[34]

> Accordingly every person re-baptised by heretics, whether he voluntarily cast off Christ his vestment [Gal. 3.27] or faltered in persecution, lost the Christ clothing that he had. Therefore while there is time let him return despoiled and naked, repenting before his merciful father, who orders that the best robe and the ring of dignity be given back at once to the returning prodigal son [Luke 15.22].[35]

Quodvultdeus identified his intended readership through his description of their favoured pastimes – fishing, board games, mimes, acrobats, plays, singing, feasting with flowers and music – activities particularly associated with wealthy educated young laymen.[36] It has been argued that his target was the noble Roman youth in Ostrogothic Italy, but there is reason to think that it was their Romano-African counterparts that he was primarily addressing.[37] The longer that Quodvultdeus and other Nicene clergy remained in exile, the bolder the claims that had to be made in order to sustain the interest and attention of their distant African congregations.

That the *Book of Promises* was so packed full of scriptural testimonies was also a deliberate strategy on the part of its author. One of the major criticisms levelled at the Homoousian position towards the Holy Trinity was that it relied heavily on non-Christian philosophical terms such as *ousia* (substance) and *homoousios* itself (consubstance). In contrast, the Arians or Homoians shunned such language and instead insisted on solely using terms that appeared in the scriptures.[38] Large quantities of African-authored anti-Arian literature that explicitly made extensive use of exempla from the scriptures to support the Nicene position began to appear.[39] The text *Against Varimadus* (*Contra Varimadum*) is one such example: a strong rebuttal of a series of objections to the Homoousian position ascribed to an Arian deacon, Varimadus.[40] The tract was written by an anonymous African exile in Naples, and reads like an instruction manual of how to counter Arianism:

> If they say to you 'the Son is not equal to the Father', you reply thus 'If the Son is not equal to the Father, then why did John the Evangelist testify about him in this manner, "Therefore", he said, "the Jews persecuted Jesus and they sought to kill him, because not only did he break the Sabbath and he also called God his father, making himself equal to God." '[41]

The author of *Against Varimadus* was clearly anxious to demonstrate the strength of the scriptural testimony that could be used against the Arians.[42]

This emphasis on scriptural quotations in African anti-Arian tracts continued for much of the second half of the sixth century and was clearly intended to protect African Homoousians from proselytizing Arians.[43] It was not just treatises and quotation crib sheets that were produced. One text purports to reproduce the exchanges from a debate between the Nicene bishop Cerealis of Castellum and an Arian bishop Maximinus in Carthage, which may have taken place in the 480s.[44] As might be expected, biblical authority was a key theme of the Nicene case, at least as it is presented here; as one scholar has recently commentated: 'He [Cerealis] proceeds to drown Maximinus in a deluge of scriptural citations drawn from almost every book in the bible and interspersed with brief commentaries, thereby reducing his opponent to silence.'[45]

Huneric, Victor of Vita and the Great Persecution

For many contemporary writers, the vicious persecutions that took place in the latter part of Huneric's reign encapsulated the hostility of the Vandals towards the Nicene Church. The most important of these authors, of course, was Victor of Vita, whose *History of the Persecutions* (*Historia Persecutionis*) was probably written in the late 480s. Little is known about Victor's background. Some scholars have argued that the references within the text suggest that he held an ecclesiastical office. At the time that he was writing there was indeed a Victor who was bishop of the see of Vita in Byzacena. However, although Victor wrote knowledgably about the Council of 484, scholars are unsure about whether this particular bishop was actually in attendance. This has led some to contend that the historian was more likely to have been a junior member of the Nicene clergy at the time of the persecution.[46] It has even been argued that Victor's particular fascination with medical terminology might indicate that he may have been a doctor.[47]

Victor portrayed the Vandals as being implacably and violently opposed to the true Catholic faith from their first arrival on the shores of North Africa. According to Victor, churches, shrines, monasteries and even cemeteries were ransacked, destroyed or turned over to the Arian priesthood.[48] Bishops, clergy and Catholic dignitaries were cruelly tortured, murdered or exiled.[49] In his work, Victor presents a marked escalation of the Vandal persecution as it mushroomed from its initial target of the Catholic ecclesiastical elite to their lay counterparts before engulfing all socio-economic groups in North Africa.[50] In sum, Victor created a coherent narrative of a Vandal persecution where previously there had been none.

Although the accession of Huneric to the Vandal throne brought with it a brief lull in the persecution, and the appointment of a new Nicene Primate of Carthage after a lacuna of 24 years, Victor made it clear that this was never anything more than a temporary respite.[51] Provoked by his Arian clergy, Huneric unleashed an even more savage repression, during which men and women of the Nicene faith were subjected to a series of torments including scalping, forced labour and execution by sword and fire.[52] Homoousian priests were banned from practicing the liturgy and nearly 5,000 bishops and clergy were sent into exile in the desert where they suffered terrible deprivation and hardships at the hands of their Moorish guards.[53]

In AD 483, the campaign against the Nicene Church was further intensified when Huneric issued a royal edict ordering all the Catholic bishops to attend a conference at Carthage where they would debate with their Arian counterparts the theological issues that divided them.[54] The Catholic Primates of Numidia and Byzacena responded by producing a lengthy document that outlined their theological position in regards to con-substance of the Father and the Son.[55] Huneric's own riposte was to order that all Nicene churches and property were to remain closed and to be handed over to either the Royal Fisc and the Arian Church.[56] Nicene clergy were forbidden to hold meetings or practice baptism or ordination on the threat of heavy fines and imprisonment. Homoousian books were to be destroyed by fire. Nicene laity lost the right to make or receive bequests. If they subsequently failed to abide by these laws, they were to be punished with the rod and exile. Palace officials, members of the civic elite, estate owners, lease-holders, tenants and the general citizenry faced dismissal and ruinous fines. Judges who failed to strictly enforce these penalties were to be punished by death, and their superiors burdened with heavy fines.[57] The Catholic bishops who had come to Carthage had all of their property seized and were sent off to work as agricultural serfs in Africa or to cut timber in Corsica for the royal navy.[58] Arian thugs were also sent throughout the kingdom in order to harass the Catholic laity where they committed many atrocities.[59]

Victor was not the only Nicene author who produced such works at this time. Also extant is a text entitled the *Passion of the Seven Monks* (*Passio Septem Monachorum*), an account of the martyrdom of seven brothers from a monastery at Gafsa which is often associated with Victor but was probably written by a later imitator.[60] This *Passion* describes how the abbot of the monastery Liberatus, a deacon Boniface, two sub-deacons Servus and Rusticus and three monks Rogatus, Septimus and Maximus were taken by force to Carthage where through flattery and the promise of honours and rewards attempts were made to get them to renounce their Nicene faith.[61] When these blandishments failed, they were thrown into prison and tortured before being loaded onto a boat that was subsequently set on fire and unmoored so that it would drift out to sea. However the fire was miraculously extinguished, so that the order was then given to beat the prisoners to death with the ship's oars. After they had achieved martyrdom, their remains were buried in the monastery of Bigua at Carthage.

Scholars have long debated the motivations that lay behind the writing of the *History of the Persecutions* and the *Passion of the Seven Monks*. It has been argued that Victor's principal ambition was to ingratiate himself with Gunthamund, Huneric's successor to the Vandal throne.[62] Victor certainly refers in the *History* to a marked improvement in the circumstances faced by the Catholics under the new king.[63] This concession to Gunthamund might well have been looked on favourably by the new Hasding ruler, and the consistent denigration of the reviled Huneric would also have won a favourable hearing at the court of his successor.[64] But Gunthamund himself remained Arian, and Victor's attempts to underscore the barbarity of the Vandals do not sit particularly comfortably with this theory.

Others have put forward the more plausible suggestion that Victor composed his text as a plea for outside intervention, and may have intended it to be read in both Rome and Constantinople.[65] The *Historia* was clearly intended to present the Vandal kingdom as the stage for widespread and longstanding religious conflict between barbarian Arians and Romano-African Catholics; Victor's *Historia* might well have been aimed at stirring up the passions of the wider Nicene community, whose attention may have drifted from events in Africa.[66] In the period which followed the publication of Victor's work, the suffering of the Nicenes in Africa enjoyed a particular prominence throughout the Mediterranean, and Victor can take some of the credit for this transformation.[67] Victor's influence has certainly been detected behind a letter written by the pope Gelasius in AD 496 that acknowledged the African Catholic Church's dogged resistance in the face of Arian persecution.[68]

Victor also intended his *Historia* to be read in North Africa, of course, particularly given the sustained challenge that the Arian clergy increasingly posed to the Nicene congregations.[69] Nicene Christians are known to have converted to Arianism, and Victor's references to this phenomenon betray his obvious anxiety.[70] The Council of Rome held in AD 487 was attended by four African bishops and discussed what should happen to both Nicene bishops and clergy who had lapsed from their faith.[71]

Other extraordinary evidence for the pressure that the African Nicene Church was now under is found in the revisions that were added in 487 to the *Notitia provinciarum et civitatum Africa*. This text was a list of the names of all 459 African Homoousian bishops who had been present at the conference in Carthage in AD 484. In a recent article Yves Modéran has convincingly argued that the acronym *prbt*, a modification found in connection with 88 of these bishops, which stood for *qui perierunt,* had nothing to do with the actual physical deaths of these individuals but rather their spiritual demise. In others words, these formerly Nicene bishops, who made up nearly 20 per cent of the total of the African Homoousian episcopate, had converted to Arianism within three years of the great conference.[72] Persecution clearly bore dividends. Such data strongly suggest that Victor wrote his *Historia* as an attempt to stem the flow not only of apostasy amongst lay congregations, but also from the ranks of the clergy and the episcopacy in the face of sustained Arian pressure.

Like his predecessors, Victor was anxious to present the cause of African Arianism as being inextricably intertwined with Vandal violence. Despite the blood-curdling nature of some of his episodes, however, the persecutions of the fifth century AD actually produced rather fewer martyrdoms than Victor seems to imply.[73] The point is illustrated by a typically dramatic introduction to one particular episode:

> I lack the ability to recount the events which happened in the town of Culusi, because it is beyond human power even to count the number of martyrs and confessors there.[74]

The one example that Victor provides is not a martyr (one who dies for their faith), but rather a confessor (who risks death, but is not killed). His account describes the torture of a married woman called Victoria, who was publicly tortured, and forced to endure her husband's pleas that she recant her faith for the sake of her children. She refused, of course, and Victor describes how she was later carried away 'completely lifeless' (*omni parte exanimam*) from her place of torture. But Victoria was not dead. Victor explains this through the intervention of the Virgin Mary, but this cannot disguise the fact that his heroine had not made the ultimate sacrifice for her faith.

This is a common strategy throughout the *Historia*. Victor repeatedly stresses the innumerable martyrs who died under the Vandals, but the detailed narratives that he provides are far more frequently related to the deeds of the confessors.[75] Victor's *Historia* is certainly littered with corpses, but when we remove those individuals who were murdered for political reasons, and discount the historian's more ambiguous accounts of mass-murder, we are left with only five specific martyrs (and only one of these individuals certainly died).[76] This is not to suggest that Victor's confessors did not suffer unutterably under Geiseric and Huneric, or to challenge the obvious intensity of their faith, but Victor's own legerdemain in representing their sufferings suggests that he was well aware of the need to dramatize their story still further.[77]

It is certainly striking how often the victims of Huneric's violence in Victor's narrative were not Romano-Africans but members of the Vandal royal family and their entourages who were clearly Arians.[78] The historian implies that the motivation behind this round of blood-letting was to secure Huneric's hold on power.[79] Nicene officials at the Vandal palace were also persecuted, of course, but this too was frequently related to political unrest, and religion may have provided little more than a convenient pretext for these purges.[80]

The persecutions affected different regions of the Vandal kingdom in different ways. For much of the Vandal period, the suppression of the Homoousian Church was restricted to Carthage and the province of Africa Proconsularis, where the ban on Nicene worship and the confiscation of church property appear to have been more rigorously enforced.[81] The numbers of bishops from dioceses in Africa Proconsularis were certainly depleted far faster than in the other parts of the kingdom, which suggests that the prohibition of new appointments there had a serious impact.[82]

Victor records the intensity of the physical damage that the Vandals caused to the Nicene Church in Carthage. He relates that the barbarians destroyed a number of important Christian monuments including the

Temple of Memoria and the Basilica Maiorum, where the celebrated martyrs Perpetua and Felicita were interred.[83] Yet archaeological excavation reveals that other ecclesiastical structures were renovated or even constructed anew during this period, including the suburban cemetery church of Bir El Knissa and possibly its counterpart at Bir Ftouah.[84] Recently another church has been added to this list at Bir Messaouda, an important neighbourhood that straddled the Decumanus Maximus, the thoroughfare which connected the administrative centre at Byrsa Hill to the ports. The basilica of this church consisted of a central nave and two other north–south orientated aisles and dates to a period after the middle of the fifth century; it was subject to a number of alterations before the Byzantine conquest.[85] Considering the strict control that the Vandal kings maintained over Carthage, it seems very likely that these building and renovation projects were undertaken by the Arian Church itself.

A very different picture of persecution emerges in Byzacena and Numidia, provinces where the Vandal presence was less marked. There the number of Homoousian bishops appears to have remained roughly constant.[86] Moreover, even the monasteries in those provinces seem to have been largely left alone despite their reputation as hotbeds of resistance to Arianism.[87]

The threat that Huneric posed to the Nicene Church was not just violence and thuggery but also came in the form of intellectual engagement. What we appear to be witnessing in Victor's extremely hostile account is evidence of a growing Vandal engagement with their own Arian faith. It is important to note that in his Royal Edict of 484 Huneric invoked the authority of two ecclesiastical councils of Ariminum and Seleucia that the Arian emperor Constantius II had convoked in 350 in an attempt to revise the Homoousian findings of Nicaea.[88] This betrays the king's pretensions to pseudo-imperial authority, of course, but also highlights a wider interest in specific issues of political theology. As one scholar has recently observed: 'Like many mainline Roman churchmen of the mid-fourth century, the fifth-century Vandals should be seen, therefore, as adherents of a more conservative theology, unhappy with the potentially embarrassing connotations of *homoousios*.'[89] In his letter to the emperor Zeno, moreover, Huneric assumed for himself mantle of the protector of all Arians, in the eastern Roman empire as well as his own kingdom. When he ordered the Nicene bishops to attend the council at Carthage it was with the expressed intention that they should engage in theological debate with their Arian counterparts.[90]

From the reactions of Quodvultdeus and others, it is clear that the Arian Church in Africa was by now engaged in a successful proselytizing

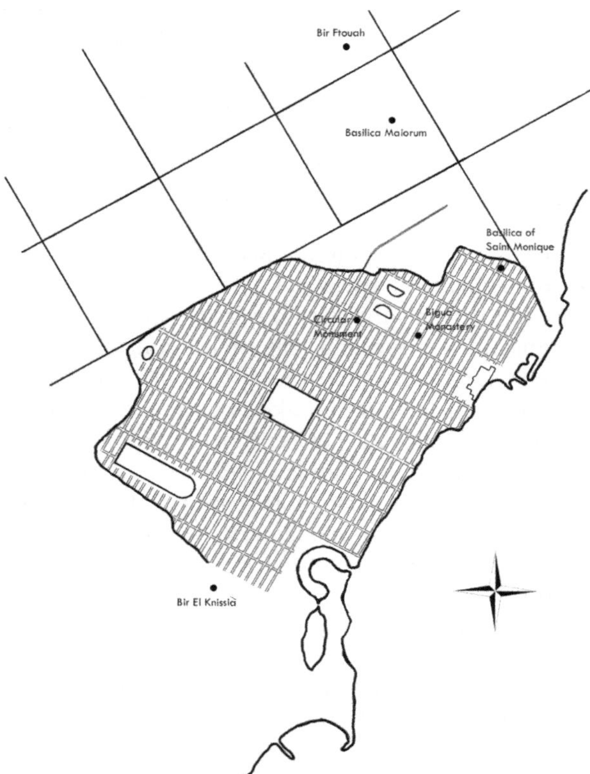

Figure 7.1 Religious buildings in Vandal Carthage

mission, which did not simply rely on state-sanctioned violence but also on a powerful intellectual assault on the theological precepts that provided the foundation for the Nicene position on the Trinity. As we have seen, the works of Quodvultdeus and the other anonymous ecclesiastical writers responded to this threat through the production of treatises, sermons and records of disputations that vigorously defended Homoousian beliefs and attacked Homoian ones. Victor, on the other hand, may also be seen as a reflection of another facet of the North African ecclesiastical polemical tradition – the martyr text. Persecution and martyrdom had played a central role in the forging of the identity of the Christian Church in North Africa since the great state-sponsored terrors of the third century AD.[91] Indeed the persecutions under the pagan emperors had been the last great period of African church unity. Victor's text should be read, at least partly, as a nostalgic attempt to reclaim a position of patient suffering that the Catholic Church had long since lost after it had come to be recognized by a series of Roman emperors in the fourth and early fifth centuries AD as the orthodox brand of Christianity in North Africa.

The Catholic Church had found itself uncomfortably cast in the role of persecutor, particularly during the first two decades of the fifth century AD. Under the implacable supervision of Augustine of Hippo and Aurelius of Carthage, the full weight of imperial censure was brought down on the 'Donatists', a breakaway sect who had split off from the established church during the early part of the fourth century.[92] This controversy was directly concerned with the whole issue of martyrdom – in particular the refusal of hardliners (who would become the 'Donatist' faction) to recognize the ecclesiastical authority of those who had abjured their Christianity during the great persecutions, and had subsequently returned to the church. The Donatists had many adherents throughout the cities, towns and villages of North Africa and had been successful in casting themselves as the true heirs of the original Christian martyrs. Now Vandal intolerance had allowed the Catholic Church to once more claim the high ground of martyrdom after a long hiatus.

It is clear that Victor himself was very aware of this long tradition and his text was consciously aligned with works of earlier Christian historians of the persecutions such as Eusebius of Caesarea and Lactantius.[93] This is particularly evident in Victor's emphasis upon the divine retribution directed at those who persecuted orthodox believers. His account of the death of a Vandal *millenarius* and his children after the former had maltreated his Catholic slaves is typical.[94] A later interpolation noted that Huneric had been consumed by worms as a direct result of his own actions[95], and the great famine that followed his persecution reflected divine judgement on the whole of his kingdom:

> This did not happen for no reason, but in accordance with the true and just judgement of God, so that where, because of the persecuting Arians, the water of the muddy whirlpool had bubbled with fire and sulphur, the rain which heaven bestows in its kindness and which had always been abundantly to hand was withheld.[96]

For Victor the Vandal Persecution presented a precious opportunity for the African Catholic Church to stand united once more under the banner of their shared suffering:

> May there now be present, I ask, people at every age, sex, and condition of life; may there now be present, I implore, the entire throng of the Catholic name carried in the womb of its mother. . . . Let them come together at the house of our grief and let us pour forth rivers of tears from our eyes together because the matter relates to the cause and faith that we have in common.[97]

But Quodvultdeus, Victor and other Nicene polemicists were also reacting to another very ancient conundrum that lay beyond not only their own control but also that of the Arians, namely the extent to which the theological divisions and loyalties which meant so much to themselves and their opponents were far less important to the laity in their congregations. Doctrinal ambivalence and the religious flexibility of African Christians was a far greater threat to the exiled Nicene Church than was Arian proselytizing during the second half of the fifth century AD.

Rough Tolerance and Religious Ambivalence in Vandal North Africa

One of the difficulties of studying a period which is so dominated by religious texts is that these sources rarely provide an accurate reflection of the interests and aspirations of the wider population. This is particularly true when examining fourth- and early fifth-century North Africa, where the works of Christian disputants, particularly Augustine of Hippo, create the erroneous impression that its inhabitants cared for little besides religious doctrine. The reality was that local political disputes in the towns, cities and villages of Late Antique North Africa were often dressed up as religious factionalism. If anything, the problem is still more acute in the study of the Vandal period.

Towards the end of his *Historia*, Victor issued a strident rejection of any pity that his plight as a persecuted Catholic might elicit from sympathetic Arians. 'I wish for no heretic to come and mourn with me . . . I do not want, no, I do not want the sympathy of strangers'.[98] However one might question the extent to which Arian Christians were really 'strangers' (*extranea*) to their Nicene counterparts in North Africa. As we have seen repeatedly, religious differences were no impediment to political and social relations in Vandal North Africa.

Vandal kings distinguished between the Nicene clergy and their congregations. A useful model for thinking about Vandal royal attitudes towards their Romano-African lay subjects is that of 'rough tolerance', recently formulated by Christopher MacEvitt in his study of interactions between the Frankish rulers of the Crusader kingdoms and the local Christian populations who resided there.[99] A striking feature of both the Frankish Levant and Vandal North Africa were the interactions between different communities that appeared to contradict religious, social and ethnic divisions and definitions provided by legal codes and other documents. 'Rough tolerance' was very far from the confrontational tenor found in many of the textual accounts of the period but rather provided an 'unspoken, undefined and amorphous' code of practice that allowed different communities to co-exist whilst also acknowledging the power relations between them.[100]

According to MacEvitt's interpretation, 'rough tolerance' was typified by periods of relative peace interspersed by bursts of localized violence and repression against indigenous communities. Silence was one of its most important aspects; separate communities of Christians simply avoided discussing the potentially serious theological differences that existed between them. Thus, 'both local Christians and Franks chose not to know, to forget, or to overlook those aspects of the other which had the most power to control and define the other'.[101]

The regional differences in the intensity of the repression that the Nicene Church suffered under Huneric have already been remarked upon. This phenomenon can also be fruitfully explored within the framework of 'rough tolerance', particularly as the persecutions continued in the later fifth and early sixth centuries. An interesting case study is the early career of Fulgentius of Ruspe, monk, bishop and theologian, who would become the most high profile member of the African Homoousian ecclesiastical establishment in the early decades of the sixth century.[102]

Conspicuously, the early part of Fulgentius' career does not seem to have been affected by the Arian persecutions. On the one occasion that the young monk was forced to flee from his monastery in the province, it was due to Moorish raids rather than Vandal persecution.[103] Later, on his return from travels in Sicily and Italy, Fulgentius received land in Byzacena from a local magnate to found a new monastery; presumably such an exchange in Africa Proconsularis would have been unthinkable. It is particularly striking that Fulgentius and his companion Felix only ran into trouble with the Arian priesthood after they were forced to relocate to Sicca Veneria in the Proconsular province. There they were quickly arrested by an Arian cleric on the suspicion that Fulgentius was a Catholic priest in disguise – evidently the area was forbidden to Nicene clergy.[104] What this episode shows is that the Vandals had little interest in controlling those regions of Byzacena where Fulgentius spent much of his African career. Indeed, Fulgentius was only exiled after he had been consecrated as a bishop. This suggests that the Vandal authorities were more concerned about those who held pastoral roles within lay communities than with the activities of the more inward-looking monastic establishments.

Then there is the question of what these doctrinal allegiances actually meant in small-town provincial North Africa. The Donatist controversy had ensured that religious sectarianism was by no means a novelty in such places. But what is more striking than the occasional outbreaks of extreme violence and legal wrangling that erupted between 'Catholics' and 'Donatists' during the fourth century was that these differences did little to disrupt the rhythm of everyday life. Despite Augustine's highly partial descriptions of towns where a rigorous form of religious apartheid was enforced by silence and boycotts, Catholics and Donatists generally worked together and lived together with little problem. These religious labels only became significant when disputes over other matters erupted and one or both of the disputants tried to enlist the support of the secular or ecclesiastical authorities. A similar state of affairs appears to have existed between Arian and Homoousian communities in much of Vandal North Africa.

At times, religious affiliation was clearly important. In a document included amongst the Albertini Tablets, which pertains to the sale of a slave boy called Fortinus, the parties involved recorded that he was not a heretic (*non erroneum*).[105] Frustratingly, we cannot say whether this suggests that Fortinus would have regarded himself as Arian or as Nicene (if indeed a six-year-old would have thought about such things), but it may indicate a standing injunction regarding the ownership of Arian or Homoousian slaves by members of different churches.[106]

It is striking how often Nicene ecclesiastical writers had to explain to their correspondents quite what the theological differences between themselves and their Arian opponents actually were.[107] This suggests that congregations constantly needed to be reminded of the doctrinal distinctions which supposedly divided their society. As one scholar has recently pointed out 'we have to imagine a much more porous border between Arian and Nicene and much more traffic than our sources are willing to disclose'.[108] Despite the efforts of both the Nicene and Arian churches, their congregations continued to eat, socialize and even worship together despite the warning issued by their clergy.[109] There was a wealth of older social, economic and cultural ties that linked individuals who were supposedly on different sides of the religious divide.

The Life of Fulgentius illustrates this well. After Fulgentius, a member of a wealthy family from Thelepte, was roughed-up by the henchmen of an Arian priest, the reaction of one particular Arian bishop was one of outrage.

> The news also reached the so-called bishops of the Arians that the blessed Fulgentius had been seriously beaten, and because a bishop knew Fulgentius' family and had loved the blessed Fulgentius himself when he had been a layman, he was motivated to take action against the priest of his own religion and diocese who instigated the beating, proposed to revenge the blessed Fulgentius if the latter were willing to swear out a complaint against the above mentioned priest.[110]

Fulgentius refused this offer. To his mind, any request for justice from an Arian bishop would not be received well by the 'little ones' (the Catholic lay congregation). But Fulgentius' concern at misinterpretation highlights the ambiguity of religious affiliation in a period when social, political and theological concerns were tightly interwoven. Evidently, Nicene members of the African provincial elite, like Fulgentius, moved in the same social circles as their Arian peers.[111] Fulgentius' family clearly had a relationship with the Arian bishop that transcended their religious differences.

There was also considerable congregational traffic between the two churches. Former Arians are reported as coming over to the Nicene Church whilst a Homoousian bishop, Revocatus, converted to Arianism.[112] Some even switched creed more than once. Elpidophorus, one of Huneric's religious enforcers, left the Arians for the Nicene Church before eventually returning to his faith.[113]

The ambiguity of local religious identities might also help to explain an intriguing group of churches recently excavated by Fathi Béjaoui in rural Byzacena. Inscriptional evidence proves that these basilicas were either built or were in use during the reigns of the Vandal kings Gunthamund and his brother Thrasamund.[114] At El Gousset an annex apparently dedicated to the veneration of saints or martyrs was added to the ecclesiastical complex there in AD 521 – in the twenty-sixth year of the reign of the Vandal king Thrasamund.[115] It has so far proved impossible to distinguish between Arian and Catholic churches through their archaeological layout.[116] It is also striking that its excavator could find no traces of the complex having been re-developed during the Byzantine period – a very common practice in this particular area. This has led to speculation about whether the complex was abandoned after the Byzantine conquest or simply continued in its Vandal-era form.[117] A similar story can be told at the nearby rural settlement of El Erg, close to the town of Thelepte, where another inscription states that a baptismal annex was built in the twenty-second year of Thrasamund's reign.[118] One must wonder whether the lack of defining architectural or architectural characteristics that might identify these buildings as either Nicene or Arian is indicative of a more general ambivalence when it came to religious allegiance. Perhaps the reality was that all of the population, Arians and Homoousians alike, worshipped there together, and the Vandal authorities generally turned a blind eye to this practice.

Thrasamund and the Development of an African Arian Church

Little is known about the religious policies of Gunthamund, Huneric's successor to the throne. What evidence there is suggests that the new king was generally better disposed towards the Catholic faith than his predecessor had been. Gunthamund restored the shrine of Agileus in Carthage and allowed bishop Eugenius to return from exile. Eugenius' then intervened and facilitated the recall of the exiled Catholic clergy and the re-opening of their churches.[119]

In 496, Gunthamund's brother Thrasamund became king, a development that had far-reaching implications for the African Nicene Church. The new monarch quickly showed that he was not willing to accept the religious status quo that appears to have operated for much of his brother's reign. Unlike his predecessors, the new king was clearly interested in theological debate. His assault on the Nicene Church was founded in the deeply held belief that it was his duty to expunge the Homoousian creed from Africa whilst at the same time doing nothing to jeopardize the stability of his thriving kingdom. Building on the initiatives of Huneric, Thrasamund sought to ensure that the Arian Church posed a serious challenge to popularity of the Nicene faith among the Romano-African population, both as a pastoral and intellectual force. The twin tenets of his campaign were the reintroduction of harsh measures against the Catholic ecclesiastical hierarchy whilst maintaining good relations with the Romano-African lay elite; his intention was to detach these two groups from one another.[120]

Thrasamund used exile to remove a considerable number of bishops from their sees. After the Nicenes had ignored a previous royal edict that forbade the consecration of new bishops, Thrasamund ordered the mass expulsion of 60 or more bishops to Sardinia in 508/509, including Fulgentius of Ruspe.[121] The majority of these exiles remained on the island until 523 AD (although Fulgentius himself was recalled to

Africa for a period of two years between 516/517–518/519 AD).[122] Simultaneously, extensive effort and resources were put into the conversion of the Nicene congregations who were left behind. What seems to have particularly concerned contemporary Homoousian commentators was that the chief weapon that would be used in this new campaign was persuasion rather than persecution. One observed that:

> Between harsh persecutions, there were deceptive measures trying, sometimes by terror, at other times by promises, to force Catholics to deny that Christ was equal to God the Father.[123]

Thrasamund further refined a strategy that had first been used against the Nicene Church by Huneric. The king ordered that a theological debate was to be held with Fulgentius of Ruspe, the best African Nicene theologian of the time. The bishop was specially recalled from exile between 517 and 519 so that he could take part in this discussion. Where Huneric had satisfied himself with the prospect of a mass debate between the assembled bishops of the two churches, however, Thrasamund put himself forward as Fulgentius' Arian disputant. First Fulgentius was given a book containing ten objections that the king had levelled regarding the question of the Trinity – issues which suggest that the king had a good knowledge of the Homoousian position.[124] The *Life of Fulgentius* portrayed its hero's responses to these questions as an emphatic victory for the Nicene champion. It suggests that Thrasamund was so out of his depth that he sought an unfair advantage by insisting that his reply to Fulgentius should only be read out to him once:

> for he was afraid that Fulgentius would put the king's words into his own responses as his arguments were refuted and that, in the eyes of the whole city (Carthage), he would be ridiculed again as having been bested.[125]

Later, after Fulgentius had overcome him, despite this considerable handicap, Thrasamund was supposedly so cowed that he had to rely on one of his own bishops to write a response, before eventually packing the turbulent priest off to Sardinia. This last action was made on the recommendation of his Arian ecclesiastical advisors who feared Fulgentius' continued presence in Carthage would lead to their defeat.[126]

The extant text of Fulgentius' responses to Thrasamund tells a somewhat different story. Fulgentius' fulsome praise of Thrasamund's intellectual prowess might reflect nothing more than the courtly language that needed be used when addressing a monarch, but the transcript of the debate itself shows that Fulgentius sometimes struggled to answer some of the Vandal king's more challenging questions.[127] Thrasamund clearly knew his Homoousian theology.

Equally worrying for Nicene writers had been the evolution the Arian Church into an identifiably *African* rival on both a pastoral and theological level. Initially it appears that the majority of the Arian bishops and clergy in Vandal Africa had been outsiders – either barbarians or Romans from other parts of the old empire. Those who were indigenous had tended to hail from rather modest professional backgrounds.[128] By the early sixth century, however, the situation had begun to change and a number of more prominent converts threatened to mark a tipping point within the establishment. These included Fastidiosus, a former Catholic monk and clergyman and Mocianus, a teacher of rhetoric.[129] There is also the intriguing testimony of an anonymous Arian theological tract, a *Commentary on the Book of Job* (*Commentarius in Iob*) that has recently been convincingly ascribed to the early decades of the sixth century.[130] The writer of this work was clearly well educated in both Latin and Greek Christian and non-Christian literature. The prose style of the tract is also unusually eloquent and the exegetical scholarship assured enough that the author could comfortably compare the Greek Septuagint Bible with a variety of Latin translations.[131] It seems likely, therefore, that the author of *Commentary on the Book of Job* was either a member of the Romano-African elite or a well-educated member of the highest echelons of Vandal society.[132] In his exhortations that they should attend church more regularly, the author sounds like Augustine, Cyprian and the other North African Christian writers of old and indeed might have held a position in the clergy or a bishopric.[133]

In the *Commentary* the Homoousians are referred to as a potent threat that spread through the world like shadows stalking and attacking the true (Arian) church.[134] This suggests that the writer was very aware that his fellow Arians were hard-pressed in the eastern empire. The commentator condemns the Nicene position on the Trinity, and also warns his audience that they should not visit the churches of the 'heretics' or take communion with them.[135] The text also contains other well-formulated rejections of the Augustinian tenets that had dominated the North African Church in the decades before the Vandal invasion. These include the theology on grace and original sin, both issues on which Augustine's position had never been very well received.[136]

The emphasis in the text on matters such as marriage, family relations, organizing inheritances, burial practices, curses and estate management further suggests that this was not intended for a cloistered audience but as a text that would be pertinent to the lives of a congregation made up of diverse socio-economic constituencies.[137] It appears that by the early sixth century, the Arians had become a serious rival to Nicene claims that they there were the true church of the Romano-African population. Tellingly, Fulgentius complained bitterly that Arian opponents had stolen sections of his own condemnation of Donatism and passed them off in their own sermons.[138]

The sophisticated threat that a genuinely African Arian Church now posed is exposed in the surviving account of one of the most high profile public confrontations in which Fulgentius was involved. His opponent was the Arian priest Fabianus, and the dispute probably took place in Carthage sometime between 523 and 533. That Fulgentius recognized Fabianus as a formidable opponent is evident from the Nicene bishop quoting the scriptures directly from the Greek.[139] In another sign that Fabianus was well educated, Fulgentius made reference to his pretensions to be a scholar of Latin literature and even went as far as quoting from the *Aeneid* at him.[140]

The tactics utilized by the Arian Church were also given a strongly African flavour by their adoption of strategies that had been used to great effect by Augustine, particularly against the Donatists.[141] Nicene opponents were to be directly engaged and challenged to public debate whenever possible. As a tactic it was clearly designed to demoralize and undermine, and the correspondence of Fulgentius shows that it clearly worked in this instance. The reaction of many Homoousians was similar to that of many of the Donatists in the early fifth century, who had been intimidated by the challenge that was issued to them and retreated into silence. Moreover, the new Arian campaign also appears to have used the dispensation of charity and a stronger pastoral ethos to win Catholics over.[142]

During the long period of exile, Fulgentius regularly acted as the chief spokesman and letter-writer for the Nicene bishops as they fought to maintain ecclesiastical discipline and doctrinal orthodoxy across the sea in Africa.[143] Fulgentius was obliged to send a number of letters and treatises to Catholic correspondents who urgently requested responses to questions and objections put forward by Arians. A letter to a certain Donatus set out the background to the latter's request.

> You say that a question was proposed to you by certain Arians concerning the Father and the Son. They asserted that the Father was greater and the Son less. But you, because of your ignorance of divine letters in which you have been given less instruction, did not come up with anything with which you might answer them in defence of the true faith. . . . Wishing to

be better prepared to answer, you ask that, instructed by our words, armed with the divine words, you know how you may be able to counter the heretics who wish to attack our faith.[144]

Fulgentius' need to furnish his correspondents with theological defences against Arian proselytizing was no different to the situation that had faced Quodvultdeus and his colleagues in the middle of the fifth century. But the frequency of these Arian challenges appears to have markedly increased. Donatus was certainly not the only one of Fulgentius' correspondents who felt under pressure from Arians.[145] One lady reported that the nature of the Trinity was now a popular topic at dinner parties.[146] Another sent Fulgentius a copy of a sermon delivered by a certain Fastidiosus, an Arian convert and former Catholic monk, in order that the bishop might refute the work.[147]

Given the strength of the challenge that Arianism now presented to the Nicene Church, and the enforced absence of many of the senior ranks of the Nicene Church, it is unsurprising that a sense of deepening crisis appears to have begun to develop amongst African Nicene circles. This was further exacerbated by the closing of the Catholic churches in Zeugitana: if Nicenes wished to worship they had to do so in Arian churches.[148] Even the highly partisan *Life of Fulgentius* makes reference to its hero having to give counsel and even re-baptize those who had lapsed and converted to Arianism:

> Those who had already been re-baptised he taught them to lament their mistake and he reconciled them. Others he warned lest they destroy their souls in exchange for worldly gains. Those who he perceived to be close to perdition, he calmed with soothing words, so that because of his kind words, they were ashamed to go through with their planned evil and turning back, they began to do penance. Others strengthened by his words and renewed in their faith by the salt of teaching confuted the Arian heretics with confidence.[149]

Fulgentius and the Nicene Fight-Back

In the first three decades of the sixth century AD, the Nicene Church was clearly under great pressure from not only the Vandal monarchy but also the increasingly organized Arian establishment. There seems to have been a general recognition within the Nicene ecclesiastical hierarchy that new tactics would be required to counter the threat posed by the Arians, and in particular that those who had lapsed were to be won back by gentle encouragement not chastisement or threats.[150] Along with his letters of advice and encouragement, Fulgentius worked hard to communicate the importance of resistance to the Catholic flock. He prepared sermons written in *sermo humilis*, plain Latin that could be easily understood by less-educated members of the congregation, and even produced an anti-Arian rhyming psalm, as his hero Augustine of Hippo had once done against the Donatists.[151]

In AD 523 an unexpected respite came in the form of the new Vandal king Hilderic, who was praised in the *Life of Fulgentius* for his 'marvellous goodness' (*mirabilis bonitas*).[152] Going against the dying wishes of his predecessor, Thrasamund, Hilderic recalled all of the Nicene bishops from exile, granted them freedom of worship and restored much of their property to them. He also allowed the appointment of a new bishop of Carthage as well the resumption of episcopal elections for the multitude of see that lay unfilled due to the policies of his predecessor.[153] According to his biographer, Fulgentius returned to Carthage with the other exiled bishops to a hero's welcome, before going back in triumph to his home province of Byzacena.[154] The African Nicene Church took full advantage of its new freedoms and held two provincial councils in Byzacena in 523 and a general synod at Carthage in 525. For the first time for a very long period, new Nicene churches were consecrated in Africa Proconsularis, including a new basilica in the town of Furnos Maius built by the Homoousian bishop Symeon in 528.[155]

However, despite the triumphal tone of the Nicene restoration, the years of exile and repression had inflicted considerable damage on its infrastructure, authority and internal cohesion. The proceedings of the Byzacenan Council at Iunci in AD 523 and the General Council at Carthage in AD 525 shine a light on the severity of the problems which now faced the church.[156] These were the first Nicene ecclesiastical meetings to be held in Vandal Africa for nearly 40 years, and there was much to be done. At Iunci, the assembled bishops deliberated over the boundaries of ecclesiastical jurisdiction between Byzacena and Tripolitania. They also adjudged a dispute between their Primate, Liberatus, and the abbot of a monastery, Peter, before finding in the former's favour and confirming the authority of bishops over monks in their dioceses. It appears that the monasteries in Byzacena, which had operated for so long without the interference of the pastoral church, were far from enthusiastic about allowing bishops to assert their traditional authority over them. In the Council of Carthage, however, this decision was reversed by the assembled bishops. Of those present, only three bishops were from Byzacena, and Liberatus was conspicuous among the absentees.

Boniface, the new bishop of Carthage, had attempted to impose his primacy over the bishops of Byzacena by sending a letter to their council at Iunci establishing the date of Easter for that year. However, when it came to decisions over jurisdiction, it was certainly not clear that Liberatus and the other Byzacenan bishops were willing to accept his authority.[157]

It is striking how few delegates from outside Africa Proconsularis attended the Carthage conference: nine from Numidia, three from Byzacena, two from Tripolitania and just one from Mauretania. This might suggest that the authority of Carthage was not immediately welcomed in the other African provinces, but practical issues of transport and travel would certainly have played their part in keeping the numbers of bishops from distant dioceses down. It should also be noted that the 37 bishops who attended from Africa Proconsularis itself compares poorly with the 164 who had attended the council held at Carthage in 439.[158] Clearly many sees were yet to be filled after falling vacant in the preceding years.

It was not just council documents that highlight the damage inflicted on the African Nicene Church. After returning home to Byzacena, Fulgentius' considerable energies seem to have been taken up with restoring ecclesiastical discipline in his see of Ruspe. Divisions that had arisen between monks and clerics were partly healed by the appointment of a brother from his own monastery into pastoral roles. The lifestyle of these new priests and their congregations was also strictly controlled in an effort to maintain ecclesiastical discipline:

> Each week, he set the Fast on Wednesday and Friday for all clergy and widows, as well as for whomever of the laity was able. All were commanded to be present at the vigils each day as well as at morning and evening prayers. Some turbulent souls he lashed with words, but others whose faults were public he had beaten with blows. Thus he attacked the vices of all with salutary words, so that while not mentioning names, he would cause all to be afraid and because of that salutary fear to abandon their hidden sins.[159]

Indeed, we might well want to view the *Life of Fulgentius* by the Carthaginian deacon Ferrandus, from which this extract derives, with its emphasis on its hero's devotion to ascetic practice and pastoral duties, as exhortation for a damaged African Nicene Church to start restoring itself, rather like Possidius' biography of Augustine a century before.

In another sign of the problems that now beset the Nicene Church, Fulgentius became embroiled in a dispute over episcopal precedence with another Byzacenan bishop, Quodvultdeus.[160] Even on his death, the protracted wrangling over who should be his successor meant that the bishopric of Ruspe would remain embarrassingly vacant for a whole year. Indeed, even 11 years later the triumphal tone of the Byzantine conquest would be quickly muted by a growing awareness on the part of Justinian and his officials that the African Catholic Church, rather than being united in adversity, was in fact a deeply troubled and divided body.

8

Cultural Life Under the Vandals

The literary life of Vandal North Africa has not always attracted the attention that it deserves. Scholars, exasperated by what they considered to be bad Latin poetry and shoddy artistic endeavour, have often been quick to dismiss what has survived as the laboured efforts of a society increasingly devoid of inspiration or technical expertise. In the introduction to his study of the works of the sixth-century North African writer, Fulgentius 'the Mythographer', L. G. Whitbread perfectly encapsulated the rather damning verdict that much of nineteenth- and twentieth-century scholarship had delivered on the literary output of the period:

> At worst, the Latin is appalling – decadent, involved, littered with wasteful connectives and rhetorical extravagances, pompous, inflated, pretentious, prolix, infested with Asianic exaggeration. The colours of rhetoric turn psychedelic; enormous sentences confront lucidity like barbed wire entanglements. And as the style is without grace, so are the purposes and methods muddleheaded and dubious, and displays of learning second hand and suspect.[1]

Fulgentius does not stand alone in attracting such harsh criticism, and many of the other writers of poetry and prose in this period have attracted the caustic comments of generations of modern scholars brought up on Vergil and Cicero.[2] But what is remarkable is that so many writers flourished in North Africa in this period, and that so many of their works have survived. In sheer volume alone, the literary output of Vandal Africa is impressive, and in some specific cases the productions of the period deserve to rank alongside any from the late Roman and post-Roman west.

The study of Latin poetry in the Vandal kingdom is dominated by two collections of verse. The first – and in purely literary terms the superior

– is the collected oeuvre of the poet Blossius Aemilianus Dracontius, who wrote in the second half of the fifth century during the reigns of Huneric, Gunthamund and Thrasamund. His works, which include short occasional pieces as well as two long Christian verses, certainly rank among the best literature of the age. But much of Dracontius' poetry was written from a prison cell in Carthage, where he was incarcerated during the reign of Gunthamund. Rather less accomplished, but striking in its variety and vivacity is the *Latin Anthology* or *Anthologia Latina*, a surprising and varied medley of poetry which survives in a single ninth-century manuscript, and which would seem to have been compiled at the time of the fall of the Vandal kingdom or shortly thereafter.[3] The collection includes some material by classical writers such as Vergil, Propertius and Ovid, as well as a considerable body of work which was certainly composed under the Vandals. To judge from the sheer number of writers assembled in the collection – 15 named poets are listed within the *Anthology* who can probably be dated to the Vandal period – there was a considerable fashion for poetry of this kind within the Hasding kingdom. None of these poets was as accomplished as Dracontius in purely literary terms, but they seem to have enjoyed a rather more fruitful relationship with their patrons. It is something of a paradox that Dracontius – the 'best' poet working in the kingdom – was overshadowed politically by his less-talented contemporaries; this is an issue which we shall explore in depth in this chapter.

Equally important to the culture of North Africa in this period was the fate of the cities under the Vandals. Like the literature of the period, post-Roman urban life was long dismissed by scholars more attuned to the spectacular ornaments of the classical world, but a recent generation of scholars has been more inclined to view the civic society of the Vandals more positively. We have already seen how the gradual transformation of the economic landscape within North Africa had an effect upon the region's cities, but these changes also had a cultural dimension. Here again, our image is mixed and occasionally puzzling, and impressive foundations did not always ensure lasting success. Carthage, for example, provides a mixed picture of continuity and change. Many prominent public buildings, including some of the most prominent landmarks of the city, were abandoned or put to new uses, others seem to have continued in use down to the vast urban regeneration campaign of Justinian in the mid-sixth century. Likewise, some neighbourhoods survived and flourished under the Vandals, while others fell into desuetude. Much the same pattern is apparent throughout the Vandal kingdom, indeed throughout North Africa as a whole.

The present chapter will examine continuity and change within the secular culture of North Africa. It will look first at the evidence for urban life within North Africa in this period, and then will explore the literary culture which continued to flourish within the towns themselves. The image which emerges is by no means straightforward. Depending on where we focus – the poems or buildings which we choose to examine – the culture of the Vandal period can be viewed as a triumph or as a disaster. Clearly, we cannot treat these two imposters just the same, and a balanced image of the Vandal kingdom must incorporate images of decay and decline alongside the striking evidence for a continued classical tradition.

Urban Culture and 'The Good Life'

For the Christian moralists of the fifth century, the Vandal invasion ended the urban civilization of North Africa. Quodvultdeus' sermon on the subject recalls nothing so much as the evocative description of Oran in Albert Camus' *The Plague*:

> Where is the thing that you were unwilling to part with? Where is Africa, that for the whole world was like a garden of pleasures? Where are her many districts? Where are her great most splendid cities? . . . when this dreadful calamity strikes our eyes, and there is no-one going out to bury the bodies of the dead, and when a black death has befouled every quarter and every square, and in some fashion the whole city; considering moreover evils like these – mothers of families led away captive, pregnant women slain, nursing mothers who, with their little ones torn from their hands and thrown half-dead in the street, neither could keep their sons who were still living nor were permitted to bury their dead ones.[4]

A generation later, Victor provided a more specific account of Vandal destruction:

> In some buildings, namely great houses and homes where fire had been of less service to them, they smashed the roofs in pieces and levelled the beautiful walls to the ground, so that the former beauty of towns cannot be deduced from what they look like now. And there are very many cities with few or no inhabitants, for after these events the ones which survive lie desolate; for example, here at Carthage they utterly destroyed the Odeon, the theatre, the temple of Memoria and what people used to call the *Via Caelestis*.[5]

Victor vividly evokes a dramatically changed cityscape, but his account deserves careful analysis.[6] It is clear from the archaeological record that both the Odeon and the theatre were abandoned, although in each case the dating is unclear.[7] The Temple of Memoria (*Aedes Memoriae*) has posed more problems for scholars, not least because the historian later alludes to a gathering at the temple during the reign of Huneric.[8] This later reference may simply allude to the neighbourhood in which the temple had once stood, but Victor's insistence upon the destruction of the temple in AD 439 is surprising. It has been suggested that the temple is to be identified with the so-called 'Circular Monument', which was constructed in the early fourth century and would seem to have been abandoned and robbed out during the fifth, but this identification has been disputed.[9] The destruction of the *via Caelestis* is also peculiar, simply because Victor's meaning here is not completely clear. As has already been discussed in the examination of the Vandal economy, this is perhaps best read as further evidence for the changing urban topography of Carthage elsewhere revealed in the encroachment of small buildings onto the grand boulevard of the *Kardo Maximus*.[10]

In Carthage, and in many African cities, the gradual erosion of the classical cityscape had long pre-dated the arrival of the Vandals, and the

Figure 8.1 The theatre at Carthage. Reproduced by permission of Professor David Mattingly

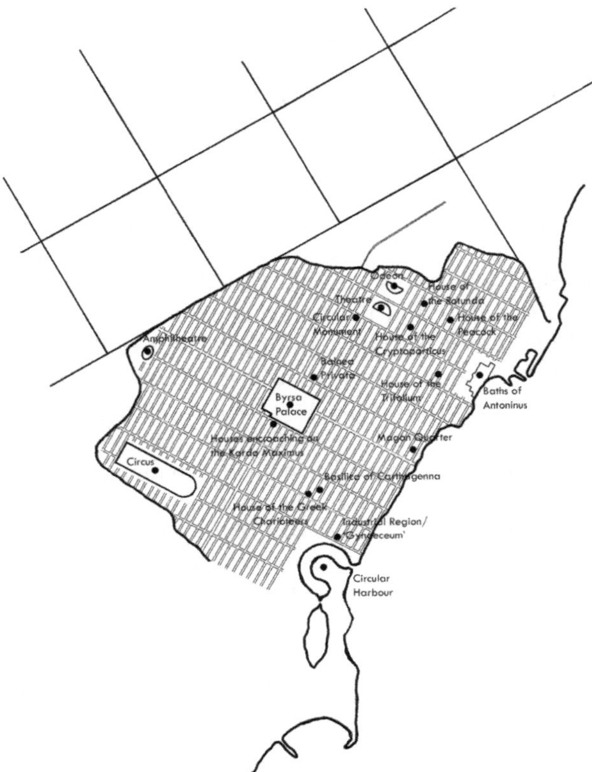

Figure 8.2 Private and public spaces in Vandal Carthage

invasion of AD 439 was simply one stage in an ongoing narrative of transformation. The Theodosian Code clearly shows that that the desertion and stripping of smaller urban centres was already enough of a problem in Africa by the second half of the fourth century AD that the emperor Constans II felt the need to intervene.[11] Imperial legislation had already ordered the closing of all pagan temples, a move that must have had a serious impact on many city centres.[12] Moreover through the teachings and interventions of Christian preachers such as Augustine of Hippo, there is little doubt that the public entertainments, although not banned, had become an increasingly less popular mode of evergetism for the local worthies who had previously bankrolled them.[13] This was probably what lay behind the imperial rescript issued by the emperors

Figure 8.3 The Antonine Baths at Carthage. Reproduced by permission of Professor David Mattingly

Honorius and Arcadius in 418 AD which reminded the provincial governor of Africa that the provision of public entertainment should not be confused with the continuing effort to uproot pagan practice.[14] Furthermore, the more mundane problem of city councils not having sufficient funds to carry out necessary work can also be traced back through the Code to at least a century before the arrival of the Vandals in North Africa.

In spite of this, it would be a mistake to explain away Victor's account of Vandal occupation as nothing more than the savage exaggeration of a hostile critic. Dramatic changes certainly took place within fifth-century cities in North Africa, and while the Vandals were not responsible for all of them, their period of occupation may have acted as an important catalyst. There is clear evidence that the large basilica of Carthagenna in the southern part of the city was destroyed during the occupation.[15] Similarly, the famed Antonine Baths – the largest such complex in Carthage and one of the major monuments of the city – had fallen out of use by the Vandal period, although they may have been in some disrepair at the time of the conquest.[16] Similarly, and most striking of all, perhaps, is the frequency with which fifth-century burials are found within what had once been prominent civic landmarks, including the Odeon, several large houses and the island at the centre of the circular harbour.[17] These burials certainly testify to a transforming civic landscape, but they should not be read as evidence for chaos or anarchy under the Vandals. They were not, in other words, the unburied dead of Quodvultdeus' lamentation, but were bodies which had been interred according to changing ritual conventions. We do not know enough about the society of Vandal-period Carthage to know why individuals and small groups were interred within specific buildings, but this practice does suggest that these sites retained an ideological significance, even if it had radically changed from familiar classical norms.

Earlier in this volume we discussed the remarkable resilience of light industry within the Vandal cities and the astonishing rapidity with which abandoned fora and bath buildings were frequently overgrown with craft activities.[18] But the cultural dimensions of this phenomenon also deserve some attention. While presses in streets and fora hint at widespread economic deregulation, and may mark the triumph of the small entrepreneur, the loss of large public spaces did profoundly affect the cities, politically and ideologically as well as visually. It has been suggested that the disappearance of many civic fora reflects the decline of the municipal authorities who once ruled them, and the case is persuasive.[19] Again, this may not be traceable directly to the Vandal occupation – some fora certainly remained in use, and others were probably obsolescent long before 439 – but the change was conspicuous.

The living inhabitants of Carthage did not surrender the whole of their city to the dead, however. There is ample evidence that the circus in particular remained an important focus of civic pride throughout the kingdom. Archaeological evidence suggests that the circus was not abandoned until well into the Byzantine period, and a series of poems from the *Latin Anthology* indicate that the charioteers and horse-racers of Carthage retained a celebrity status. The poems of Luxorius not only praise and mock the achievements of individual charioteers but also take as their subject actual places associated with the circus. Two poems refer to the figures of Fama and Victoria situated on the threshold of the circus stables.[20] Another celebrates a fountain that stood in the courtyard of the circus from which the horses drank.[21] The fountain not only beautified the circus and served a useful function in watering horses, it also promised good luck for the future.[22] Although it does appear that the circus in Carthage was in use throughout the Vandal period, it would be dangerous to take these poems as an actual description of what was taking place there at this time.[23]

This pattern of survival and decay is apparent throughout the North African kingdom. Some cities clearly suffered during the Vandal period – there is evidence for example that Leptiminus on the coast of Byzacena underwent massive economic decline until the Byzantine occupation allowed its fortunes to recover.[24] Other cities in the same province witnessed the widespread abandonment of suburbs during the later fifth century, perhaps in response to increased rural unrest. But elsewhere the image was more mixed. In Thuburbo Maius, for example, it is the contrasting fate of very similar sites which is most striking, and which underscores the peculiar nature of urbanism in this period. The private 'Winter Baths' seem to have remained in use throughout the fifth century, and parts of the structure were refurbished in the later fifth or early sixth century.[25] The 'Baths of the Stars', similarly, were enlarged during the fifth century and may have remained in use throughout the Vandal period.[26] The complex known as the 'Baths of the Labyrinth', however, had fallen out of use by the early Vandal period, and was reused as a light industrial centre, a common enough fate for bath houses in North Africa, as we have already seen.[27]

Private Architecture in Carthage

Carthage was still the focus of intense civic pride, and remained a city in which the elite still had a substantial material and ideological investment. Although some rich houses were abandoned during the fifth century, it is clear that throughout the period the private house had maintained its place as a primary symbol of wealth and status. The House of the Cryptoporticus, located close to the theatre, and the nearby House of the Rotunda were both large townhouses which had been constructed during the first or second centuries and had remained occupied thereafter; significantly, both underwent some substantial renovation during the Vandal period.[28] Nearby on the Hill of Juno, the House of the New Hunt was decorated with a new mosaic, and also underwent some change in its ground plan. Critically, this was not simply the ossified preservation of an obsolescent lifestyle. In each of these cases, patterns of renovation suggest that practices of habitation were changing, and that rooms which had once been peripheral increasingly became focal within the social display of the fifth century. New houses were also built.[29] One example close to the Antonine Baths, known as the House of the Trifolium, was probably constructed during the Vandal period, and subsequently extended through the addition of a triconch (a small dining room with three apsidal sides) and a further reception room. Close to the circular harbour, the House of the Greek Charioteers had originally been constructed towards the end of the fourth century, and was expanded and refurbished with two new mosaics under the Vandals.[30]

Less exclusive residential areas in Carthage also remained occupied through the Vandal period, although here again different regions of the city suffered different fates.[31] In several cases, the abandonment of public spaces or prominent structures led to a proliferation of low-status housing in wood and mud-brick. One such neighbourhood in the north-eastern area of town was disrupted by the construction of the city wall in 425, but occupation continued there at least until the end of the century.[32] Similar small buildings also accumulated within the abandoned theatre and the Odeon.[33] Elsewhere urban occupation declined, even on the most basic level. In the southern part of the walled city, for example, there is little evidence for occupation until the Byzantine conquest.[34]

Institutional Continuity

The classical city was defined by its political institutions as well as its physical infrastructure. At the height of the imperial period, the *curiae*, or city councils had provided the administrative backbone of the empire, but by Late Antiquity their position was increasingly eroded.[35] Curial power was already in crisis at the time of the Vandal occupation, and there is little to suggest that they survived the century which followed. Municipal positions are almost entirely absent from the textual and epigraphic record, and many scholars have assumed that they disappeared completely.[36] Towards the end of the fifth century we hear that the young Fulgentius of Ruspe had benefited from the patronage of prominent civic figures in Byzacena but the ambiguity of their titles and the absence of corroborative evidence from elsewhere in the kingdom suggests that such institutions were not especially common within the kingdom.[37]

But if the political infrastructure of the cities was in abeyance, or was increasingly dominated by ecclesiastical figures, secular aristocrats retained an unusual attachment to the ideological associations of the city. This is most apparent in the abundant evidence for the survival of one very peculiar civic institution of the *flamen perpetuus*, or the 'keeper of the imperial flame'.[38] This title was held by Flavius Geminius Catullinus, the landowner whose records are preserved in the Albertini Tablets and may well have been held in the nearby city of Cillium. A series of epitaphs from a basilica at Ammaedara commemorate three members of the same family: Astius Mustelus, Christian and *flamen perpetuus* who died in 526 AD; Astius Vindicianus, *vir clarissimus et flamen perpetuus*; and Astius Dinamius, *sacerdotalis provinciae Africae*.[39] The position of *flamen perpetuus* which these men shared was originally instituted to preserve the imperial cult within the cities of the empire, and it was an important civic position within pre-Christian society. Naturally, the survival of this institution into Christian (and post-imperial) North Africa has provoked some considerable speculation. Why would prominent civic leaders in Ammaedara commemorate their devotion to the imperial cult in a Vandal-period Christian epitaph? And why would Geminus declare his own imperial duties within documents of sale which also asserted his loyalty to the Vandal king? The most convincing explanation is still the one put forward by André Chastagnol and Noël Duval. They have argued that after the Christian emperors of the fourth century banned imperial worship, the provincial councils preserved only a secularized version of this practice as a manifestation of civic pride. It was this secularized practice which the Vandal kings tolerated as a way of creating a link between themselves and the Romano-African elite.[40]

Education, Education, Education

The foundations for the extraordinary literary productivity of Vandal Africa were laid by the educational system within the kingdom. Education continued to mean a great deal in Vandal North Africa. In the 470s or 480s, the polymath Martianus Capella composed a long allegorical treatise on the seven liberal arts entitled *On the Marriage of Philology and Mercury*.[41] In one particularly memorable passage, Martianus illustrates the power of learning through the personification of Philology herself:

> The girl strained hard and with great effort retched up the weight that she was carrying in her breast. Then that nausea and forced vomit turned into a stream of literature of all sorts. One could see what books and great manuscripts and the works of how many languages flowed from the mouth of the maiden. There were some made of papyrus which had been smeared with cedar oil, other volumes were woven of rolls of parchment, and a very few were written on Linden bark. . . . But while the girl was bringing up such matter in spasms, several young women, of whom some were called the Arts, and others the Disciplines, were straightaway collecting whatever the maiden brought forth from her mouth, each one of them taking material for her own essential use and her particular skill.[42]

This repulsively compelling episode reveals Martianus' conviction that learning should not just be stored away as an anonymous dead weight, but should be transmitted through scholarship, instruction and publication.[43]

Indeed, the whole of Martianus' long project could be read in these terms. *The Marriage of Philology and Mercury* provides an entertaining and compelling overview of the seven traditional subjects of the classical curriculum, namely the three principal disciplines of grammar, dialectic and rhetoric (the *trivium*), and the four supplementary subjects of geometry, arithmetic, astronomy and music (the *quadrivium*). If a work as ambitious as this could be written in Vandal Africa, clearly education remained a prized asset. Martianus clearly knew his stuff, was capable of presenting it in a compelling manner, and evidently expected to write for an audience with tastes similar to his own.

A good education had long been essential for any member of the Roman provincial elite of the western empire if they desired a career in either the civil service or the law.[44] At the most basic level tuition was undertaken by a *grammaticus* who taught his young charges correct Latin usage and familiarized them with a number of key works of literature of which by far the most important were those of Vergil. As well as Latin, students would also gain some familiarity with Greek language and literature although the extent of their proficiency in the language in Late Antique North Africa is open to question.[45] Later these young men would come under the guidance of a *rhetor* who would instruct them in the art of public speaking which involved studying text books and set exercises.

The institutionalization of North African Christianity during the fourth century saw this curriculum change, but did not remove the pagan classics from the schoolroom. Prominent churchmen like Augustine certainly regarded the old canon with mixed feelings, and reflected upon the power that the *grammaticus* wielded over impressionable young minds. There was Vergil:

> who is read by small boys precisely so that when their minds are steeped in this great and most famous and best of all poets, he may not easily be abolished into forgetfulness; as Horace says 'new vessels long retain the taste of what they first contained'.[46]

Even the more mechanistic arts of rhetoric and grammar were considered by some Christian authors to be potentially dangerous because of their ethical and philosophical underpinnings. They were means through which young Romans learned how to obey the laws of civilized life.[47] Indeed, many of the rhetorical exercises with which schoolboys were presented contained difficult moral problems which they were expected to explore comprehensively.[48] Quodvultdeus discusses this ambivalence in his sermon *On Barbarian Times* in which he implies that the lessons of the schoolroom had left a generation ill-prepared for the brutal realities of contemporary life:

> But if even the lessons that you recited by rote in the schools, and that to this day you have heard your children reciting, cannot recall you from your vainglory and ungodliness, then may the present age teach you a lesson.[49]

Yet it was precisely this training in rhetoric and dialectic which had provided the Christian Church with its firmest intellectual foundations, and nowhere was this debt more apparent than in North Africa. Augustine himself, who was by then bishop of Hippo, had been the recipient of a first class education at Thagaste and had previously served as the chief *rhetor* in Milan.[50]

The Vandal occupation of North Africa left the educational infrastructure of the region relatively unscathed. There were certainly some educated individuals among the exiles who fled from Carthage in 439, and some schoolboys may have found their lessons interrupted by the barbarian invasion, but they were ushered back into the classroom soon enough.[51] Indeed, the pupils of this generation were soon joined by some unfamiliar faces. The poet Dracontius was educated during the early years of the Vandal kingdom, and he was later to recall Roman and 'barbarian' youths rubbing shoulders in the lecture theatre of his teacher, Felicianus.[52] We know from Victor of Vita that at least one member of the Hasding family was sufficiently well-educated to earn the respect of the historian, and such a background may not have been unusual.[53] Other evidence for continuity in education seems conclusive. Luxorius dedicated a collection of his poems to his own teacher Faustus, and included an angry *grammaticus* among the subjects of his epigrams.[54] Another anonymous verse gently mocks an elementary school teacher (*magister ludi*) who was unable to keep order amongst his students. Although we may doubt whether some of these teachers were anything more than the conceits of playful poets, the literary training that lay behind these compositions was not imagined. Rightly could the poet Florentinus celebrate the Vandal city as 'Carthage adorned with schools and teachers'.[55]

Fulgentius 'the Mythographer', who was probably educated during the last years of the Vandal kingdom, not only reminisced about the state of his swollen hands after the beatings meted out by his teacher, he also presented Vergil as a rather grumpy *grammaticus* wearily trying to teach a school student in a short study of the great poet's work.[56] Fulgentius' cheeky plea that Vergil, still the mainstay of the school curriculum during this period, only teach 'the slight things that schoolmasters expound, for monthly fees, to boyish ears', would surely have brought a smile to the lips of his readership who would have endured a similar pedagogic regime.[57] Moreover, Fulgentius was clearly anxious to prove that he was the beneficiary of a good education in other more subtle ways. He peppered his work with scholastic Latin and little vignettes in Greek, which added little to the general argument but rather acted as a reminder to his readership that they were in the presence of a well-schooled author.[58] All of the writers of the period were writing for an audience who must have been expected to pick up on these clever rhetorical tricks and learned allusions which suggests that the standard of education, at least amongst the elite, was still high. Indeed one gets the impression of a rather self-contained world where members of the literati read each other's work and dedicated books to one another.[59]

In many cases, the poets themselves may well have been *grammatici* when they were not composing their verses.[60] The majority of Vandal-era poets collected in the *Latin Anthology* were representatives of the educated Romano-African elite. Superscriptions on the manuscript inform us that Luxorius was a *vir clarissimus et spectabilis*, a rank which had traditionally been reserved for the highest senatorial class within the empire, and two other poets are described as *viri clarissimi*. By the fourth century AD, these titles were commonly used by members of the North African municipal elite, and increasingly marked educational achievement, as well as social standing.[61] A law of 425 preserved in the *Theodosian Code* states that *grammatici* who had taught with distinction for 20 years service in a noted school could be rewarded with similar promotion.[62] A number of the *Latin Anthology* poets might have received their titles in this way.

For others, social standing could be taken for granted, but education could still be an important mark of status. Fulgentius of Ruspe was born into the upper echelons of African society, but nevertheless benefited from a first-class education. According to the *Life* of the saint, Fulgentius was initially educated at home, because his mother wished him to have a firm grounding in Greek, which could no longer be provided by the public schools. Nevertheless, Fulgentius too went on to study under a *grammaticus*, and Ferrandus' account implies that this was perfectly normal among the African aristocracy.[63]

Outside the urban elite, the importance of education is rather less clear. The Bir Trouch *ostraka* and the Albertini Tablets clearly indicate that a documentary culture was very much alive within Vandal North

Africa at the end of the fifth century and was probably widespread. Internal evidence within the Albertini Tablets themselves, moreover, suggests that a significant minority (over 15%) of the community at the remote farming community at Tuletianos in Byzacena had at least basic literacy. Moreover at least nine scribes are attested on the sales documents and two parties who identify themselves as *magistri* might well have been the local school masters.[64] If comparable patterns may be assumed from elsewhere in the Vandal kingdom, the image of educational continuity seems impressive.

Some suggestion of the nature of education in this period is provided by the work of Pompeius, the author of a commentary on the fourth-century grammarian Donatus. Although much of his treatise was clearly plagiarized and peppered with embarrassing howlers, it highlights just how important a Classical education still was for the elites in North Africa in the late fifth and early sixth century AD.[65] As well as holding forth on numerous points of grammar, Pompeius stands as a convincing example of a society where exuberant rhetorical style was still highly prized even when used in rather dry discussions of points of grammar:

> Don't let anyone tell you, 'If we sometimes use an adverb as a noun, we are also obliged to decline the adverb itself.' Impossible! For when a *nomen* is put in place of an adverb, it maintains its cases; but when an adverb passes into place of a *nomen*, there's no way that it can take on a case. . . .[66]

In fact it appears that Pompeius' targeted readership were not schoolboys but those that taught them. Pompeius clearly saw himself as the school masters' school master. Texts like this may imply that education was not what it had once been in the golden age of Roman Africa, but it clearly remained an important social reality for many. Thus many of the examples that he gave were clearly intended to resonate with his pedagogic audience, and included images such as teachers scuttling off across the town square to their classes, choosing which texts to lecture on and conducting question and answer sessions with pupils.[67]

Again, Dracontius and the poets of the *Latin Anthology* suggest how wide-ranging the African curriculum is likely to have been. As well as containing a number of poems that can definitely be attributed to Vandal North Africa, the *Latin Anthology* also includes a number of anonymous works and others by poets such as Vergil, Propertius, Ovid, Petronius, Seneca and Martial.[68] These were all names which would have been familiar to Dracontius, and his various works allude to earlier profane

Latin writers, particularly Vergil, Ovid, Lucan, Statius, Juvenal and Claudian, as well as Christian writers such as Prudentius, Paulinus of Nola, Augustine, Tertullian and Ambrose.[69] In his long *De Laudibus Dei* Dracontius self-consciously borrowed a number of expressions from Vergil's *Georgics* and *Aeneid* as well as Ovid's *Metamorphosis.* In the *Satisfactio*, in which the poet implored Gunthamund to release him from prison, it was Ovid's *Tristia*, the series of poems written begging the emperor Augustus to recall him from his Black Sea exile, that provided much of the frame of reference.[70] Moreover Dracontius' version of the story of Orestes had clearly been based on the original Greek tragedy rather than excerpts or summaries, suggesting that his command of that language must have been good.[71] Further evidence of the continuing strength of the rhetorical schools can be seen in his use of *controversia* (set exercises based on seemingly intractable problems) in a number of his poems.[72]

Continuity within the educational system of North Africa is also demonstrated by the surprising efflorescence of professional training throughout this period. Late Roman North Africa was particularly well-endowed with medical writers, for example, and this tradition continued under the Vandals. The venerable Vindicianus was known to the young Augustine in the 370s or early 380s and was also the tutor of Theodorus Priscianus, author of the influential Latin *Euporista* in the early years of the fifth century.[73] This tradition was continued in the work of Caelius Aurelianus and later Cassius Felix who wrote under the Vandal Kings.[74] The latter's extant work *De Medicina* (*On Medicine*) was written in AD 447 as a working medical text on the different diseases of the body and their cures. Cassius was probably born in Cirta (Constantine), although his work was probably composed in Carthage: at the start of the text, Cassius defines the human head as the 'capital city' (*summa civitas*) of the body.[75] Volumes such as these were the mainstay of medical education in this period. A poem of the *Latin Anthology* mocks a mixer of medicines who spent more time in the brothel than at his books; another jokes about the instruction of students in Hippocratic practice (through a laboured pun on *hippos* = horse), and a third makes fun of an impotent doctor.[76]

Lawyers, too, remained perennial figures of fun within the Vandal kingdom. Included among the most scurrilous verses of the *Anthology* are two poems concerning Filager, a lawyer from Vita who enjoyed tender intercourse with his own horse, others concerning an advocate who was mocked for his effeminacy and a third who had a concubine with the pet-name 'Charity'.[77] That the African legal system survived well enough to be generating its own 'lawyer' jokes into the sixth century should not be surprising. It was certainly fully operational at the time of the Vandal conquest, and was probably in better shape than virtually anywhere else in the western empire. In the 420s and 430s, when the compilers of Theodosius II's great legal code set about piecing together the legislation of the previous century and a half, they relied particularly on the rich archives of the North African cities.[78] Some of these lawyers did not remain long in Africa: many fled the region at the time of the Vandal invasion and one of Valentinian's edicts relates to their future property rights.[79] But others stayed, and legal professionals proved to be a resilient group.

Evidently, the educational system of Vandal Africa remained in a relatively healthy state, at least in the larger cities, and probably remained so down to the Byzantine occupation. At the time of the reconquest, Justinian insisted in his legislation that Carthage should be provided with two *rhetors* and two grammarians at the public expense.[80] Evidently, these new teachers were not intended to reintroduce formal education to a region which had forgotten the practices of the schoolroom. Justinian, it would seem, was offering his official support to an unusually healthy feature of North African society.

In Praise of the King: The Survival of Imperial Panegyric in Vandal North Africa

The Vandal court at Carthage drew many educated African aristocrats within its orbit. For many, politics and administration provided an obvious route to power and influence; for others, poetry and literary expression offered a means of promotion. Throughout the Roman period, court patronage had provided a powerful stimulus to literary creativity, and this pattern continued in the successor kingdoms. Within Vandal Africa, Thrasamund has long been recognized as an important supporter of the arts – a *soi-disant* intellectual with ambitions as a theologian and architect – but it seems likely that all of the Hasding kings appreciated the importance of culture to the ideology of their rulership.[81]

The ambitious poet in Vandal Africa had a difficult path to navigate. While some of the more successful poems in honour of the Hasdings might hint at Vandal and Roman aristocracies in perfect concert, this was an illusion which both sides had done much to create. In reality, negotiating the complex cultural rifts between the civic and military aristocracy could be difficult. This is most clearly illustrated by the life of Blossius Aemelius Dracontius, whom we have already met briefly in this chapter. Dracontius was the most productive and the most accomplished of the poets of Vandal Africa, and deserves to be considered among the top rank of Latin poets writing anywhere in the fifth century.[82] But this talent did not save him from an ignominious fate. After completing his education, probably during the reign of Geiseric, Dracontius served briefly as a lawyer (*advocatus*) under Pacideius, the proconsul of Carthage, and apparently enjoyed some social cachet to judge from his title of *vir clarissimus*.[83] But things fell apart soon afterwards. At some point during Huneric's reign, Dracontius composed a long panegyric – a formal poem of praise – to an unknown ruler, a political *faux pas* that was to result in his imprisonment for 12 years during the reign of Gunthamund.

The intention of Dracontius' lost poem, and the figure for whom he wrote it, have been much disputed. Some scholars have argued that this anonymous patron must have been from outside Africa – either the barbarian leaders Odoacer or Theodoric in Italy or the eastern emperor Zeno.[84] However, the most plausible candidate was Huneric, the Vandal king at the time of the composition.[85] Gunthamund is unlikely to have been particularly well disposed towards his uncle who had conducted a brutal purge of his immediate family in 481 and had attempted to redefine the succession in favour of his son, Hilderic.[86] When his own turn came to assume the throne, Gunthamund may well have instituted some political house-keeping of his own, albeit on a rather less bloody scale. Dracontius may have been a victim of this regime change, something that had been an occupational hazard for members of the Roman elite since Augustus, the first emperor. It appears that by trying to ingratiate himself with Huneric and his particular branch of the Hasdings, Dracontius had paid a heavy price when it was his nephew who secured the Vandal throne. Such was the cruel fate of being a good poet. Having praised one king, Dracontius found himself alienated by his successor, and spent much of the remainder of his life trying to atone for these mistakes. The spoken word could be forgotten or covered up in the way that the skilfully-written one could rarely be.

In some senses, posterity should be glad that Dracontius suffered in prison: his poetic output during this period was certainly unusually accomplished, and much of it was motivated by his understandable anxiety to be set free.[87] His first major production of this period was the long *Satisfactio* ('*Apology*' or '*Reparation*'), written in elegiac couplets, which he dedicated to Gunthamund in formal apology for his folly in composing the earlier poem. It is here that he laments his youthful folly most clearly:

> Mine was the blunder, being silent about forbearing lords, to celebrate one, though sovereign, long-forgotten to me; such a fault as attends those ungrateful men who worship vain idols with unholy hearts, even though they know their Lord.[88]

The pleas of the *Satisfactio* fell on deaf ears, and the poem was followed some years later by the still longer *De Laudibus Dei* (*On the Praises of God*). This was an exposition of the Nicene Creed in three books of hexameters which has justifiably been regarded as his masterpiece. The poem displays an extraordinary ability to vary style and literary genre that includes a daring confluence of Christian hymn and epic poetry. At the heart of the first book is a Hexameron, a celebration of the six days of the Creation which are represented in a series of poems based on the Book of Genesis. Although transforming parts of the Bible into epic poetry was hardly a new pastime (it had been a favourite pursuit of learned Christians since the first half of the fourth century AD), a number of the poetic passages show a dazzling originality with no clear parallels with other contemporary or earlier poems that were inspired by the same material.

Dracontius' imprisonment, and the difficulty that he found in obtaining his release, demonstrate that politics could be a dangerous world for poets in this period, but they also show how anxious writers were to enter into it. By the time of his imprisonment, of course, the poet would have been primarily concerned with securing his release from jail, but before and after his incarceration Dracontius clearly regarded political poetry as a means for direct social advancement. The fact that the poet's imprisonment was the direct result of his writing – whomever his patron may have been – also indicates how important poetry was politically in this period; if Dracontius' works were an academic irrelevance, he would hardly have been imprisoned for more than a decade for a perceived slight. Equally important is the fact that Dracontius continued to seek a royal patron throughout his career, despite the difficulties which he had encountered. Vandal Africa could be a difficult environment for poets, but it could also be a rewarding one.

Other poets in Vandal Africa may have lacked Dracontius' poetic skill, but they showed a far greater finesse in the political sphere. The *Latin Anthology* includes several poems which were written in honour of the Hasding kings and their preservation may well indicate that they were favourably received. The earliest of these is a short poem by one Cato written in praise of Huneric.[89] The ostensible subject of this poem is the king's construction of a *coclea*, a manually powered water-lifting device commonly known as an 'Archimedes Screw'.[90] The verse describes the operation of the *coclea*, and may very well reflect a genuine improvement of Huneric's, either in the harbour at Carthage or elsewhere on the African coast. Of rather more interest to Cato, however, and perhaps to those among his audience with a taste for the unusual, were the incongruities which the construction brought to mind. At the heart of the poem is the observation that the power of the king has turned water into land – a vivid demonstration of royal, if not divine, power. Cato also notes that it was through the power of a hand-turned *coclea* that a man could set his feet upon the dry sea bed, although this is admittedly rather less impressive a poetic paradox.

To a Nicene audience, a greater irony may have been found in Cato's reference to the 'clear faith' (*manifesta fides*) of the king in the poem's opening line. This allusion to Huneric's religious belief is passed over quickly, but can scarcely be accidental, and it has been persuasively suggested that the poem was a whole contains a guarded allusion to the famous story of Moses' parting of the Red Sea waters in Exodus 14.21–22. The use of similar language in an anonymous 'Poem Against the Marcionites', preserved independently of the *Latin Anthology*, has led one scholar to suggest that both of these verses were composed in celebration of Huneric at the time when his persecution of the Manichaean Sect within North Africa made him popular amongst Arians and Nicenes alike.[91] If this is correct, Dracontius' likely decision to look to Huneric for patronage seems much more understandable.

Fifty years later, Huneric's son Hilderic also proved to be a popular literary patron. Luxorius composed a short elegiac poem on the king's construction of a new palace at Anclae, a suburb of Carthage, presumably in the mid-520s.[92] Another poet, Felix, composed a short verse celebrating the wall decorations of the same building.[93] This poem – a variation on the classical *ekphrasis* – describes images of Valentinian III, Theodosius and Honorius that Hilderic had commissioned to celebrate his own descent from the Theodosian imperial line. This poem provides our principal evidence that Hilderic was attempting to redefine the Hasding law of succession in favour of his own side of the Hasding family, and hence has a considerable political significance, but its cultural resonances are also profound.[94] A Latin poem written to celebrate a wall painting, which was in turn a dramatic assertion of Roman imperial identity, is a clear illustration of the cultural aspirations of the Hasding kings, even in the third decade of the sixth century.

It was under Thrasamund, however, that the Latin poets of North Africa enjoyed their fullest support. The king cultivated a reputation as a thoughtful man of letters; he was remembered as a sensitive ruler by Procopius and his own fascination with theological issues led to the disputes with Fulgentius of Ruspe which marked a turning point in the religious history of the kingdom.[95] The clearest illustration of Thrasamund's royal aspirations, however, is found in a poem composed in his honour by Florentinus, probably towards the beginning of his reign. The opening is typical of its flavour:

> The imperial splendour of Thrasamund, ruler of Libya, is the world's renown – just as the sun glittering more brightly than the entire radiate universe, stands forth above all the stars. Reverence and foresight converge in this man, as do good character, bravery, handsome appearance, distinction, spirit, vigorous education, and a very adroit intelligence that watches over everything.[96]

Florentinus goes on to flatter this intelligence with a full tour of the common tropes of Late Antique panegyric. Thrasamund, the poet insists, is celebrated throughout the world, as far as the Chinese 'silk people' – and might take due credit for the extraordinary fertility of his African kingdom. No less importantly, Thrasamund is also praised through the medium of Carthage itself, a fusion of Hasding and Punic imagery which was central to the ideology of Vandal kingship as it developed within North Africa:

> Carthage, yes, Carthage, retains her fame by her high places and her king. Carthage the victress. Carthage the mother city of the Hasdingi triumphs. Carthage glitters, In all of Libya's lands, Carthage, Yes, Carthage is eminent.[97]

Florentinus' verse may lack the nuance of Dracontius' ill-starred Christian poems – indeed his relentless repetition can seem almost deranged – but he was a writer who seems to have realized the full potential of his work, in both senses of the verb.

In the middle of Florentinus' panegyric is a brief allusion to a pet project of the king – the renovation of the bath complex in the suburb of Alianae:

> With you as king, the citadel of Carthage shines forth steadily. Her offspring Alianae follows her with uneven step, her equal in esteem and distinction.[98]

Despite a number of different hypotheses, the exact location of Alianae is unknown. It is also unclear whether Thrasamund's baths were newly constructed or a restoration of existing buildings, but whatever form it took, this royal patronage was an important cultural event. The bathing complex at Alianae was the subject of a series of five poems preserved in the *Latin Anthology* and attributed to the *vir clarissimus* Felix.[99] Three of these poems are elegiac and two hexameters, but all are 12 lines long, and they were clearly composed as a sequence. In them, the poet celebrates the prodigious feat which saw the buildings completed in a year, and delights in the paradoxes that the baths represent.[100] Through the buildings, Thrasamund is shown to have power over nature, to have brought barren landscapes to life and to submit even the water itself to his will.[101] Under the king's aegis, the two antagonistic elements, fire and water, were forced to co-operate with one another creating a benign force which brought relaxation and restored well-being to those who come to the baths.[102]

The last poem in the sequence, written in hexameters, provided a fitting climax. The grandeur and scale of the new baths was emphasized with its high roofs and gleaming marble rising up over the cliffs.[103] In the baths fire and water came together for the well-being of the king's subjects.[104] The baths at Alianae stand as a testament to the illustrious Vandal name which Thrasamund has renewed through his munificence.[105] There is a strong possibility that all five of these poems were originally intended as decorations for the rooms of the baths themselves, either as a carved inscription or as a mosaic epigraph.[106] This practice is known from Sullectum and Hippo in pre-Vandal North Africa and the consistent length of the Felix poems strongly supports this interpretation.[107] This seems particularly likely in the case of the fifth poem, which celebrates the king and his construction together. This poem is constructed around an acrostich *Thrasamundus*, a mesotich *cun[c]ta innovat* and the telestich *vota serenans*, with the result that the viewer can read the definitive statement 'Spreading light, Thrasamund renews all his vows' through the first, middle and last letters of each line. If these letters were picked out in red when the poem was displayed, as has been argued, the message would have been particularly clear.[108]

This was public verse writ large. Not long after the most talented poet of his generation had been freed from prison, the Vandal king was literally surrounding himself with Latin poetry. Away from the affairs of the royal court, there was a renewed emphasis on Carthage having regained its reputation as a centre for the secular arts. Once again the city would play host to the poetry of its elite. In the introductory poem to his book of epigrams, the poet Luxorius, remembers how his youthful verse had been written in the Forum itself.[109]

None of the Late Antique poems in the *Latin Anthology* can compare with *De Laudibus Dei* for ambition or accomplishment, but Dracontius' verse did not win the audience it sought. It may be that this was because of its subject matter. What Dracontius may not have realized in his attempts to gain political patrons was that Latin learning within the Vandal kingdom was an increasingly secularized affair. Indeed, one might see the problems faced by Dracontius, the one poet who consistently wrote major poems on overtly Christian themes, as something of a cautionary tale in this respect. Perhaps Dracontius' failure to secure his own release from prison shows that this was a man who for all his political experience, had profoundly misunderstood the current political climate. After all, the *Satisfactio* was fundamentally a Christian *deprecatio*, a plea for pardon. Although full of the usual classicizing rhetoric, its tone is religious. The text opens with an evocation to the Highest God and in the text over 50 references are made to His divine powers.[110] There are also numerous biblical references.[111] For a Catholic Romano-African to present such a work to his Vandal king was politically crass. It is hardly surprising that Dracontius was left languishing in his prison cell.[112] In *De Laudibus Dei*, written in prison after the *Satisfactio* had failed to make the required impression, one senses that Dracontius had completely given up any hope of release but had instead decided to set himself up as a martyr for Nicene Christianity rather than merely as a courtier who had backed the wrong prince. This would explain the overtly Christian themes and the extraordinary attack on the Arian position on the Trinity.[113] These were the defiant words of an imprisoned man who had run out of options. The fact that Thrasamund would latter release him on his accession to the throne suggests just how peripheral a figure he may have become.[114]

Creating the Secular Middle Ground

One of the striking features of the considerable amount of Latin literature that survives from the Vandal period is the scarcity of explicit reference to Christianity. Although there are works within the *Latin Anthology* that do have avowedly Christian themes including poems on baptism, the Cross, the virgin birth and the Judgement of Solomon, it is far from clear whether these were produced in Vandal North Africa.[115] Most of the poems which can be attributed to named poets of the Vandal period, or which refer to contemporary themes, are almost completely secular in their language and themes.[116] Indeed in some works, such as

Martianus Capella's *Marriage of Philology and Mercury*, a long treatise that shows a deep fascination with divination, oracles, theurgy and magic, the absence of Christianity is so marked that some textual critics have suggested that its author must have been a pagan.[117] When considered alongside the other literature of the period, however, such a conclusion becomes far less secure. As one literary scholar has recently noted, even the work of clearly Christian authors often shows an 'indifference to theology and to the Church as an institution', a discretion which may not have been accidental.[118] Given the peculiar religious tensions within the Vandal kingdom, this is perhaps not surprising. In such difficult circumstances it is understandable that ambitious writers tended to shy away from controversial themes within their work. Indeed, the extraordinary renaissance of Latin literature in fifth- and sixth-century Africa appears to have been driven by the need for the Vandal monarchs and Romano-African elite to create a political *modus vivendi*.[119]

Whether it was through religious apathy or political pragmatism or both, the Roman lay elite colluded in the promotion of the profane in the Vandal kingdom. They were, after all, old hands at it. Religious conflict was not a new phenomenon in North Africa. Much of the fourth and early fifth centuries had seen the hounding and eventual banning of non-Christian religious observance as well as an incredibly bitter dispute between the Nicene Church and Donatist rigorists. Yet in spite of these major upheavals, the lay elites had continued running the towns and cities of Africa and sending their best and brightest overseas to Italy. They had managed to do it by ring-fencing and celebrating the secular and ignoring religion. It is a striking feature of the surviving inscriptions put up by the North African municipal elite during this period that any mention of Christianity is almost entirely absent.[120] Moreover, the inscriptions that celebrate the renovation of public buildings used for pagan worship were, without exception, put up in a private capacity.[121] At a time when pagan-Christian and Catholic-Donatist tensions were high, it is appears that the public places of the city were essential in recreating a much-needed secularly based consensus for the municipal elites of Late Antique North Africa.[122]

This strategy proved to be invaluable under the Vandals. The reigns of Thrasamund and Hilderic were marked by an interest in secular poetry which seems to have been shared by many different groups within the population of the kingdom. The fact that Luxorius stuck rigidly to secular themes in his verses in honour of the wall paintings of the barbarian Fridamal, or his lament for the young daughter of Oageis, does not indicate that the poet was Nicene and his patrons were Arians (although this could have been the case); the crucial point is that the secular aristocracies of North Africa had developed a form of cultural interaction and engagement that all could share, irrespective of their religious outlook.[123]

In the same way we might also view the diatribes written by Catholic ecclesiastical writers such as Victor of Vita, Fulgentius and Ferrandus as being more peripheral to the concerns of the Romano-African lay elite than has often been thought. It is always tempting in a period when so many of our meagre sources are Christian texts to view it as an age when religious concerns were absolutely paramount. However the secular poems and treatises of the Latin writers of the Vandal kingdom should warn against such an approach. It would be misleading to view the celebrations of the building schemes, weddings and hunts of the king and his nobles as nothing more than obsequious displays dictated by their masters' interests. It is equally misguided to see what was essentially an exercise in power and patronage amongst Late Antique elites through the lens of modern identity politics. Unlike their Nicene ecclesiastical counterparts and modern scholars, these poems show their authors to be a good deal less vexed by ethnic difference than they were by other social and cultural distinctions.

What lay behind much of the cultural renaissance in fifth- and sixth-century North Africa was the need for a coherent agenda that promoted a relationship between the Romano-African elite and Vandal kings built on resolutely secular foundations. Paradoxically, considering the portrayal of the Vandals as ill-educated barbarians in both ancient and modern works, it was Classical literature and learning that provided that common ground.

9

Justinian and the End of the Vandal Kingdom

In AD 565, the glittering funeral of the emperor Justinian took place in the imperial capital, Constantinople. On the orders of Sophia, the wife of his successor Justin, the body of the dead emperor was carried in a decorated pall, a magnificent piece of needlework which is described by the court poet Corippus:

> And she [Sophia] brought a pall stitched with precious purple, where the whole vista of Justinian's achievements was picked out in woven gold and glittered with gems. On one side the artist had skilfully represented with his sharp needle barbarian phalanxes bending their necks, slaughtered kings and subject peoples in order. And he made the yellow gold stand out from the colours, so everyone looking at it thought that they were real bodies. The faces were in gold, the blood in purple. And Justinian himself he had depicted as a victor amongst his courtiers, trampling on the brazen neck of the Vandal king, and Libya, applauding, bearing fruit and laurel.[1]

As a North African, Corippus, the author of this panegyric, might well have been expected to privilege the 'liberation' of his homeland. But amongst the population as a whole the conquest of North Africa, over three decades earlier, was still considered to be one the most impressive achievements of Justinian's long and eventful reign, despite the years of military campaigning against the Moors and religious dissension that had followed it.[2]

The origin for the Byzantine invasion of the Vandal kingdom had been the usurpation and imprisonment of Hilderic by his cousin Gelimer in 530, a political fracas that initially looked like just another episode in the long internecine struggle between the two main branches of the Hasding family.[3] On learning of the usurpation, Justinian immediately intervened by sending envoys to North Africa with a strongly worded letter of protest. In his missive, the emperor not only pointed out the moral improbity of Gelimer's actions but also argued that, by deposing Hilderic, the new king had broken the custom of royal succession established by Geiseric. Gelimer, confident that Justinian's complaint would translate into little more than an official protest, cursorily dismissed the imperial ambassadors, placed Hilderic and the king's nephew Oageis in close confinement and blinded his other nephew Hoamer. Justinian responded with a second delegation who delivered what was in essence an ultimatum. Gelimer was to send Hilderic and his nephews to the safety of Constantinople or face war with the eastern Roman empire. Rather disingenuously, the emperor concluded the document by re-iterating that in attacking the Vandal king, he would be avenging the memory of Geiseric whose constitutional arrangements had been ignored by Gelimer.[4]

Gelimer was not prepared to cede any ground and probably calculated that the disastrous conclusions to the previous attempts by the eastern Roman empire to wrest control of North Africa would discourage Justinian from making good on his threats. He sent a letter to the emperor which robustly defended his actions and pointed out that it had, in fact, been Hilderic who had challenged the Vandal tradition of royal succession by promoting his own nephews at Gelimer's expense. The communiqué concluded with a warning that any attack would be strongly resisted.[5]

In his account of the rupture of relations between Carthage and Constantinople, Procopius strongly implies that Justinian's intervention was connected to the fact that Hilderic was a long-standing personal guest-friend of the emperor.[6] Hilderic was, of course, the grandson of Valentinian III through his mother Eudocia, and the edict of toleration that he had issued towards the Nicene Church in AD 523 must also have been popular at the eastern imperial court. Justinian might also have been tempted by the renowned agricultural wealth of the region. Until the early fifth century Africa had been the bread basket of the western Roman Empire, and the emperor may well have believed that Africa could once more function as an agricultural powerhouse for his restored Roman Empire. All of these considerations might have played their part in Justinian's decision to attempt an invasion of the Vandal kingdom, but the emperor's principal motivation was probably the desire to deflect the mounting discontent within Constantinople at his high-handed style of rule and the unpopular fiscal policies of his senior officials.[7] The previous year Justinian had only been saved from being overthrown during the so-called Nika riots by the brutal intervention of his generals who had massacred of 30,000 of his subjects in the

Hippodrome.[8] A mission to restore Africa to the Roman Empire represented something of a fresh start for an emperor conscious that even his supporters would not tolerate any more blunders.

Justinian's decision to invade North Africa would have been determined by the sources of information available to him. First there were merchants who plied their trade throughout the Mediterranean: on at least two occasions in Procopius' narrative, merchants are represented as conduits of crucial strategic information.[9] Then there were Roman refugees who had made their way to the imperial court. Procopius mentions a certain Apollinarius, a greatly favoured confident of Hilderic, who after the king's fall:

> came to the Emperor Justinian with other Libyans, who were working in the interests of Hilderic, in order to entreat his favour as a suppliant.[10]

The Syrian chronicler Zacharias the Rhetor, a contemporary of Justinian, also recorded the major role that Romano-Africans had played in the emperor's decision to send an expeditionary force:

> There was then in Constantinople certain African nobles, who because of a quarrel that they had with a prince of that land [Gelimer], had quit their land and sought refuge with the emperor, and they had given him information about this country and urged him to act, saying that this country was extremely vast and very peaceful, and it was dreamt of a war with the Romans, but was locked in a war with the Moors, a people established in the desert and living like the Arabs on brigandage and raids. They emphasised in front of the emperor that this land had been snatched and stolen from the Roman Empire in the time of Geiseric, who had also taken Rome, carried off the objects of value in gold and silver, and retired to Carthage, in Africa. A fine city which he had seized and occupied.[11]

Such informants can only have furnished the emperor with a very partial account of affairs in Africa in order to encourage him to act. In his legislation, Justinian even made reference to the suffering inflicted by the Vandals on African exiles that he had encountered:

> We have seen worthy men, with tongues cut off at the root, eloquently describe the punishment visited upon them. Others dispersed through the various provinces after different tortures and ended their life in exile.[12]

Procopius describes the gradual processes by which the empire geared up for a vast western war. Justinian immediately put into action a new foreign policy initiative designed to free up troops and resources for a military expedition against the Vandal kingdom. A new treaty, optimistically termed 'the Eternal Peace', was concluded with Persia in September 532. But as these preparations were made, few members of Justinian's inner circle of advisors thought that the invasion was a sound idea. There were good reasons for this lack of enthusiasm. Although the potential rewards of the African campaign were high, the previous imperial expeditions to conquer the province had been unmitigated disasters and were hugely expensive. Whatever the economic potential of Africa, the initial expedition would demand a significant outlay in terms of manpower and money. Furthermore, there were concerns about how soldiers who had only just returned from a long hard war against the Persians would react to being immediately sent on what all knew to be an extremely risky enterprise.[13]

Despite these grave misgivings only John the Cappadocian, Justinian's Praetorian Prefect, had the nerve to try and dissuade the emperor from this course of action:

> You are planning to launch a mission against Carthage, to which if one goes by land, the journey takes one hundred and forty days, and by water, one is forced to cross the full extent of the open sea and go its very extremity. So whoever brings news to you from the camp will take a full year to deliver it. One might also add that if you are victorious over your enemies, you could not secure Africa whilst Sicily and Italy remain in the hands of others. At the same time if any reverse befalls you, O Emperor, the treaty having already been broken by you, you will bring danger to your own realm. In fact, pulling all of these thoughts together, it will be impossible for you to enjoy the fruits of victory whilst at the same time any defeat will jeopardise what is already well established.[14]

Initially it appeared that Justinian heeded these words of caution, but after the intervention of one of his own priests, who informed the emperor of a dream that revealed divine support for the campaign, preparations were recommenced. Justinian entrusted command of the expedition to his best general, Belisarius. At the same time encouraging news reached Constantinople that a serious revolt led by a certain Pudentius had broken against the Vandals in the territory of Tripolis in Libya. Justinian sent Pudentius the troops that he requested with the result that the easternmost reaches of the Vandal kingdom were permanently lost to the Hasdings. Further encouragement also arrived from Sardinia where the Vandal governor Godas had decided to break with Gelimer; on learning of the planned invasion, he sought an alliance with the eastern empire.[15]

Procopius served as an *assessor* in the expeditionary force commanded by Belisarius. The historian states that the general's command comprised around 18,000 men, made up of both regular and federate infantry and cavalry. The army was transported on a convoy of 500 ships which was protected by a fleet of 92 warships. Having left Constantinople towards the end of June 533, the fleet landed at Caput Vada to the east of Carthage in the last days of August. On the way, they had been able to stop and take on new supplies in Sicily. Welcome intelligence was received there that Gelimer was away from his capital and that much of the Vandal army had been sent to deal with the revolt in Sardinia.

Belisarius wished to capitalize on this lack of preparation and was conscious of his troops' lack of enthusiasm for a maritime engagement; consequently, he opted to disembark his force immediately and march on Carthage. Gelimer only learned of the invasion some four days after the landing, and immediately instructed his brother Ammata to take up a position at Ad Decimum, ten miles to the east of Carthage, with the intention of heading off Belisarius. Meanwhile, Gelimer and his cavalry caught up with the rear of the Byzantine army and shadowed it with the intention of entrapping it between the two Vandal forces. The Byzantine vanguard reached Ad Decimum far faster than Ammata expected, however; the Vandal commander was caught by surprise, killed and his army routed.[16]

Gelimer won a minor victory of his own, but instead of driving home his advantage, the king paused to bury Ammata – a moment of sentiment which gave the Byzantine forces time to rally and counter-attack. The Vandals were again surprised and retreated in total disarray. After this surprisingly easy victory, Belisarius led his troops into Carthage completely unopposed on 14 September. Climbing the Brysa Hill, Belisarius entered the royal palace where he took his ease on the throne of the absent Vandal king and feasted on the food that had been prepared in the royal kitchens.[17]

Meanwhile Gelimer had managed to rally his troops close to the city of Bulla Regia. He also recalled 5,000 troops who had been campaigning in Sardinia under the command of another brother, Tzazo. The Vandal king then marched on Carthage where he attempted to mount a blockade by cutting off its aqueduct whilst also attempting to induce the Arian soldiers in the Byzantine army and the inhabitants of the city to come over to his side. This initiative proved inconclusive. In December, Belisarius secured the defences of the city, satisfied himself that the Moors would not provide any aid to the Vandal king, marshalled his troops and marched out to confront Gelimer's army. The two sides met at Tricamarum some 20 miles outside the city and the Vandal army was once again defeated. The king, with most of his troops killed or scattered, his treasure seized and his brother dead, fled to Mons Pappua in Numidia with a handful of followers and he sought sanctuary with the Moors. In Carthage, Hippo Regius and other African cities most of those Vandals who were still at large had taken refuge at Christian sanctuaries from where they were disarmed and taken into custody. A further blow to Gelimer's fortunes was dealt by the handing over of what amounted to his reserve funds to Belisarius by one of his officials, Boniface.[18]

Gelimer's last days of freedom saw him a broken man. After three months of harsh winter and starvation in his mountain hideout, the Vandal king was ready to surrender. In a peculiar passage, Procopius describes how the king asked Belisarius for gifts of bread to alleviate his hunger, a sponge to bathe an infected eye, a harp with which to lament his misfortune and assurances for his own safety. Gelimer received his gifts, bemoaned his fate and was brought before the imperial general in Carthage. The depredations that he had suffered had clearly affected him; Procopius describes how the defeated king broke out into fits of uncontrollable laughter during his audience with the general. Sympathizers protested that he was of sound mind and his amusement was merely a result of his realization, after the dramatic change in fortune that he had endured, that 'man's lot was worthy nothing else apart from much laughter'. In the summer of 534, Belisarius returned to Constantinople with Gelimer and 2,000 Vandal warriors.[19]

In the imperial capital, Justinian was so confident of final victory that he had assumed the imperial titles of *Vandalicus* and *Africanus* a full month before the decisive victory at Tricamarum.[20] Now a great victory triumph was held in Constantinople, the centrepiece of which saw Gelimer stripped of his purple robe and forced to do obeisance to Justinian in the Hippodrome.[21] In a display of calculated imperial clemency, the defeated king was retired to an estate in Galatia. His former subjects were deported en masse to the empire's eastern frontiers where they were organized into cavalry cohorts charged with its defence against the Persian threat.[22] The Vandal kingdom was at an end but the memory of the great Byzantine victory, and the role that Justinian had played within it, would be kept alive on a mural that decorated the vaulted ceiling of vestibule of the imperial palace which showed the emperor and empress being approached in supplication by the defeated Vandal king.[23]

Justinian the Saviour of Africa

Procopius was anxious to highlight the efforts that Justinian expended on the physical restoration of his new realm following the military victory over the Vandals. In the *Buildings*, his tribute to the multifarious empire-wide building projects of Justinian, Procopius reserved a significant section for the programme of prudent reconstruction and foundation carried out in post-conquest North Africa.[24] Fittingly, he began his account with Carthage, the capital of the new Praetorian Prefecture:

> First, then, he took care for Carthage, which now, very correctly, is called Justinianê, rebuilding the whole circuit wall, which had collapsed, and excavating around it a moat which it had not had before. He also dedicated shrines, one to the Mother of God in the palace, and one outside this to a certain local saint, Saint Prima. Furthermore he built stoas on either side of what is called the Maritime forum, and a public bath, a fine sight, which they have named Theodorianae, after the empress. He also constructed a monastery on the shore inside the circuit-wall, close to the harbour which they call Mandracium, and by surrounding it with very strong defences he made it an impregnable fortress.[25]

The strong emphasis on the construction and re-development of religious centres, fortifications and public utilities is a consistent theme throughout the text. Indeed, *The Buildings* is so formulaic that scholars have justifiably shrunk from using it as a guide to Justinian's construction programmes.[26] A recent survey of the epigraphic evidence from the eastern and North African provinces during the reign of Justinian has confirmed the difficulty of identifying building projects as part of a coherent imperial blueprint. This caution is particularly pertinent regarding Justinian's building activities in Carthage. Although a number of structures broadly dating to this period have been excavated, none of them accurately correlates with Procopius' account. There are many building inscriptions in which Justinian's name was mentioned which did not appear on Procopius' list.[27] In Carthage itself there has been considerable scepticism as to whether a coherent 'Justinianic' Building Program really existed. As one archaeologist who worked in the city for many years observed: 'In the Byzantine period, while there may have been some Justinianic revival, the whole city cannot have been rebuilt or redecorated within only twenty-five years.'[28]

It is precisely because of its formulaic nature, however, that the *Buildings* may be regarded as a powerful testament to imperial aspiration.

Figure 9.1 The topography of early Byzantine Carthage

As a panegyric, the work sought to create the fiction of a perfect imperial building programme that underlined the emperor's care for security and comfort of his subjects both new and old. That the citizens of the Roman Empire now lived in safety, protected from worldly threats such as barbarians, misery, diseases, poverty and other misfortunes that lay beyond the human sphere of influence, was a recurrent theme in the work. Hence the establishment of a common pattern within the *Buildings* which attributed to Justinian the restoration or erection of a city wall, a basic infrastructure (water supply and streets) and a church or shrine for the Virgin Mary in numerous towns and cities across the empire.

Archaeology has shown that the restoration and new construction of public utilities, Christian buildings and fortifications did take place in many towns and cities across North Africa during this period, although not in the precise form that Procopius suggests. At Carthage, commercial ports were extensively redeveloped, a sign that the imperial authorities were anxious to exploit Africa's agricultural productivity.[29] There is evidence of the improvement of some public amenities including several bath complexes which show signs of extensive refurbishment.[30] The Byrsa Hill, the administrative heart of the city since the Punic era, appears to have been fortified by walls and on its summit the Proconsular Palace, which might have also served as the Vandal royal palace, was re-furbished.[31] Furthermore, there is evidence that at least eight churches, two monasteries and a martyr complex were also either built or underwent renovation in the city during this period.[32]

This building activity was not limited to just Carthage. At Leptis Magna, the forum was fortified and part of the city enclosed by walls. In the time of Justinian the old judicial basilica was transformed into a very large and richly decorated church dedicated to Mary Theotokos. In addition a further four small churches were built.[33] At Sabratha a similar pattern of building activity during the Justinianic period has been identified: the city walls were re-built and extended, the judicial basilica transformed into a church and a considerable number of other churches were either renovated or constructed anew.[34]

Outside the main cities there is also evidence of renewed activity in urban centres, albeit of a new kind. In the port city of Leptiminus, for example, large-scale amphora production took place in kilns built in the disused East Baths. Whilst it is certainly possible that the revived prosperity of Leptiminus was stimulated by the need to supply the army, the scale of the imperial revival within the city remains striking.[35] Evidence for butchery, meat processing and iron working has also been found in the East Baths complex. Regardless of the situation on the frontiers, Leptiminus appears to have been thriving.[36]

In many of the larger towns and cities of Africa, the literary and physical transformation of the urban topography supported the varied justifications for the invasion that the administration put about in the period after the conquest. The first of these was set out clearly by John Lydus, two decades after Belisarius' victory, in his study of the magistracies of the Roman state:

> While the government was being buffeted by such tsunamis and storms of trouble, Fortune brought forth diligence as a counterweight to the idleness of the past, for it had put Justinian in charge of the state, the most vigilant of all emperors who . . . fought for the state in order that they might

> capture not merely whatever had once belonged to the Romans that because of past indolence was completely lost, but besides whatever belonged to the enemy, in addition to the former . . . and when he suddenly waged war upon the Vandals, a Germanic people, who were devouring Africa, he both captured them in just two months, and after taking them in war, presented them to the empire, having delivered to the Romans for servitude Gelimer himself along with the most illustrious men of his people, whom the barbarians called Hasdings, his wife and children, and huge wealth just as though they were worthless skivvies.[37]

Justinianic imperial rhetoric sought to conflate the idea that it was an emperor's duty to reunite the long fragmented parts of the old Roman empire with the claim that this was also part of a divinely ordained plan.[38] Justinian himself proclaimed:

> We are inspired with the hope that God will grant us rule over the rest of what, subject to the ancient Romans to the limits of both seas, they later lost by their neglect.[39]

The invasion of North Africa was represented as part of this divine schema by the emperor. In an edict issued in 534, the emperor stated:

> What thanks and praise we should offer up to our Lord Jesus Christ, neither the mind can formulate or the tongue speak of. We already received many bounties from God and we acknowledge His innumerable gifts showered upon us and we recognise that we have done nothing worthy of them, but, above all that which the omnipotent God has now, for His praise and glory, deemed proper to demonstrate through us exceeds all wonderful acts which have happened in the course of time – namely that freedom should, through us, in so short a time be received by Africa, which 105 years before was captured by the Vandals who were enemies of both mind and body. . . . By what language, therefore, or by what works worthy of God that He deemed it proper that the injuries of the Church should be avenged through me, the least of His servants.[40]

The conquest of Africa was cast as a crusade to unite the orthodox Romano-Africans with their church, while restoring the lands of the old western Roman Empire. Justinian's was a divine mission to save the orthodox Romano-Africans from their savage persecution by the heterodox Arian Vandals.[41] Indeed, it did not take long before a story began to circulate that Justinian himself had been persuaded to undertake the conquest after the African bishop Laetus of Nepta, who had been martyred by Huneric, had appeared to him in a dream.[42]

This link between the Vandal persecution and the imperial programme of reconquest was widely accepted by contemporaries. When Cassiodorus sent a letter on behalf of the Roman senate pleading with Justinian to hold off from a similar invasion of Italy, he was anxious to create a clear distinction between the treatment that he and his colleagues received from the Ostrogothic king and the state of affairs that had existed in Vandal North Africa:

> My religion, which is your own, is known to be thriving; why then do you try and do more for me? . . . For Africa deserved to receive its freedom from you, It is cruel for me to lose a freedom that I already have.[43]

Very swiftly the new regime presented itself as the divinely-sanctioned deliverer of the Romano-Africans from the heresy and barbarism of the Vandals, and supported this with an ambitious building programme. But once the initial euphoria of Belisarius' great victory had died down, Justinian and his officials would find that tackling the Vandal legacy in North Africa required more than glittering triumphs and deportations.

The Problem of the Vandal Past

Deep political and religious divisions remained in North Africa which could not be spirited away by the power of imperial rhetoric. As we have seen, many African aristocrats had prospered under the Vandal kings and had held prominent positions at court and in the royal administration. Even Gelimer, who was said to have represented an aristocratic faction hostile to Hilderic's friendly relations with Constantinople, continued to maintain strong relations with his Roman subjects. Although Romano-African supporters of Hilderic such as Apollinarius did go to Constantinople to enlist Justinian's support, Procopius refers to others who remained loyal, including one Boniface, a native of Byzacena, who was entrusted by Gelimer with the transportation of the royal treasury to Visigothic Spain in the event of the king's defeat.[44]

Procopius indicates that Gelimer received some support from the Roman population of Africa, although he explains this in terms of the king's bribery and the cunning of the Africans, rather than the essential interdependence of the region's population. The historian states that many Roman camp followers and non-combatants were killed by local farmers who had been promised a fixed sum of gold for each Byzantine head they presented to the Vandal king. Even if this did not translate into active support for the Vandal king, it certainly implies some ambivalence towards the invaders from the East.[45] Nor did Belisarius assume that his army would automatically enjoy the support of their fellow 'Romans'. Early in his account of the campaign, Procopius relates an incident in which Belisarius severely punished soldiers who had stolen fruit from the fields. Summoning together his army the general warned that such larceny would simply unite the Romano-Africans and Vandals in their opposition: his was a campaign to win hearts and minds.[46] Later in the campaign, Belisarius adopted a different solution to the same problem and had a local grandee named Laurus impaled on a hill overlooking Carthage for plotting with Gelimer. Procopius would observe that this very public execution had its desired effect:

> and as a consequence of this the rest came to feel a kind of uncontrollable fear and stopped their treason.[47]

Even after the final defeat and deportation of the Vandals, Justinian did not take the loyalty of his new Romano-African subjects for granted. In his first legislation directed at the new provinces explicitly the emperor warned his judges and officials not to prey on his new African subjects:

> For although we try to ensure through the aid of God that the tax payer should remain unscathed in all the provinces, we especially consult the interests of the tax payers of the African diocese who after a captivity of so long a time, are through us, with the aid of God, allowed to look through the light of freedom.[48]

This rhetoric was primarily intended to appease the Romano-African population, but it also highlights a potential source of tension. Under the Vandal kings, Romano-African elites had been close to the centre of power; Carthage was a royal capital and aristocrats living in its orbit could expect to hold positions of real influence. The incorporation of North Africa into the Byzantine Empire suddenly placed the same elites on the opposite side of the world from the epicentre of imperial rule. Just as they had in the late empire, the most ambitious Romano-Africans would have to travel overseas to seek out preferment and patronage. Now it would not be a journey across the Tyrrhenian Sea to Rome, Milan or Ravenna, however, but a long and arduous voyage to Constantinople.

But it was the thorny question of religious allegiance which posed the greatest problem for the new administration. The correspondence of members of the African Nicene ecclesiastical elite from this period was dominated by one issue – the integration of Arian clergy and congregations into their church.[49] With the majority of Vandals having been forced out, it seems clear that these recalcitrant Arians were themselves Romano-Africans: evidence of the widespread impact of the heresy during the Hasding kingdom. Justinian's own legislation explicitly refers to the conversion of Romano-Africans to Arianism.[50] But as we have seen, religious allegiances could be exceptionally fluid in the Vandal period and this continued to be the case in the years which followed. Despite the disapproval of both Nicene and Arian ecclesiastical establishments, the period had been marked by a large degree of interconnectivity between Arian and Homoousian congregations. Indeed, outbreaks of violent religious factionalism had tended to be prompted by other local tensions and disputes. What faced Justinian, then, was the prospect of integrating a lay population which was unusually adept at exploiting religious differences for political ends, while under the intense scrutiny of a Nicene establishment that was anxious to assert its own primacy in Africa.

Maintaining good relations with the African Nicene Church was clearly a priority for Justinian, but the lay elite were also a key constituency of support for his administration. In an edict issued in 534, Justinian had set out the new complex administrative arrangements for the government of the new Praetorian Prefecture of Africa.[51] At its head was a Praetorian Prefect himself, supported by a staff of 396.[52] Below the Prefect were 7 provinces each administered by a governor with a staff of 50.[53] A military structure was instituted in parallel with this civil government and authority was split between 6 *duces* (dukes) each of whom had an extensive staff and military contingent under his command.[54] Although the most senior positions in the new imperial administration were filled by appointees from Constantinople, the vast majority of this infrastructure was to be staffed by local Romano-Africans.[55] If the province was to be administered and exploited, the empire would require the cooperation of a landholding elite who continued to enjoy considerable economic clout, but who had their own religious and political aspirations. Clearly, this was a sector of society which Justinian could not offend if he was to integrate North Africa within his empire.

The majority of Romano-African 'Catholics' had peacefully co-habited and fraternized with their Arian counterparts. This important group had been deeply implicated in the successful running of the Vandal kingdom, politically, economically and culturally, and would be needed for the new imperial state. For them, the prospect of religious retribution after the Vandal period was distinctly unattractive. Overly harsh treatment of ex-Arians would have run the risk of alienating an important section of society who might have viewed it as a witch-hunt against those who had close links with the previous Vandal regime. There was already considerable turmoil in North Africa caused by the legal complexities of claim and counterclaim over property that had been purportedly been seized by the Vandals sometimes nearly a century before.[56] Reconciliation rather than retribution would have to be the byword of the new Byzantine regime.

Fiction and Reconciliation in Post-Conquest Africa

Architecture provided one medium in which a true image of religious unity could be presented, and an extraordinary building programme lay at the centre of Justinian's drive for reconciliation in post-conquest Africa. This project allowed the emperor and both secular and ecclesiastical religious elites to unite publicly around their shared commitment to doctrinal orthodoxy whilst at the same studiously ignoring the compromises and collaborations of the past.

Despite the scholarly scepticism about the very existence of a large-scale Justinianic building programme in Africa, recent excavations in Carthage indicate that, in the religious sphere at least, there was some kind of coordinated initiative that was clearly shaped by both architectural and liturgical influences from the eastern Mediterranean. At least eight churches and a number of Christian cult buildings in the city show clear traces of varying degrees of re-modelling in this period.[57] There is a certain uniformity to many of these modifications that strongly hints at the powerful influence of the imperial government, if not its direct involvement. Particularly striking is the re-orientation of many of the basilicas towards the east through the construction of new (eastern) apses, something that had long been the architectural orthodoxy in the eastern Mediterranean.[58] A renewed emphasis on the veneration of relics during this period also points to eastern Mediterranean influence. North Africa had long been the locus for the veneration of martyrs, of course, thanks to its strong and vexed history of martyrdom.[59] Indeed, a major feature of fourth- and early fifth-century church architecture in the region had been the placing of relics in caskets that were deposited in a vault below the altar, or in a large vault below the apse. Usually they remained inaccessible underground, although in some cases the relics were accessible through a crypt.[60] During the Justinianic period, however, the redevelopment of churches in Carthage reflected a marked change in the form in which these relics were venerated.

The Damous El Karita was a very large cemetery church and pilgrimage centre which lay just outside the city walls of Carthage, and provides a clear illustration of this process. During the Justinianic period, the basilica was expanded from nine to eleven aisles and a new eastern apse and atrium were also added. To the south, a subterranean rotunda was constructed which acted as the spiritual centre of the restored complex. Entering through a semi-circular forecourt screened by a portico, pilgrims would process into the circular martyrium. Access to and departure from the circular crypt, where the relics were housed under a marble ciborium, was gained by lateral, counter-rotating staircases. What is clear is that the rotunda at the Damous El Karita was specifically designed for large-scale circulation with a constant flow of pilgrims processing past the relics. The prototype for this architectural schema seems to have been the palace architecture of Constantinople.[61]

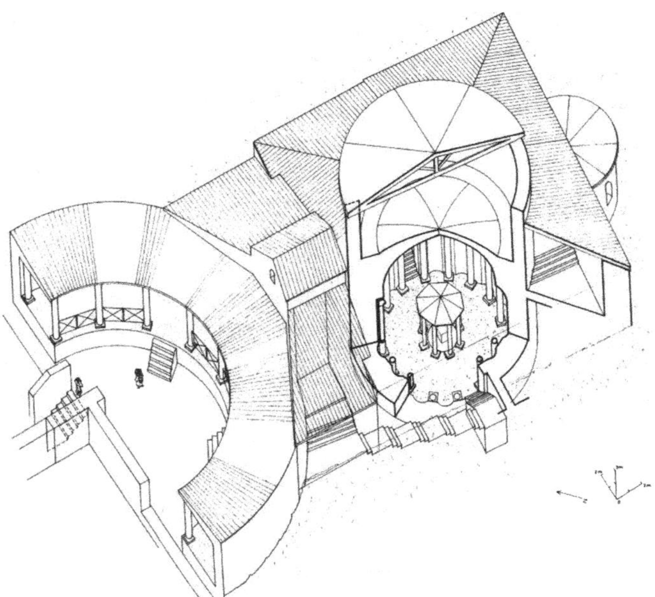

Figure 9.2 Isometric illustration of the Basilica at Damous El Karita. Reproduced courtesy of the Austrian Archaeological Institute

Damous El Karita was not the only Christian centre in Justinianic Carthage that was designed for pilgrim circulation. At Bir Ftouha, another large cemetery church just outside the city walls, a very large pilgrimage complex was constructed in the 640s. The overall architectural plan of the complex resembled a Latin cross with a baptistery at its head in the east, peristyle courtyards as the arms, a basilica as the main body and a usual nine-sided hall as its base. What the excavators of this extraordinary complex have demonstrated is that its plan was framed around the concept of movement, and particularly circumambulation. Starting from the nine-sided hall, pilgrims would process through a gallery into the main basilica where an ambulatory provided a path for pilgrims around the screened-off sanctuary, which contained the tombs of presumably martyrs and other saints. This architectural ensemble was connected to the basilica by peristyle courtyards, and culminated in a large baptistery. This was divided internally by a circular colonnade which may have allowed for further rotation. Architecturally, the baptistery acted as the counterpoint of the polygonal western complex of the church. As the excavators have pointed out: 'Since the baptistery was the termination of the design, baptism was likely to have been the primary goal of some pilgrims, catechumens and penitents'.[62] They conclude that: 'As a newly-founded basilica *ad corpus*, Bir Ftouha may have commemorated Carthage's official return to orthodoxy, this major metropolis having recently been incorporated into the Byzantine empire . . . a pilgrimage to Bir Ftouha may have been a statement of orthodoxy, a celebration of the victory over Arianism'.[63]

These large new Byzantine pilgrimage sites were also found inside the city walls of Carthage. The so-called Circular Monument, situated between *Cardines* II and III east and just south of the Decumanus IV north in the east end of the city, was comprehensively restored in the mid-sixth century and, according to its most recent excavators, acted together with the adjacent basilica as a church-*memoria*-complex rather like that at Damous El Karita.[64] Another important basilica complex with an unusual ground plan was constructed at Bir Messaouda – an important central neighbourhood of Carthage, which straddled the Decumanus Maximus, the main thoroughfare of the city connecting the Byrsa Hill to the ports to the north, and *Cardines* IX and X east to the west and east respectively. This was a transept basilica with three north–south aisles 69 × 17 metres in size and five east west aisles of 34.5 × 22.5 metres. Where the inner colonnades of the east–west oriented aisles met the axis of the north–south colonnades stood four substantial pillars which supported a central tower or dome. At the central

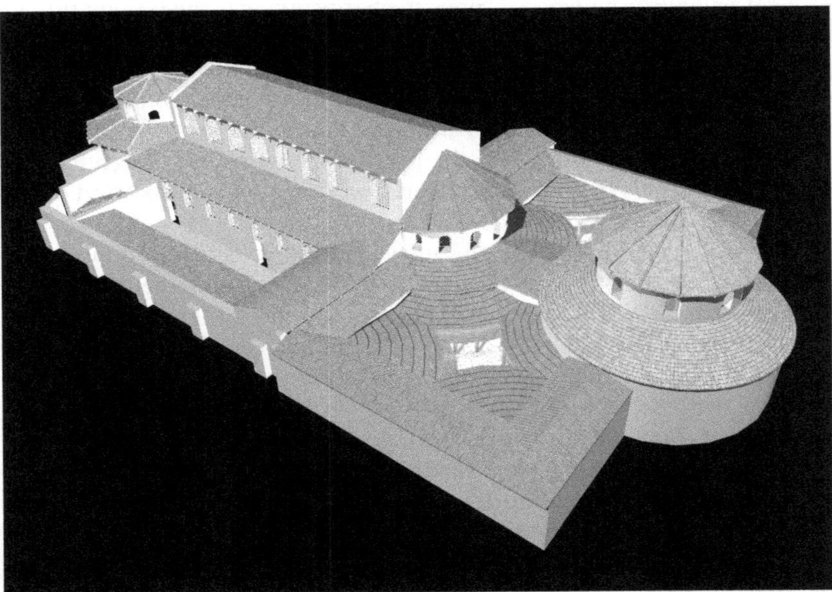

Figure 9.3 Reconstruction of the Basilica at Bir Ftouha. Reproduced courtesy of the *Journal of Roman Archaeology*. Source: Stevens, S. T. et al. (eds.), *Bir Ftouha. A Pilgrimage Church Complex at Carthage, JRA* Suppl. 59 (Rhode Island, 2005). © JRA

confluence of the aisles stood the altar, with some kind of canopy or *ciborium* over it. The building was orientated by an apse to the east of this central sanctuary. Like the other Justinianic era basilicas at Carthage, its floors and walls were richly decorated with mosaics, marble *opus sectile* and painted plaster. On the northern and southern flanks the basilica equidistant from the central nave of the east–west aisles were a very large baptistery with colonnaded walkways and a subterranean crypt with walls decorated with various motifs, including a Greek cross, which was clearly used to house martyr relics. Although it followed a very different architectural plan to Bir Ftouha, the two complexes were united by the emphasis on circulation through well-placed ambulatories that pushed the faith down channels created by ambulatories, chancels and colonnaded aisles between the baptistery and the saints' *memoria*.[65]

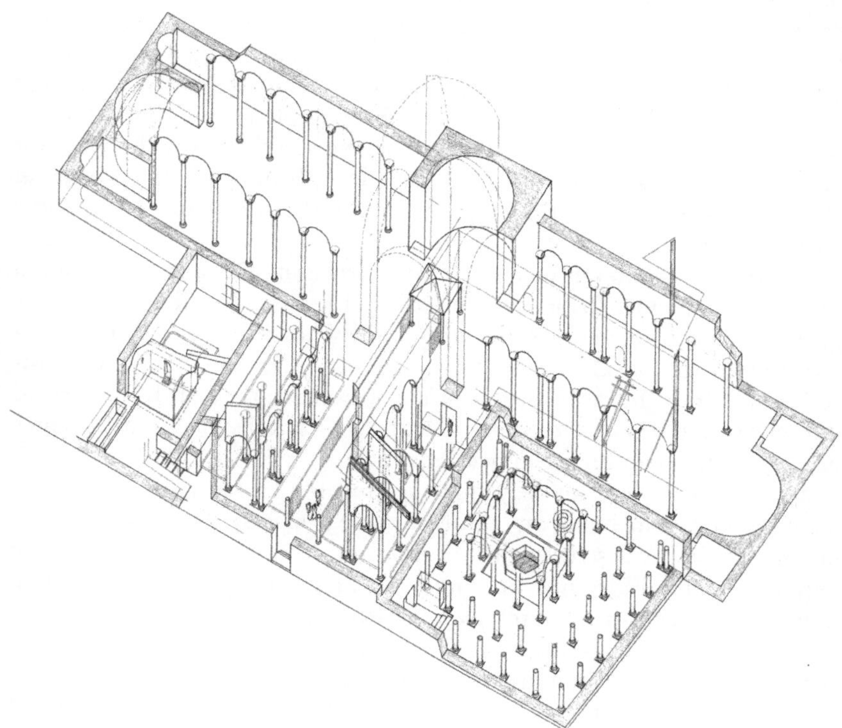

Figure 9.4 Isometric illustration of the Basilica at Bir Messaouda

The design of these buildings suggests that African Christianity was becoming increasingly synchronized with current developments in the eastern Roman empire. Despite the differences in their ground plans, there was a shared emphasis on rotation, martyr veneration and baptism in these buildings. In the east there was a growth in interest in pilgrimage in the second half of the sixth century and a particular emphasis on what has been termed a 'tactile piety'. This involved the faithful worshipping in close proximity to – or even handling – holy relics or an object that had been in contact with them. The east also witnessed developments in processional liturgies. Such parades had evolved in the great churches of Jerusalem in the fourth century AD before spreading to Rome and Constantinople, but had never been an important part of the African liturgy. By the sixth century in the eastern imperial capital, the Eucharistic service included two processions of the clergy during the service. Indeed in Constantinople many of the churches in whose construction or re-development Justinian was involved were specifically designed to accommodate elaborate liturgical processions. There were the processions that went from church to church through the various neighbourhoods of the city.[66] Now, in post-conquest North Africa, the same liturgical blueprint seems to have been implemented through these 'superchurches'. This period also witnessed a discernible growth in interest in eastern saints such as Tryphon, Theodore, Pantaleon, and Menas in Africa.[67] It seems likely that the imperial authorities had played some part in this process.

Yet these new developments were more than the one dimensional top-down implementation of doctrinal and liturgical conformity. These processions and ceremonies provided a finely orchestrated affirmation of the sacred and secular order that governed the new order in post-conquest Africa. In these awe-inspiring structures, the faithful witnessed the representatives of the emperor and their ecclesiastical and lay elites processing in a carefully planned sequence.

Although it is very unlikely that the emperor had any direct involvement with or contributed any funds to these projects, the construction of major ecclesiastical structures in important cities would certainly have required imperial blessing. Procopius' comment that 'it was impossible to build or to restore a church except with imperial support, not only in Constantinople but everywhere in the empire', was probably more accurate than modern commentators have often suggested.[68] Justinian's legislation suggests that he saw his role as the overall co-ordination of his grand religious project, rather than the direct control of specifics. In *Novella* 67, for example, the emperor ordered potential *evergates* to turn their attentions to the necessary task of repairing the decaying churches of Constantinople and the provinces, rather than endowing yet more small churches.[69]

The well-documented process of imperial rebuilding following the Byzantine conquest of Italy sheds important light upon the contemporary situation in North Africa. Here, church building and renovation was generally undertaken on the joint initiative of local ecclesiastical and secular elites (who usually funded the projects) and the imperial officials sent to govern them. Structures such as the basilica of San Vitale at Ravenna were loci for a complicated confluence of local, regional and imperial interests, both secular and religious.[70] There is no reason to suppose that the situation in Africa was any different. Certainly inscriptional evidence from outside Carthage reveals the considerable input of Solomon, Justinian's Praetorian Prefect in Africa, for two separate spells in the 530s and 540s.[71] In cities such as Sufetula inscriptions indicate that local clergy were involved in the construction of churches and baptisteries in the Byzantine period.[72] Rather more epigraphic evidence exists for the construction of forts in Africa in this period. A variety of institutions seem to have taken responsibility for these constructions, including the imperial administration and the praetorian prefecture as well as local military and civil authorities.[73]

Each group had much to gain. The ambitious building schemes that followed the re-conquest were not merely about the reconfiguration of the urban landscape but also the past. This vision of Christian orthodoxy gloriously restored helped to shift the focus away from compromises and collaborations that had been the reality of the recently departed Vandal regime. At Bir Messaouda, Dermech I and many of the other basilicas built in Justinianic Carthage, the old churches that symbolized the collaborations and compromises under the Vandal regime were quite literally subsumed under these new superstructures. All that would remain would be carefully selected vignettes that told of terrible persecution and brave resistance. New buildings were constructed to hold the relics of Nicene churchmen reputed to have been martyred by the Vandals such as the baptistery-chapel of bishop Iucundus and perhaps the baptistery of Vitalis at Sufetula.[74]

Most famously in Carthage, at the so-called Monastery of Bigua, an inscription to the seven Macchabeen brothers, martyrs of the Old Testament who died in the second century BC in Antioch, was laid into a mosaic floor.[75] The decision to commemorate the seven Macchabees in North Africa may at first seem bizarre, but the anonymous account of the seven monks of Gafsa who were martyred in AD 483 provides a possible context. According to this text, the monks were killed and thrown into the sea, but their bodies miraculously found their way back to the shore and were buried in the monastery. The writer repeatedly compared these two sets of martyrs and mentioned them in the same context. Some of the remains of the original Macchabeen martyrs had been brought to Constantinople in the mid-fifth century AD.[76] One might therefore speculate about whether some of these relics were subsequently brought from the imperial capital after the Byzantine conquest once the popular association had become known. Whatever that particular connection, it seems likely that this was intended as a reminder of the martyrdoms suffered during the Vandal persecutions.

In the great new churches of Carthage, pilgrims would not just be reminded of Christian orthodoxy gloriously regained but also the part that the emperor, his high officials, the African Nicene Church and the lay elite had supposedly played in that great victory. In the cemetery churches such as Bir Ftouha, as pilgrims processed towards the great baptismal font past the sanctuary and apses screened off by a grille, they might catch a glimpse of the tombs of these honoured people close to the sacred relics of martyrs. At Bir Messaouda and Dermech I, it would have been the living representatives of these groups who stood in glorious seclusion behind the chancels. The message, like that of the great mosaic at S. Vitale, was a simple one. It was these groups under the protection of God, Jesus and the martyr saints who had restored Africa to peace, security and doctrinal orthodoxy.

The Limits of Compromise

The spectacular church buildings of the early Byzantine period created a spectacular façade of religious and political unity, but the contrasting interests of the worshippers within them posed genuine problems to the new administration. On the one side was a motivated and triumphant Nicene clerical elite, anxious to flex its muscles after the dark days of the past, on the other a selection of secular and Arian interests more concerned with maintaining a tacit *status quo*. In his extraordinary and scurrilous satire *The Secret History*, written as a steamy counterpoint to the classicism of *Wars* and *The Buildings*, Procopius directly accused Justinian of bringing unrest to North Africa through his harsh treatment of the Arians.[77] He could scarcely have been more wrong. In fact, despite the Christian triumphalism of the emperor's edicts, Justinian's initial religious policies in Africa were primarily informed by a deep political pragmatism, and had little to do with zealotry. If the new prefecture was to be a success, the emperor needed the lay and ecclesiastical elites within North Africa to remain unified. No less serious was the issue of the large number of Arians in the Byzantine army, a group who already had an uneasy relationship with the emperor, if Procopius' account is to be trusted.[78] It is hardly surprising that the emperor chose to tread lightly as he approached Africa's Arian problem.

The first challenges faced by the imperial authorities concerned the status of the Arian clergy who remained in Africa and who wished to join the Nicene Church, and the difficult issue of the restoration of Nicene ecclesiastical assets that had been seized by the Arians. The emperor's initial solutions to both of these problems were compromises. Justinian's crucial edict on these issues no longer exists, but reference to it in later laws allows us to piece the legislation together. The Arian clergy, it would seem, were ordered to hand over the sacraments to their Nicene counterparts immediately, but other property was to be surrendered only after a significant time delay. It seems likely that the Arian clergy were also allowed to keep their former offices once they had been re-baptized and admitted within the Nicene Church. The delay that the legislation allowed for the handover of church property was presumably to enable the orderly conversion of the Arian ecclesiastical hierarchy and their congregations, and to avoid the turmoil and bitterness that the sudden transfer of assets would create.[79]

The African Nicene Church represented the most obvious impediment to such a compromise. Correspondence and council records from this period highlight the anxieties of its leaders towards these re-baptized Arian converts. There was particular resistance to the suggestion that the Arian clergy might be integrated seamlessly within the existing ecclesiastical hierarchy. Within 18 months, Justinian's compromise had begun to unravel. The African Nicene Church mobilized against a proposal which failed to recognize the sacrifices that they had made for their faith during the long years of persecution. As early as 533, leading theologians were writing to important ecclesiastical figures in Italy, rehearsing the doctrinal case against Arianism with the clear intention of galvanizing winder western support.[80] A general ecclesiastical council was summoned to meet between January and August 535 under the leadership of Reparatus, the new Primate of *Proconsularis*.[81] The choice of venue for the proceedings was a provocative one. The meeting was to take place in the Basilica Fausti, one of the Nicene churches that had been seized by Huneric, and represented a pointed physical reminder of the issues at stake.[82] After addressing a number of other disciplinary issues, the council sent a petition to Justinian which requested the full and immediate restitution of the church properties confiscated by the Arians. At the same time a letter was sent to Pope John II, which appealed for his support against the imperial policy of allowing re-baptized Arian clerics to maintain the status of their office after their conversion.[83] It took little to persuade the papacy of the strength of the African Church's position. John had died before the African church envoys arrived in Rome, but his successor Agapetus was anxious to assert his own ecclesiastical authority over Africa and acceded to the demands of the council, confirming that converted Arian priests could not simply remain in office.[84]

News quickly followed from Constantinople that Justinian had backed down on the issue of the immediate restitution of church property. *Novel* 37 issued in August 535 ordered:

> that they [the African Nicene Church] might firmly in accordance with the tenor of the law already promulgated in connection therewith, hold the property of the churches of all Africa, which were taken from them in the time of the tyrants, and which, after the victories granted us by the help of God over the Vandals, were returned to them by pious order of our majesty, subject to the payment of taxes fixed in each place, we deem it proper, willingly and gladly to grant their request.[85]

All churches were to be returned to the Nicene fold. But this was by no means the only victory for the African Nicene Church within this particular law. The Praetorian Prefect Solomon was also instructed that:

> Your Sublimity must take care that no Arians, Donatists or Jews or others who are known not to adhere to the orthodox religion, share in any manner of ecclesiastical rites, but that impious persons are entirely excluded from sacred things and temples and no permission whatever shall be granted them to ordain bishops or clergymen, or to baptise any persons, making them adherents of their error, because such sects have been condemned not only by our, but also by former laws and are followed only by impious and pollute men.[86]

Arians, even those who had re-baptized, were also to be banned from public office and from any imperial administrative post for fear that 'heretics may seem to govern the orthodox'. Anyone who violated this law was to pay a fine of ten pounds of gold.[87]

For the Pope and the African Church this apparent *volte face* represented an important victory over an emperor who until then had shown little propensity for listening to their opinions or acting upon them.[88]

There is a marked triumphalism in the letter that Agapetus subsequently sent to Justinian congratulating him for acting so decisively in the interests of doctrinal orthodoxy.[89] Yet one might question whether the emperor had really been forced into a humiliating retreat. Justinian had framed his new legislation within the traditional model of imperial laws relating to heretics, schismatics, pagans and Jews; in so doing, he created the impression that he was acting decisively on a crucial issue while sidestepping the suggestion that the African Arians represented a unique and intractable problem. *Novel* 37 strongly suggests that, in granting a stay on the handing over of formerly Nicene property, the emperor had unwittingly encouraged the Arians to launch a barrage of lawsuits in an attempt to retain these possessions. Conspicuously, Justinian also issued an edict which limited any claims to the restitution of other Vandal confiscations to property taken within the last two generations and to those who could prove their paternal and maternal parentage.[90] Justinian acted because he realized that his attempts at reconciliation were having the opposite effect, and not because of any pressure from the pope. Faced with this resistance, and attracted by the opportunity to portray himself as a pious Christian prince, Justinian acted decisively and very much on his own terms.

Once these vexed questions had been resolved, there was a general consensus that the Arian congregations needed to be integrated into Nicene orthodoxy as quickly as possible, and that the Nicene Church needed to set its own house in order. There was little appetite for further retribution. In the years immediately before and after the imperial conquest, attempts had been made to repair the internal infrastructure of a church establishment which had been badly damaged by the years of exile; this had focused particularly upon the restoration of both clerical and pastoral discipline.[91] Conciliar records from both Byzacena and Numidia suggest that the primates of these provinces were particularly active in articulating their ecclesiastical authority in a form that would be visible in both Rome and Constantinople. We hear of five provincial councils in Byzacena and Numidia in the sixth century and it is implied that those in Numidia were to be held annually. Although only one provincial council is known to have met in Proconsularis in this period, four general councils were held there.[92]

In the longer term, Justinian's handling of the Arian issue severely compromised his standing with the African Nicene Church, and this situation did not improve. His unilateral legislation raised suspicions among the African ecclesiastical community that Justinian felt intervention into Christian doctrinal affairs to be within his jurisdiction as emperor. These views were later confirmed by the 'Three Chapters' controversy which convulsed the church in the 540s and 550s. This crisis was precipitated by the emperor's clumsy attempts to address the controversial issue of the relative humanity and divinity of Christ, despite widespread opposition within the western church. This issue was a particularly sensitive one for African Nicenes, who had already tangled with the Arians on similar issues relating to Christ's divinity. Their long struggle with what had become an intellectually sophisticated and well-organized threat had hardened them against the prospect of any compromise with a new opponent. After more than a century of conflict, the self-identity of the Nicene African Church was bound up in an active sense of suspicion and victimhood when it came to secular authority. Perhaps inevitably, the Three Chapters controversy was to be defined by bribery and repressive tactics, deposition, imprisonment and exile.[93]

Mutiny and the Moors

The imperial administration also faced a succession of military crises in North Africa. By 534 Moorish groups took advantage of the turmoil created by the Vandal collapse and resumed their raids on Byzacena and Numidia.[94] The Byzantine response was placed in the hands of the general Solomon, after Belisarius had withdrawn to Constantinople for political reasons.[95] Solomon was initially successful: he won a number of emphatic victories in Byzacena which temporally checked the Moorish threat, although Numidia proved harder to pacify. In AD 536, however, the nascent Byzantine administration in Africa imploded, as a direct result of Justinian's religious policies. According to Procopius, there were about a thousand Arians serving in the imperial army in North Africa. These troops had previously been exempt from imperial legislation against their faith, but the new edicts included no such allowance. Arian soldiers found themselves fighting for an empire that banned them from attending church services or holding public office.[96]

> For it was not possible for them to worship God in their usual manner, but they were excluded both from all sacraments and from all sacred rites. For the Emperor Justinian did not allow any Christian who did not espouse the orthodox faith to receive baptism or any other sacrament. But most of all they were stirred up by the feast of Easter, during which they found themselves unable to baptise their children with the sacred water or do anything else pertaining to this festival.[97]

These religious tensions were exacerbated by serious pay arrears and concerns about property ownership. A number of these soldiers had married the wives and daughters of the Vandals, who had not been subject to the deportation order placed on the men.[98] These women had inherited the property of their former husbands and fathers, and they sought to transmit these rights of ownership to their new spouses. The imperial treasury, however, had other ideas.[99] A plot was soon hatched to assassinate Solomon at the Easter ceremony in Carthage. This failed, and Solomon managed to escape to Sicily, but the mutineers assembled in the Hippodrome and attacked the prefect's palace.

Belisarius returned to Carthage, but by the time he arrived the rebels had elected Stotzas as their new leader and had mustered a force said to have been 10,000 strong. According to Procopius, this included Byzantine deserters as well as around 1,000 Vandals, 400 of whom had managed to escape deportation to the eastern frontier.[100] Belisarius drove this army back in disarray, but further mutinies were festering in Sicily and the general was forced to return there. This allowed the African mutineers time to regroup in Numidia, where their numbers were strengthened by the rebellion of the troops of the *dux* of Numidia. In an attempt to quell this second rising, Belisarius sent his cousin Germanus to take command of what remained of the African army. Over the next two years Germanus won several emphatic victories over the rebels until eventually Stotzas was forced to take refuge amongst the Moors in Mauretania.

The fragmentary sources make it very difficult to assess the impact that these conflicts – and the further wars of the 540s – had on the Praetorian Prefecture of Africa. Procopius refers to the heavy burden of Justinian's new tax assessments even before the outbreak of these campaigns, and this cannot have improved as the disruptive war continued.[101] The North African poet Corippus, whose long epic *Iohannidos* celebrates the Byzantine general John Troglita and provides an unusually detailed narrative of many later episodes in these campaigns, presents a sobering picture of a ravaged landscape:

> The wretched ploughmen wept as they fled, to see the enemy unyoke their cattle and drive them away, and all their houses were destroyed with all they contained. The poor were not the only victims of this disaster for they sank beneath it with the wealthy besides them. . . . On all sides, in a frenzied rage, the bandits set fire to cities and fields. Nor did the crops and trees only perish in the flames, for whatever escaped that disaster the herds consumed.[102]

Corippus may have exaggerated in order to accentuate the triumph of the hero of his poem, but Procopius echoes this gloomy impression. The Christian optimism which marked the initial stages of the Byzantine reconquest had dissipated after years of war:

> Thus it happened that those of the Libyans who survived, few as they were in number and very impoverished, at last and after great effort found some peace.[103]

A large number of forts were constructed in Byzacena and Numidia in this period, both by imperial decree and under local initiative.[104] Typical of these is the fortification at Ain Tounga, which overlooks the main road between Carthage and Constantina, and was probably created under Justinian and developed under his successors.[105] Similar structures have been excavated across North Africa and often include barrack rooms as well as storage facilities and cisterns: clearly they were designed

Figure 9.5 The Byzantine fort at Ain Tounga. Reproduced by permission of Professor David Mattingly

to protect local populations. The fact Byzacena has the greatest number of forts which date securely from the reign of Justinian concurs with the literary testimony that it was in that province that the heaviest fighting took place.[106] In many cities, moreover, forts were constructed in disused public buildings such as forums, baths, amphitheatres, theatres and pagan temples. A number of cities were also refortified with smaller, more defendable city walls.[107]

Concluding Remarks

The Byzantine conquest of Africa brought the Vandal kingdom to an abrupt and surprising end. A kingdom which had once dominated the politics of the western Mediterranean was shattered within a matter of weeks by a small but well-organized imperial army. But the triumphal imperial rhetoric, which depicted Hasding power as a flimsy and tyrannical regime to be swept aside by the bold new rule of Justinian, could not disguise the long legacy of the Vandal kingdom. Most of the Vandals were deported immediately to the other side of the Mediterranean; those few who remained disappeared with the defeat of Stotzas' rebellion in the later 530s. Yet the continuing Vandal influence on the political, economic, religious and cultural life of Byzantine Africa is undeniable. In the decades that followed, the newcomers from the east sought to bridge the religious and cultural divisions which separated them from a Romano-African elite which had been far more integrated into the Vandal regime than either side cared to admit.

If North Africa was ever to be a viable imperial province, the authorities in Constantinople needed the financial and political support of the Romano-African elite. The re-building programme that they instituted was thus concerned with the collective forgetting of a troubling past, as a well as the construction of a glorious new present. The imperial regime could portray itself as the great saviour of North Africa whilst the Romano-African elite basked in the invented memory of a courageous resistance to the heresies of their barbarous overlords. But the reality was more complex. The Three Chapters controversy and the military mutinies that blighted Africa for much of the 540s and 550s showed that there were limits to the extent to which grievances, both historical and present, could be smoothed over by the seductive re-writing of the Vandal past.

Notes

NOTES TO CHAPTER 1

1 The bibliography on the political and social changes of the fifth-century west is immense. Excellent general introductions include Halsall (2005) – perhaps the clearest general overview of the 'barbarian invasions' – and Burns (1994).
2 Raven (1993) provides a useful overview of Roman North Africa in English. Cf. also Prévot et al. (2006).
3 Mart. Cap., *De Nupt.* VI.669; *Exp. Tot. Mun.* 61.
4 On the background to the composition of the *Getica*, and its debts to the lost *History* of Cassiodorus, see Merrills (2005), pp. 100–15.
5 Jordanes, *Getica* 115, 161, 166, 173.
6 On Procopius, see esp. Cameron (1985).
7 Procopius, *BV* IV.6–9, tr. Dewing. On this image, see further Merrills (2004a), pp. 17–18.
8 On Isidore's *Gothic History*, see Merrills (2005), pp. 170–228; on the role of his Vandal History, see also Merrills (2006).
9 *Origo*, 1. On this text see Goffart (1988), pp. 329–70, and pp. 382–8.
10 Paul, *HL* I.7–8. Paul's apologetic preface to this episode: *refert . . . antiquitas ridiculam fabulam* ('old men tell ridiculous stories') is not an indication that the tradition was a long-preserved oral tradition.
11 Greg. Tur., *LH* II.2–3. On his likely source for this material, see Cain (2005).
12 Agnellus, *LP* 87. I am grateful to Simone Spedale Latimer for bringing this passage to my attention.
13 Courtois (1955), pp. 43–7.
14 Cervantes, *Don Quixote*, II.12–14.
15 On the dubious etymology of *Al-Andalus*, see Courtois (1955), pp. 56–7.
16 For a fuller discussion of this material, see Merrills (forthcoming a).
17 D'Urfé, *L'Astrée* V.8. See Edelman (1946), pp. 165–8, 182–4.
18 De Scudéry's own epic *Alaric, ou Rome vaincue* appeared in 1655.
19 On Deshoulières' play, see Gethner (2002), pp. 159–70.
20 Brady, *The Rape*. On gender ambivalence (which is central to the meaning of this play) see esp. Marsden (2007), pp. 76–9.

21 For discussion, see Loewenberg (1978).
22 *Critica Musica*, vol. 1 pt. 3 (July 1722).
23 This material is discussed in detail by Steinacher and Donecker (forthcoming).
24 The account here is largely drawn from Abernethy (1959), pp. 40–54; Sakolski (1932), pp. 1–17; and Livermore (1968), pp. 119–22. See also the further discussion in Merrills (forthcoming a).
25 Other proposed names included 'Charlotta' and 'Pittslyvania'.
26 On the details of this coinage, see Merrills (forthcoming b).
27 A translation of the letter appears in Holt (1957), p. 291. Cited and discussed by Sax (1990), pp. 1148–9.
28 Cowper, 'On the Burning of Lord Mansfield's Library I'.
29 Pope, *An Essay on Criticism*, p. 40; Desaguliers, *Course in Experimental Philosophy*, pp. 1–2. Other examples are manifold and would be too tedious to list here.
30 Gibbon, *Decline and Fall*, ch. 10.
31 Compare Dubos, *Histoire Critique* I.18; III.3; Montesquieu, *Considerations*, 20, *Espirit*, VI.30.7. And see the discussion in Merrills (forthcoming a).
32 Grégoire, *Mémoires*, p. 60.
33 Meyer, *Fragments*, pp. 189–90.
34 For a brief overview of the importance of Tacitus to the humanist antiquarians (and much Germanic prehistory since), see Goffart (2006), pp. 48–50.
35 Rives (1999) provides a useful overview of the text.
36 On Lipsius' popular edition see Beck (1934), pp. 64–8. Borchardt (1971) sets this rediscovery in context.
37 On the publication history of the *Historia Persecutionis*, see Lancel (2002), pp. 78–80.
38 Cameron (1985) remains the best general introduction to Procopius and his works.
39 On the publication history of Procopius, see esp. Kalli (2004), pp. 4–7.
40 Beck (1934), pp. 75–86 provides a stimulating survey of this French 'pangermanism'.
41 Johannesson (1991) provides an important overview of the Magnus brothers and their contribution to this scholarship.
42 Beck (1934), pp. 45–9.
43 See, for example, Olaus Magnus, *Historia* V.32.
44 On the *Wandalia*, see Nordmann (1934). See also the discussion in Steinacher and Donecker (forthcoming).
45 Discussed in Steinacher and Donecker (forthcoming) and Steinacher (2006).
46 Nugent, *The History of Vandalia*.
47 Mannert, *Geschichte der Vandalen*.
48 On the development and intellectual context of the *MGH*, see Knowles (1963), ch. 4.

49 Pingel (2006) provides an excellent overview of this archaeological scholarship. On the shortcomings of this material for the study of the Vandals specifically, see Martens (1989).
50 See esp. Kossinna (1911) idem (1929).
51 Jahn (1940); Hald (1942).
52 On the colonial programme within the archaeology of French North Africa, see esp. Mattingly (1996). On the implications of this for the study of the Vandals particularly, cf. Merrills (2004a).
53 Haaren (1904), pp. 46–54.
54 It is worth stressing that, while the view of 'Germanic' identity as something fixed and immutable was received warmly in Hitler's Germany, the assumption was by no means limited to Nazi sympathizers. Goffart (2006), pp. 40–1, provides a short discussion of Ernst Stein – a Jewish professor of ancient history at Berlin from 1927, who left Germany at the time of Hitler's rise to power and wrote his most famous work in French as a protest at the cultural policies of his homeland. Stein nevertheless regarded Germanic culture as something essentially monolithic, and charted its imposition onto post-Roman Europe in his *Histoire du Bas Empire.*
55 Theiss (1938); Blunck (1937).
56 Bigelow (1917), p. 1.
57 Courtois et al. (1954).
58 The phrase itself was taken from Gautier (1929).
59 See Merrills (2004a), esp. pp. 7–8.
60 For an overview of these projects (with bibliography), see Mattingly and Hitchner (1995), and Merrills (2004a), pp. 8–16.
61 Lepelley (2004) sets Courtois within the context of his time.
62 Benabou (1976), developed in idem (1980) and (1981); a similar approach is adopted in Laroui (1970). For discussion, see Mattingly and Hitchner (1995), p. 170, and Merrills (2004a), pp. 14–16.
63 For a survey of these changes, and their implications, see Mattingly (1996).
64 Altschul (2008) provides a stimulating overview of the importance of postcolonial approaches to the study of the Middle Ages more generally.
65 The papers in David Mattingly's edited volume *Dialogues in Roman Imperialism* (1997), usefully introduce many of these topics. And see also Webster (2001) on the notion of 'creolization'. The implications of this scholarship for Late Antiquity have yet to be explored in detail.
66 Wenskus (1961) is generally regarded as seminal in the evolution of this approach.
67 See, for example, Pohl (1991) and idem (2002) for an explanation and defence of the methodology (against harsh criticism). Pohl (2004) and Berndt (2007) investigate the Vandals from this perspective. Geary (1988) was an influential adoption of the ethnogenesis model in the Anglophone world.
68 See the discussion of the continued relevance of identity studies in Geary (2002).

69 The edited collection of Andrew Gillett (2002a) provides a convenient collection of these challenges, but see also Gillett (2006) and Goffart *passim*.
70 'Moorish' identity in the period is discussed in detail in Modéran (2003a).
71 *ND*, Or. 28.25.
72 For a recent and thorough engagement with much of this scholarship, see esp. Berndt (2007), pp. 52–135, who adopts an appropriately cautious line.
73 Tacitus, *Germania* 2; Pliny, *HN* IV.98.
74 Pohl (2004) provides a convenient overview of this discussion. And see now Berndt (2007), esp. pp. 79–80.
75 Martens (1989) provides a brief, but vivid demonstration. On the problems of viewing ethnicity through the material record, see more generally Jones (1997), Brather (2004) and the recapitulation in Brather (2008), and cf. Curta (2007).

NOTES TO CHAPTER 2

1 The best introduction is in Birley (1987), pp. 159–78.
2 Cassius Dio 72.11–12. For discussion, see esp. Berndt (2007), pp. 31, 79.
3 Pet. Patr., Fr. 7; Eutropius, *Brev.* VIII.12.1. A similar list in *Hist. Aug.*, M. Ant. 22.1. omits them, although the group may have been lost in a textual lacuna.
4 Cassius Dio 72.2–4; 77.20.3–4 and discussion in Mócsy (1974), pp. 191–3.
5 On these historians see esp. Millar (1969), Millar (1964) and Barnes (1984).
6 A useful summary of the *Historia Augusta* and its interpretation is provided by the introduction to Chastagnol (1994).
7 Jordanes, *Getica* 113–15.
8 Although Jordanes implies that his source is Dexippus, the geographical passage at *Getica* 114 is stylistically identical to other geographical digressions elsewhere in the text and is certainly Jordanes' own. Cf. Merrills (2005), pp. 155–62. On the problems associated with this episode, compare Courtois (1955), pp. 33–5 and Berndt (2007), pp. 79–80.
9 Courtois (1955), p. 33, notes this may be Jordanes' misunderstanding (and misdating) of the peace treaty with Aurelian in AD 270 referred to by Dexippus, Fr. 24.
10 He did this a lot. See Goffart (1988), and the bibliography therein.
11 The principal primary sources on this episode are Zosimus I.48 (who identifies the invaders as 'Scythians'), Dexippus, Fr. 7; Pet. Patr., Fr. 12M and *Hist. Aug.*, Aurel. 18.2 and 33.1. An excellent overview (and provocative reinterpretation) of these events is provided by Watson (1999), pp. 49–50 and 216–20.
12 Dexippus, Fr. 7; Berndt (2007), pp. 78–9.

13 On these campaigns see Drinkwater (2007), pp. 51–79.
14 Wilkes (2005), pp. 159–62, provides an archaeological context for these changes.
15 Zosimus I.68 and cf. *Hist. Aug.*, Probus 18.1.
16 This is stated in Jordanes, *Getica* 113. This was probably taken from Dexippus, although his subsequent account of the defeat of the Vandal kingdom was probably his own invention.
17 Márkus (2003) provides a typical example of this.
18 See the discussion in Oltean (2007), pp. 41–56.
19 Velkov (1977), pp. 261–4.
20 For further discussion of these problems on the ground, see Ellis (1996), and Vaday, Istvánovits and Kulcsár (1989). The latter article argues persuasively that changes in dress in this region were determined primarily by changing cultural and economic influences, rather than by widespread shifts in the population.
21 For overviews of this archaeology, see Matei and Stanciu (2000), and esp. the ongoing publication of the Upper Tisza Project at http://ads.ahds.ac.uk/catalogue/resources.html?uppertisza_ba_2003. I am grateful to Mark Gillings and Rob Wanner for their advice on this material.
22 See Vaday (2003), pp. 267–80, although the article retains a peculiar confidence in the ethnographic identification of graves, settlements and material culture.
23 Istvánovits and Kulcsár (2005); Wilkes (2005), pp. 171–2.
24 On the Alamanni, see esp. Drinkwater (2007). On the Goths, compare the stimulating introductory discussion in Kulikowski (2007), the overview in Heather (1991) and the useful collection of translated texts in Heather and Matthews (1991).
25 On these constructions see Wilkes (2005), pp. 161–2, with the bibliography therein.
26 On these events, compare Heather (1991) and Kulikowski (2007), pp. 123–53.
27 Jerome, *Ep.* 60.16.
28 See *PLRE* II, Radagaisus. See Burns (1994), pp. 195–9, for a brief narrative of these events.
29 Augustine, *De Civ. Dei*, V.23; Orosius, *Hist.* VII.37.
30 Burns (1994), pp. 183–223, and Kulikowski (2007), pp. 154–77, provide useful narrative overviews of these events.
31 Claudian, *Get.* 419–23. Stilicho was widely blamed in antiquity for having betrayed the Rhine frontier to the barbarians. Cf. Orosius, *Hist.* VII.38.3–7; Marcellinus Comes a.408; Jordanes, *Getica* 115. His 'barbarian' origins were frequently cited, see esp. Claudian, *De Cons Stil.* I.35–8; Jerome, *Ep.* 123.16.2 (which terms him *semibarbarus*) and the comments in Courtois (1955), p. 39; Burns (1994), p. 207, and O'Flynn (1983), p. 56.

32 Schmidt (1953), pp. 20–2, and Courtois (1955), pp. 39–41, propose routes that may have been taken by the Vandals. On the different causes proposed to explain this movement, see Goffart (2006), pp. 86–96.
33 Greg. Tur., *LH*, II.9. Wynn (1997) proposes a radically different dating for this conflict.
34 Orosius, *Hist.* VII.40.3; Orosius dates this battle to AD 408.
35 Zosimus VI.3.1 states that the Vandals, Sueves and Alans crossed the 'trans-Alpine' regions in 406, rather than the Rhine. This either represents a geographical error in Zosimus' (unfinished) final book, or the likely presence of several different invading groups in Gaul at this time. For discussion see Paschoud (1989), p. 22. Still other groups of Vandals may have been present in Gaul in a third capacity; Jerome, *Ep.* 123.16 refers to 'Pannonians' among the peoples who troubled Gaul from 406 onwards. The identity of this group is uncertain, although Jerome's language does imply that they had previously been allied with the empire. Burns (1994), p. 205, suggests that they may have been Vandal federates, sent by Stilicho in response to the threat posed by Constantine or the invaders of 406.
36 The British usurpations have prompted considerable scholarship, in part because of their iconic significance to the 'end' of Roman Britain. On these events compare Kulikowski (2000), and now Birley (2005), pp. 455–60. Zosimus' crucial (but confused) testimony is discussed in detail in Paschoud (1989), pp. 19–23.
37 Zosimus VI.2.1. Paschoud (1989) and Birley (2005), p. 458, on the dating.
38 Kulikowski (2000). A provocative thesis, persuasively challenged by Birley (2005), pp. 455–60.
39 Gibbon, *Decline and Fall*, ch. 30. The transformation of this sentence from narrative aside to established historical fact was noted by Kulikowski (2000a), p. 326.
40 Fredegar II.60, cautiously followed by Schmidt (1953). On the problems with this source, see Courtois (1955), p. 43, and Alemany (2000), p. 125.
41 After Jerome, *Ep.* 123. Courtois (1955), p. 38, and Burns (1994), p. 203, are representative.
42 Orosius, *Hist.* VII.42.1.
43 Freeman (1904) was the first to attempt a coherent narrative of the usurpation and associated events. Stevens (1957), Demougeot (1979), and Matthews (1975), pp. 307–22 remain essential. Burns (1994), pp. 208–14 and 249–55, provides a further interpretation. The certainties (such as they are) of the mid-twentieth-century model have recently been challenged by the work of Drinkwater (1998) and Kulikowski (2000a). See also Kulikowski (2004), pp. 156–67, and (more radically) Wynn (1997).
44 Drinkwater (1998), pp. 276–8, who traces Constantine's likely route through his coin issues.
45 Olympiodorus, Fr. 13, and Sozomen, *HE* IX.11, on the appointment of Justin[ian] and Nebiogast. On Sarus' campaign, see Zosimus VI.2.3–5. On

the passage (and the campaign), see Paschoud (1998), pp. 25–9, and Burns (1994), p. 214. As Freeman (1904) rightly states of the episode: 'We are told just enough to awaken our curiosity without satisfying it.'

46 Zosimus VI.3.2. refers only to 'a very large group of barbarians'. For interpretation, compare Courtois (1955), p. 49. Kulikowski (2000a), p. 333, and Paschoud (1989), pp. 28–30.

47 Orosius, *Hist.* VII.40.4. On this passage see Drinkwater (1998), p. 282.

48 Zosimus VI.5.6.

49 *Chron. Gall.* 452. a.408.

50 Jerome, *Ep.* 123.16 modified from the translation of Mierow.

51 Kulikowski (2000), pp. 331–2.

52 Courtois (1955), p. 43.

53 Jerome, *Ep.* 125.20.

54 Zosimus VI.5.2. Drinkwater (1998), pp. 283–5; Paschoud (1989), p. 36, compare Burns (1994), p. 254, and Wynn (1997), p. 90, n.83, for different interpretations.

55 On Britain and Armorica, see Paschoud (1998), pp. 38–41, following Salway (1981), pp. 434–44.

56 S. Paulini, *Epigramma*. The translation is the elegant verse of Lindsay (1948), pp. 199–200. For a more literal rendering compare Alemany (2000), p. 65.

57 Hyd., *Chron.* 297.15 Lem. 42 (IIII Kal. Oct. and III Id Oct. respectively). As Alemany (2000), p. 53 notes, Hydatius also specifies that the date of the invasion was a Tuesday. The latter date in its present form was a Wednesday (presumably IIII Id. Oct. was intended).

58 See esp. Fernández-Ochoa and Morillo (2005), pp. 331–40.

59 Orosius, *Hist.* VII.40.7. Kulikowski (2004), p. 363, n.30 infers from the title that they must have been regular military units (by analogy with known units of *Honoriani*).

60 Sozomen, *HE* IX.12.

61 See Constantius, *Vita Germani*, 28 on the Alan presence in Armorica; Paul Pell, *Euch* 377–85 on Alan presence in Aquitaine c. 417; Sid. Ap., *Carm.* 5.474–5 notes the presence of Alans and Sueves among the federated people involved in Majorian's campaign against Vandal Africa in AD 460.

62 Olympiodorus, Fr. 17.2. The direct involvement of the barbarians in the usurpation of Maximus is also stated directly by Renatus Frigeridus in Greg. Tur. *LH* II.9.

63 Hyd., *Chron.* 297.16 Lem. 48, tr. Burgess.

64 Kulikowski (2004), pp. 162–3. Kulikowski's study argues for some level of urban and administrative continuity within Spain (and especially Tarraconensis), down to the early 460s. Cf. also the collected essays in Kulikowski and Bowes (2005).

65 Hyd., *Chron.* 297.17 Lem 49, tr. Burgess.

66 Gallaecia was not tiny, however. On definitions (and importance) of the region, see Díaz and Menéndez-Bueyes (2005), esp. pp. 266–9.

67 This is the consensus among modern scholars. See for example Gautier (1929), p. 102; Arce (2002), p. 79; Goffart (2006), pp. 101–3.
68 Hyd., *Chron.* 299.24 Lem 68.
69 Burns (1994), p. 268, and Goffart (2006), pp. 101–3, are sceptical about the role of the state in the settlement. For further discussion see Kulikowski (2004), pp. 365–6 n.62. But the suggestion that the barbarians were settled by *foedus* persists. Cf. Arce (2002), p. 79.
70 Orosius, *Hist.* VII.43.14. Cf. Courtois (1955), p. 54.
71 Orosius, *Hist.* VII.42.5. Olympiodorus, Fr. 17.1 and cf. Prosper, *Chron.* s.a.412.
72 Hyd., *Chron.* 298.22 Lem 60.
73 On the relationship between Athaulf and Ravenna, see Burns (1994), pp. 247–9 and 257–60.
74 Orosius, *Hist.* VII.43.4–6 on the famous speech made by Athaulf. Possibly when drunk.
75 Orosius, *Hist.* VII.43.1–3.
76 Olympiodorus, Fr. 26.1 states that he was killed by a servant, and most other accounts provide variations on the same theme. See Prosper, *Chron.* a.415; Hyd., 298.22 Lem. 60; Isidore, *Hist. Goth.* 19. Jordanes, *Getica* 163 claims (incredibly) that Athaulf was killed in combat with the Vandals.
77 Olympiodorus, Fr. 29.1.
78 Orosius, *Hist.* VII.43.11.
79 Orosius, *Hist.* VII.43.15–6. Orosius finished his *History* before news of Wallia's campaigns had reached North Africa (or before the implications of his victory were apparent in Hippo).
80 Hyd., *Chron.* 299.24 Lem. 67–8.
81 Arce (2002), pp. 79–80; Kulikowski (2004), pp. 170–2.
82 The identification of the Siling king as 'Fredbal' is based on a corrupt recension of Hydatius. Noted by Courtois (1955), p. 237.
83 Hyd., *Chron.* 299.24. Lem 68.
84 Arce (2002), p. 80.
85 Burns (1994), p. 262.
86 Wallia's victory may have been commemorated in an ivory diptych of AD 417, which depicts Constantius alongside captives, who may well be Alans or Vandals. Cf. Courtois (1955), p. 54, n.4. The victory was certainly sufficiently important to be remembered by Sidonius Apollinaris on New Year's Day 468. Sid. Ap., *Carm.* 2.362–5. On the settlement of the Visigoths in Aquitaine, see now Kulikowski (2002).
87 On Maximus' refuge with the barbarians, see n. 71 above. The second 'Maximus' usurpation is recorded in *Chron. Gall.* 452.85 [a.416]. This usurper is listed as Maximus 7 in *PLRE* II.
88 Hyd., *Chron.* 299.26 Lem. 74. Gregory of Tours was familiar with a historical tradition (certainly Suevic in origin) which suggested that the

Vandals had been pushed out of Gallaecia after suffering a defeat in single battle. Greg. Tur., *LH* II.2.

89 Greg. Tur., *LH* II.9, and cf. Marc. Com. a.422.

90 Kulikowski (2004), pp. 173–4.

91 Aug., *Ep.* 11*. Kulikowski (2004), p. 174 after Van Dam (1986).

92 *Chron. Gall.* a.452. 89.

93 On Castinus' campaign, see *PLRE* II Bonifatius 3, Castinus 2.

94 Boniface's quarrels with Castinus and departure for Africa are noted in Prosper 395.1278; *Chron. Gall.* 511. 571 and Hyd., *Chron.* 77.

95 Hyd., *Chron.* 300.28 Lem. 77; Prosper 395.1278. Cf. also *Chron. Gall.* 452.107, which states that 20,000 troops were lost in a campaign against the Vandals, but dates this to 430.

96 Arce (2002), p. 81.

97 Courtois (1955), p. 50 notes this. And cf. Burns (1994), pp. 206–7: 'There were several different groups of "Vandals" and other barbarians moving about in 406–7; some were under Roman control, others not.'

98 Compare Schmidt (1953), p. 9; Liebeschuetz (2003), pp. 61–2, and the note of caution sounded by Goffart (2006), p. 86. Berndt (2007), pp. 146–56 provides a through discussion of the references to the groups in the literary sources.

99 See the references in n. 61 above. Matthews (1975), p. 308, n.5, also notes the presence of a breakaway group of Sueves in north-west Gaul in the mid-fifth century.

100 Zosimus VI.3.2; Orosius, *Hist.* VII.40.9.

101 Vict. Vit., *HP* I. 2 See esp. Goffart (1980), pp. 231–4, and compare Gil Egea (1998), pp. 189–92.

102 Procopius, *BV* III.5.18–20. On the full significance of this passage, see pp. 69 below.

103 Zosimus VI.13.2; Olympiodorus, Fr. 6; Sozomen, *HE* IX.9.

104 See Burns (1994), p. 247.

105 McLynn (2005) on the background of Theodosius II.

106 Olympiodorus, Fr. 17.1–2; Sozomen, *HE* IX.13. This may not have been unusual.

107 Paul. Pell., *Euch.* 377–8.

108 Greg. Tur., *LH* II.2 provides a peculiar account of the Vandal succession in Gaul and Spain, which is nevertheless accurate in structure, if not in names. If we overlook his hopeless confusion with the proper names of kings, his account is essentially identical to Procopius, *BV* III.3.2 and 23–4. Procopius, however, notes the existence of alternative traditions which circulated among the Vandals at *BV* III.33–4 (which places the death of Gunderic in Spain).

109 Procopius, *BV* III.3.23. states simply that Godigisclus died without mentioning any battle, although Wynn (1997), p. 80, argues reasonably that the reference to the Vandal myth that Gunderic died in battle with the

Germani may be a transposition of his father's death in battle with the Franks.

110 Hyd., *Chron.* 301.4 Lem. 89. Procopius, *BV* III.3.23–4 implies that Gunderic died in Africa, and Greg. Tur., *LH* II.2 apparently worked from the same tradition in his account.

111 Procopius, *BV* III.3.24 implies that Geiseric was the elder.

112 Hyd., *Chron.* 301.1. Lem. 86, tr. Burgess.

113 Hyd., *Chron.* 301.4. Lem. 89, tr. Burgess.

114 On this unity, see esp. Shaw (2005) and Spaul (1997).

115 Arce (2005).

116 Kulikowski (2004), pp. 69–76.

117 Arce (2002), p. 83.

118 Carr (2002) discusses the fieldwork of Michel Posnich in the Guadalquivir Valley.

119 *Chron. Gall.* 452 a.425 refers to the rebuilding of the walls of Carthage in this year, but there is nothing to connect this to the perceived Vandal threat.

120 Jordanes, *Getica*, 166; Hyd., *Chron.* 302.5 Lem. 90; Greg. Tur., *LH* II.2.

121 On these disputes see esp. O'Flynn (1983), pp. 76–82.

122 The likely strength of the Roman military in North Africa is discussed in Gil Egea (1998), pp. 186–9, 195–215.

123 On Boniface, see *PLRE* II, Bonifatius 3. Boniface's popularity is reflected in Olympiodorus, Fr. 40. Augustine's correspondence with Boniface is preserved as *Ep.* 17*; 185; 189 and 220.4.

124 Augustine, *Ep.* 189.4 and 220.7 refer to Boniface's conduct of these campaigns, although the latter implies that the fighting wasn't going particularly well in 427 AD. Boniface's military reputation is indicated in Prosper 395.1278 and Olympiodorus, Fr. 22.2.

125 The narrative which follows is a summary of Procopius, *BV* III.3.14–36.

126 Prosper, *Chron.*, 400.1294.

127 For discussion of these missions, see the excellent study of Mathisen (1999).

128 Darius was the recipient of Augustine, *Ep.* 429 and 431 (c. 429 AD), and his reply is preserved as Augustine, *Ep.* 430.

129 Procopius, *BV* III.3.25, tr. Dewing.

130 Jordanes, *Getica* 167; *Romana* 330; Joh. Ant., Fr. 196; Theoph. AM 5931. For discussion and bibliography, see Courtois (1955), pp. 155–8, and Gil Egea (1998), pp. 180–2.

131 Hyd., *Chron.* 302.5 Lem. 90 which dates the expedition to May 429 AD is generally preferred. See the discussion in Courtois (1955), p. 155; Mathisen (1997), p. 177, n.16, and esp. Gil Egea (1998), pp. 179–81.

132 See for example, Courtois (1955), pp. 158–60; Arce (2002), p. 83; and Pohl (2004), p. 38. The common assumption that the reference to *Iulia Traducta* at Greg. Tur., *LH* II.2 indicates that this was the likely port of embarkation seems mistaken. This port was the southernmost point of

Spain, and Gregory probably intended his comment to be read as a colourful assertion that the Sueves chased the Vandals 'right the way out of Spain', as modern Britons might refer to their country 'from Land's End to John O'Groats'.

133 Gautier (1929), pp. 167–73.
134 As suggested by Le Gall (1936) and followed by Courtois (1955), pp. 159–60.
135 These diplomatic links proved crucial in Geiseric's diplomacy in the 440s. On this see below pp. 113–14.
136 Procopius, BV III.3.30–36 provides the fullest narrative.
137 Aug., *Ep.* 228, cf. Possidius, *VA* 29–30. On this activity, see González-Salinero (2002), pp. 81–5.
138 Leo, *Ep.* 12.8.
139 See esp. Theoderet, *Ep.* 22, 29–36, 70. *Nov. Val.* 2; 12; 13.6 legislate for those who had fled to Italy. For a full discussion of this material, see Conant (2004a), pp. 83–110.
140 Possidius, *VA* 28; Vict. Vit., *HP* I.3–7.
141 Possidius, *VA* 28.
142 The narrative of this second campaign is provided in Procopius, *BV* III.3.35–6. Boniface's death is variously described in Prosper, a.432; Prosp. Haun. a.432; Hyd., *Chron.* 303.8. Lem. 99; Marc. Com. s.a.432; *Chron. Gall.* 452. a.432.
143 Procopius, *BV* III.4.2–11.

NOTES TO CHAPTER 3

1 Jordanes, *Getica*, 168.
2 See Merrills (2004b), pp. 160–1.
3 Steinacher (2004), pp. 175–7 discusses this material.
4 See below, pp. 219–20.
5 On this aspect of Thrasamund's reign, see esp. Hen (2007), pp. 74–93, and the discussion in chapter 8 below.
6 See chapter 5, below.
7 See pp. 133–4, 201–2 below.
8 See Merrills (forthcoming b) and below, pp. 76–7.
9 Shown most obviously in Marmontel's eighteenth-century novel, *Belisaire*, in which the eponymous hero meets Gelimer in straitened circumstances, and is praised by the defeated king. A similar sentiment is apparent in Longfellow's short poem *Belisarius*, first published in Longfellow (1875).
10 The principal source is Prosper 1321. cf. *LRV* and Isidore, *Hist. Goth.*, 74. and the discussion in Courtois (1955), pp. 169–70.
11 See Heather (1997) and Chrysos (1989).
12 Prosper 1327.a.435. This passage provides our only indication of the extent of Vandal territory by the *foedus* of 435. Prosper is explicit that all

three bishops came from 'the regions in which [Geiseric] lived' (*intra habitationis suae limites*). On the identification of the bishops see Courtois (1955), p. 170, n.2.

13 Prosper 1329 a.437. The Spaniards are named as Arcadius, Paschasius, Probus and Eutycianus.

14 Prosper 1330 a.438 refers to barbarian 'deserters of the federates' (*barbari foederatorum desertas*) turning to piracy. 1332 describes attacks on Sicily in AD 438 by further pirates. On which cf. Marc. Com., a.438 who refers to the leadership of one Contradis. Croke (1995), p. 82, n.a.438, and Schmidt (1953), p. 84, note the possible identification of Marcellinus' Contradis as the plausibly 'Vandal' sounding Guntharix.

15 The dating is secure. See Prosper 1339 a.439; Marc. Com., a.439; Cassiodorus, *Chron.* 1231. See also the comments in Steinacher (2004), p. 175.

16 Aug., *Ep.* 228; Possidius, *VA* 28; Vict. Vit., *HP* I.3–8. On this material see esp. González-Salinero (2001) and (2002), pp. 77–94.

17 Vict. Vit., *HP* I.8. Von Rummel (2008), pp. 153–7; González-Salinero (2002), pp. 92–3.

18 Courtois (1955), p. 173, rightly terms these events 'the true moment of birth of the Vandal state' ('véritablement l'acte du naissance de l'État vandale'). On this treaty, see esp. Modéran (2002), pp. 92–5 and 102–7.

19 Prosper 1347 a.442. *Cum Gisirico ab Augusto Valentiniano pax confirmata et certis spatiis Africa inter utrumque divisa est.*

20 Procopius, *BV* III.4.12–14. Procopius' dating for the treaty is confused; he evidently conflates the treaties of 435 and 442. The details, however, certainly relate to the later treaty. Merobaudes, *Carm.* I.7–8 and cf. *Pan.* II.23–9. On these poems see esp. Clover (1971), pp. 20–7 and 41–59.

21 Procopius, *BV* III.4.13.

22 Vict. Vit., *HP* I.13: *Disponens quoque singulas quasque prouincias, sibi Bizacenam, Abaritanam atque Getuliam et partem Numidiae reseruauit, exercitui, uero Zeugitanam uel Proconsularem funiculo heriditatis diuisit, Valentiniano adhuc imperatore reliquas licet iam exterminatas prouincias defendente. . .* , tr. Moorhead.

23 Some confusion is generated by Victor's peculiar formulation *Zeugitanem uel Proconsularem*: 'Zeugitana *or* Proconsularis' and cf. also Vict. Vit., *HP* I.29. In fact, the two provincial names appear to have been synonymous and refer to the same region. Compare *HP* I.39 and the provincial divisions established after the Byzantine conquest in *Cod. Iust.* I.27.1.12 which confirm this. For discussion, see Schmidt (1953), p. 55.

24 *Abaritana* is also known from Quodvultdeus, *Lib. Prom. Dei* III.38.45. The text implies that it was a province at the time of composition – generally assumed to be between AD 445 and 451.

25 Definitions: Modéran (1999), p. 245, after Desanges (1984) and (1995). Gil Egea (1998), pp. 238–9 suggests that *Gaetulia* might be the broad area north of the Hodna Chotts – not an administrative district, per se, but a *limes* region and economic zone.

26 Vandal control of Tripolitana was certainly established by 455, when Vicis of Sabratha and Cresconius of Oea were both expelled from their dioceses (*HP* I.23). The fact that no imperial legislation relates to the region from the 440s (in contrast to eastern Numidia and the Mauretanias) would seem to imply that Tripolitana fell under Vandal jurisdiction from 442.

27 *Nov. Val.* 12; 13; 34.3. cf. also Leo, *Ep.* 12. This papal letter, which is addressed to the bishops of Mauretania, suggests that the papacy shared the imperial sense of responsibility toward the western African provinces.

28 *Nov. Val.* 2; 12; 13.6.

29 Vict. Vit., *HP* I.13. On the expansion cf. Gil Egea (1998), pp. 244–5, and esp. Modéran (1999), pp. 249–63. Courtois (1955), p. 183, argues to the contrary that the frontiers of the Vandal state were established in AD 442 and remained substantially unchanged thereafter.

30 *AE* 1967 no. 596; Modéran (1999), p. 249.

31 Marc. Com. a.484; Modéran (1999), pp. 252–57. The text of the Notitia Provinciarum is published and discussed in Lancel (2002), pp. 251–72.

32 Vandal control over the Aurés massif, and the later loss to the Moors, is recorded in Procopius, *Aed.*, VI.7.2–6 and *BV* III.8.5 which states that the region was lost during the reign of Huneric. See Modéran (2008), pp. 219–22. On the *ostraka*, see chapter 6.

33 Vict. Vit., *HP* III.29–30. See also chapter 6 below on the circulation of Vandal coinage in the region.

34 The exile's name was Reparatus. *CIL* VIII.9286; cf. Handley (forthcoming).

35 For a summary of recent scholarship on the issue, see Gil Egea (1998), pp. 251–8, and Modéran (2002). The dispute has largely been framed by the important scholarship of Goffart (1980), who argues (primarily from the Ostrogothic evidence) that the settlement of the barbarians within the western empire was enabled by fiscal restructuring, rather than the direct confiscation of land: barbarians in other words received designated portions of specific rents as their allowances, rather than the lands themselves, as had previously been assumed. To a large extent this is a dispute that has been fought away from Africa, for a variety of reasons. Two attempts to impose the model on the region have been Durliat (1981a) and (1988) and more recently Schwartz (2004), both of whom accept that the Vandals were later to acquire lands, but suggest that they were initially accommodated by fiscal redistribution. This view has been demolished by Modéran (2002), pp. 97–112, based on the clear evidence for actual land confiscation within Africa.

36 Vict. Vit., *HP* I.14; Ferrandus, *VF* 1; NV 34.3–4. The Byzantine evidence (notably Nov. Just. 36) is less useful, simply because the Vandals are

known to have acquired lands (by purchase, rather than confiscation) after 442. Regardless of the initial settlement pattern, some form of land restitution must have taken place after 534.

37 Gil Egea (1998), pp. 259–62. On these estates see esp. Kehoe (1988).

38 On the problems faced by the Byzantines with the redistribution of lands, see Modéran (2002), pp. 112–18, and below, chapter 9.

39 Vict. Vit., *HP* I.13.

40 Procopius, *BV* III.5.11–15, tr. Dewing.

41 The term appears in Huneric's legislation at Vict. Vit., *HP* II.39 and III.4.

42 Vict. Vit., *HP* I.13. Procopius, *BV* III.5.14 (free from taxation); *HP* I.35 hints that lands were inherited, and see also *BV* IV.14.8.

43 See for example Vict. Vit., *HP* I.30–36 on the estates and slaves of one Martinianus, a Vandal *millenarius*, whose slaves (if not his lands) were handed over to a minor Hasding by his widow following his death and that of their heirs. The only other known Vandal estate is that of Fridamal, noted in the poetry of Luxorius from the later Vandal period *AL R* 304 [s. 299]. Cf. also the discussion of the 'Vandal widows' in chapter 4 below.

44 See Modéran (2003b), pp. 24–5, and (2002), pp. 107–10.

45 Modéran (2002), pp. 107–10.

46 Mines – Vict. Vit., *HP* III.68 and *Not. Prov.*, Num 76; vineyards *HP* I.44 and II.16. Cf. Schmidt (1953), p. 220, n.5.

47 Despite the assertion of Procopius, *BV* III.5.11 Theoderic certainly survived into Huneric's reign, cf. Vict. Vit., *HP* II. 12.

48 Procopius, *BV* III.5.18. Courtois (1955), pp. 217ff. and p. 235, on some of the implications of this passage.

49 The dating of this episode is unclear, although it seems to relate more closely to Procopius, *BV*, III.5.17 (related to the events of AD 442) than to III.5.22 (AD 454).

50 Isidore, *Orig.* IX.3.30, writing in the early seventh century, certainly regards the terms as synonymous.

51 Gil Egea (1998), p. 332. Compare Schmidt (1953), p. 207 who argues that the position may also have had a judicial function.

52 Prosper 1348.a.442, tr. Murray.

53 Jordanes, *Getica* 184. On this episode, see chapter 5, below.

54 Jordanes, *Getica* 170.

55 Theoph. AM 5941. On this passage, see Clover (2003), pp. 46–7.

56 Jordanes, *Getica* 169.

57 Procopius, *BV* III.5.25.

58 See, for example Vict. Vit., *HP* II.39 and III.3.

59 Vict. Vit., *HP* II.4.

60 Vict. Vit., *HP* II.1.

61 Dracontius, *Satisf.* 113.4.

62 On the history of these relations, see esp. Modéran (2008), and the discussion at pp. 124–9 below.

63 Procopius, *BV* III.25.3–6, tr. Dewing.
64 *Contra* Modéran (2008), pp. 218–19, who implies that this was the norm only down to AD 484.
65 On the political significance of the term *dominus*, see Merrills (2004b), p. 157.
66 *AL R* 371 [S.366]. See the discussion in chapter 8 below.
67 *AL R* 215 [S.206]. On this passage see the translation and discussion in Merrills (forthcoming b).
68 Procopius, *BV* III.9.4–10.
69 On the dating, see Gil Egea (1998), pp. 240–3 and Clover (2003), pp. 50–60.
70 Only two genealogies appear in the literature of Vandal Africa. Dracontius' brief allusion to Gunthamund's lineage in the *Satisfactio* 49–52 is cursory and does not seem to invoke any 'official' family tree. On this see Merrills (2004b), p. 158. The anonymous celebration of Hilderic at *AL R* 215 [S.206] probably *did* employ officially propounded material, but this emphasized the Roman heritage of the king, and not his Vandal ancestors.
71 Vict. Vit., *HP* II.14.
72 The institution was praised hyperbolically in the two major works on the Vandals of the twentieth century. Schmidt (1953), p. 194, terms the succession 'among the most important constitutional acts in history'; Courtois (1955), p. 238, 'almost like a constitution in the modern sense of the term'. On the succession (and later crises) see also Schultze (1859) and now Merrills (forthcoming b).
73 On the principles behind the Frankish system, see the discussion in Wood (1977).
74 Vict. Vit., *HP* II. 12–16; on this episode, see Merrills (forthcoming b).
75 Vict. Vit., *HP* III.17–20.
76 Procopius, *BV* III.9.6–26; cf. Theoph. AM 6062; Evagrius, *HE* IV.17; *Vict. Tun.* A.531; Isid., *Hist. Goth.* 82–3.
77 Hilderic's great age is suggested by Corippus, *Ioh.* III.262–4. Hilderic must have been conceived between the arrival of Eudocia in Carthage in 455 and her departure in 472. Most scholars assume an earlier date is more likely.
78 *AL R* 215 [S.206].
79 Procopius, *BV* III.9.2 and cf. *AL R* 345 [S.340], which was written in honour of Hoageis' daughter.
80 Procopius, *BV* III.9.14. On the punishment see Lascaratos and Marketos (1992) and Bührer-Thierry (1998).
81 *Cod. Iust.*, 27.3–4; and cf. *SEG* 9.356 on a constitution of Anastasius c. AD 501 relating to the ducal bureau in Libya (Which was to be restricted to 40). Translated with comments in Johnson et al. (1961), pp. 253–5.

82 On wider court culture in the period, see esp. McCormick (2000) and Smith (2007). On the communication networks that bound these courts together, see Gillett (2003).

83 Procopius, *BV* III.4.2 (the future emperor Marcian); Jordanes, *Getica* 184 (the unnamed Visigothic princess); *BV* III.5.3 (Eudoxia and her daughters); *BV* III.8.1 (Amalafrida and her retinue); Cassiodorus, *Variae* V.43–4 (the Visigothic pretender Gesalic). The western emperor Olybrius is unlikely to have been in Carthage, but this has been argued. See *PLRE* II, Olybrius 6.

84 Procopius, *BV* III.4.13 (Huneric); III.9.5 (Hilderic's friendship with Justinian).

85 On the Byrsa Hill complex, see Leone (2007), p. 159, and Ben Abed and Duval (2000), p. 189.

86 See Vict. Vit., *HP* I.17 (Geiseric at Maxula); *AL R* 376 [S.371] and *AL R* 210–14 [S.201–5] (Thrasamund at Alianae); *AL R* 203 [S.194] (Hilderic at Anclae); Procopius, *BV* III.14.10 (Gelimer at Hermiana). Further foundations (which may have been royal) are alluded to at *BV* III.17.8 (Grasse) and *AL R* 291 [S.286] (an unknown estate with a fish-pond).

87 Vict. Vit., *HP* II.29; II.43. For discussion, see Gil Egea (1998), pp. 276–9.

88 *Referendarius: AL R* 380 [S.375]; *Primiscrinarius: AL R* 254 [S.248]. Schmidt (1953), p. 215, compares the latter to the *primicerius notariorum* of Ostrogothic Italy and see also Gil Egea (1998), pp. 281–2.

89 Cf. for example, Procopius, *BV* III.9.8; 21.1; 22.9–11; IV.3.14.

90 See above, pp. 73.

91 Vict. Vit., *HP* II.10.

92 Vict. Vit., *HP* III.13.

93 Vict. Vit., *HP* II.8. For different interpretations of the significance of these ranks, see Courtois (1955), p. 252ff., who assumes that they were domestic staff, and Gil Egea (1998), pp. 325–9, who regards them as high status individuals. Schmidt (1953), p. 217, sees it as a generic term for high ranking courtiers.

94 Procopius, *BV* III.4.7.

95 On administrative systems in the later Roman empire, see Barnish et al. (2000); Gil Egea (1998), pp. 12–157, provides a useful overview of Roman African administration.

96 Quodvultdeus, *De Temp. Barb.*, I.10.

97 Vict. Vit., *HP* III.62.

98 See Lepelley (2002), pp. 66–71.

99 Overbeck (1973), and see also the discussion in Conant (2004a), pp. 13–17.

100 Dracontius, *Rom.* V.

101 Vict. Vit., *HP* III.27.

102 Gil Egea (1998), pp. 283–4.

103 Vict. Vit., *HP* III.10–11. And cf. *C.Th.* 16.5.52. (issued in AD 412).

104 See chapter 8, below.

NOTES TO CHAPTER 4

1 *ILC* 2652. The best general introduction to the burial is von Rummel (2005), pp. 337–42.

2 On Arifridos' name, see Francovich Onesti (2002), p. 148.

3 Ghalia (2008a) provides a useful short introduction to this material. Duval (1976) provides a more thorough discussion.

4 The traditional interpretation of Arifridos' grave and a handful of others like it is that the dress accessories were typically 'Vandalic' or 'barbarian'. Koenig (1981) provides the classic formulation, re-interpreted by Kleeman (2002). The position taken here – that these were typically 'Roman' dress accessories – follows the important scholarship of von Rummel (2007).

5 On the constitution of this group, and the circumstances in which they joined together, see pp. 47–50 above.

6 Procopius, *BV* III.5.21–2, tr. Dewing.

7 The estimated population is taken from Wolfram (1997), p. 167.

8 Barth (1969). For useful discussions of this research and its importance to history and archaeology, see esp. Emberling (1997), and the recent discussion in Curta (2007). Geary (2002) provides a vivid discussion of the political importance of these theories as they are applied to the early medieval period.

9 See, for example, Geary (1983).

10 Merlin (1912). This grave is briefly discussed in Ghalia (2008b), although the assumption that both of the Thuburbo Maius graves were 'Vandalic' cannot be sustained.

11 The bibliography is vast. Gillett (2002a) and Pohl (2002) vividly illustrate the complexities (and frequent hostility) of this debate. The papers collected in Noble (2006), pp. 29–232, provide a useful starting point. Halsall (2007), pp. 455–98, gives a balanced survey of much of this scholarship, and proposes provocative new directions for this study. Many of his suggestions have been followed here.

12 See for example Pohl (1991), on means of definition, Goffart (2002) on the importance (or otherwise) of history, and Amory (1997) for a provocative interpretation of the political importance of ethnic formation. Useful general overviews of recent directions in this study are provided by Halsall (2007), esp. pp. 35–62 and 455–98, and Curta (2007).

13 Pohl (2004) and Liebeschuetz (2003) both hint at the possibility of applying the 'ethnogenesis' approach to the study of the Vandals without developing this fully. Berndt (2007) provides a thought-provoking recent application of the model.

14 Woolf (1998) provides an excellent introduction.

15 See esp. Gleason (1999); Montserrat (2000); and the stimulating discussion by Cooper (1996) on engendered Roman identity.
16 Woolf (1998) and Webster (2001) provide thought-provoking models.
17 Cherry (1998) provides a provocative interpretation.
18 Conant (2004a), pp. 126–40.
19 See for example Markus (1990), pp. 107–23; Brown (1995), pp. 1–26; González-Salinero (2002), pp. 50–8; Lepelley (2001), pp. 361–6; Van Slyke (2005). Lepelley (2002) discusses the spaces in which these differences might be put aside.
20 On changing balance of the Roman aristocracy cf. Cameron (1993a); Banaji (2002); Goffart (2006), pp. 189–91. MacMullen (1965) provides a stimulating overview of the changing nature of Roman military identity in this period. See also the observations of Halsall (2007), pp. 101–10.
21 von Rummel (2007).
22 *C.Th.* XIV.10.1–4. On this passage see esp. von Rummel (2007), pp. 156–66.
23 See above pp. 52–3 and 124–5. On the earlier period see also Blackhurst (2004).
24 On these mosaics see esp. Duval (2002), who argues that these need not have been 'Vandals', and reflect late Roman dress styles; Berndt (2007), pp. 271–4, argues that a Vandal date should not be excluded. The uncertainty reflects the continuity of ideology discussed below.
25 The importance of the invasion of AD 429 for the development of a 'Vandal' identity forms the central argument of Berndt (2007).
26 On Hasding identity, see above pp. 68–70. On Roman aristocratic identity under the Vandals, see esp. Conant (2004a).
27 See, for example, Procopius, *BV* III.16.3–4 and III.20.18–20.
28 This is a controversial issue. See the important study of Heather (1998).
29 See below, pp. 102–5.
30 Amory (1997) provides the clearest articulation of this idea.
31 The processes by which the settlement of AD 442 was enacted, and the scholarly controversies surrounding this event, are discussed at pp. 66–9 above.
32 Vict. Vit., *HP* I.13; II.39; III.4.
33 Procopius, *BV* III.5.12.
34 Francovich Onesti (2002) is fundamental. See also Markey (1989) and the brief discussions in Berndt (2007), pp. 234–7, and Steinacher (2008), pp. 253–4.
35 *AL R* 285 [S.279], modified from the translation of Rosenblum.
36 For discussion see Francovich Onesti (2002), pp. 140–3.
37 Sid. Ap., *Carm.* XII.
38 Amory (1997), pp. 102–8.
39 Vict. Vit., *HP* II.4.
40 Vict. Vit., *HP* II.55. On this passage, see Conant (2004a), p. 78.
41 Vict. Vit., *HP* I.43 (Armogas); I.48 (Marivadus); II.3 and II.41 (Vitarit); II.43 (Obadus); II.15 (Gamuth); II.15 (Heldica); III.24 (Maioricus); III.33 (Dagila); III.34 (Muritta).

42 Francovich Onesti (2002), p. 166.
43 Vict. Vit., *HP* III.24.
44 Francovich Onesti (2002), p. 151.
45 There are no obvious examples of Romans assuming Vandal names in this period, but cf. Halsall (2007), pp. 466–7, for comparanda from elsewhere in the post-Roman Mediterranean.
46 See, for example, Liebeschuetz (2003), p. 58, and the discussion in Merrills (2004a), pp. 19–20.
47 Procopius, *BV* III.3.33–4.
48 Discussed by Gillett (2002a), p. 109, n.30, and Alemany (2000), pp. 192–3. Cf. Nov. Just. XXX.11.2.
49 Vict. Vit., *HP* II.13; III.12. The title is also employed in Prosper, *Add. Af.* a.455 with respect to Geiseric, although this need not imply that that king had used it. For discussion, see esp. Berndt (2007), pp. 203–7.
50 *CIL* VIII 10862.
51 For discussion of the dual title see Schmidt (1953), pp. 33–4; Clover (1989a), p. 58; Modéran (2002), p. 95.
52 Gillett (2002), pp. 92–3 and 109–10.
53 Francovich Onesti (2002), pp. 179–85, provides a (very) short Alanic prosopography.
54 *AE* 1951.267. Discussed by Courtois (1955), p. 375, n.70; On the name see Francovich Onesti (2002), p. 182.
55 Vict. Vit., *HP* I.30, tr. Moorhead.
56 Vict. Vit., *HP* I.31–5.
57 On the rank of *millenarius*, see above pp. 69. On the possible importance of weapons as markers of ethnic identity, see Halsall (2007), pp. 466–7.
58 On the name Fridamal, see Francovich Onesti (2002), pp. 153–4.
59 *AL R* 304 [S.299], tr. Rosenblum.
60 Sigisteus, *Ep. ad Parth.*; Parthemius, *Resc. ad Sig.*
61 On Sigisteus' name see Francovich Onesti (2002), p. 172. On the rank of *comes* in Vandal Africa (and the fact that several non-Vandals held the position), see above, pp. 78–80.
62 Parthemius *Resc. ad Sig.*; Hays (2004), p. 126.
63 Procopius, *BV* III.9.2.
64 Luiselli (1992), pp. 538–41, 553–5, provides the obvious illustration. See also Conant (2004a), pp. 61–8.
65 See above, pp. 70–3.
66 Procopius, *BV* IV.6–9, tr. Dewing. On this image, see further Merrills (2004a), pp. 17–18.
67 Pohl (2004), p. 45. Conant (2004a), pp. 74–5, is more cautious.
68 See, for example, Salvian, *De Gub. Dei.*, VI; Quodvultdeus, *De Temp. Barb.* And the references at n. 19 above.
69 Noted by Pohl (2004), p. 46. For discussion of some of this material, see pp. 16–20 above.

70 von Rummel (2007), pp. 183–91, and Berndt (2007), pp. 238–44, are fundamental on this passage. See also von Rummel (2002) and (2005).
71 Vict. Vit., *HP* II.8, tr. Moorhead.
72 Vict. Vit., *HP* II.9, tr. Moorhead.
73 There is some evidence that hairstyle could be an important marker of identity in early medieval Gaul. Compare Sid. Ap., *Ep.* IV.20; *Carm.* V.238–53; Greg. Tur., *LH* II.9, 41; III.10; VIII.10.
74 Vict. Vit., *HP* II.9, tr. Moorhead.
75 Vict. Vit., *HP* II.10.
76 Vict. Vit., *HP* II.27; II.32–3.
77 Vict. Vit., *HP* I.28; I.40; I.48–49; II.10; III.33.
78 Vict. Vit., *HP* III.63. *totum subuertere uoluerunt*. Cf. also *HP* I.6 and 18 for explicit statements of Vandal hostility to social rank.
79 Vict. Vit., *HP* III.21, tr. Moorhead.
80 Cf. Vict. Vit., *HP* II.24.
81 Vict. Vit., *HP* I.15.
82 Vict. Vit., *HP* I.14. '*laicos nobiles*'.
83 Vict. Vit., *HP* II.16, tr. Moorhead.
84 Vict. Vit., *HP* III.62, tr. Moorhead.
85 Vict. Vit., *HP* I.1: *senes, iuuenes, paruuli, serui uel domini*. Most commentators on this passage have assumed that it does refer to women as well as men, but this is clearly not the case. Hyd., *Chron.* 302.5 Lem. 90. States that Geiseric crossed 'with all of the Vandals and their families' (*cum Vandalis omnibus eorumque familiis*).
86 Vict. Vit., *HP* III.33 (Dagila); CIL VIII.13800 (Munifrida); *AL R* 345 [S.340] (Damira).
87 Procopius, *BV* III.5.6 (Eudocia); *BV* III.8.11 (Amalafrida); Jordanes, *Getica* 184 (Visigothic princess); *AL R* 345 [S.340] (Damira).
88 See above p. 97. Ermengon's epitaph is one of only two which explicitly identifies a woman by an ethnonym in this period. The other is *CIL* XI.1731 which commemorates an Alamanna in Florence. On these inscriptions as exceptional, see Halsall (2007), p. 486, n.124.
89 Procopius, *BV* IV.14.8–9, tr. Dewing.
90 Procopius does not use the term in this section, presumably because this might imply that the women had a justifiable legal claim over these lands. The imperial legal position on the issue, by contrast, is explained at length at *BV* IV.14.10.
91 Vict. Vit., *HP* I.35. For discussion of this passage, see above pp. 98.
92 See, for example, *AL R* 298 [S.293] (eunuchs); *AL R* 317 [S.312] (hermaphrodites); *AL R* 309[S.304], 322 [S.317] (cuckolds); *AL R* 301 [S.296]; 364 [S.359] (chaste women); *AL R* 362 [S.357] (promiscuous women); *AL R* 317 [S.312] (a man with a large penis). On the absence of religious themes from the *Latin Anthology*, see below, pp. 225–7.

93 See, for example, *AL R* 296 [S.291], 310 [S.305] (dwarfs); *AL R* 315 [S.310] (hunchbacks); *AL R* 300 [S.295], 329 [S.324], 361 [S.356] (ugly people); *AL R* 338 [S.333], 357 [S.352], 364 [S.359] (beautiful people).

NOTES TO CHAPTER 5

1 The two best discussions of Vandal foreign policy are Clover (1967) and Gil Egea (1997), both of which are largely restricted to the reign of Geiseric. On diplomacy and foreign relations in general in this period, see esp. Blockley (1992) on eastern foreign policies and Gillett (2003) on the west, with the bibliographies therein.

2 Procopius, *BV* II.14.20 on the shipyard at Misuas in Carthage.

3 Prosper 413.1342 a.440; Hyd., *Chron.* 304.16. Lem. 120; Cassiodorus, *Chron.* 1235. Salvian, *DGD* VI.12 describes the impact of the Vandal raids on Sicily and Sardinia in apocalyptic terms: 'they have devastated and overthrown cities'. In the light of Salvian's haphazard information on events overseas, the details need not be taken too seriously, but the impact of the early attacks on the islands was evidently felt widely.

4 Leo, *Ep.* III.1. On the date of this letter, see Courtois (1955), p. 191. *Nov. Val.* I.2. The date of the *novella* is uncertain, but is perhaps best suited to the immediate aftermath of the Vandal attack. Cf. Clover (1967), p. 69.

5 Hyd., *Chron.* 304.16, Lem. 120; Isidore, *Hist.* 75.

6 *Nov. Val.* 9.1. *Nov. Val.* 5.1 (issued on March 3, 440) offers Greek merchants refuge in Rome 'during these critical times'.

7 *Nov. Val.* 9. This legislation came on the back of a law of March 440 (*Nov. Val.* 6.1.) which substantially tightened the procedures of military recruitment. Aetius' recall is mentioned in *Chron. Gall.* 452 a.440.

8 Cassiodorus, *Variae* I.4. The date of this heroism is not completely clear. Evidently it either preceded the signing of the treaty of 442 or post-dated the sack of Rome in 455 (Vandal raids on Sicily and Bruttii are not known between these dates, and are unlikely to have happened for reasons outlined in the text). Ruggini (1980), pp. 497–8 prefers the earlier date; Clover (1967), p. 71, n.1. prefers the later.

9 Naples: the inscription is preserved as *CIL* X.1409. For recent discussion of it and the defences see Christie (2003), pp. 346–7, and Arthur (2002), pp. 34–8. Terracina: Christie and Rushworth (1988), arguing from historical as well as archaeological grounds that the Vandal threat of the early 440s provides the best context for the construction (and thus challenging the traditional Byzantine dating of the wall circuit).

10 Priscus, Fr. 9.4 [=Theoph. AM 5942]. Prosper 413.1342 names Areobindus, Ansila and Germanus as the leaders of the expedition.

11 Theoph. AM 5941 provides the details of the expedition. For likely sources compare Blockley, I. p. 381, n.20, and Clover (1967), pp. 83–4, who

doubts the veracity of Geiseric's embassy, given the silence of contemporary western sources on the tradition.

12 Prosper 413.1344. According to *Nov. Theod.* 7.4. Areobindus was still in Constantinople on 6 March 441, which would have been the beginning of the sailing season.

13 On the Persian attack see Theod., *HE* V.37 and Marc. Com. s.a. 441. The dating of this attack is disputed. Croke (1977), p. 349, n.9, proposes a dating of 421–2 on the strength of Theodoret's chronological ambiguity. Compare Blockley (1992), p. 61, for the dating followed here.

14 Prosper a.442; *Chron. Gall.* 452. a.441; Theoph. AM 5942 = Priscus, Fr. 9.4. The redeployment of the troops from the Vandal expedition to the struggle in Thracia is indicated by the statement that Areobindus retained a position of command in both campaigns. The campaign against the Huns was a humiliating defeat (cf. Priscus, Fr. 13.2), and the struggle against the Huns continued to be an important distraction for the eastern empire. According to Priscus, Fr. 19 Aspar enjoyed notable success in the theatre before his elevation at court.

15 Prosp. 1347 a.442 and compare Procopius, *BV* I.4.12–14. Procopius here confuses the settlements of 435 and 442 AD. The provisions that he lays out, including the payment of an annual 'tribute' from Libya, fit the circumstances of 442 far more closely than they do 435 AD.

16 Merobaudes, *Carm.* I.7–8 and cf. *Pan.* II.23–9. On these poems see esp. Clover (1971), pp. 20–7 and 41–59.

17 Jordanes, *Getica* 184. On this marriage cf. Clover (1967), pp. 107–8.

18 Prosp. 415.1348. Firmly suggested by Wolfram (1988), p. 177.

19 Conspicuously, Jordanes explains Geiseric's negotiations with Attila prior to the Hunnic campaign of 451 as an attempt to prevent Visigothic reprisals for the episode of 442.

20 Procopius' grasp on early Vandal diplomacy is notoriously feeble, however, and too much should not be read into the omission.

21 Priscus, Fr. 10. On the dating, contrast Croke (1983), and Bayless (1979). The passage is best read as a reflection of the general threat posed by the Vandals, rather than as a reference to a specific attack.

22 Hyd., *Chron.* 306.21, Lem. 131.

23 As suggested by Clover (1967), pp. 103–4.

24 See the discussion in Clover (1967), p. 75.

25 *Vita Dan.* 56. The *Life* is explicit that these attacks never took place, but the threat was sufficient the cause panic in the imperial court and in Egypt alike. In fact, the reference to troop mobilization in the province may relate to the preparations for the campaign of Heracleius in 470.

26 Greg. *Dial.* III. 1.

27 Priscus, Fr. 11.2. For discussion, see *PLRE* II 'Attila'.

28 On these claims see Priscus, Fr. 17 = Joh. Ant., Fr. 199 and *PLRE* II Iusta Grata Honoria.

29 Jordanes *Getica*, 184 The episode is discussed in Clover (1967), pp. 113–17, and 127–8, and Berndt (2007), pp. 136–7. *Nov. Val.* 36.1 may hint at Vandal activity off Sardinia in July 452, but the reference is not conclusive.

30 Procopius, *BV* I.4.24 notwithstanding, who implies (surely incorrectly) that Aetius' victory over the Huns had given him a stature which made him dangerous to Maximus. The obvious parallels with Belisarius' experiences in the court at Constantinople may have shaped Procopius' understanding here.

31 The dynastic implications of this match are alluded to (retrospectively) in Sidonius panegyric to Majorian of AD 458. Sid. Ap., *Carm.* V.203–6. Cf. Oost (1964), p. 24, on the union itself.

32 Procopius, *BV* I.4.16–28 propounds an improbable myth involving Valentinian's rape of Maximus' wife. While the story seems oddly plausible in the context of pre-, post- and extra-marital intrigue in the political accounts of the period, less colourful (but more trustworthy) accounts are provided by Prosp. Add. Haun. 1373 (which gives the date September 21).

33 Detailed accounts are given in Prosp. Add. Haun. 1375 and *Vict. Tun.* a.454.

34 Hyd., *Chron.* 308.31 Lem. 162 provides the only reference to the betrothal of Palladius to a daughter of Eudoxia. The identification of this daughter (whether it was Placidia or Eudocia) has been the matter of some dispute. For discussion, and the case for Placidia, see Oost (1964), p. 28; Clover (1978), p. 181, n.46. Maximus' marriage is better attested by Prosper 428.1376 (or 1375); Procopius, *BV* I.4.36–7. Theoph. AM 5947 refers to the rape of Eudoxia without stating that the usurper married the imperial widow.

35 Hyd., *Chron.* 308.31 a.455 and Priscus, Fr. 20 = Joh. Ant., Fr. 201 are both clear that they did not themselves believe the tradition. Jord., *Rom.* 334, Marc. Com. a.455, Theoph. AM 5947, Procopius, *BV* I.4.38–9 and Malalas XIV.26 all reproduce the tradition without comment. Sidonius Apollinaris may also allude to the same tradition at *Carm.* V.61–2 (composed in the following year). For discussion see Clover (1967), pp. 151–2.

36 The precise dating is disputed. Clover (1967), pp. 140–1, concludes that June 2–15 provides the most convincing date for the sack itself. Cf. Courtois (1955), p. 195, n.8.

37 Prosp. 428.1376 states that Maximus was killed by royal slaves, Procopius, *BV* I.5.2 and Priscus, Fr. 30.1 that he was killed by a mob of citizens. Sid. Ap., *Carm.* VII.442–3 makes an intriguing allusion to the scheming of a Burgundian, which caused Maximus' death. *Vict. Tun.* a.455 simply states that Maximus was killed.

38 Leo's meeting with Geiseric is recorded in Prosp. 428.1376; Vict. Tun. a.455. The meeting of Leo and Attila appears in Priscus, Fr. 22 = Jordanes, *Getica*, 223; Vict. Tun. a.449.

39 The sources on the sack are varied. *Chron. Gall.* 511.65 [623]; Theoph. AM 5947; Procopius, *BV* I.5.4.
40 Procopius, *BV* II.9.5.
41 Procopius, *BV* I.5.4; that the scale of the plunder was still remembered in Constantinople 80 years later is evident both from Procopius' account and from the legislation in *Cod. Iust.* I.27.1.
42 Procopius, *BV* I.5.3. and see also Vict. Vit., *HP* I.25.
43 The date of Olybrius' union with Placidia is *hugely* complex. Cf. Clover (1978) for what would seem to be a definitive discussion (her possible marriage to Palladius notwithstanding).
44 Berndt and Steinacher (2008), p. 260.
45 Blockley (1992), pp. 161–3. This was not simply an imaginative interpretation of Geiseric's own, as is often supposed.
46 Sid. Ap., *Carm.* V.385–430. The same poem includes an evocative description of a raid. See discussion below.
47 Procopius, *BV* I.5.22.
48 Procopius, *BV* I.5.23–5, tr. Dewing.
49 Vict. Vit., *HP*. I.13.
50 Vict. Vit., *HP* I.13.
51 Vict. Vit., *HP* I.51. Cf. *The Oracle of Baalbek*. And compare Procopius, *BV* I.3.23: '. . . he plundered Illyricum and most of the Peloponnesus and the rest of Greece and all the islands which lie near it.'
52 Priscus, Fr. 19 (On Aspar and the rise of Marcian); Priscus, Fr. 31.1 (On the treaties).
53 Discussion in Blockley (1992), p. 69, and Clover (1967), pp. 170–2. Only Theodore Lector, *HE* I.7. associates Marcian with a direct act of hostility against the Vandals. This states that Marcian was preparing a major campaign against Carthage at the time of his death. While the tradition cannot be discounted entirely, it reads best as a retrospective attempt to rehabilitate the foreign policies of an otherwise popular emperor.
54 Hyd., *Chron.* 309.2 Lem. 176 refers to Ricimer's victory by subterfuge over a the attack of a Vandal fleet of 60 ships on Italy and Gaul. Cf. also Priscus, Fr. 31.1 and perhaps Sid. Ap., *Carm.* V.89–90. The victory was evidently sufficiently well-remembered to be alluded to in a panegyric ten years later: *Carm.* II.366–80.
55 Prosp. Add. Haun. 1383.
56 On Majorian see Oost (1964).
57 Hyd., *Chron.* 310.3 Lem. 197; Isid., *Hist. Goth.* 33; Joh. Ant., Fr. 203 = Prisc. 36.2. On the circumstances of Majorian's election, see Oost (1964) and *PLRE* II 'Maiorianus'. On his early diplomacy, see the discussion in Gil Egea (1997), p. 117.
58 On Marcellinus, see Procopius, *BV* IV.6.7.
59 That a major campaign against the Vandals was common knowledge throughout the west as early as 458 is demonstrated by Sidonius'

panegyric to Majorian. The poem was written late in 458, fully two years before the attack took place, yet alludes at length to the coming campaign (*Carm.* V.53–273) and the diplomatic preparations that had already gone into it (lines 441–603). Given this publicity, Geiseric's detailed knowledge of the campaign preparations should probably not be regarded as evidence for the betrayal of Majorian's expedition.

60 Hyd., *Chron.* 309.2. Lem. 192 refers to Vandal and Gothic envoys at the Suevic court at this time.

61 These events are narrated in Priscus, Fr. 36.1 = Joh. Ant., Fr. 203. The source is oblique on the eventual defeat of the expedition.

62 *Chron. Gall.* 511.71 [634] (Burgess) states that the fleet was captured near Carthago; Hyd., *Chron.* 310.4 Lem. 200 suggests that the Vandals seized ships offshore on the strength of information given by spies. Marius of Avrenches a.460 also agrees that some ships were captured, and claims that this happened near 'Elche'. The most detailed account is also the least reliable. Procopius, *BV* IV.7.4–17 gives an almost novelistic narration of Majorian's preparation for the expedition, on which see Max (1982). The campaign itself is wrongly dated to c. 474 and is erroneously said to have ended when Majorian died of dysentery. Among the modern interpretations of these events, see esp. Morazzani (1966), p. 553.

63 Priscus, Fr. 36.2 = Joh. Ant., Fr. 203. *Chron. Gall.* 511.72 [635–6].

64 These attacks (which are repeatedly alluded to in the embassies of the early 460s) argue strongly against the suggestion that Majorian's defeat resulted in the signing of a treaty which favoured the Vandals. *Pace* Schmidt (1953), p. 107, and Courtois (1955), p. 200.

65 The return of the women is alluded to in Hyd., *Chron.* 310.5 Lem. 216; Priscus 38.1. Later sources perpetuate a tradition that the hostages were returned under Marcian. Cf. Evagrius Schol., *HE* II.7; Malalas, *Chron.* XIV; Zonaras, *Epit.* 13.25.

66 Priscus, Fr. 38.2 = Joh. Ant., Fr. 204 and Priscus, Fr. 39.

67 Hyd., *Chron.* 310.1 Lem. 216. The date of the marriage is uncertain – on which see Clover (1978). Clover suggests that Olybrius may have travelled to Carthage before 461 in order to formalize their long-standing betrothal. Olybrius certainly had the standing (and the personal connections) to make him an ideal candidate for an embassy to the Vandals, but there is no firm evidence to support this supposition.

68 Blockley (1992), p. 72, developing Stein (1959), p. 387. Such a political agreement is implied in Priscus, Fr. 39.1 and 52 in which Geiseric accuses Leo of breaking an agreed treaty by supporting the elevation of Anthemius to the western throne in 467. Without a clause such as that proposed by Blockley, it is difficult to see the grounds on which Geiseric made this claim.

69 This was certainly the opinion of Priscus, Fr. 39.1.

70 *PLRE* II Libius Severus 18.

71 This period of compromised diplomacy is discussed in Priscus, Fr. 38, Fr. 39.1 and Fr. 41.
72 Priscus, Fr. 41. and cf. Theoph. AM 5943 on Tatian and his brother Julius with obvious parallels to Procopius, *BV* IV.4.5–11. Cassiodorus, *Chron.* a.464.
73 Priscus, Fr. 50; Evagrius, *HE* II.16 and cf. Procopius, *BV* I.6.5. Anthemius' difficult reign is discussed by O'Flynn (1991).
74 Priscus, Fr. 52. Cf. Priscus 39.1.
75 Hyd., *Chron.* 311.3 Lem. 224 is the only known source on Vandal negotiations with Aegidius.
76 Continuation of Vandal raiding is implied in Sid. Ap., *Carm.* II.348–50 (written in early 468) and cf. Theoph. AM 5961 = Priscus, Fr. 53. This would support the contention of Procopius, *BV* I.6.1–2 that the campaign of 468 was partly in direct response to these threats. The Alexandrian episode appears in *Vit. Dan*, 56.
77 The precise dates of Marcellinus' campaigns are uncertain. Hyd., *Chron.* 311.3 Lem. 227 implies that Marcellinus occupied Sicily in 465, but it seems more likely that his initial campaign was in Sardinia at some point between 466 and 468 as is suggested by Procopius, *BV* III.6.8 = Priscus, Fr. 53.3. Cf. *Chron. Const.* a.464. For comments see Courtois (1955), p. 187, who suggests that the campaign may have been proposed originally by the Sardinian Pope, Hilarius.
78 Hyd., *Chron.* 311.1 Lem. 232 implies that an invasion of Africa was proposed in 467 AD, and was foiled only by poor weather. While this may indeed be a reference to an otherwise unknown campaign (or a misunderstanding of the Sardinian expedition), it seems more likely that this is a distortion of the 468 expedition – defeated (indirectly) by the change of wind which allowed the Vandal fire-ship attack.
79 Theoph. AM 5961; Joh. Lyd., *De Mag.* III.43.
80 The confiscation of African shipping is implied by Malchus, Fr. 17, which discusses Huneric's later renunciation of claims over this shipping in an embassy to Constantinople.
81 Joh. Ant., Fr. 207 refers to 6,000 troops in Italy intended for the attack on Africa. On which see Clover (1967), p. 202. Marcellinus' capture of Sicily in 468 is suggested by Procopius, *BV* III.6.7–8 = Priscus, Fr. 53.3. The general seems to have been killed while in possession of the island. Compare Marc. Com. a.468. Cassiodorus, *Chron.* 1285.
82 Procopius, *BV* IV.6.11 implies as much. (He states that Geiseric was awestruck and ready to surrender.)
83 This is implied in Theoph. AM 5961, although it is possible that Theophanes is simply alluding here to the successful operation in Sicily under Marcellinus, and not to naval victories under Basiliscus.
84 Compare Procopius, *BV* IV.6.2–4, 10–16; Malalas, *Chron.* XIV.44; Theoph. AM 5961 (probably drawing upon Priscus).

85 The date of Heracleius' campaign is disputed. Courtois (1955), p. 204, follows Theoph. AM 5963 for a date of AD 470; Blockley (1992), p. 76, follows Hyd., *Chron.* 312.2 Lem. 247 and the problematic text of Procopius, *BV* IV.6.9 and suggests that the overland campaign was coordinated with the naval action of Basiliscus.

86 Theoph. AM 5963 states that Basiliscus, Heracleius and Marsus were all recalled by Leo to aid in a plot against Aspar. Cf. Evagrius, *HE* II.16 = Priscus, Fr. 61.

87 Suggested by Theoph. AM 5963.

88 Ennodius, *Vita Epiphanius* 51–75.

89 *Vict. Tun.* a.472. Malalas, *Chron.* XIV.45 includes an improbable (but intriguing) suggestion that Olybrius was sent to Italy in order that Anthemius might have him assassinated. Ricimer apparently intercepted the message and so gained Olybrius' support. For discussion, see Clover (1978).

90 Procopius, *BV* IV.7.16–17 sums up the political position well: 'There were, moreover, still other emperors in the west . . . but though I know their names well, I shall make no mention of them whatever. For it so fell out that they lived only a short time after attaining the office, and as a result of this accomplished nothing worthy of mention.' The principal primary source for events in the period is Ennodius' *Life of Epiphanius.* Even this text recommends brevity in dealing with the imperial politics of the mid-470s at chapters 79–80.

91 Procopius, *BV* IV.7.26.

92 Jordanes, *Getica* 244 describes Geiseric's embassies to the Goths. Although discredited by Clover (1967), p. 202, Jordanes' account is supported by a clause in Zeno's treaty with Theoderic Strabo (the ruler of one faction of Balkan Ostrogoths) recorded in Malchus, Fr. 2. Theoderic Strabo's insistence that his Goths would never be used in a conflict against the Vandals has been variously read as an indication that Leo planned an imminent engagement against Carthage (as by Clover [1967], p. 207, and Blockley [1992], p. 77), or that the Goths were frightened of the sea (thus Wolfram [1988], p. 269). The most likely motive for the insertion of such a clause would surely be that Theoderic Strabo had reached a prior arrangement with Geiseric, as Jordanes suggests.

93 Malchus, Fr. 5; Procopius, *BV* IV.7.26. The date is disputed. For a discussion of the case for AD 476 rather than 474, see Berndt (2007), pp. 200–1.

94 Vict. Vit., *HP* I.51.

95 Malchus, Fr. 17. Vict. Vit., *HP* II.2. suggests that at the same time Huneric acceded to the request of Zeno and Placida and accepted the appointment of a Catholic bishop in Carthage. This was later followed with demands for reciprocal Arian appointments in the empire, but it seems clear that the African appointment was made first (cf. Vict. Vit., *HP* II.2 and II.4).

96 Vict. Vit., *HP* II.4 (AD 478); II.38–9; and III.32 (both AD 484).

97 Malchus, Fr. 17.

98 Modéran (2003a) is crucial with references to the abundant earlier literature (much of it in French). Brett and Fentress (1996), pp. 70–7, provide a useful overview in English.
99 Procopius, *BV* III.25.5–7. On the historical context of this passage, see pp. 72 above.
100 Procopius, *BV* III.5.22.
101 Sid. Ap., *Carm.* V.337–8; Vict. Vit., *HP* I.25. Cf. Priscus, Fr. 38 and the discussion of the Moorish presence in Sardinia in pp. 137–8 below.
102 On the adoption of Christianity in the region (and other Roman cultural practices), see Morizot (1979) and (1991) and the useful synthesis in Modéran (2003a), pp. 389–96.
103 Assuming that *Abaritana* in Vict. Vit., *HP* I.13 refers to this region. See the discussion at pp. 63–4 above.
104 Procopius, *BV* I.8.1–2, 5. And compare Procopius, *Anec.* VI.7.5.
105 On the Bir Trouch ostraka, see pp. 00. On the Vandal dating system, see pp. 00.
106 *D.M.S. EGO MASTIES DUX | ANN[IS] LXVII ET IMP[E]R[ATOR] ANN[IS] X QUI NUN | QUAM PERIURAVI NEQUE FIDE[M] | FREGI NEQUE DE ROMANOS NEQUE | DE MAUROS, ET IN BELLU PARUI ET IN | PACE, ET ADVERSUS FACTA MEA | SIC MECU[M] DEUS EGIT BENE.* I follow the reading of Modéran (2003a), p. 399, here which suggests that Masties was *imperator* for X (10) years, and not XL (40), as was previously thought.
107 On the inscription and its interpretation see Modéran (2003a), pp. 396–415, with the discussion of earlier scholarship.
108 *CIL* VIII.9835. The identity of this king has been much disputed. See Camps (1984) and Modéran (2003a), pp. 374–8.
109 *CIL* VIII.8379 and 20216. On this inscription, see esp. Modéran (2003a), pp. 468–9, and Camps (1984), pp. 199–200.
110 Vict. Vit., *HP* II.26–8. Cf. Lancel (2002), pp. 301–2, n.170.
111 *Vict. Tun.* a.479. For discussion, see Modéran (2003a), p. 395.
112 Vict Vit., *HP* I.35. On the identification of *Caprapicta*, see Lancel (2002), p. 290, n.81, and Modéran (2003), pp. 544–6.
113 Procopius, *BV* III.8.7.
114 Procopius, *BV* III.8.15–29.
115 Ferrandus, *VF* 5.
116 Procopius, *BV* III.3–4 and *Anec* VI.5.1–5; Corippus, *Ioh.* III.184–97.
117 Hoamer's victories are alluded to at *BV* III.9.2; Gelimer's at Joh. Mal. 459. The discontent at Hilderic is suggested in Procopius, *BV* III.9.1 and Corippus, *Ioh.* III.198–200.
118 On settlement patterns in late Roman and early medieval Sicily, see esp. Ruggini (1980) and Bejor (1986).
119 Prosp., *Chron.* 1330 and 1332 on 'barbarian' attacks on Sicily. Marc. Com. a.438 refers to the defeat of pirates under the command of one

'Contradis': perhaps a corruption of the Vandal name Guntharix. Discussed by Croke (1995), p. 82.

120 *Nov. Val.* I.2.

121 Wilson (1990), pp. 331–3, provides a detailed summary. A survey of some of the key named sites in Late Antique Sicily is provided by Lagona (1982).

122 Christie (2003), p. 348.

123 Cassiodorus, *Variae* III.4. With discussion in Wilson (1990), p. 333.

124 On Valentinian's legislation, see Ruggini (1980), p. 496, who regards this as evidence of the political influence of Sicilians in Rome, rather than a genuine crisis in Sicily. On the archaeology, compare Wilson (2000) on a small production/distribution centre at Campanaio (destroyed c. 460, but subsequently reoccupied); Bernadini et al. (2000), pp. 120–33, on small settlements around Segesta which disappeared around this time; Castellana and McConnell (1990) on the villa complex of Contrada Saraceno, which changed in function c. 400 and was heavily damaged in the mid-fifth century.

125 Cf. Wickham (2005), p. 270, and Vera (1986), pp. 418–22. See also Salvian, *DGD* VI.68; Cassiodorus, *Variae* IV.7.2; Jordanes, *Getica* 50.

126 Vict. Vit., *HP* I.14, tr. Moorhead.

127 Compare Courtois (1955), pp. 192–3; and the more cynical assessment of Clover (1999).

128 Schmidt (1953), pp. 115–16, and Giunta (1958), pp. 72–3, identify Lilybaeum as this *pars*. Courtois (1955), p. 192, reads *pars* as a Vandal fiduciary interest in the island, represented by Odoacer's tributary payments. For discussion, see Clover (1991), p. 114, n.5.

129 Dracontius, *Satisf.* 211–4. The text is allusive, and interpretations have been varied. Cf. Moussy (1988), pp. 214–15; Schmidt (1953), p. 153; Courtois (1955), p. 193, n.2; and *PLRE* II Ansila, 2. Other proposals put forward include Martroye (1907), p. 33; McCormick (1986), pp. 265–6; Gil Egea (1998), p. 334, n.398, and p. 366; and Modéran (2002), pp. 551–2.

130 Cassiodorus, *Chron.* a.491.

131 *CIL* X.7232: *fines inter Vandalos et [Go]thos*. The allusion is undated, and could relate to a division of territories at some stage in the early sixth century.

132 Procopius, *BV* IV.8.11–13, tr. Dewing. The marriage is also mentioned in Anon Vales. 68 and Jordanes, *Getica*, 299.

133 Ennodius, *Pan.* XIII.70; Cassiodorus, *Variae* I.4.14. For discussion see Moorhead (1992), pp. 64–5.

134 Jordanes, *Getica* 299; *BV* I.8.14.

135 Procopius states at *BV* IV.8.11 that Thrasamund's proposal was made in an effort to shore up his kingdom in a period of difficulty. On the escalating problems with the Moors in the late 490s, see pp. 129 above.

136 Procopius, *BV* IV.8.14 on Thrasamund's close relations with Anastasius. Moorhead (1992), pp. 63–4, provides a thought-provoking discussion of the wedding of AD 500 as a mutually beneficial alliance, rather than the imposition of Ostrogothic power over the African kingdom.
137 Marc. Com. a.508; Jordanes, *Romana*, 356. The destruction caused by these attacks is alluded to in Cassiodorus, *Variae* I.16 and II.38. For discussion, see Moorhead (1992), pp. 182–3.
138 Cassiodorus, *Variae* V.43. Discussion in Moorhead (1992), pp. 190–1.
139 Procopius, *BV* IV.9.3. Procopius' statement that Amalafrida was imprisoned with 'all the Goths' implies an obvious change of political alignment was intended by the act.
140 Cassiodorus, *Variae* IX.1. The fact that a formal protest at the execution of Amalafrida was only lodged after Athalaric's succession does suggest that the murder took place only after Theoderic's death.
141 Moorhead (1992), pp. 207–8.
142 For discussion, see Moorhead (1992).
143 Ruggini (1961), pp. 548–61, provides the best general assessment of Theoderic's navy. See also Uggeri (1993) on the associated development of infrastructure at Ravenna and Classe.
144 Cassiodorus, *Variae* V.17. *non habet quod nobis Graecus impute taut Afer insultet.*
145 Ruggini (1961), p. 551; Vasiliev (1950), pp. 330–3.
146 Lulliri and Urban (1996) provides the best general overview of the island in this period. See also Dyson and Rowland (2007), pp. 173–87 for a useful overview of the archaeology in English.
147 Palladius, *Opus agriculturae*, IV.10.16.
148 Mastino (2005), pp. 499–507, provides the best recent overview of Sardinia in this period. Pergola (1988) and Lulliri and Urban (1996), pp. 33–6, provide useful discussions of urbanism in the island under the Vandals, with references.
149 See *Nov. Val.* 36.1 on the difficulties of navigation around Italy and Sardinia in July 452, with the discussion at n. 29 above.
150 By far the best discussion of Vandal Sardinia is provided by Lulliri and Urban (1996), esp. pp. 23–53.
151 Lulliri and Urban (1996), pp. 24–5 and 49–50. Their proposal rests upon analogies with rule in Sicily as implied in the treaty of AD 476. If the *praeses* was the *de facto* ruler of the island, however, his absence in the literary sources of the period is worthy of comment. One would expect Fulgentius in particular to have made the most of his contacts with a genuinely influential administrator.
152 Procopius, *BV* III.10.25–7. Lulliri and Urban (1996), p. 24, deduce from a coin bearing the inscription VBER CVDA that Godas may well have styled himself *gobernator* in a conscious break from the Vandal state and the existing system of administration.

153 Procopius, *BV* IV.13.43.
154 On this group see Lulliri and Urban (1996), pp. 25–7, which sets forth the argument broadly followed here. And see also *BV* II.5.1f on the resistance to the occupation of Cyril.
155 The involvement of the Moors in the conquest of the island is implied in *Cod. Iust.* I.27.1.
156 Lulliri and Urban (1996), p. 26.
157 Vict. Vit., *HP* II.23. Victor also mentions bishops sent into exile in Sicily in the same year: remarkable given its formal transfer to Odoacer six years earlier. Nevertheless, it seems clear that the majority of exiles were sent to Sardinia in the years that followed.
158 On this literature, see esp. Mastino (2005), pp. 502–4.
159 Mastino (2005), pp. 502–4; Pergola (1988).
160 Folliet (1988) and Meloni (1988).
161 Secular exiles to Sardinia should not be neglected. Ferrandus, *VF* 25 refers to 'senators and widows and virgins whose good reputations were unknown' among the exiles lent succour by the teaching of Fulgentius. Further indication of these refugees is provided by Dracontius, *Rom.* VII: an epithalamium dedicated to an African couple John and Vitula, in exile in Sardinia at the time of writing. See esp. *Rom.* VII.140–54.
162 Ferrandus, *VF* 8.
163 Moorhead (1992), pp. 208–9.
164 This is implied by Greg., *Ep.* 7.3 on complaints about corruption from imperial officials in the late sixth century.
165 Pergola and Vismara (1989).
166 Procopius, *BV* IV.5.6.
167 Procopius, *BV* IV.5.7–9.
168 Vict. Vit., *HP*. III.19 on some bishops who were sent to Corsica (to cut wood for the royal navy) before 484. On the later exiles see Courtois (1955), p. 186.
169 *AL R* 237 [S.229] lines 7–8: *Non panis, non haustus aquae, non ultimus ignis; | Hic sola haec duo sunt: exul et exilium.*
170 Discussion in Pergola (1981), pp. 913–14, which develops that of Courtois (1955), p. 186, n.12.
171 Pergola (1981), p. 915.
172 Summarized in Pergola (2000), esp. pp. 815–24.
173 Greg., *Ep.* 1, 50, 76, 77, 79; 6.22 and 8.1, cf. Pergola (1981), p. 916; idem (2000), pp. 811–14.
174 Following Courtois (1955), pp. 185–6.

NOTES TO CHAPTER 6

1 Treasure from Rome: Procopius, *BV* IV.5.3–5; III.9.4–5, and see the discussion in ch. 4 above; Gelimer's attempts to save the treasure: *BV*

IV.4.34–41, and see the discussion at pp. 165 below; Belisarius' attempts to restrict plunder: *BV* III.16.5 and esp. IV.4.3–4.

2 See esp. Vict. Vit., *HP* III.59. On the theft of senators' riches: *HP* I.5, I.6; I.12, III.15; robbery of churches: *HP* I.5, I.15, I.16, I.39, II.23, III.2, III.15; taxation: *HP* II.2; ransoms: *HP* I.25; piracy (and the sack of Rome): *HP* I.24.

3 On catastrophes in the Mediterranean world, see esp. Horden and Purcell (2000), pp. 298–341. On their relation to longer-term economic change – what Wickham terms the 'catastrophe flip' – see Wickham (2005), p. 13 (and *passim*). Ladtstätter and Pülz (2007) provide an exemplary illustration of this on the ground in the city of Ephesus.

4 See above chapter 4.

5 The Vandal occupation itself rarely features more than incidentally in the major archaeological surveys of the economy: compare Keay (1984) and (1998); Reynolds (1995) and Bonifay (2004). But cf. Panella (1986) and (1993) for a more positive assessment.

6 The work of John Hayes has been crucial in the establishment of fineware typologies. See Hayes (1972) and (1980) with the reflections of Hayes (1998). Keay (1984) was of comparable importance in establishing typologies for late Roman amphorae.

7 See (for example), Carandini (1970) and (1986); Fulford (1990); Panella (1986) and (1993); Reynolds (1995).

8 The best general survey of North African archaeology remains Mattingly and Hitchner (1995). See also the bibliography in von Rummel (2003) and Merrills (2004a), and the discussion below.

9 Crucial here is the work of David Mattingly. See esp. Mattingly (1988), (1989), (1990).

10 See esp. the sobering assessment of Bonifay (2004), pp. 443–9, after Bonifay (2003).

11 Recent excavations at Leptiminus highlight the dramatic impact that changing ceramic chronologies may have upon archaeologists' interpretations. See esp. Stone et al. (forthcoming) I am grateful to David Mattingly and David Stone for letting me see sections of this work in advance of publication.

12 The production complex in the east baths in Leptiminus provides a striking illustration of this process. Initially dated to the Vandal period on the strength of the presence of Keay Type LXII amphorae; the kiln and associated features found in the building are now thought to date from the early Byzantine occupation.

13 See the important discussion in Bonifay (2004), pp. 463–86, and Bonifay (2003).

14 Hopkins (1980) is the classic formulation of taxation as a stimulus for the monetization of the early empire. Wickham stresses that state redistribution was – if anything – a still more significant agent for change in the later empire. Cf. Wickham (1984), esp. pp. 8–15; Wickham (1988) and now

Wickham (2005), in which the disappearance of late Roman taxation occupies a central role.

15 Wickham (2005), p. 87.

16 The operation of the *annona* and its aftermath have been the subject of considerable recent study. See esp. Panella (1993); Manacorda (1977); Sirks (1991); McCormick (1998). Loseby (2005) provides a stimulating recent overview.

17 Jones (1964), p. 825 (with references).

18 Hurst (1994) and Peña (1998).

19 Carandini (1986) developing Carandini (1970) notes the strong link between ARS exports and the *annona* shipment: an observation which has directed all recent work on the phenomenon.

20 The practice is illustrated most clearly by *C.Th.* XIII.5.26 (AD 396) which curbed slightly the freedom of the *navicularii* to transact their own business while the *annona* was awaiting delivery. *C.Th.* XIII.5.24 (AD 395) on exemption from customs laws; XIII.5.23 (AD 393) on exemption from the *vectigalia*; XIII.5.17 (AD 386) on exemption from curial duty and taxes. On these laws see esp. McCormick (1998), pp. 80–92.

21 *C.Th.* XIII.8 (AD 395) ostensibly prohibits the practice of adding private goods to a public cargo. On this compare Reynolds (1995), p. 127, and McCormick (1998), pp. 85–7, who argues that this law may have been exceptional.

22 Carandini (1986); Mattingly (1988), pp. 52–3.

23 Viticulture: see esp. Brun (2003) and (2004); fish products: Slim et al. (2004), with comments also in Wilson (2006).

24 See esp. Peacock et al. (1990).

25 *C.Th.* XIII.5.27 (AD 397); XIII.9.5 (AD 397); XIV.15.3 (AD 397). Cf. Sirks (1991), p. 147.

26 Zosimus VI.11.1; Orosius, *Hist.* VII.42.12.

27 See Wickham (2005), p. 87, contra Sirks (1991), pp. 162–3 (who argues for a continuation in the form of the *dasmos* alluded to by Procopius, *BV* I.4.13).

28 Wickham (2005), p. 88. See, for example, *Nov. Val.* XIII (AD 445); I.3 (AD 450); XXXIV (AD 451), all of which reflect the financial difficulties that resulted for provincials from intensive taxation.

29 Procopius, *BV* IV.3.26, tr. Dewing.

30 Bonifay (2004), pp. 480–2, which revises the chronology of Panella (1993). Cf. also Bourgeois (2002).

31 Bonifay (2004), p. 481, and Reynolds (1995), pp. 112–13.

32 Reynolds (1995), p. 112; Bonifay (2004), pp. 481–2.

33 Ps. Fulg., *Sermo*. 38: *quam pulchram apparet litus dum repletur mercibus, et trepidat mercatoribus! Exponuntur de navibus sarcinae uestium diuersarum, laetantur innumeri cantantium in iucunditate nautarum.* With discussion in Isola (1990), pp. 110–11, and McCormick (2001), pp. 84–5.

34 Procopius, *BV* IV.14.7–13 (on the merchant from Syracuse).
35 Procopius, *BV* III.20.6–16; III.20.22–3.
36 See the discussion and references in Bonifay (2004), pp. 445–9, and the survey of Loseby (2005).
37 Reynolds (1995), pp. 113–14; cf. Tortorella (1998).
38 Spain: identified and discussed by Keay (1984), pp. 424–7 and *passim*, and developed in Keay (1998); Reynolds (1995), pp. 107–17. Islands: McCormick (1998), pp. 95–6; Panella (1993), pp. 641–4; Wilson (2000). And see also the general survey of Loseby (2005).
39 Identified and discussed by Panella (1993), pp. 641–51; Reynolds (1995), pp. 116–18; Fulford (1990), pp. 71–3. Compare the more positive account in Loseby (2005).
40 On late antique urbanism in general, see esp. Liebeschuetz (2001); Christie and Loseby (1996); Rich (1992). On African towns Leone (2007) is fundamental. Cf. also the discussion in Leone (2003) and the useful survey of Potter (1995).
41 *Kardo Maximus* – Leone (2007), p. 136; Deneauve and Villedieu (1977), (1979); *via Caelestis* – Vict. Vit., *HP* I.8. Cf. Quodvultdeus, *Lib. Prom. Dei*, III.44 on the same subject. On the location of the *via Caelestis* see the discussion and references in Lancel (2002), p. 276. The *Platea maritima* was a third public space in Carthage, referred to in Augustine, *De Civ. Dei* XVI.8. The identification of the *platea*, and hence its fate after the Vandal occupation, are not certain. See Gros (1985) and Leone (2007), pp. 124 and 159 for discussion.
42 Leone (2003), pp. 263–4; Vismara (1999), pp. 73–5; Gelichi and Milanese (1997), pp. 71–82; (1998), pp. 462–3.
43 Leone (2007), p. 143; Guéry (1981), p. 98; Guéry et al. (1982), pp. 11–13.
44 Leone (2007), p. 128; Mackensen (1993), pp. 27–32; Mackensen and Schneider (2002), pp. 128–30; Barraud et al. (1998); Bonifay (2004), pp. 53–5.
45 Rakob (1991), pp. 242–51.
46 Hurst (1994) and see the brief discussion in Leone (2007), p. 80.
47 For an overview, see esp. Leone and Mattingly (2004) which surveys the surveys.
48 Hitchner (1988a), (1988b), (1990) and (1995). The discussion of specific sites which follows is drawn largely from Rob Wanner's (2006) unpublished gazetteer of the survey area. I am grateful to him for allowing me to use this valuable synthesis.
49 Mattingly (1988), p. 45, provides a summary of the exploitation of the Sahel.
50 Mattingly (1989).
51 Hitchner (1988a).
52 Peacock et al. (1989) and (1990).

53 Panella (1993) suggests the possibility of a Vandal policy. Compare Reynolds (1995), pp. 112ff., and Bonifay (2004), pp. 483–4, citing the excavations at Nabeul.
54 Discussion (with references) in Leone and Mattingly (2004), pp. 154–5.
55 Carthage survey: Greene (1983), (1992); Dougga: De Vos (1997), (2001); El Mahrine: Mackensen (1985), (1993), (1998a), (1998b).
56 Mackensen and Schneider (2002), pp. 131–4; Peacock et al. (1990), pp. 66–74.
57 The standard edition (and important commentary) is Courtois et al. (1952). Recent studies include Mattingly (1989); Ørsted (1994); Vitrone (1994–5); and Conant (2004b).
58 The origins of the law would seem to lie in the distinction between tenants' obligations to landlords (on estates) and the fisc (on marginal land) – an interpretation based largely on the references to the law in the Bagradas Valley. For discussion, see Kehoe (1984), and Kehoe (1988), pp. 48–51, with discussion in Duncan-Jones (1990). A radically different interpretation is put forward by Ørsted (1994) who argues that the tablets may represent records of annual sales of produce, and not trees or plots of land. This helps to explain the (very) low prices on offer, but leaves a great deal unexplained (as Ørsted acknowledges), not least the particular emphasis placed in the documents on irrigation construction and land improvements.
59 TA 5; Mattingly (1989), p. 411, calculates that this field may have been between 100 and 200 m^2, that is somewhere between the size of a cricket strip and a small municipal swimming pool (or rather less than a quarter of the size of a baseball diamond). The difficulties of assessing the likely sizes of these land plots are discussed in Mattingly (1988).
60 The relevant documents are (in chronological order) TA 17, 13, 31, 15. The illiteracy of Processanus and Siddana is stated explicitly TA 13 and 31. To judge from TA 15 their son Quodvultdeus was also illiterate. As Conant (2004b) discusses the inhabitants of the region display a relatively high level of literacy. The prices for trees and plots cited in the tablets compare poorly with those of Ianuarilla's dowry – a point made by Courtois et al. (1952), p. 204, and cf. Grierson (1959) and Ørsted (1994).
61 TA 2.
62 On this title, see pp. 212–3 below.
63 TA 1.
64 Bonnal and Fevrier (1966–7) provide a short edition of the *ostraka* along with brief commentary.
65 Bir Trouch, *Ostraka* 1, 2, 3. Discussion in Wickham (2005), pp. 266, 273–4.
66 Other examples include the collections from Henchir Bou Gornine (AD 359); Ksar Koutine (AD 419) and Negrine (AD 542–3). A list of isolated and unpublished *ostraka* is provided by Bonnal and Fevrier (1966–7), p. 246, n.1.

67 Procopius, *BV* IV.8.25.
68 This is the conclusion of Wickham (2005), p. 91 and *passim*.
69 The 50% estimate is taken from Wickham (2005), p. 73.
70 Vict Vit., *HP* II.38; Procopius, *BV* III.16.12 refers to the use of the *cursus publicus*. On this institution in the empire, see Kolb (2001), and under the Vandals, see Diesner (1968).
71 See ch. 3, above.
72 Wickham (2005), p. 89.
73 Ferrandus, *VF* 1; 2.
74 Ferrandus, *VF* 14. Cf. Gil Egea (1998), p. 305.
75 Procopius, *BV* III.5.14.
76 Procopius, *BV* III.5.15–17.
77 Vict Vit., *HP* II.2.
78 *AL R* 341 [S.33], 342 [S.33].
79 See Rosenblum (1961), p. 219., cf. also *PLRE* II Eutychus 2 and *PLRE* III Bonifatius 1.
80 *Vict. Tun.* a.533.
81 Procopius, *BV* IV.4.33–41.
82 *AL R* 137 [S.126], tr. Kay. Compare the epigram on the same theme at *AL R* 138 [S.127].
83 Cf. Isidore, *Orig.* 11.1.105. And the discussion in Kay (2006), p. 232, who argues that the poem alludes to a medical condition of scrotal swelling, rather than to a more common phenomenon.
84 As is suggested by the specific remission at *C.Th.* XIII.1.10. (AD 374). Cf. Keay (2006), p. 232.
85 See for example *C.Th.* XIII.18–19 (AD 400).
86 On this treaty, see pp. 131–2 above.
87 Vict. Vit., *HP* III.11, tr. Moorhead.
88 *C.Th.* XVI.5.54.5.
89 Cf. Gil Egea (1998), p. 299.
90 Vict. Vit., *HP* II.23.
91 Cf. Wickham (2005), pp. 60–1, on the basic principles discussed here.
92 On the form of the Vandal settlement, see the discussion in ch. 3 above.
93 Procopius, *BV* IV.13.43; Lulliri and Urban (1996), pp. 25–7.
94 As Kay (2006), p. 203 notes, the term echoes *C.Th.* VIII.4.8 on the provincial military supply of the *pastus*.
95 Fulgentius, *Ad Tras.* 1.1.3.
96 Vict. Vit. *HP* III.29–30.
97 Turcan (1961), pp. 207–34, and cf. Morrisson (1976).
98 Morrisson (2003), pp. 80–1.
99 General introductions to Vandal numismatics may be found in Blackburn (2005), Hendy (1985) and Grierson and Blackburn (1986). Salama (1985) provides an important overview of these coins in circulation.

100 The scholarship on the ideology of Vandal coinage is also voluminous. For an assessment of the current state of play compare Morrisson (2003), Clover (2003) and the summary comments of Duval (2003).
101 The importance of the *solidus* to the later Roman state is highlighted strongly by Banaji (2002), on which see the helpful summary and discussion of Sarris (2005). Morrisson (1987) provides a fundamental study of the circulation of gold coinage in Vandal Africa.
102 Morrisson (1987), p. 327. Although note that much of the gold deposited in the fifth century was minted in the fourth, and may have been in circulation for some time.
103 Morrisson (1987), p. 332.
104 Compare, for example, Wolfram (1997), pp. 167–8; Hendy (1995); Grierson and Blackburn (1986), p. 19. And (brief) discussion in Morrisson (1987), p. 333.
105 Salama (1985), pp. 192–3.
106 Discussed most fully in Morrisson and Schwartz (1982). These issues have frequently been dated to the pre-Vandal period, but the consensus now places them either in the reign of Geiseric or Huneric.
107 See Clover (2003) and Duval (2003) for discussion and bibliography.
108 Hendy (1985), pp. 478–84, provides a systematic overview. Cf. Morrisson (2003), pp. 70–2.
109 *Nov. Val.* XVI. (AD 455).
110 Morrisson (2003), pp. 67–9.
111 The discussion here broadly follows Hendy (1985), pp. 478–84, developing Grierson (1959). Cf. also Morrisson (2003), pp. 70–1.
112 Hendy (1985), p. 486.
113 On this debate see Morrisson (2003), pp. 72–4, and Hendy (1985), pp. 486–9. Cf. also the discussion in Clover (1991), pp. 117–32.
114 See esp. Hendy (1995), pp. 475–8.
115 Reynolds (1995), p. 140, n.3; Morrisson (2003), pp. 81–4.
116 Morrisson (2003), pp. 80–1.
117 See esp. Grierson (1959).

NOTES TO CHAPTER 7

1 Possidius, *VA* 28.
2 Possidius, *VA* 29–31; *'hostili neci extinctos'*.
3 See, for example, Quodvultdeus, *De Temp. Barb*, I.8.7; Augustine, *Ep.* 228.5; Vict. Vit., *HP* I.3–7.
4 For accounts of different aspects of the Arian controversy see Barnes (1993); Williams (2001); Ayres (2004); Parvis (2006).
5 On these missions, see Sozomen, *HE* VI.37; Socrates, *HE* IV.33.; Orosius, *Hist.* VII.33.19.
6 Van Slyke (2003), pp. 182–3; Heather (2007), p. 143.

7 Hyd., *Chron.* 89; Greg. Tur., *LH* II.2.
8 Prosper, *Chron.* 2.747.a.439.
9 Possidius, *VA* 28.8–10.
10 Augustine, *Ep.* 228.5 quoting from the letter of Honoratus. The letter appears in Possidius, *VA* 30.
11 Capreolus, *Ep.* 1.
12 Prosper, *Chron.* 1327.a.437.
13 Vict. Vit., *HP* I.15.
14 Eno (1989), p. 153; Van Slyke (2003), pp. 24–30.
15 Vict. Vit., *HP* I.23.
16 Augustine, *Ep.* 170; 238; 239; 240; 242; *Serm.* 140; *Contra Max.Ar.; Coll.Cum. Max.* For Augustine and his confrontations with Arianism see Lancel (2002), pp. 368–90; Bonner (1997), pp. 141–4. On Arian bishops and clergy see Mathisen (1997).
17 Quodvultdeus, *De Temp. Barb.* II.14.4–6, tr. Kalkmann.
18 Quodvultdeus, *De Symb.* 1.13.4–5; *Lib. Prom. Dei* 13.22.
19 Jordanes, *Getica* 25.132.
20 Hyd., *Chron.* 301.4, Lem. 89.
21 Heather (2007), p. 145.
22 Courtois (1954), p. 292.
23 Vict. Vit., *HP* I.4–16. On the confiscations, see above pp. 66–9.
24 Vict. Vit., *HP* III.63; Heather (2007), 139–40.
25 Vict. Vit., *HP* I.24–29. For the dates of the consecration and death of Deogratias, bishop of Carthage, see Mandouze (1982), p. 271.
26 Heather (2007), p. 141.
27 Possidius, *VA* 27 (Visitations); *VA* 23 (Care of the poor); *VA* 24 (Care of church property); *VA* 21 (Attendance of Church Councils); *VA* 20 (Discerning intercession on behalf of others); *VA* 20 (As a judge).
28 Hamilton (2004), pp. 86–90.
29 Possidius, *VA* 30; Hamilton (2004), p. 90.
30 Possidius *VA* 22 (Augustine's ascetic lifestyle); *VA* 25 (Ascetic lifestyle of the Cleric-Monks who lived with him); Hamilton (2004), pp. 98–105.
31 Quodvultdeus, *Lib. Prom. Dei* 5.7. See also *Lib. Prom. Dei* 10.18;
32 Quodvultdeus, *Lib. Prom. Dei* 2.21.41; 2.27.57.
33 Quodvultdeus, *Lib. Prom. Dei* 2.27.57; 1.26.50; 2.31.69.
34 Quodvultdeus, *Lib. Prom. Dei* 2.6.11;
35 Quodvultdeus, *Lib. Prom. Dei* 14.23; 2.6.11. For Quodvultdeus' emphasis upon the apocalypse see Van Slyke (2003).
36 Quodvultdeus, *Lib. Prom. Dei* G.13.1516.
37 For the noble youth of Italy as Quodvultdeus' audience see Van Slyke (2003), pp. 84–5.
38 Van Slyke (2003), pp. 187–8.
39 Mapwar (1994).
40 *Contra Varimadum.*

41 *Contra Varimadum* 1.6.
42 *Contra Varimadum Praef.*
43 See for instance *Testimonia de patre et filio et spiritu sancto*; *Liber de Trinitate.*
44 Cerealis Castellensis, *Contra Maximinum Arianum Libellus*. For a study of this text see Caserta (1986).
45 Van Slyke (2003), p. 76.
46 On Victor's background see Lancel (2002), pp. 9–12; Pastorino (1980), pp. 48–53; Costanza (1980), pp. 231–9; Courtois (1954), pp. 5–10.
47 Shanzer (2004), p. 278.
48 Vict. Vit., *HP* I.4; 9; 10; 15; 16;
49 Vict. Vit., *HP* I.5–7; 19–21; 23.
50 See, for example, Vict. Vit., *HP* I.30–35.
51 Vict. Vit., *HP* II.1–7.
52 Vict. Vit., *HP* II.8–9; 23–25.
53 Vict. Vit., *HP* II.26–37; *Vict. Tun.* a.479 puts the number at 4,000.
54 Vict. Vit., *HP* II.39.
55 Vict. Vit., *HP* II.56–101.
56 Vict. Vit., *HP* III.2.
57 Vict. Vit., *HP* III.3–14.
58 Vict. Vit., *HP* III.15–20.
59 Vict. Vit., *HP* III.21–54.
60 *Passio Septem Monachorum*, M. Petschenig (ed.), CSEL 7 (1881). On the authorship of the work see Lancel (2002), pp. 69–71.
61 For the later importance of this text, See below, p. 247–8.
62 For the convincing argument that at least part of Victor's history was written after the death of Huneric see Lancel (2002), pp. 9–12; Shanzer (2004), pp. 272–3. For the theory that the *History* was aimed at Gunthamund see Schwarcz (1994), p. 118.
63 Vict. Vit., *HP* III.40.
64 On the tensions between Huneric and his successor, see Vict. Vit., *HP* II.12–13, and above pp. 75–6.
65 For the *HP* as a plea to Constantinople see Schwarcz (1994), pp. 117–18; Constanza (1980), pp. 246–9; Courtois (1954), pp. 17–22. It has been speculated that Eugenius, the new bishop of Carthage might himself have been from the east. Shanzer (2004), pp. 272–8, however, questions the role of Eugenius in the commission of this work, on the grounds that at least two sections of the prologue, previously thought to be addressed to Eugenius, would appear to have been taken from a letter addressed to Victor himself.
66 On Victor's definitions of 'barbarian' and 'Roman', see ch. 4, above. Earlier examples of stirring up this wider interest in the African cause include Quodvultdeus, *Lib. Prom. Dei* 5.7; *De Temp. Barb.* I.8.7.

67 Other texts do seem to have circulated, however. On a lost *passio* which was known in Merovingian Gaul, see Cain (2005).
68 Gelasius, *Ep. ad episc. Dard.*
69 Courtois (1954), p. 51; Courcelle (1948), p. 194.
70 Vict. Vit., *HP* III.48; III.60.
71 *Mansi*, VII, Col, 1171. For a list of references to the Arian conversion see Courtois (1955), p. 225, n.3 and p. 227, n.3.
72 Modéran (2006), pp. 165–82.
73 Shanzer (2004), pp. 281–6.
74 Vict. Vit., *HP* III.26, modified from the translation of Moorhead.
75 Assertions of the scale of martyrdoms are numerous, details are rather rarer. Cf. Vict. Vit., *HP* I.5; I.7; I.9; I.10; I.30; III.21; III.33.
76 These are: *HP* II.52 (Laetus who was burned to death); III.24 (Majoricus, who *may* have been killed); III.27 (Victorinus, ditto); and III.28 (two brothers, ditto). We might also add the anonymous lector killed by an arrow to the throat during an assault on a church in *HP* I.41.
77 The ambiguity of Victor's application of the terms 'martyr' and 'confessor' is indicated by *HP* II.34.
78 See esp. Vict. Vit., *HP* II.12–15. On these deaths, see pp. 75 above.
79 Cf. Vict. Vit., *HP* II.14.
80 His formerly close advisor, Count Sebastian, probably met his end because he was the son-in-law of the last Roman military governor of North Africa (Vict. Vit., *HP* I.19–21). One might also wonder whether it was political infighting that brought about the disgrace of Saturus, another Romano-African who was superintendent of the household of Huneric (Vict. Vit., *HP* I.48–50).
81 Modéran (1998).
82 Modéran (2002), p. 108. More generally on the Vandal concentration on Africa Proconsularis 107–110. For the funerary epitaph of an exiled African Nicene bishop found in Mauretania Caesarea see Modéran (2006), pp. 182–5.
83 Vict. Vit., *HP* I.8–9.
84 Stevens (2000); Stevens et al. (2005); Leone (2007), p. 155.
85 Miles (forthcoming).
86 Modéran (1998), pp. 255–7.
87 As well as Fulgentius' work we also have an exegesis on the Book of Psalms written by an anonymous Catholic abbot in the same period which appears to make allusive references to both spiritual and temporal 'enemies'. Cf. Ferguson (1999), pp. 30–5. However. Ferguson's thesis that Fulgentius was himself the author of these collects remains unproved.
88 Vict. Vit., *HP* III.5.
89 Heather (2007), p. 138.
90 Vict. Vit., *HP* II.39.
91 Grig (2004).

92 For accounts of different aspects of the Donatist controversy see Frend (1952); Tilley (1997); Markus (1983), esp. chs. 6–9; Shaw (1992) and (2004).
93 Vict. Vit., *HP* III.61; Wynn (1990); Shanzer (2004), pp. 278–9. Eusebius' *Ecclesiastical History* had been translated from Greek into Latin by Rufinus of Aquileia in the late fourth century, and this is the text which would seem to have been known to Victor.
94 Shanzer (2004), p. 279; Vict. Vit., *HP* I.30–35.
95 Vict. Vit., *HP* III.71. On this tradition, see esp. the discussion in Steinacher (2004), pp. 175–7.
96 Vict. Vit., *HP* III.55, tr. Moorhead.
97 Vict. Vit., *HP* III.64, tr. Moorhead.
98 Vict. Vit., *HP* III.65.
99 MacEvitt (2007). I am grateful to Professor Peter Brown for drawing my attention to this book.
100 MacEvitt (2007), p. 22.
101 See in particular MacEvitt (2007), pp. 23. The argument that the roots of Frankish 'Rough Tolerance' in the Holy Land hailed from the successor kingdoms of early medieval Europe appears to be borne out by the situation in Vandal North Africa.
102 Stevens (1982).
103 Ferrandus, *VF* 5.
104 Ferrandus, *VF* 5–6. Modéran (2002), p. 108.
105 AT 2.
106 We do not know whether the community at *Fundus Tuletianos* was Arian or Nicene (or both). For further discussion of this society, see pp. 159–61 above.
107 See above, p. 182–4.
108 Shanzer (2004), p. 287.
109 Vict. Vit., *HP* II.46 for Arians and Nicenes eating together.
110 Ferrandus, *VF* 7; *'multa parvula'*, tr. Eno.
111 For more on the network of Fulgentius see Stevens (1982). On Fulgentius' upbringing, Ferrandus, *VF* 1–2.
112 Vict. Vit., *HP* III.33; 3.38; 3.39. Courtois (1954), pp. 224–7; Greg. Tur, *LH* II.3.
113 Vict. Vit., *HP* III.34.
114 Béjaoui (2008), pp. 239–43.
115 Béjaoui (1995).
116 Leone (2007), p. 148.
117 Béjaoui (2008).
118 Béjaoui (2003), pp. 147–61. See also a funerary inscription for a deacon Lucilianus found at the church of El Ounaissia in the same region which gives the date of seventh year of the reign of Gunthamund (AD 491), discussed in Béjaoui (2008). Other churches which excavators considered to

be Catholic were also built during the Vandal epoch at Thibiuca, Thala, Sufetula and Utica during the later fifth century; see Leone (2007), pp. 150–4.

119 *Laterculus Regum Vandalorum et Alanorum* (Reichenau Version), Fol. 49 v. Steinacher (2004), pp. 165–6; Courtois (1955), p. 300. The recall of the Catholic clergy is also mentioned by *Vict. Tun.* a.479.2. It has been argued that that Eugenius himself did not return until AD 487 and the Catholic clergy only returned to their posts in 494.

120 Cf. Vict. Vit., *HP* III.13 on the precedent for these actions under Huneric.

121 Ferrandus, *VF* 17.; Courtois (1955), p. 302.

122 Ferrandus, *VF* 20–21. I have used the dating of Eno (1997), pp. xv–xvii, for the events recorded in the text. On the impact of the bishops in Sardinia, see above pp. 137–9.

123 Ferrandus, *VF* 20, tr. Eno. See also Procopius' similar assessment at *BV* III.8. 8–11.

124 *Obiectiones Regis Trasamundi* (CC 9167–70). Ferrandus, *VF* 20.

125 Ferrandus, *VF* 21, tr. Eno.

126 Ferrandus, *VF* 21.

127 Fulgentius, *Ad Trasamundum* 1.2.1.

128 Vict. Vit., *HP* III.29, records a *Notarius*; Mathisen (1997), pp. 686–7.

129 Fulgentius, *C. Fastid.* 1.1; Facundus, *C. Mocianum* 64.

130 Pseudo Origen, *Comment. in Iob* (*PG* 17.371–522). For the arguments placing this text in the Vandal period see Dossey (2003). It is more difficult to argue that this text was a response to the freedoms that were granted to the Catholic Church by Thrasamund's successor, Hilderic, as Dossey suggests at pp. 120–1.

131 Dossey (2003), pp. 63, 89–104.

132 See ch. 8 on elite education in Vandal North Africa.

133 Pseudo Origen, *Comment. in Iob* 512B.

134 Pseudo Origen, *Comment. in Iob* 428B.

135 Pseudo Origen, *Comment. in Iob* 428B; 382A.

136 Dossey (2003), pp. 105–6.

137 Dossey (2003), pp. 63–4.

138 Fulgentius, *Ep. ad Victor* 10.1. For accusations of Donatism during unconnected ecclesiastical disputes in the late sixth century AD see Markus (1991), pp. 159–66.

139 Fulgentius, *Contra Fabianum* 2.1; 2.3; 2.4; 3.11; 3.12; 3.13; 12.3; 4.115.4; 15.5 (CC 91A 765, 766, 770, 771, 782, 783, 786).

140 Fulgentius, *Contra Fabianum* 3.10 (CC 91A: 770); 34.8 (CC 91A: 839).

141 Cf. Shanzer (2004), pp. 285–6.

142 Fulgentius, *Abecedarium* 236–240 (CC 91A: 883); 256–257 (CC 91A: 884). Shanzer (2004), p. 288, n.134.

143 Ferrandus, *VF* 20.

144 Fulgentius, *Ep. ad Don.* 2, tr. Eno.

145 See also Fulgentius, *Ad Mon.* 2.1.
146 Fulgentius, *De Incarn* 2.
147 Fulgentius, *Contra Serm. Fast.*
148 Fulgentius, *Abecedarium* 294–296.
149 Ferrandus, *VF* 20, tr. Eno.
150 Fulgentius, *Abecedarium* 269–270.
151 For the use of sermons in order to maintain resistance to Arianism see Isola (1990). For the rhyming anti-Arian psalm of Fulgentius see *Abecedarium* (CC 91A: 877–885). Courcelle (1948), p. 198.
152 Ferrandus, *VF* 25.
153 *Vict. Tun.* a.523.2; Ferrandus, *VF* 25.
154 Ferrandus, *VF* 26–27.
155 *ILT*, 620; Courtois (1955), p. 382, n.125,
156 *Mansi* 8: 633; *Mansi* 8 635–656; *Conc. Carthag.* A.525 (CCL 149: 254–282); Courtois (1955), pp. 304–9; Massigli (1912).
157 *Mansi* 8: 633; Massigli (1912).
158 *Mansi* 8: 635–656; Courtois (1955), pp. 304–9. *Conc. Carthag.* A.525 (CCL 149: 254–282)
159 Ferrandus, *VF* 27, tr. Eno.
160 Ferrandus, *VF* 27.

NOTES TO CHAPTER 8

1 Whitbread (1971), p. ix. On the dating of the text, see the discussion in Hays (2004), who argues that Fulgentius was writing some time after the middle of the sixth century AD.
2 See Raby (1957), p. 100. On Martianus and his contemporaries (thought by Raby to be later fourth century or early fifth century): '[M]any of the others had sunk into an intellectual darkness, deepened by the literary obscurity which they cherished for its own sake.'
3 Reynolds (1983), pp. 9–13, provides a helpful overview of the transmission of the *Anthologia Latina*. Hen (2007), pp. 78–83, sets the collection within its historical context. The African provenance and dating of many of the anonymous poems are uncertain. See esp. Courtney (1980) and Stevens (1988) for discussion of the possibility of an African provenance.
4 Quodvultdeus, *De Temp. Barb.* II.5, tr. Kalkmann.
5 Vict. Vit., *HP* I.8, tr. Moorhead.
6 Leone (2007), pp. 154–7, provides an excellent recent overview.
7 Leone (2007), p. 159; Leone (2002), p. 240; von Rummel (2008), p. 154; Lancel (1988), pp. 654–7.
8 Vict. Vit., *HP* III.17. On this passage see Lancel (2002), pp. 317–18, n.394.
9 Senay (1992); Hallier (1995); and see the discussion in Lancel (2002), p. 317, n.394, and Leone (2007), pp. 155–7.

10 See above, pp. 154.
11 *C.Th.* XV.1.1.
12 *C.Th.* XVI.10.3.
13 On Late Antique Christian attitudes to the theatre see Easterling and Miles (1999).
14 *C.Th.* XVI.10.17.
15 The function of this basilica is not completely clear. Cf. Leone (2007), pp. 77–8; 155 after Ennabli (2000).
16 Lézine (1968), pp. 71–2. Cf. von Rummel (2008), pp. 155–6.
17 Leone (2007), p. 160.
18 Cf. above pp. 153–4.
19 See esp. Leone (2009), pp. 87–95 with references.
20 *AL R* 312 [S.307]; 313 [S.308].
21 *AL R* 320 [S.315].
22 Stevens (1988), pp. 153–4.
23 Stevens (1988), pp. 173–8. For an archaeological study of the Circus at Carthage in Late Antiquity see Humphrey (1988), pp. 25–31.
24 See Stone et al. (forthcoming).
25 Leone (2007), pp. 140–1; Thébert (2003), p. 418.
26 Leone (2007), p. 141; Thébert (2003), p. 419.
27 Leone (2007), pp. 140–1; Thébert (2003), p. 172.
28 Ben Abed and Duval (2000), pp. 198–200; Leone (2007), pp. 162–3; Balmelle et al. (1990), pp. 11–18.
29 Ben Abed and Duval (2000), p. 198.
30 See Leone (2007), p. 162 [House of the Trifolium] and 161 [House of the Greek Charioteers].
31 See esp. Stevens (1996).
32 Leone (2007), pp. 160–1; Wells (1992).
33 Leone (2007), p. 161; Stevens (1995a), p. 210.
34 Leone (2007), p. 161.
35 On the fate of *curiae* in Late Antiquity, see Lepelley (2006).
36 On the survival of the curial elite in Vandal North Africa see Modéran (1996), pp. 108–111.
37 On these passages, see pp. 193 above.
38 On this title see the discussions of Chastagnol and Duval (1974); Clover (1982) and the summary in Ben Abed and Duval (2000), pp. 171–2.
39 The inscriptions are quoted and discussed in Duval (1975), nos. 413, 401 and 424.
40 Chastagnol and Duval (1974), developed in Duval (1984).
41 On the possible background of Martianus see Shanzer (1986), pp. 2–3.
42 Martianus Capella, *De Nuptiis*, II.135–8. Translation Gehl (2002), p. 4.
43 Gehl (2002), pp. 4–5.
44 Brown (1992), pp. 35–70.

45 Augustine, *Confessions* 1.13–14, recalls the experience of learning Greek in provincial Africa.
46 Augustine, *De Civ. Dei,* I.3.
47 See for example Cicero, *De Invect.* 1.1.1–3; Quintilian 1.4.2–3; 2.1.4–5. Gehl (2002), pp. 3–9.
48 Seneca's *Controversiae* & *Suasoriae* provide good illustration of this.
49 Quodvultdeus, *De Temp. Barb.* II.4, tr. Kalkmann.
50 Brown (1967), pp. 35–9; Lancel (1999), pp. 14–19.
51 Cf. Riché (1976), pp. 38–9.
52 Dracontius, Praef, *Rom.* 1.12–15.
53 Vict. Vit., *HP* II.13. This was the nephew of Huneric who died in the purge of 481. On the circumstances of this purge see above pp. 75–6.
54 *AL R* 287 [S.282]; 294 [S.289].
55 *AL R* 376.32 [S.371.32].
56 For the arguments for a later dating see Hays (2003).
57 Fulgentius, *Mito* 8.19; *Cont.* 86.4.
58 Hays (2002).
59 Shanzer (1986), pp. 12–13, demonstrates that Fulgentius had read Martianus. On the literary closed circle of the anthology poets, see Hays (2004), p. 127.
60 Raby (1957), p. 113.
61 For example, in AD 363, the town council of Timgad contained 10 *viri clarissimi*. *CIL* VIII.1, 2403; Suppl. 2, 17903.
62 *C.Th.* VI.21,1.
63 Ferrandus, *VF* 1.
64 Conant (2004b).
65 For a close study of Pompeius see Kaster (1988), pp. 137–68. The plagiarized work was an earlier commentary of the same work by Servius who was teaching in Rome in the 390s.
66 Pompeius 136.18–21.
67 Pompeius 235.16–24; 236.19–21; 142.35–143.8.
68 Rosenblum (1961), pp. 28–32, 97–101; Schubert (1875), p. 17.
69 Moussy and Camus (1985), pp. 68–75.
70 Moussy and Camus (1985), pp. 56–66.
71 Bright (1987), p. 217.
72 Bright (1987), p. 218.
73 On the medical writers of the period, see Langslow (2000).
74 Langslow (2000), pp. 56–60.
75 Langslow (2000), p. 57.
76 *AL R* 159 [S.148] (the teacher of students); 309 [S.304] (the impotent doctor); 302 [S.297] (the brothel-creeper).
77 *AL R* 148 [S.137] and 149 [S.138]; (Filager and his horse); 295 [S.290] (the effeminate lawyer); 340 [S.335] (the lawyer and his concubine).
78 Jones (1964), pp. 474–5; Matthews (1993); Lepelley (2002), pp. 62–5.

79 *Nov. Val.* XIII.9.
80 *Cod. Iust.* I.27.
81 See esp. Hen (2007), pp. 74–93.
82 On Dracontius see esp. Moussy (1988), Bright (1999), and Bustamente (1978).
83 Dracontius, *Rom.* V, and cf. *De Laud.* III.653–7. On this background, cf. Bustamente (1978), pp. 42–8, and Moussy (1985), pp. 9–11.
84 For a full account of the different theories regarding the recipient of Dracontius' *Carmen* see Moussy (1985), pp. 18–26, and Merrills (2004b).
85 For the argument for Huneric as Dracontius' first royal patron see Merrills (2004b).
86 On these purges, see above, pp. 75–6.
87 On the dating of these poems, cf. Bright (1999), pp. 199–205, and the discussion in Merrills (2004b).
88 Dracontius, *Satisf.* 93–98, tr. st. Margaret.
89 *AL R* 387 [S.382]. The poem is translated into French in Chalon et al. (1985), pp. 222–3.
90 On this poem see esp. Chalon et al. (1985), pp. 242–4, and Malaspina (1994–5). A similar object appears in Vitruvius, *De Arch.* V.12.5 and X.6.2–3.
91 *Carmen adversus Marcionem*, III.57. Malaspina (1994–5), pp. 49–52.
92 *AL R* 203 [S.194]. On this poem see Chalon et al. (1985), p. 243.
93 *AL R* 215 [S.206]; Chalon et al. (1985), pp. 244–7.
94 On this episode, see pp. 76 above, and Merrills (forthcoming b).
95 Procopius, *BV* III.8.8 and see above pp. 196–8.
96 *AL R* 376.2–7 [S.371.2–7], tr. Clover.
97 *AL R* 376.28–31 [S.371.28–31], tr. Clover.
98 *AL R* 376.19–20 [S.371.19–20], tr. Clover.
99 *AL R* 210–14 [S.201–5]. The best general discussion is provided by Chalon et al. (1985), pp. 226–41.
100 *AL R* 211.3 [S.202].
101 *AL R* 210.3–4 [S.201.3–4]; *AL R* 214.3–5 [S.205.3–5].
102 *AL R* 211.5–12 [S.202.5–12]; *AL R* 213.8–12 [S.204.8–12]; *AL R* 214.9 [S.205.9].
103 *AL R* 214. 3–8 [S.205.3–8].
104 *AL R* 214.9–10 [S.205.3–8].
105 *AL R* 214.11–12 [S.205.11–12].
106 Chalon et al. (1985), p. 230, and cf. Courtney (1980), pp. 39–41. The poems are also usefully discussed in Hen (2007), pp. 80–1.
107 Chalon et al. (1985), p. 230; Thebért (2003), p. 494.
108 Courtney (1980), pp. 39–41.
109 *AL R* 287.5–6 [S.282.5–6].
100 Moussy and Camus (1985), pp. 40–2.

101 Dracontius, *Satis.* 151–74; Clover (1989a), pp. 64–5.
102 Courtois (1955), pp. 299–301, discusses Gunthamund's religious policies. Clover (1993), pp. 68–9, on the contrast in tone between the *Satisfactio* and the *Anthologia Latina.*
113 Moussy and Camus (1985), pp. 26–9, on the probable dating of the *Satisfactio* and *De Laudibus Dei.*
114 Dracontius' bitter complaints about being deserted by his friends and family litter his poetry. See esp. Dracontius, *Rom.* 7, 118–136; *De Laud.* III. 602–606. On the circumstances of his release see *Rom.* 6, 37–40.
115 *AL R* 378 [S.373]; 379 [S.374]; 380 [S.375]; 93 [S.82].
116 *AL R* 387 [S.382] represents one exception, discussed at pp. 221–2 above. The only other allusion is the reference to altars in one of the bath poems of Felix, but this is scarcely unambiguous. *AL R* 213.5–6 [S.204.5–6].
117 Shanzer (1986), pp. 16–28.
118 Hays (2004), p. 131.
119 This argument is explored in more detail in Miles (2005).
120 Lepelley (1979–81); (2002), p. 272.
121 Lepelley (2002), pp. 272–8.
122 Lepelley (2002), pp. 277–8.
123 *AL R* 304 [S.299]; 345 [S.340].

NOTES TO CHAPTER 9

1 Corippus, *Laud. Iust*, 1.274–287, tr. Cameron.
2 Corripus, *Ioh.* III.13.44; *CIC* I, *Inst* 21; Procopius, *BV.* III.21.8.
3 On the origins of this dispute see above pp. 76. And Merrills (forthcoming b).
4 Procopius, *BV* III.9.10–19.
5 Procopius, *BV* III.9.19–23.
6 Procopius, *BV* III.9.5.
7 Honoré (1978), pp. 53–6.
8 Greatrex (1997); Evans (1996), pp. 119–25.
9 Procopius, *BV* III.14-7-17; III.24-10-15.
10 Procopius, *BV* IV.5.8, tr. Dewing.
11 Zacharias, *HE* IX.17, tr. Hamilton and Brooks.
12 *Cod. Iust.* 1.27.1.4.
13 Procopius, *BV* III.9.24–1.10.6.
14 Procopius, *BV* III.10.14–16, tr. Dewing.
15 Procopius, *BV* III.10-18-34. On Godas, see above, pp. 136–7.
16 Procopius, *BV* III.11.1–19.33.
17 Procopius, *BV* III.20.1–21.6. For a general historical account of the military campaigns see Pringle (1981), 1, pp. 16–22.
18 Procopius, *BV* III.25.1–2.3.28. On the possible location of Mons Pappua, see Desanges (1963).

19 Procopius, *BV* IV.4.26–31; 2.7.1–17.
20 *CIC* I, *Inst* 21; Cameron (2000), p. 559, n.40.
21 Procopius, *BV* IV.9.1–14; McCormick (1986), pp. 64–8, on Justinian's victory triumphs.
22 Procopius, *BV* IV.4.9.
23 Procopius, *Aed.* I.10.11. A commemorative medallion might also have been struck, cf. McCormick (1986), p. 65, n.105.
24 For Procopius' *Buildings* see the excellent collection of essays in *Antiquité Tardive* 8 (2000), pp. 7–180. Also Cameron (1985), pp. 84–112; Downey (1947), (1950); Irmscher (1977); Croke and Crow (1983).
25 Procopius, *Aed.* VI.5.8–11, tr. Dewing.
26 Cameron (1985), pp. 84–112.
27 Feissel (2000); Durliat (1981b).
28 Humphrey (1980), p. 88.
29 Hurst (1979), p. 43; (1994), p. 63. A new inner colonnade and two cisterns were also built.
30 The famous Antonine Baths were restored in this period. During the Vandal occupation a potter's workshop was installed in the Caldarium. After the Byzantine re-conquest the baths were put back into operation, with a partly new plan and repairs in the mosaic floor. Lézine (1956) and (1968).
31 Leone (2007), p. 174; Lézine (1968).
32 Ennabli (1997).
33 Leone (2007), pp. 185–6.
34 Leone (2007), pp. 276–9.
35 Leone (2007), pp. 220–3.
36 On this site, see now Stone et al. (forthcoming).
37 John Lydus, *De Mag.* 3.55, tr. Bandy.
38 Maas (1992), pp. 45–8.
39 *Nov. Just.* 30.11.2.
40 *Cod. Iust.* 1.27.1.1–2.
41 See, for example, Procopius, *BV* III.10–21.
42 *Vict. Tun.* a.534.
43 Cassiodorus, *Variae* II.3.
44 Procopius, *BV* IV.4.33–41. On this Boniface, see above, pp. 165.
45 Procopius, *BV* III.23.1–4.
46 Procopius, *BV* III.16.1–8.
47 Procopius, *BV* IV.1.7–8, tr. Dewing.
48 *Cod. Iust.* 1.27.15.
49 See for instance *Epistolae passim.*
50 *Cod. Iust.* 1.27.2.
51 *Cod. Iust.* 1.27. 1.1–3.
52 *Cod. Iust.* 1.27.1.13.
53 *Cod. Iust.* 1.27.1.12.
54 *Cod. Iust.* 1.27.2. 19–34.

55 *Cod. Iust.* 1.27.13–42; Administrators, accountants, clerks, couriers, sheriffs, lawyers, law court clerks, messengers, stenographers, bailiffs, jailors, heralds, record keepers, banner carriers, bureau of public works, physicians, orators and grammarians are all mentioned within the text. See Diehl (1896), pp. 97–137. On the appointment of external Greek-speaking outsiders to senior administrative positions see Cameron (1993b). It is striking that much of this evidence is from the seventh rather than sixth century.

56 *Nov. Just.* 36.

57 The basilicas Dermech I, Dermech II, Mcidfa, Bir Ftouha, Damous el-Karita Bir Messaouda, Carthagenna and Bir el Knissa.

58 The basilicas Dermech I, Mcidfa and possibly also Carthagenna were originally east–west orientated but with an apse in the west, and were rebuilt with the main apse in the east. The basilicas Damous el-Karita and Bir Messaouda were turned from a north–south alignment into an east–west one, reusing parts of the old structures. Others, such as the basilicas Dermech II, Dermech III and Bir Ftouha, have insufficient archaeological evidence to establish a clear ground plan. Cf. Ennabli (1997), pp. 152–4. For eastern apses in fifth-century eastern Mediterranean basilicas see Krautheimer and Ćurfić (1986), pp. 99–166.

59 Duval (1981).

60 Krautheimer and Ćurfić (1986), pp. 189–90; Duval (1972), pp. 1155–6. In Carthage see Ben Abed-Ben Khader et al. (1999), pp. 106–7 (Dermech I); Ennabli (1997), pp. 132–3 (Basilica Mcidfa).

61 Dolenz (2001).

62 Stevens et al. (2005), p. 573.

63 Stevens et al. (2005), p. 574.

64 Senay (1980), pp. 7–37; (1992), pp. 109–10.

65 Miles (forthcoming).

66 For a good overview of all of these developments see Krueger (2005), pp. 300–11.

67 Duval (1981) 2, 657ff. Cameron (1989), p. 177, is too quick to dismiss the possibility of a deliberate imperial policy at work here.

68 Procopius, *Aed.* 1.8.

69 *Nov. Just.* 67.

70 Ward-Perkins (1984), p. 53, n.5; pp. 81–3; pp. 243–4; Andreescu-Treadgold and Treadgold (1997). For a similar situation in Rome see Coates-Stephens (2006).

71 This is the case at Calama, Cululis (Theodoriana) and Timgad.

72 Duval (1971).

73 Pringle (1981); Durliat (1981b), pp. 96–100.

74 Duval (1971), pp. 99–323.

75 Bairam-Ben Osman and Ennabli (1982), pp. 8–18; (1997), p. 90; Duval (1997), pp. 328–34, is sceptical of Ennabli's thesis. The text reads *LOCUS*

SA | N(C)TORUM | SEPT(EM) FRAT(R)UM | MENACA | BEORUM or LOCUS SA | NTORUM | SEPTE(M) FRATRUM | IC ME(MORIA-AE) MACA | BEORUM.

76 Bairam-Ben Osman and Ennabli (1982), p. 11; (1997), p. 38, no. 26, pp. 91–3.
77 Procopius, *Anec.* XVIII. 11–12.
78 Procopius, *BV* IV.1.4; Kaegi (1965).
79 Saumagne (1913).
80 See for instance Ferrandus, *Ep. ad Eugippi.*
81 *Mansi* 8.841. For a discussion of the date of the council see Saumagne (1913), pp. 84–85; Champetier (1951), p. 104.
82 *Collect. Avell.* 85.1–2.
83 *Collect. Avell.* 85.3–6.
84 *Collect. Avell.* 87.5.
85 *Nov. Just.* 37.1.
86 *Nov. Just.* 37. 5–6.
87 *Nov. Just.* 37. 6–7.
88 Sotinel (2005) pp. 275–9.
89 *Collect. Avell.* 88.7.
90 *Nov. Just.* 36.
91 Ferrandus, *VF* 27.
92 Champetier (1951) pp. 108–11.
93 The full extent of the Three Chapters Controversy lies outside the scope of this book. For recent studies of the controversy from a variety of different perspectives see Chazelle and Cubitt (2007) and Sotinel (2000).
94 Modéran (2003a), pp. 565–606, provides an excellent account of the military clashes between the Byzantine authorities and various Moorish groups.
95 Procopius, *BV* IV.8.1–2.
96 *Nov. Just.* 37.5.
97 Procopius, *BV* IV.14.11–15, tr. Dewing.
98 On this dispute, see above pp. 107–8.
99 Procopius, *BV* IV.14.8–10.
100 Procopius, *BV* IV.15.1–8.
101 Procopius, *BV* IV.8.25.
102 Corippus, *Ioh.* 3.443–452, tr. Shea.
103 Procopius, *BV* IV.52, tr. Dewing.
104 Pringle (1981); Durliat (1981b), pp. 96–100.
105 Pringle (1981), I, pp. 270–2.
106 Pringle (1981), I, p. 99.
107 Leone (2007) pp. 187–98.

Pre-1800 Sources

Agnellus, *LP. Liber pontificalis Ravennatis.* O. Holder-Egger (ed.), MGH. Scriptores rerum Langobardicarum (Hannover, 1878).

Anonymous Valesianus, *Pars Posterior*, J. C. Rolfe (ed. and tr.), *Ammianus Marcellinus Vol. III*, LCL (Cambridge, MA, 1936), 530–69.

Augustine, *De Civitate Dei*, B. Dombart and A. Kalb (eds.), CCSL 47–8 (Turnhout, 1955); tr. H. Bettenson, *St Augustine. City of God* (Harmondsworth, 1972).

Augustine, *Epistulae*, A. Goldbacher (ed.), CSEL 34 (Vienna, 1895–1911); tr. Wilfrid Parsons, FC 12, 18, 20, 30, 32, 81 (Washington DC, 1951–89).

Augustine, *Sermones*, J. P. Migne (ed.), *PL* 38, 39 (Paris, 1841); tr. E. Hill, *The Works of Saint Augustine. A Translation for the 21st Century. Sermons.* 10 vols. (New Rochelle, NY, 1990–5).

Bir Trouch, *Ostraka*, P.-A. Fevrier (ed. and tr.), 'Ostraka de la région de Bir Trouch', *Bulletin d'archéologie algérienne*, 2 (1966–7), 239–49.

Brady, Nicholas, *The Rape* (London, 1694).

Capreolus, *Epistolae, PL* 54, cols. 843–858.

Carmen adversus Marcionem, R. Willems (ed.), *CCL* 2 (Turnhout, 1954), cols. 1417–1454; tr. S. Thelwall, *The Writings of Tertullianus*, Ante-Nicene Christian Library (Edinburgh, 1870), 318–83.

Cassiodorus, *Chronicon*, T. Mommsen (ed.), MGH, AA IX (Berlin, 1894).

Cassiodorus, *Variae*, T. Mommsen (ed.), MGH, AA XII (Berlin, 1894), partially tr. S. Barnish. *Cassiodorus: Variae* (Liverpool, 1992).

Cassius Dio, *Historia Romana*, E. Cary (ed. and tr.), LCL, 9 vols. (Cambridge, MA, 1967).

Cerealis Castellensis, *Contra Maximinun Arianum Libellus, PL* 58, cols. 757–768.

Cervantes, Miguel de *Don Quixote. El ingenioso hidalgo Don Quijote de la Mancha* (Madrid, 1604–15); tr. Edith Grossmann, *Don Quixote* (London, 2007).

Chron. Const., *Consularia Constantinopolitana*, R. W. Burgess (ed. and tr.), *The Chronicle of Hydatius and the Consularia Constantinopolitana* (Oxford, 1993).

Chronica Gallica a.452, R. Burgess (ed.), 'The Gallic Chronicle of 452: A New Critical Edition with a Brief Introduction', in Ralph W. Mathisen and Danuta Shanzer (eds.), *Society and Culture in Late Antique Gaul: Revisiting the Sources* (Aldershot, 2001), 52–84.

Chronica Gallica a.511, R. Burgess (ed.), 'The Gallic Chronicle of 511: A New Critical Edition with a Brief Introduction', in Ralph W. Mathisen and Danuta Shanzer (eds.), *Society and Culture in Late Antique Gaul: Revisiting the Sources* (Aldershot, 2001), 85–100.

Claudian, *Opera*, Maurice Platnauer (ed. and tr.), LCL, 2 vols. (Cambridge, MA, 1922).

Collectio Avellana, O. Guenther (ed.), CSEL 35 (Prague, Vienna, and Leipzig, 1895).

Concilia Africae, C. Munier (ed.), CCSL 149 (Turnhout, 1974).

Constantius, *Vita Germani*, R. Borius (ed. and tr.), SC 112 (Paris, 1965); tr. F. H. Hoare, *The Western Fathers* (London, 1954).

Contra Varimadum, B. Schwank (ed.), CCSL 90 (Turnhout, 1961), cols. 1–134.

Corippus, *Iohannidos*, J. Diggle and F. D. R. Goodyear (eds.), *Flavii Cresconii Corippi Iohannidos seu de Bellis Libycis Libri VIII* (Cambridge, 1970); tr. G. W. Shea, *The Iohannis or De bellis Libycis of Flavius Cresconius Corippus* (Lewiston, 1998).

Cowper, William, 'On the Burning of Lord Mansfield's Library', in *The Poetical Works Of William Cowper, Volume 1* (Boston, 1859).

Desaguliers, J. T., *A Course on Experimental Philosophy* (London, 1745).

Dexippus, Fragments, Karl Müller (ed.), *FHG* III (Paris, 1849).

Dracontius, *De Laudibus Dei*, Claude Moussy and Colette Camus (ed. and tr.), Budé (Paris, 1985–8).

Dracontius, *Romulea*, J. Bouquet and E. Wolff (ed. and tr.), Budé (Paris, 1995–6).

Dracontius, *Satisfactio*, Claude Moussy (ed. and tr.), Budé (Paris, 1988); tr. (into English) M. St Margaret, *Dracontii Satisfactio. With Introduction, Text, Translation and Commentary* (Philadelphia, 1936).

Dubos, *Histoire Critique*, Jean-Baptiste Dubos, *Histoire Critique de l'établissement de la monarchie française dans les Gaules* (Paris, 1734).

D'Urfé, Honoré, *L'Astrée*, Hugues Vaganay (ed.), 5 vols. (Paris, 1925–8).

Ennodius, *Panegyricus*, ed. and tr. (into Italian), Simona Rota, *Magno Felice Ennodio, Panegirico del dementissimo re Teoderico* (Rome, 2002).

Ennodius, *Vita Epiphanius*, ed. Friedrich Vogel, MGH, AA, VII (Berlin, 1885).

Epigramma Paulini, C. Schenkl (ed.), CSEL 16 (Vienna, 1888); tr. Jack Lindsay, *Song of a Falling World* (London, 1948).

Eusebius, *HE. Historia Ecclesiastica*, T. Mommsen and E. Schwartz (eds.), *Eusebius Werke. Die Kirchengeschichte*, GCS (Leipzig, 1903–8); tr. J. E. L. Oulton and H. J. Lawlor (Oxford, 1926).

Eutropius, *Breviarum ab urbe condita*, Franz Rühl (ed.) (Stuttgart, 1887); tr. H. W. Bird, *Eutropius: Breviarum* (Liverpool, 1993).

Evagrius, *Historia Ecclesiastica*, Joseph Bidez (ed.) (Amsterdam, 1964); tr. Michael Whitby, *The Ecclesiastical History of Evagrius Scholasticus* (Liverpool, 2000).

Expositio Totius Mundi, Jean Rougé (ed. and tr.), SCNC 124 (Paris, 1966).

Facundus, *Contra Mocianum*, J.-M. Clément and R. Vander Plaetse (eds.); tr. A. Solignac, SC (2006).

Ferrandus, *Epistola dogmatica adversus Arrianos alioque haereticos ad Eugippium*, Adalbert Hamman, *PL* Supplementa, 4 (Paris, 1967).

Ferrandus, *Epistolae*, A. Hamman (ed.), *PL* Supplementa, 4 (Paris, 1967), cols. 36–9; J. P. Migne (ed.), *PL* 67 (Paris, 1848), 887–950; tr. R. B. Eno, FC 95 (Washington, DC, 1997).

Ferrandus, *VF. Vita S. Fulgentii episcopi Ruspensis*, G.-G. Lapeyre (ed.), *Vie de Saint Fulgence de Ruspe* (Paris, 1929); tr. R. B. Eno, FC 95 (Washington, DC, 1997).

Fredegar, *Chronicon*, ed. B. Krusch, MGH, SRM, II (Berlin, 1888).

Fulgentius, *Continentia, De aetatibus, Mitologiae Sermones*, R. Helm (ed.), *Fabii Planciadis Fulgentii V.C. Opera* (Leipzig, 1898); tr. L. G. Whitbread, *Fulgentius the Mythographer* (Cincinnati, 1971).

Fulgentius of Ruspe, *Abecedarium, Ad Monimum, Contra sermonem Fastidiosi Ariani, De incarnatione et gratia*, J. Fraipont (ed.), CCSL 91 and 91A (Turnhout, 1974); partially tr. R. B. Eno, *Fulgentius. Selected Works*, FC 95 (Washington, DC, 1997).

Gelasius, *Epistulae, PL* 59, cols. 13–140.

Gibbon, Edward, *History of the Decline and Fall of the Roman Empire* (London, 1776–1789), ed. David Wormesley, 3 vols. (London, 1994).

Greg. Tur., *Decem Libri Historiarum*, B. Krusch and W. Levison (eds.), MGH, SRM I.2 (Berlin, 1885); tr. O. M. Dalton, *The History of the Franks by Gregory of Tours* (Oxford, 1927).

Grégoire, *Mémoires de L'Abbé Grégoire*, Jean-Michel Leniaud (ed.) (Paris, 1834, repr. Paris, 1989).

Historia Augusta, André Chastagnol (ed. and tr.), *Histoire Auguste* (Paris, 1994).

Hydatius, *Chronicle*, T. Mommsen (ed.), MGH, AA, XI (Berlin, 1894); ed. and tr. R. W. Burgess, *The Chronicle of Hydatius and the Consularia Constantinopolitana* (Oxford, 1993).

Isidore, *Etymologiarum Sive Originum Libri XX*, W. M. Lindsay (ed.), OCT (Oxford, 1911); tr. Stephen A. Barney, W. J. Lewis, J. A. Beach and Oliver Berghof, *The Etymologies of Isidore of Seville* (Cambridge, 2006).

Isidore, *Historia Gothorum, Wandalorum, Sueborum*, Cristóbal Rodríguez Alonso (ed. and tr.), *Las Historias de los Godos, Vandalos y Suevos de Isidoro de Sevilla* (Leon, 1975); partially tr. (into English), Guido Donini and Gordon B. Ford, *Isidore of Seville's History of the Goths, Vandals and Sueves* (Leiden, 1970).

Jerome, *Epistulae*, I. Hilberg (ed.), CSEL 54 (Vienna, 1910); partially tr. C. C. Mierow, *The Letters of Saint Jerome*, Ancient Christian Writers, 33 (Westminster, MD, 1963).

John of Antioch, Fragments, Karl Müller (ed.), *FHG* IV (Paris, 1851).

John of Biclarum, *Chronicon*, T. Mommsen (ed.), MGH, AA, XI (Berlin, 1894); tr. K. B. Wolf, *Conquerors and Chroniclers of Early Medieval Spain*, Translated Texts for Historians, 9 (Liverpool, 1991).

John Lydus, *De Magistratibus*, A. C. Bandy (ed. and tr.), *Ioannes Lydus On Powers* (Philadelphia, 1982).

Jordanes, *Getica, De Origine Actibusque Getarum*, T. Mommsen (ed.), MGH, AA, V.1 (Berlin, 1882); tr. (into French) O. Devillers, *Jordanès: Histoire Des Goths* (Paris, 1995); tr. (into English) C. C. Mierow, *The Gothic History of Jordanes* (Princeton, NJ, 1915).

Jordanes, *Romana. De summa temporum vel origine actibusque gentis Romanorum*, T. Mommsen (ed.), MGH, AA, V.1 (Berlin, 1882).

Leo I, *Epistula*, *PL* 54.

Liber de trinitate, J. Fraipont (ed.), CCSL 90 (Turnhout, 1961), cols. 239–260.

LRV, Laterculus Regum Vandalorum, Roland Steinacher (ed.), 'The so-called Laterculus Regum Vandalorum et Alanorum: A Sixth-Century Addition to Prosper Tiro's Chronicle?', in A. H. Merrills (ed.), *Vandals, Romans and Berbers: New Perspectives on Late Antique North Africa* (Aldershot, 2004), 163–80.

Mai, A. (ed.), *Scriptorum veterum nova collection*, III.2 (Rome, 1828).

Malalas, *Chronicon*, Ludwig Dindorf (ed.), Corpus Scriptorum Historiae Byzantinae. (Bonn, 1831); tr. Elizabeth Jeffreys, Michael Jeffreys and Roger Scott, *The Chronicle of John Malalas*, Australian Association for Byzantine Studies, Byzantina Australiensia, 4 (Melbourne, 1986).

Malchus, Fragments, R. C. Blockley (ed. and tr.), *The Fragmentary Classicizing Historians of the Later Roman Empire,* Vol. II (Liverpool, 1983).

Mannert, Konrad, *Geschichte der Vandalen* (Leipzig, 1785).

Mansi, G., *Sacrorum Conciliorum nova et amplissima collection*, 31 vols. (Florence and Venice, 1758–98).

Marcellinus Comes, *Chronicon*, T. Mommsen (ed.), MGH, AA, XI (Berlin, 1894); tr. B. Croke, *The Chronicle of Marcellinus* (Sydney, 1995).

Marius of Avenches, *Chronicon*, Theodor Mommsen (ed.), MGH, AA, XI (Berlin, 1894).

Martianus Capella, *De Nuptiis Philologiae et Mercurii*, J. Willis (ed.), Teubner (Leipzig, 1983); tr. W. H. Stahl, R. Johnson and E. L. Burge, *Martianus Capella and the Seven Liberal Arts.* Vol. II. *The Marriage of Philology and Mercury* (New York, 1977).

Merobaudes, *Carmina* and *Panegyrici*, Frank M. Clover (ed. and tr.), *Flavius Merobaudes. A Translation and Historical Commentary,* Transactions of the American Philosophical Society; n.s. 61 (Philadelphia, 1971).

Meyer, F. J. L. *Fragments sur Paris*, 2 vols. (Hamburg, 1798).

Montesquieu, *Considérations sur les causes de la grandeur des Romains et de leur décadence* (Amsterdam, 1734); tr. David Lowenthal, *Montesquieu, Considerations on the Causes of the Greatness of the Romans and their Decline* (New York, 1965).

Montesquieu, *De l'esprit des lois* (Geneva, 1748); ed. and tr. Anne M. Cohler, Basia Carolyn Miller and Harold Samuel Stone, Montesquieu, *The Spirit of the Laws,* Cambridge Texts in the History of Political Thought (Cambridge, 1989).
Notitia Dignitatum, Otto Seeck (ed.) (Paris, 1876).
Nugent, Thomas, *The History of Vandalia* (London, 1761).
Olaus Magnus, *Historia. Historia de gentibus Septentrionalibus* (Rome, 1555); tr. Peter Fisher and Humphrey Higgens, *Olaus Magnus. Description of the Northern Peoples* (London, 1996–8).
Olympiodorus, Fragments, R. C. Blockley (ed. and tr.), *The Fragmentary Classicizing Historians of the Later Roman Empire, Vol. II* (Liverpool, 1983).
Origo, *Origo Gentis Langobardorum*, ed. Georg Waitz, MGH, SRL (Hannover, 1878).
Orosius, *Historiarum Adversus Paganos Libri Septem*, M.-P. Arnaud-Lindet (ed. and tr.), Budé (Paris, 1990); tr. (into English) R. Deferrari, FC 50 (Washington, DC, 1964).
Palladius, *Opus Agriculturae*, Enrico Di Lorenzo, Bruno Pellegrino and Saverio Lanzaro (ed. and tr.), *Opus Agriculturae* (Salerno, 2006).
Parthemius, *Resc ad. Sig. Rescriptum ad Sigisteum*, K. Buechner (ed.), *Fragmenta Poetarum Latinorum epicorum et lyricorum praeter Ennium et Lucilium* (Leipzig, 1982), p. 201, and A. Hamman (ed.), *PL* Supplementa, 3 (Paris, 1963), cols. 447–8.
Paul, *Historia Langobardorum*, Ludwig Berthemann and Georg Waitz (eds.), MGH, SRL (Hannover, 1878); tr. William Dudley Foulke, *Paul the Deacon: History of the Lombards* (Philadelphia, 1907).
Paulinus Pellaeus, *Eucharisticon*, Hugh G. Evelyn White (ed. and tr.), *Ausonius II*, LCL (Cambridge, MA, 1949).
Peter the Patrician, *Fragments*, Karl Müller (ed.), *FHG* IV (Paris, 1928).
Pliny, *HN. Historia Naturalis*, H. Rackham, W. H. S. Jones and D. E. Eichholz (ed. and tr.), LCL, 10 vols. (Cambridge, MA, 1989).
Pompeius Grammaticus, H. Keil (ed.), *Grammatici latini*, t. 5 (Leipzig, 1868), 95–312.
Pope, Alexander, *An Essay On Criticism* (London, 1711).
Possidius, *VA. Vita Augustini*, M. Pellegrino (ed.), *Vita di S. Agostino*, Nerba semiorum, 4 (Alba, 1955); tr. A. Fellowes, *The Life of Saint Augustine by Possidius Bishop of Calama* (Villakova, PA, 1988).
Priscus, Fragments, R. C. Blockley (ed. and tr.), *The Fragmentary Classicizing Historians of the Later Roman Empire, Vol. II* (Liverpool, 1983).
Procopius, *De aedificiis*, H. B. Dewing (ed. and tr.), LCL (Cambridge, MA, 1914).
Procopius, *Anecdota*, H. B. Dewing (ed. and tr.), LCL (Cambridge, MA, 1914).
Procopius, *De bello Gothico*, H. B. Dewing (ed. and tr.), LCL (Cambridge, MA, 1914).
Prosp. Add. Haun., *Chronicon*, Theodor Mommsen (ed.), MGH, AA, IX (Berlin, 1894); tr. Steven Muhlberger, 'The Copenhagen Continuation of Prosper', *Florilegium* 6 (1984), 71–95.

Prosper, *Chron.*, *Prosperi Tironis epitoma chronicon*, T. Mommsen (ed.), MGH, AA, IX (Berlin, 1892); partially tr. A. C. Murray, *From Roman to Merovingian Gaul: A Reader* (Peterborough, 2000).

Pseudo-Fulgentius, *Sermones*, *PL* 65, cols. 855–954.

Pseudo-Origen, *Commentarium in Iob, PL* 17, cols. 371–522.

Quodvultdeus, *De tempore barbarico*, ed. R. Brown, CCSL 60 (Turnhout, 1976); tr. Richard George Kalkmann, 'Two sermons: "De Tempore Barbarico" attributed to St. Quodvultdeus, bishop of Carthage. A Study of the Text and attribution with Translation.' Unpublished Ph.D. thesis, Catholic University of America, 1963.

Quodvultdeus, *Liber promissionum et praedictorum dei*, R. Braun (ed. and tr.), SC 101 and 102 (Paris 1964).

Quodvultdeus, *Opera*, R. Braun (ed.), CCSL 60 (Turnhout, 1976).

Rufinus, *Historia Ecclesiastica*, T. Mommsen and E. Schwartz (eds.), *Eusebius Werke. Die Kirchengeschichte*, GCS (Leipzig, 1903–8); M. Simonetti (ed.), CCSL 20 (Turnhout, 1961); partially tr. P. R. Amidon, *The Church History of Rufinus of Aquileia. Books 10 and 11* (New York, 1997).

Salvian, *De gubernatione Dei*, C. Halm (ed.), MGH, AA, I (Berlin, 1877); tr. J. F. O'Sullivan, FC 3 (New York, 1947).

Sidonius, *Carmina, Epistulae*, W. B. Anderson (ed. and tr.), LCL, 2 vols. (Cambridge, MA, 1968).

Sigisteus, *Epistola ad Parthemium*, A. Hamman (ed.), *PL* Supplementa, 3 (Paris, 1963), cols. 447–8.

Socrates Scholasticus, *Historia Ecclesiastica*, *PG* 67.

Sozomen, *Historia Ecclesiastica*, ed. and tr. (into French), J. Bidez, André-Jean Festugière and Guy Sabbah, *Sozomene: Histoire Ecclesiastique* (Paris, 1983); tr. (into English), Chester D. Hartranft, NPNF II (Oxford, 1891).

Tacitus, *Germania*, M. Hutton and E. H. Warmington (ed. and tr.), LCL (Cambridge, MA, 1970).

Testimonia de patre et filio et spiritu sancto, D. De Bruyne (ed.), CCSL 90 (Turnhout 1961), 227–33.

Theodore Lector, *Historia Ecclesiastica*, Guenther Christian Hanson (ed.), *Theodoros Anagnostes Kirchengeschichte*, Die griechische christliche Schriftsteller der ersten Jahrhunderte (Berlin, 1971).

Theophanes, *Chronicle,* Cyril Mango and Roger Scott (ed. and tr.), *The Chronicle of Theophanes Confessor: Byzantine and Near Eastern history, AD 284–813* (Oxford, 1997).

Vict. Tun., *Victorius Tunnunensis Chronicon cum reliquiis ex Consularibus Caesaraugustanis*, C. Cardelle de Hartman (ed.), CCSL 173A (Turnhout, 2001); ed. and tr. A. Placanica, *Vittore da Tunnuna. Chronica. Chiesa e Impero nell'età di Giustiniano* (Florence, 1997).

Vita Sancti Danielis Stylitae, Hippolyte Delehaye (ed.), Subsidia Hagiographica, 14 (Brussels, 1923).

Vitruvius, *De Arch. De Architectura*, Frank Granger (ed. and tr.), LCL, 2 vols. (Cambridge, MA, 1962); tr. Rowland Howe, *Vitruvius. Ten Books on Architecture* (Cambridge, 1999).

Zacharias, *HE. Historia Ecclesiastica*, E. W. Brooks (ed.), *Historia Ecclesiastica Zachariae Rhetori vulgo adscripta* (Louvain, 1924); F. J. Hamilton and E. W. Brooks (tr.), *The Syriac Chronicle: Known As That Of Zachariah Of Mitylene* (London, 1899).

Zonaras, *Epitome historiarum*, M. Pinder and T. Büttner-Wobst (eds.), 3 vols. (Bonn, 1841–97); Thomas Banchinch and Eugene Lane (tr.), *The History of Zonaras. From Alexander Severus to the Death of Theodosius the Great* (London, 2009).

Zosimus, *Historia Nova*, F. Paschoud (ed. and tr.), Budé (Paris, 1971–89); tr. R. T. Ridley, *Zosimus. New History* (Sydney, 1982).

Works Post 1800

Abernethy, Thomas Perkins. 1959. *Western Lands and The American Revolution* (New York).

Albertini, E. 1955. *L'Afrique Romaine* (Algiers).

Alchermes, J. 2005. 'Art and Architecture in the Age of Justinian', in M. Maas (ed.), *The Cambridge Companion to the Age of Justinian* (Cambridge), 343–75.

Alemany, Agustí. 2000. *Sources on the Alans. A Critical Companion.* Handbook of Oriental Studies. Section 8. Central Asia. 5 (Leiden).

Altschul, Nadia. 2008. 'Postcolonialism and the Study of the Middle Ages', *History Compass*, 6, 588–606.

Amory, Patrick. 1997. *People and Identity in Ostrogothic Italy, 489–554* (Cambridge).

Andreescu-Treadgold, I. and W. Treadgold. 1997. 'Procopius and the Imperial Panels of S. Vitale', *The Art Bulletin*, 79, 708–23.

Arce, Javier. 2008. 'Los vándalos en Hispania (409–429 AD): Impacto, actividades, identidad', in Guido M. Berndt and Roland Steinacher (eds.), *Das Reich der Vandalen und seine (Vor-) Geschichten*, Österreichische Akademie der Wissenschaften. Forschungen zur Geschichte des Mittelalters, 13 (Vienna), 97–104.

Arce, Javier. 2005. 'Spain and the African Provinces in Late Antiquity', in Kim Bowes and Michael Kulikowski (eds.), *Hispania in Late Antiquity. Current Perspectives* (Leiden), 341–68.

Arce, Javier. 2002. 'Los Vandalos en Hispania (409–429 AD)', *Antiquité Tardive*, 10 (2002), 75–85.

Arthur, Paul. 2002. *Naples. From Roman Town to City-State: An Archaeological Perspective.* Archaeological Monographs of the British School at Rome, 12 (London).

Ayres, L. 2004. *Nicaea and its Legacy: An Approach to Fourth-Century Trinitarian Theology* (Oxford).

Bachrach, Bernard S. 1967. 'The Alans in Gaul', *Traditio*, 23, 476–89.

Bairam-Ben Osman, W. and L. Ennabli. 1982. 'Note sur la topographie chrétienne de Carthage: Les mosaïques du monastère de Bigua', *Revue des études augustiniennes*, 28, 3–18.

Balmelle, C., A. Ben Abed-Ben Khader, A. Bourgeois, C. Brenot, H. Broise, J.-P. Darmon, M. Ennaïfer and M.-P. Reynaud. 2003. 'Vitalité de l'architecture domestique à Carthage au Ve siècle: l'exemple de la maison dite le Rotonde, sur la colline de l'Odeon', *Antiquité Tardive*, 11, 151–66.

Balmelle, C., A. Ben Abed-Ben Khader, S. Ben Mansour, W. Ben Osman, J.-P. Darmon, M. Ennaïfer, S. Gozlan, R. Hanoune, N. Jeddi and M.-P. Raynaud. 1990. 'Recherches franco-tunisiennes dans la maison du cryptoportique', *CEDAC*, 11, 11–18.

Banaji, Jairus. 2002. *Agrarian Change in Late Antiquity. Gold, Labour, and Aristocratic Dominance* (Oxford).

Barnes, T. D. 1993. *Athanasius and Constantius: Theology and Politics in the Constantinian Empire* (Cambridge, MA).

Barnes, T. D. 1984. 'The Composition of Cassius Dio's Roman History', *Phoenix*, 38, 240–55.

Barnish, Sam, A. D. Lee and Michael Whitby. 2000. 'Government and Administration', in A. Cameron, B. Ward-Perkins and M. Whitby (eds.), *The Cambridge Ancient History, XIV. Late Antiquity: Empire and Successors, AD 425–600* (Cambridge), 164–206.

Barnwell, P. S. 1992. *Emperors, Prefects and Kings. The Roman West, 395–565* (London).

Barraud, D., M. Bonifay, F. Dridi and J. F. Pichonneau. 1998. 'L'industrie céramique de l'Antiquité tardive', in H. Ben Hassen and L. Maurin (eds.), *Oudhna (Uthina). La rédecouvert d'une ville antique de Tunisie* (Bordeaux, Paris and Tunis), 139–67.

Barth, F. 1969. 'Introduction', in F. Barth (ed.), *Ethnic Groups and Boundaries: The Social Organization of Culture Difference* (Boston), 1–38.

Bayless, William N. 1979. 'The Chronology of Priscus Fragment 6', *Classical Philology*, 74.2, 154–5.

Beck, Thor. J. 1934. *Northern Antiquities in French Learning and Literature (1755–1855). A Study in Preromantic Ideas. Volume I. The Vagina Gentium and the Liberty Legend* (New York).

Béjaoui, Faithi. 2008. 'Les Vandales en Afrique: Témoinages archéologiques. Les récentes découverts en Tunisie', in Guido M. Berndt and Roland Steinacher (eds.), *Das Reich der Vandalen und seine (Vor-) Geschichten*, Österreichische Akademie der Wissenschaften. Forschungen zur Geschichte des Mittelalters, 13 (Vienna, 2008), 197–212.

Béjaoui, Faithi. 2003. 'Recherche archéologique à Thelepte et ses environs. Note sur les récentes découvertes', in *Histoire des Hautes Steppes. Antiquité et Moyen Age. Actes du Colloque à Sbeïtla 2001* (Tunis), 147–61.

Béjaoui, Fathi. 1995. 'Une église d'époque vandale à Henchir el Gousset (région de Thelepte-Tunisie)', *AFRICA*, XIII, 101–22.

Bejor, Giorgio. 1986. 'Gli insediamenti della Sicilia romana: distribuzione, tipologie e sviluppo da un primo inventario dei dati archeologici', in A. Giardina (ed.), *Società romana e impero tardantico*, III (Bari), 463–519.

Ben Abdallah, Z. and H. Ben Hassen. 1991. 'Rapport preliminaire sur la fouille du port marchand de Carthage', *CEDAC*, 12, 6.

Ben Abed, Aïcha and Noel Duval. 2000. 'Carthage, la capitale du royaume et les villes de Tunisie à l'époque vandale', in Gisela Ripoll and Josep M. Gurt (eds.), *Sedes regiae (ann. 400–800)*, (Barcelona), 163–218.

Ben Abed-Ben Khader, A., M. A. Alexander, R. L. Alexander, W. Bairem-Ben Osman, N. Duval, A. Gonosova, C. Condoleon and G. Métraux. 1999. *Corpus des mosaïques de Tunisie, IV.1. Karthago (Carthage): les mosaïques du parc archéologique des thermes d'Antonin* (Tunis).

Bénabou, M. 1981. 'L'Afrique et la culture romaine: le problème des survivances', *Cahiers de Tunisie*, 29, 9–21.

Bénabou, M. 1980. 'L'imperialisme et l'Afrique du Nord, le modèle romain', in D. Nordman and J-P. Raison (eds.), *Sciences de l'homme et conquête coloniale consitution et usage des sciences humaines en Afrique XIXe–XXe siècles* (Paris), 15–22.

Bénabou, M. 1976. *La résistance africaine à la romanisation* (Paris).

Bernadini, Sandra, Cambi, Franco, Molinari, Alessandra and Neri, Ilaria. 2000. 'Il Territorio di Segesta fra l'età arcaica e il medioevo. Nuovi dati dalla carta archeologica di Calatafimi', in *Terze Giornate Internazionali di Studi sull'area Elima. Atti I* (Pisa), 91–133.

Berndt, Guido M. 2007. *Konflikt und Anpassung. Studien zu Migration und Ethnogenese der Vandalen*. Historische Studien, 489 (Husum).

Berndt, Guido M. 2008. 'Gallia-Hispania-Africa: Zu den Migrationen der Vandalen auf ihrem Weg nach Nordafrika', in Guido M. Berndt and Roland Steinacher (eds.), *Das Reich der Vandalen und seine (Vor-) Geschichten*, Österreichische Akademie der Wissenschaften. Forschungen zur Geschichte des Mittelalters, 13 (Vienna), 131–47.

Berndt, Guido M. and Roland Steinacher. 2008. 'Minting in Vandal North Africa: Coins of the Vandal Period in the Coin Cabinet of Vienna's Kunsthistorisches Museum', *Early Medieval Europe*, 16, 252–98.

Bigelow, Poultney. *Genseric: The First Prussian Kaiser* (New York, 1917)

Birley, Anthony. 2005. *The Roman Government of Britain* (Oxford).

Birley, Anthony. 1987. *Marcus Aurelius. A Biography*, rev. edn. (London).

Blackburn, Mark. 2005. 'Money and Coinage', in Paul Fouracre (ed.), *The New Cambridge Medieval History, I* (Cambridge), 660–74.

Blackhurst, Andy. 2004. 'The House of Nubel: Rebels or Players?', in A. H. Merrills (ed.), *Vandals, Romans and Berbers: New Perspectives on Late Antique North Africa* (London), 59–76.

Blockley, R. C. 1992. *East Roman Foreign Policy. Formation and Conduct from Diocletian to Anastasius*. ARCA, 30 (Leeds).

Blockley, R. C. 1981. *The Fragmentary Classicising Historians of the Later Roman Empire. Eunapius, Olympiodorus, Priscus and Malchus*. Vol I. ARCA, 6 (Liverpool).

Blunck, Hans F. 1937. *König Geiserich. Eine Erzählung von Geiserich und dem Zug der Wandalen* (Hamburg).

Bonifay, Michel. 2004. *Etudes sur la céramique romaine tardive d'Afrique*. BAR Int. Ser. 1301 (Oxford).

Bonifay, Michel. 2003. 'La céramique africaine, un indice du développement économique?', *Antiquité Tardive*, 11, 113–28.

Bonnal, J.-P. and P.-A. Février. 1966–7. 'Ostraka de la région de Bir Trouch', *Bulletin d'archéologie algérienne*, 2, 239–49.

Bonner, G. 1997. *Saint Augustine of Hippo: Life and Controversies* (Norwich).

Borchardt, Frank L. 1971. *German Antiquity in Renaissance Myth* (Baltimore).

Bourgeois, Ariane. 2002. 'La ceramique Africaine aux époques Vandale et Byzantine', *Antiquité Tardive*, 10, 177–95.

Bourgeois, C. 1980. 'Les Vandales, le vandalisme et l'Afrique', *Ant. af.*, 16, 213–28.

Brather, Sebastian. 2008. 'Kleidung Grab und Identität in Spätantike und Frühmittelalter', in Guido M. Berndt and Roland Steinacher (eds.), *Das Reich der Vandalen und seine (Vor-) Geschichten*, Österreichische Akademie der Wissenschaften. Forschungen zur Geschichte des Mittelalters, 13 (Vienna), 283–94.

Brather, Sebastian. 2004. *Ethnische Interpretationen in der frühgeschichtlichen Archäologie. Geschichte Grundlagen und Alternativen* (Berlin and New York).

Brett, M. and E. Fentress. 1996. *The Berbers* (Oxford).

Bright, D. F. 1999. 'The Chronology of the Poems of Dracontius', *Classica et Medievalia*, 50, 193–206.

Bright, D. F. 1987. *The Miniature Epic in Vandal Africa* (Norman, OK and London).

Brown, Peter. 1995. *Authority and the Sacred in Late Antiquity* (Cambridge).

Brown, Peter. 1992. *Power and Persuasion in Late Antiquity, Towards a Christian Empire* (Madison, WI).

Brown, Peter. 1967. *Augustine of Hippo: A Biography* (London).

Brun, Jean-Pierre. 2004. *Archéologie du vin et de l'huile dans l'Empire romain*, Collection des Hespérides (Paris).

Brun, Jean-Pierre. 2003. *Le vin et l'huile dans la Méditerranée antique: viticulture, oléiculture et procédés de transformation*, Collection des Hespérides (Paris).

Bührer-Thierry, Geneviève. 1998. ' "Just Anger" or "Vengeful Anger"? The Punishment of Blinding in the Early Medieval West', in Barbara H. Rosenwein (ed.), *Anger's Past. The Social Uses of an Emotion in the Middle Ages* (Ithaca), 75–91.

Burns, Thomas. S. 2003. *Rome and the Barbarians, 100 BC–AD 400* (Baltimore, MD).

Burns, Thomas. S. 1994. *Barbarians within the Gates of Rome: A Study of Roman Military Policy and the Barbarians, ca. 375–425 AD* (Bloomington, IN).

Bury, John B. 1923. *History of the Later Roman Empire, from the Death of Theodosius I to the Death of Justinian (AD 395 to AD 565)* (London), 2 vols.

Bustamente, J. M. Diaz de. 1978. *Draconcio y sus carmina profana* (Santiago de Compostela).

Cain, Andrew. 2005. 'Miracles, Martyrs and Arians: Gregory of Tours' Sources for his Account of the Vandal Kingdom', *Vigiliae Christianae*, 59, 412–37.

Cameron, Averil. 2000. 'Vandal and Byzantine Africa', in A. Cameron, B. Ward-Perkins and M. Whitby (eds.), *The Cambridge Ancient History, XIV. Late Antiquity: Empire and Successors,* AD *425–600* (Cambridge), 552–69.

Cameron, Averil. 1993a. *The Mediterranean World in Late Antiquity, 395–600* (London).

Cameron, Averil. 1993b. 'The Byzantine Reconquest of North Africa and the Impact of Greek Culture', *Graeco-Arabica*, 5 (1993), 153–65; repr. in A. Cameron, *Changing Cultures in Early Byzantium* (Aldershot, 1996).

Cameron, Averil. 1989. 'Gelimer's Laughter: The Case of Byzantine Africa', in F. M. Clover and R. S. Humphreys (eds.), *Tradition and Innovation in Late Antiquity* (Madison, WI, 1989), 171–90; repr. in A. Cameron, *Changing Cultures in Early Byzantium* (Aldershot, 1996).

Cameron, Averil. 1985. *Procopius and the Sixth Century* (London).

Camps, G. 1984. 'Rex gentium, Maurorum et Romanorum. Recherches sur les royaumes de Maurétanie des VIe et VIIe siècles', *Ant. af.*, 20 (1984), 183–218.

Carandini, A. 1970. 'Produzione Agricola e produzione ceramica nell'Africa di età imperial. Appunti sull'economia della Zeugitana e della Byzacena', *Studi Miscellanei*, 15, 97–119.

Carandini, A. 1986. 'Il mondo della tarda antichità visto attraverso le merci', in A. Giardina (ed.), *Società romana e impero tardantico*, III (Bari), 3–19.

Carr, Karen Eva. 2002. *Vandals to Visigoths. Rural Settlement Patterns in Early Medieval Spain* (Ann Arbor, MI).

Caserta, A. 1986. 'Cereale di Castello (Sec. V) in difesa del dogma trinitario', in G. Lorizio and V. Scippa (eds.), *Ecclesiae sacramentum: studi in onore di P.Alfredo Marranzini S.J.* (Naples), 91–109.

Castellana, Giuseppe and Brian E. McConnell, 1990. 'A Rural Settlement of Imperial Roman and Byzantine Date in Contrada Saraceno near Agrigento, Sicily', *AJA*, 94, 25–44.

Chalon, M., G. Devallet, P. Force, M. Griffe, J.-M. Lassère and J.-N. Michaud. 1985. '*Memorabile factum*: Une célébration de l'évergétisme des rois Vandales dans l'Anthologie Latine', *Ant. af.*, 21, 207–62.

Champetier. P. 1951. 'Les Conciles africains durant la période byzantine', *Revue africaine*, 95, 103–19.

Chastagnol, André. 1994. *Histoire Auguste* (Paris).

Chastagnol, A. and N. Duval. 1974. 'Les survivances du culte impérial dans l'Afrique du Nord à l'époque vandale', *Mélanges d'histoire ancienne offerts à William Seston* (Paris), 87–118.

Chazelle, C. and C. Cubitt (eds.). 2007. *The Crisis of the Oikoumene: The Three Chapters and the Failed Quest for Unity in the Sixth-Century Mediterranean* (Turnhout).

Cherry, D. 1998. *Frontier and Society in Roman North Africa* (Oxford).

Christie, Neil. 2003. *From Constantine to Charlemagne. An Archaeology of Italy AD 300–800* (London).

Christie, Neil and Simon Loseby (eds.). 1996. *Towns in Transition: Urban Evolution in Late Antiquity and the Early Middle Ages* (London).

Christie, N. and A. Rushworth. 1988. 'Urban Fortification and Defensive Strategy in Fifth and Sixth Century Italy: The Case of Terracina', *JRA*, 1, 73–88.

Chrysos, Evangelos K. 1989. 'Legal Concepts and Patterns for the Barbarians' Settlement on Roman Soil', in Evangelos K. Chrysos and Andreas Schwarcz (eds.), *Das Reich und die Barbaren*. Veröffentlichungen des Instituts für Österreichische Geschichtsforschung, 29 (Vienna and Cologne), 13–24.

Clover, F. M. 2003. 'Timekeeping and Dyarchy in Vandal Africa', *Antiquité Tardive*, 11, 45–63.

Clover, F. M. 1999. 'A Game of Bluff: The Fate of Sicily After AD 476', *Historia*, 48.2, 235–44.

Clover, F. M. 1991. 'Relations between North Africa and Italy AD 476–500: Some Numismatic Evidence', *Revue Numismatique*, 33 (1991), 112–33.

Clover, F. M. 1989a. 'The Symbiosis of Romans and Vandals in Africa', in E. Chrysos and A. Schwarcz (eds.), *Das Reich und die Barbaren, Veröffentlichungen des Instituts für Österreichische Geschichtsforschung* (Vienna), 57–73; repr. in F. M. Clover *The Late Roman West and the Vandals* (Aldershot, 1992).

Clover, F. M. 1989b. 'Felix Karthago', in F. M. Clover and R. S. Humphreys (eds.), *Tradition and Innovation in Late Antiquity* (Madison, WI), 129–69; also in *Dumbarton Oaks Papers*, 40 (1986), 1–16; repr. in F. M. Clover, *The Late Roman West and the Vandals* (Aldershot, 1992).

Clover, F. M. 1982. 'Emperor Worship in Vandal Africa', in G. Wirth, K.-H. Schwarte and J. Heinrichs (eds.), *Romanitas-Christianitas: Untersuchungen zur geschichte und Literatur der römishen Kaiserzeit* (Berlin), 663–74; repr. in F. M. Clover, *The Late Roman West and the Vandals* (Aldershot, 1992).

Clover, F. M. 1978. 'The Family and Early Career of Anicius Olybrius', *Historia*, 27 (1978), 169–76.

Clover, F. M. 1971. *Flavius Merobaudes. A Translation and Historical Commentary*, Transactions of the American Philosophical Society, n.s. 61 (Philadelphia, PA).

Clover, F. M. 1967. 'Geiseric and Statesman: A Study of Vandal Foreign Policy', unpubl. PhD. thesis, University of Chicago.

Coates-Stephens, R. 2006. 'Byzantine Building Patronage in Post-Reconquest Rome', in C. Goddard, et al. (eds.), *Les cités de l'Italie tardo-antique (IVeme–VIeme siècle): institutions, économie, société, culture et religion* (Paris).

Conant, Jonathan P. 2004a. 'Staying Roman: Vandals, Moors and Byzantines in Late Antique North Africa, 400–700', unpubl. Ph.D. thesis, Harvard University.

Conant, Jonathan P. 2004b. Literacy and Private Documentation in Vandal North Africa: The Case of the Albertini Tablets', in A. H. Merrills (ed.), *Vandals, Romans and Berbers: New Perspectives on Late Antique North Africa* (London), 199–224.

Cooper, Kate. 1996. *The Virgin and the Bride. Idealized Womanhood in Late Antiquity* (Cambridge, MA).

Costanza, Salvatore. 1980. 'Vittore di Vita e la *Historia persecutionis Africanae provinciae*', Veterum Christianorum, 17, 230–68.

Courcelle, Pierre. 1948. *Histoire Littéraire des Grandes Invasions Germaniques* (Paris).

Courtney, E. 1980. 'Observations on the Latin Anthology', *Hermathena*, 129, 41–2.

Courtois, C. 1955. *Les Vandales et L'Afrique* (Paris).

Courtois, C. 1954. *Victor de Vita et son oeuvre. Étude Critique* (Algiers).

Courtois, C., L. Leschi, C. Perrat and C. Saumagne (eds.). 1952. *Tablettes Albertini: actes privés de l'epoque vandale* (*fin du Ve siècle*), 2 vols. (Paris).

Croke, Brian (tr.). 1995. *The Chronicle of Marcellinus* (Sydney).

Croke, Brian. 1983. 'The Context and Date of Priscus Fragment 6', *Classical Philology*, 78, 297–308.

Croke, Brian. 1977. 'Evidence for the Hun Invasion of Thrace in AD 442', *Greek, Roman and Byzantine Studies*, 18, 347–67.

Croke, B. and J. Crow. 1983. 'Procopius and Dara', *JRS* 73, 143–59.

Curta, Florin. 2007. 'Some Remarks on Ethnicity in Medieval Archaeology', *Early Medieval Europe*, 15.2 (2007), 159–85.

Curta, Florin. 1997. 'Slavs in Fredegar and Paul the Deacon: Medieval *gens* or "Scourge of God"?', *Early Medieval Europe*, 6, 141–67.

Deloum, S. 1990. 'L'économie monétaire de l'Afrique du Nord: les trésors monétaires des V et VIe siècles ap. J.C.', *L'Africa Romana*, 7, 961–72.

Demougeot, E. 1979. *La formation de l'Europe et les invasions barbares* (Paris, 1979), Vol. 2.2.

Deneauve, J. 1990. 'Le centre monumental de Carthage', in *Carthage et son territoire. Histoire et archéologie de l'Afrique du Nord. IVe Collque* (Paris).

Deneauve, J. and F. Villedieu. 1977. 'Le Cardo Maximus et les edifices situés à l'est de la voie', *Ant. af.*, 11, 95–130.

Deneauve, J. and F. Villedieu. 1979. 'Le Cardo Maximus et les edifices situés à l'est de la voie', in Serge Lancel (ed.), *BYRSA I: Rapports preliminaries des fouilles* (Rome), 143–76.

Desanges, J. 1995. 'Une mention des *Abaritani* dans Arnobe?', in *L'Afrique, la Gaule, la Religion à l'époque romaine. Mélanges à la mémoire de Marcel Leglay* (Brussels), 95–9.

Desanges, J. 1984. 'Abaritana ou Avaritana provincia', *Encyclopédie berbère*, 1 (Aix), 57–9.

Desanges, J. 1963. 'Un témoignage peu connu de Procope sur la Numidie vandale et byzantine', *Byzantion*, 33 (1963), 41–69.

De Vos, Mariette (ed.). 2001. *Rus Africum. Terra acqua olio nell'Africa settentrionale Scavo e ricognizione nei dintorni di Dougga (Alto Tell tunisino)*, Labirinti, 50 (Trent).

De Vos, Mariette. 1997. 'Gli Antichi insediamenti rurali nei dintorni di Dougga e il riciclaggio delle epigrafi', in M. Khanoussi and L. Maurin (eds.), *Dougga (Thugga) étude epigraphiques* (Paris).

Devréesse, R. 1940. 'L'église d'Afrique durant l'occupation byzantine', *MEFRA*, 57, 147–66.

Díaz, Pablo C. and Luís R. Menéndez-Bueyes. 2005. 'The Cantabrian Basin in the Fourth and Fifth Centuries: From Imperial Province to Periphery', in Kim Bowes and Michael Kulikowski (eds.), *Hispania in Late Antiquity. Current Perspectives* (Leiden), 265–97.

Diehl, C. 1896. *L'Afrique byzantine: histoire de la domination byzantine en Afrique (533–709)* (Paris).

Diesner, Hans-Joachim. 1968. 'Zum vandalischen Post- und Verkehrswesen', *Philologus*, 112:3/4, 282–7.

Diesner, Hans-Joachim. 1966. *Das Vandalenreich. Aufstieg und Untergang* (Stuttgart).

Dietz, S. L., Ladjimi Sebaï and H. Ben Hassen (eds.). 1995. *Africa Proconsularis. Regional Studies in the Segermes Valley of Northern Tunesia.* 2 vols. (Copenhagen).

Dolenz, H. 2001. *Damous-el-Karita: Die österreichisch-tunesischen Ausgrabungen der Jahre 1996 und 1997 im Saalbau und der Memoria des Pilgerheiligtumes Damous-el-Karita in Karthago* (Vienna).

Donecker, Stefan and Roland Steinacher. 2006. 'Rex Vandalorum – The Debates on Wends and Vandals in Swedish Humanism as an Indicator for Early Modern Patterns of Ethnic Perception', in Robert Nedoma (ed.), *Der Norden im Ausland – das Ausland im Norden. Formung und Transformation von Konzepten und Bildern des Anderen vom Mittelalter bis heute,* Wiener Studien zur Skandinavistik 15 (Vienna), 242–52.

Dossey, L. 2003. 'The Last Days of Vandal Africa. An Arian Commentary on Job and its Historical Context', *JTS*, n.s. 54.1, 60–138.

Downey. G. 1950. 'Justinian as Builder', *ARTB*, 3, 262–6.

Downey. G. 1947. 'The Composition of Procopius' *De Aedificiis'*, *TAPA*, 78, 171–83.

Drinkwater, J. F. 2007. *The Alamanni and Rome 213–496. Caracalla to Clovis* (Oxford).

Drinkwater, J. F. 1998. 'The Usurpers Constantine III (407–411) and Jovinus (411–413)', *Britannia*, 29, 269–98.

Duncan-Jones, R. 1990. *Structure and Scale in the Roman Economy* (Cambridge).

Durliat, J. 1988. 'Le salaire de la paix sociale dans les royaumes barbares', in Herwig Wolfram and Andreas Schwarcz (eds.), *Anerkennung und Integration. Zu den wirtschaftlichen Grundlagen der Völkerwanderungszeit 400–600,*

Veröffentlichungen der Kommission für Frühmittelalterforschung, 11 (Vienna), 21–72.

Durliat, J. 1981a. 'Les grands propriétaires africains et l'état byzantin', *Cahiers de Tunisie*, 29, 517–31.

Durliat, J. 1981b. *Les édifices de Justinien au témoignage de Procope et de l'épigraphie*, Ecole Française de Rome Collection de l'Ecole Française de Rome, 49 (Rome).

Duval, N. 2003. 'Les dates régnales des Vandales et les structures du Royaume Vandale', *Antiquité Tardive*, 11, 85–96.

Duval, N. 2002. 'Deux mythes de l'iconographie de l'antiquité tardive: la villa fortifée et la "chasseur vandale"; le "chasseur barbare" de Borj Jedid et sa "villa" ', in *Humana Sapit: mélanges offerts à L. Cracco Rugginni*, Bibliothèque de l'Antiquité tardive, 3 (Turnhout), 333–40.

Duval, N. 1997. 'L'état actuel des recherches archéologiques sur Carthage chrétienne (Etudes d'archéologie chrétienne nord-africaine, 25)', *Antiquité Tardive*, 5, 309–50.

Duval, N. 1984. 'Culte monarchique dans l'Afrique vandale: culte des rois ou culte des empereurs?', *Revue des études Augustiniennes*, 30, 269–73.

Duval, N. 1976. *La mosïque funéraire dans l'art palaeochrétien* (Ravenna).

Duval, N. 1975. *Les inscriptions chrétiennes. Recherches archéologiques à Haïdra I* (Rome).

Duval, N. 1972. 'Etudes d'architecture chretienne Nord-Africaine', *MEFRA*, 84, 1071–2.

Duval, N. 1971. *Les Basiliques de Sbeitla a deux sanctuaires opposes (Basiliques I, II et IV)* (Paris).

Duval, Y. 1981. *Loca sanctorum Africae: le culte des martyrs en Afrique du IVe au VII siècle*. 2 vols. (Rome).

Dyson, Stephen L. and Robert J. Rowland Jr. 2007. *Archaeology and History in Sardinia from the Stone Age to the Middle Ages. Shepherds, Sailors and Conquerors* (Philadelphia, PA).

Easterling, P. and R. Miles. 1999. 'Dramatic Identities: Tragedy in Late Antiquity', in R. Miles (ed.), *Constructing Identities in Late Antiquity* (London), 95–111.

Edelman, Nathan. *Attitudes of Seventeenth-Century France toward the Middle Ages* (New York, 1946).

Ellis, Linda. 1996. 'Dacians, Sarmatians and Goths on the Romano-Carpathian Frontier: Second-Fourth Centuries', in Ralph W. Mathisen and Hagith S. Sivan (eds.), *Shifting Frontiers in Late Antiquity* (Aldershot), 105–25.

Emberling, Geoff. 1997. 'Ethnicity in Comparative Societies: Comparative Perspectives', *Journal of Archaeological Research*, 5.4, 295–344.

Ennabli, L. 2000. *La basilique de Carthagenna et le locus des sept moines de Gafsa. Nouveaux édifices chrétiens de Carthage* (Paris).

Ennabli, L. 1997. *Carthage: une métropole Chrétienne* (Paris).

Eno, R. B. 1997. *Fulgentius. Selected Works*. FC, 95 (Washington, DC).

Eno, R. B. 1989. 'Christian Reaction to the Barbarian Invasions and the Sermons of Quodvultdeus', in David G. Hunter (ed.), *Preaching in the Patristic Age. Studies in Honour of Walter J. Burghardt* (New York), 139–61.

Evans, J. A. S. 1996. *The Age of Justinian: The Circumstances of Imperial Power* (London).

Fasoli, Gina. 1982. 'Le città siciliane tra Vandali, Goti e Bizantini', *Felix Ravenna*, 119, 95–110.

Feissel, D. 2000. 'Les édifices de Justinien au témoignage de Procope et de l'épigraphie', *Antiquité Tardive*, 8, 81–104.

Fentress, Elizabeth, Sergio Fontana, R. Bruce Hitchner and Philip Perkins. 2004. 'Accounting for ARS Fineware and Sites in Sicily and Africa', in Susan E. Alcock and John F. Cherry (eds.), *Side-by-Side Survey. Comparative Regional Studies in the Mediterranean World* (Oxford), 147–62.

Fentress, Elizabeth and Philip Perkins. 1988. 'Counting African Red Slip Ware', *L'Africa Romana*, 5, 205–14.

Ferguson, T. S. 1999. *Visita Nos. Reception, Rhetoric, and Prayer in a North African Monastery* (New York).

Fernández-Ochoa, Carmen and Ángel Morillo. 2005. 'Walls in the Urban Landscape of Late Roman Spain: Defense and Imperial Strategy', in Kim Bowes and Michael Kulikowski (eds.), *Hispania in Late Antiquity. Current Perspectives* (Leiden), 299–340.

Février, P.-A. 1989–90. *Approches du Maghreb Romain*, 2 vols. (Aix-en-Provence).

Folliet, Georges. 1988. 'Fulgence de Ruspe. Temoin privilégié de l'influence d'Augustin en Sardaigne', *L'Africa Romana*, 6, 561–9.

Francovich Onesti, Nicoletta. 2002. *I Vandali. Ligua e Storia* (Rome).

Freeman, E. A. 1904. *Western Europe in the Fifth Century* (London).

Frend, W. H. C. 1952. *The Donatist Church* (Oxford).

Fulford, M. 1990. 'Carthage: Overseas Trade and the Political Economy', *Reading Medieval Studies*, 6, 68–80.

Gaggero, G. 1994. 'Gli Alani nel Nord Africa', *L'Africa Romana*, 11, 1637–42.

García Moreno, Luis A. 1982. 'La invasión del 409 en España: nuevas perspectivas desde el punto de vista germano', in A. del Castillo (ed.), *Ejército y Sociedad* (Léon), 63–86.

Gautier, E.-F. 1929. *Genséric Roi des Vandales* (Paris).

Gautier, E.-F. 1927. *Les siècles obscurs du Maghreb: L'islamisation de l'Afrique du Nord* (Paris).

Geary, Patrick. J. 2002. *The Myth of Nations. The Medieval Origins of Europe* (Princeton, NJ).

Geary, Patrick J. 1988. *Before France and Germany. The Creation and Transformation of the Merovingian World* (New York).

Geary, Patrick. J. 1983. 'Ethnic Identity as a Situational Construct in the Early Middle Ages', *Mitteilungen der anthropologischen Gesellschaft in Wien*, 113, 15–26.

Gehl, P. 2002. 'Latin orthopraxes', in C. Lanham (ed.), *Latin Grammar and Rhetoric. From Classical Theory to Medieval Practice* (London), 1–21.

Gelichi, S. and M. Milanese. 1997. 'Uchi Maius: la cittadella e il Foro. Rapporto Preliminare sulla campagna di scavo 1995', in M. Khanoussi and A. Mastino (eds.), *Uchi Maius 1, Scavi e ricerche epigrafiche in Tunisia* (Sassari), 49–82.

Gelichi, S. and M. Milanese. 1998. 'Problems in the Transition Towards the Medieval in the Ifriqya: First Results from the Archaeological Excavations at Uchi Maius (Teboursouk, Beja)', *L'Africa Romana*, 12, 457–86.

Gethner, Perry. 2002. *Femmes dramaturges en France (1650–1750). Pièces choisies. Tome II*. Biblio 17. Band 136 (Tübingen).

Ghalia, Taher. 2008a. 'Christian Funerary Mosaics in Africa', in Jean-Jacques Aillagon (ed.), *Rome and the Barbarians: The Birth of a New World* (Venice), 328–30.

Ghalia, Taher. 2008b. 'The Grave Goods of Thuburbo Maius', in Jean-Jacques Aillagon (ed.), *Rome and the Barbarians: The Birth of a New World* (Venice), 334–6.

Gil Egea, María Elvira. 1998. *África en tiempos de los vándalos: continuidad y mutaciones de las estructuras sociopolíticas romanas*, Universidad de Alcalá, Servicio de Publicaciones (Alcalá de Henares).

Gil Egea, María Elvira. 1997. 'Piratas o estadistas: La política exterior del reino vándalo durante el reinado de Genserico', *Polis*, 9, 107–29.

Gillett, A. 2006. 'Ethnogenesis: A Contested Model of Early Medieval Europe', *History Compass 4/2*, 241–60.

Gillett, A. 2003. *Envoys and Political Communication in the Late Antique West, 411–533* (Cambridge).

Gillett, A. (ed.). 2002a. *On Barbarian Identity. Critical Approaches to Ethnicity in the Early Middle Ages* (Leiden).

Gillett, A. 2002b. 'Was Ethnicity Politicized in the Earliest Medieval Kingdoms?', in Andrew Gillett (ed.), *On Barbarian Identity. Critical Approaches to Ethnicity in the Early Middle Ages* (Leiden), 85–121.

Giunta, Francesco. 1958. *Genserico e la Sicilia* (Palermo).

Gleason, Maud W. 1999. Elite Male Identity in the Roman Empire', in D. S. Potter and D. J. Mattingly (eds.), *Life, Death and Entertainment in the Roman Empire* (Ann Arbor, MI), 67–84.

Godłowski, K. 1992. 'Die Przeworsk-Kultur', in Günter Neumann and Henning Seemann (eds.), *Beiträge zun Verständnis der Germania des Tacitus II*, Abhandlungen der Akademie der Wissenschaften in Göttingen, Philologisch-Historische Klasse, 3 (Göttingen), 9–90.

Goffart, W. 2006. *Barbarian Tides. The Migration Age and the Later Roman Empire* (Philadelphia, PA).

Goffart, W. 2002. 'Does the Distant Past Impinge in the Invasion Age Germans?', in Andrew Gillett (ed.), *On Barbarian Identity: Critical Approaches to Ethnicity in the Early Middle Ages* (Leiden), 21–37.

Goffart, W. 1988. *The Narrators of Barbarian History* (Princeton).

Goffart, W. 1980. *Barbarians and Romans* AD *418–584. The Techniques of Accommodation* (Princeton, NJ).

González-Salinero, Raúl. 2002. *Poder y conflicto religioso en el norte de Africa: Quodvultdeus de Cartago y los Vándalos* (Madrid).

González-Salinero, Raúl. 2001. 'La invasión vándala en los Sermones de Quodvultdeus de Cartago', *Florenta Iliberritana*, 12, 221–37.

Greatrex, G. 1997. 'The Nika Riot: A Reappraisal', *JHS*, 117, 60–86.

Greene, J. A. 1992. 'Une reconnaissance archéologique dans l'arrière – pays de la Carthage antique', in *Pour Sauver Carthage* (Tunis), 195–7.

Greene, J. A. 1983. 'Carthage Survey', in D. T. Keller and D. W. Rupp (eds.), *Archaeological Survey in the Mediterranean Area*, BAR Int. Ser. 115 (Oxford), 197–9.

Grierson, Philip. 1959. 'The Tablettes Albertini and the Value of the Solidus in the Fifth and Sixth Centuries AD', *JRS*, 49, 73–80.

Grierson, Philip and Mark Blackburn. 1986. *Medieval European Coinage I. The Early Middle Ages (5th–10th centuries)* (Cambridge).

Grig, L. 2004. *Making Martyrs in Late Antiquity* (London).

Gros, P. 1992. 'Colline de Byrsa: les vestiges romains', in A. Ennabli (ed.), *Pour sauver Carthage. Exploration et conservation de la cité punique, romain et byzantine* (Paris), 99–104.

Gsell, S. 1929. *Histoire ancienne de l'Afrique du Nord*, 1–5 (Paris).

Guéry, R. 1981. 'L'occupation de Rougga (Bararus) d'après la stratigraphie du forum', in *BCTH*, 17B, 91–100.

Guéry, R., C. Morrisson and H. Slim. 1982. *Rougga III. Le trésor de monnais d'or byzantine* (Rome).

Haasen, John H. *Famous Men of the Middle Ages* (New York, 1904).

Hald, Kristian. 1942. 'Angles and Vandals', *Classica et Mediaevalia*, 4, 62–78.

Hallier, G. 1995. 'Le Monument circulaire du plateau de l'Odéon à Carthage', *Ant. af.*, 201–30.

Halsall, Guy. 2007. *Barbarian Migrations and the Roman West 376–568* (Cambridge).

Halsall, Guy. 2005. 'The Barbarian Invasions', in Paul Fouracre (ed.), *The New Cambridge Medieval History, I. c.500–c.700* (Cambridge), 35–55.

Hamilton, Louis. 2004. 'Possidius' Augustine and Post-Augustinian Africa', *JECS*, 12:1, 85–105.

Handley, Mark A. 2003. *Death, Society and Culture. Inscriptions and Epitaphs in Gaul and Spain,* AD *300–750*, BAR Int. Ser., 1135 (Oxford).

Handley, Mark A. forthcoming. *Dying on Foreign Shores.*

Hayes, John W. 1998. 'The Study of Roman Pottery in the Mediterranean: 23 Years After *Late Roman Pottery*', in L. Saguí (ed.), *Ceramica in Italia: VI–VII secolo. Atti del Convegno in onore di John W. Hayes. Roma 11–13 maggio 1995* (Biblioteca di Archeologia Medievale, 14) (Florence), 9–21.

Hayes, John W. 1980. *Supplement to Late Roman Pottery* (London).

Hayes, John W. 1972. *Late Roman Pottery* (London).

Hays, Gregory. 2004. '*Romuleis Libicisque Litteris*: Fulgentius and the 'Vandal Renaissance', in A. H. Merrills (ed.), *Vandals, Romans and Berbers: New Perspectives on Late Antique North Africa* (London), 101–32.

Hays, Gregory. 2003. 'The Date and Identity of the Mythographer Fulgentius', *Journal of Medieval Latin*, 13, 163–252.

Hays, Gregory. 2002. 'Tales out of School: Grammatical Culture in Fulgentius the Mythographer', in C. Lanham (ed.), *Latin Grammar and Rhetoric. From Classical Theory to Medieval Practice* (London), 22–47.

Heather, Peter. 2007. 'Christianity and the Vandals in the Reign of Geiseric', in John Drinkwater and Benet Salway (eds.), *Wolf Liebeschuetz Reflected.* Bulletin of the Institute of Classical Studies, Supplement 91 (London), 137–46.

Heather, Peter. 1998. 'Disappearing and Reappearing Tribes', in Walter Pohl and Helmut Reimitz (eds.), *Strategies of Distinction. The Construction of Ethnic Communities, 300–800* (Leiden), 95–111.

Heather, Peter. 1997. '*Foedera* and *foederati* of the Fourth Century', in Walter Pohl (ed.), *Kingdoms of the Empire: The Integration of the Barbarians in Late Antiquity* (Leiden), 57–74.

Heather, Peter. 1991. *Goths and Romans. 332–489* (Oxford).

Heather, Peter and John Matthews. 1991. *The Goths in the Fourth Century* (Liverpool).

Helbling, Hanno. 1954. *Goten und Wandalen, Wandlung der historischen Realität* (Zurich).

Hen, Yitzhak. 2007. *Roman Barbarians, The Royal Court and Culture in the Early Medieval West* (London).

Hendy, Michael F. 1995. 'Coinage and Exchange', in Antonio Carile (ed.), *Teoderico e i Goti tra Oriente e Occidente* (Ravenna), 151–8.

Hendy, Michael F. 1985. *Studies in the Byzantine Monetary Economy c.300–1450* (Cambridge).

Hitchner, R. Bruce. 1995. 'Historical Texts and Archaeological Context in Roman North Africa: The Albertini Tablets and the Kasserine Survey', in D. B. Small (ed.), *Methods in the Mediterranean: Historical and Archaeological Views on Texts and Archaeology*, Mnemosyne Suppl., 135 (Leiden), 124–42.

Hitchner, R. Bruce. 1990. 'The Kasserine Archaeological Survey 1987', *Ant. af.*, 26, 231–60.

Hitchner, R. Bruce. 1988a. 'The Kasserine Archaeological Survey 1982–1986', *Ant. af.*, 24, 7–41.

Hitchner, R. Bruce. 1988b. 'The Organization of Rural Settlement in the Cillium-Thelepte region (Kasserine, Central Tunisia)', *L'Africa Romana*, 6, 387–402.

Holt, Elizabeth Gilmore. 1957. *A Documentary History of Art* (Princeton).

Honoré, A. 1978. *Tribonian* (London).

Hopkins, Keith. 1980. 'Taxes and Trade in the Roman Empire (200 BC–AD 400)', *JRS*, 70, 101–25.

Horden, Peregrine and Purcell, Nicholas. 2000. *The Corrupting Sea. A Study of Mediterranean History* (Oxford).

Humphrey, J. H. 1988. *The Circus and a Byzantine Cemetery at Carthage* (Ann Arbor, MI).

Humphrey, J. H. 1980. 'Vandal and Byzantine Carthage: Some New Archaeological Evidence', in J. Pedley (ed.), *New Light on Ancient Carthage* (Ann Arbor, MI), 85–120.

Hurst, H. R. (ed.). 1994. *Excavations at Carthage. The British Mission. Volume II.1. The Circular Harbour, North Side. The Site and Finds Other Than Pottery*, British Academy Monographs in Archaeology, 4 (Oxford).

Hurst, H. R. 1979. 'Excavations at Carthage, 1977–1978, Fourth Interim Report', *Antiquaries Journal*, 59, 19–49.

Innes, Matthew. 2006. 'Land, Freedom and the Making of the Medieval West', *TRHS*, 16, 39–76.

Irmscher, J. 1977. 'Justinian als Bauherr in der sicht der Literatur seine Epoche', *Klio*, 59, 225–9.

Isola, Antonino. 1994–5. 'A proposito dell'*inscitia* dei Vandali secondo Fulg., *ad Tras.* 1,2,2.', *Romanobarbarica*, 13, 57–74.

Isola, Antonino. 1990. *I cristiani dell'Africa vandalica nei sermones del tempo (429–534)*, Edizioni universitarie Jaca, Storia 74 (Milan).

Istvánovits, Eszter and Valéria Kulcsár. 2005. 'Gritty Pots. A Characteristic Type of Roman Provincial Import and Barbarian Pottery on the Barbarian Settlements of the Great Hungarian Plain', *Limes. XIX Roman Frontier Studies* (Pecs), 987–97.

Jahn, M. 1940. 'Die Wandalen', in H. Reinerth (ed.), *Vorgeschichte der deutschen Stamme*, III (Leipzig), 943–1032.

Johannesson, Kurt. 1991. *The Renaissance of the Goths in Sixteenth-Century Sweden: Johannes and Olaus Magnus as Politicians and Historians* (Berkeley, CA).

Johnson, Alan Chester, Paul Robinson Coleman-Norton and Frank Card Bourne. 1961. *Ancient Roman Statutes*, Corpus Juris Romani, 2 (Austin, TX).

Jones, A. H. M. 1964. *The Later Roman Empire 284–602*, 2 vols. (Oxford).

Jones, Sîan. 1997. *The Archaeology of Ethnicity. Constructing Identities in the Past and Present* (London).

Kaegi, Walter. 1965. 'Arianism and the Byzantine Army in Africa 533–546,' *Traditio*, 21, 23–53.

Kalli, Maria K. 2004. *The Manuscript Tradition of Procopius' Gothic Wars, A Reconstruction of Family in the Light of a Hitherto Unknown Manuscript (Athos, Laura H-73)*, Beiträge zur Altertumskunde, 205 (Leipzig).

Kaster, R. A. 1988. *Guardians of the Language: The Grammarian and Society in Late Antiquity* (Berkeley, CA).

Kay, N. M. 2006. *Epigrams of the Anthologia Latina. Text, Translation and Commentary* (London).

Keay, S. 1998. 'African Amphorae', in L. Saguí (ed.), *La ceramica in Italia: VI–VII Secolo. Atti del covegno in onore di John Hayes Rome 1995* (Florence), 141–55.

Keay, S. 1984. *Late Roman Amphorae in the Western Mediterranean. A Typology and Economic Study: The Catalan Evidence,* BAR Int. Ser. 196, 2 vols. (Oxford).

Kehoe, D. P. 1988. *The Economics of Agriculture on Roman Imperial Estates in North Africa* (Gottingen).

Kehoe, D. P. 1984. 'Private and Imperial Management of Roman Estates in North Africa', *Law and History Review*, 2.2, 241–63.

Kleeman, Jörg, 2002. 'Quelques réflexions sur l'interprétation ethnique des sépultures habillées considérées comme Vandales', *Antiquité Tardive*, 10, 123–9.

Knowles, David. 1963. *Great Historical Enterprises. Problems in Monastic History* (London).

Koenig, G. G. 1981. 'Wandalische Grabfunde des 5. und 6. Jahrhunderts', *Madrider Mitteilungen des Deutschen Archäologischen Instituts*, 22, 299–360.

Kolb, Anne. 2001. 'Transport and Communication in the Roman State: The *cursus publicus*', in Colin Adams and Ray Laurence (eds.), *Travel and Geography in the Roman Empire* (London), 95–105.

Kossinna, Gustaf. 1929. 'Die Wandalen in Nordjütland', *Mannus*, 21, 233–55.

Krautheimer, R. and S. Ćurčić. 1986. *Early Christian and Byzantine Architecture* (New Haven, CT).

Krueger, D. 2005. 'Christian Piety and Practice in the Sixth Century', in M. Maas (ed.), *The Cambridge Companion to the Age of Justinian* (Cambridge), 291–315.

Kulikowski, Michael. 2007. *Rome's Gothic Wars* (Cambridge).

Kulikowski, Michael. 2004. *Late Roman Spain and its Cities* (Baltimore, MD).

Kulikowski, Michael. 2002. 'The Visigothic Settlement in Aquitania: The Imperial Perspective', in Ralph Mathisen and Danuta Shanzer (eds.), *Society and Culture in Late Antique Gaul: Revisiting the Sources* (Aldershot), 26–38.

Kulikowski, Michael. 2000. 'Barbarians in Gaul, Usurpers in Britain', *Britannia*, 31, 325–45.

Kulikowski, Michael and Kim Bowes (eds.). 2005. *Hispania in Late Antiquity. Current Perspectives.* The Medieval and Early Modern Iberian World, 24 (Leiden).

Laaksonen, H. 1990. 'L'educazione a la trasformazione della cultura nel regno dei Vandali', *L'Africa Romana*, 7.1, 357–61.

Ladstätter, S. and A. Pülz. 2007. 'Ephesus in the Late Roman and Early Byzantine Period: Changes in the Urban Character from the Third to the Seventh Century AD, in A. G. Poulter (ed.), *The Transition to Late Antiquity on the Danube and Beyond* (London), 391–434.

Lafaurie, J. 1960. 'Trésor de monnaies de cuivre trouvé à Sidi-Aïch (Tunisie)', *RN*, 6, 113–30.

Lagona, Sebastiana. 1982. 'La Sicilia Tard-Antica e Bizantina', *Felix Ravenna*, 119, 111–30.

Lancel, Serge. 2002. Victor de Vita *Histoire de la Persécution vandale in Afrique* (Paris).

Lancel, Serge. 1999. *Saint Augustin* (Paris).

Lancel, Serge. 1988. 'Victor de Vita et la Carthage vandale', *L'Africa Romana*, 6, 649–61.

Langslow, D. R. 2000. *Medical Latin in the Roman Empire* (Oxford).

Laroui, A. 1970. *L'histoire du Maghreb, un essai de synthèse* (Paris).

Lascaratos, John and S. Marketos. 1992. 'The Penalty of Blinding During Byzantine Times', *Documenta Ophthalmologica*, 81, 133–44.

Le Gall, Joël. 1936. 'L'itinéraire de Genséric', *Revue de philologie*, ser 3.10, 268–73.

Leone, Anna. 2007. *Changing Townscapes in North Africa from Late Antiquity to the Arab Conquest* (Bari).

Leone, Anna. 2003. 'Topographies of Production in North African Cities During the Vandal and Byzantine Periods', in L. Lavan and W. Bowden (eds.), *Theory and Practice in Late Antique Archaeology* (Leiden), 257–87.

Leone, Anna. 2002. 'Le sepolture nello spazio urbano a Cartagine tra V e VII secolo d.C', *Antiquité Tardive*, 10, 233–48.

Leone, Anna and David Mattingly. 2004. 'Vandal, Byzantine and Arab Rural Landscapes in North Africa', in Neil Christie (ed.), *Landscapes of Change. Rural Evolutions in Late Antiquity and the Early Middle Ages* (Aldershot), 135–62.

Lepelley, Claude. 2006. 'La cité africaine tardive', in J. Krause, C. Witschel (eds.), *Die Stadt in der Spätantike – Niedergang oder Wandel? Akten des internationalen Kolloquiums in München am 30. und 31. Mai 2003*, Historia Einzelschriften Bd. 190 (Stuttgart), 13–31.

Lepelley, Claude. 2004. 'The Perception of Late Roman Africa. From Decolonization to the Re-Appraisal of Late Antiquity', in Carole Straw and Richard Lim (eds.), *The Past Before Us. The Challenge of Historiographies of Late Antiquity*, Bibliothèque de l'Antiquité Tardive, 6 (Turnhout), 25–32.

Lepelley, Claude. 2002. 'L'Afrique à la veille de la conquête Vandale', *Antiquité Tardive*, 10, 61–72.

Lepelley, Claude. 2001. *Aspects de l'Afrique romaine. Les cites, la vie rurale, le Christianisme* (Bari).

Lepelley, Claude. 1992. 'The Survival and Fall of the Classical City in Late Roman Africa', in J. Rich (ed.), *The City in Late Antiquity* (London), 50–76.

Lepelley, Claude. 1979–81. *Les cités de l'Afrique romaine au Bas-Empire*, 2 vols. (Paris).

Letizia, P. E. 1985. 'La Sardegna e l'Africa nel perido vandalico', *L'Africa Romana*, 2, 105–22.

Lézine, A. 1968. *Carthage-Utique, Études d'architecture et d'urbanisme* (Paris).

Lézine, A. 1956. 'Observations sur la ruine des Thermes d'Antonin à Carthage', *CRAI*, 425–30.

Liebeschuetz, J. H. W. G. 2003. '*Gens* into *Regnum*: The Vandals', in H.-W. Goetz, J. Jarnut and W. Pohl (eds.), with S. Kaschke, *Regna and Gentes. The Relationship Between Late Antique and Early Medieval Peoples and Kingdoms in the Transformation of the Roman World* (Leiden), 55–83.

Liebeschuetz, J. H. W. G. 2001. *Decline and Fall of the Roman City* (Oxford).

Lindsay, Jack. 1948. *Song of a Falling World* (London).

Livermore, Harold. 1996. 'Honorio y la restauración de las Hispanias', *Boletín de la Real Academia de la Historia*, 193, 443–501.

Livermore, Shaw. 1968. *Early American Land Companies. Their Influence on Corporate Development* (New York).

Loewenberg, Alfred. 1978. *Annals of Opera 1597–1940* (London).

Longfellow, Henry Wadsworth. 1875. *Masque of Pandora and Other Poems. Birds of Passage, Flight the Fourth* (Boston).

Loseby, S. T. 2005. 'The Mediterranean Economy', in Paul Fouracre (ed.), *The New Cambridge Medieval History. Vol. I, c.500–c.700* (Cambridge), 605–38.

Luiselli, Bruno. 1992. *Storia Culturale dei Rapporti tra Mondo Romano e Mondo Germanico* (Rome).

Lulliri, Giuseppe and Maria Bonaria Urban. 1996. *Le Monete della Sardegna Vandalica. Storia e Numismatica* (Rome).

Maas, M. 2003. *Exegesis and Empire in the Early Byzantine Mediterranean. Junillus Africanus and the Instituta Regularia Divinae Legis*, Studien und Texte zu Antike und Christentum, 17 (Tubingen).

Maas, M. 1992. *John Lydus and the Roman Past: Antiquarianism and Politics in the Age of Justinian* (London).

MacEvitt, Christopher. 2007. *The Crusades and the Christian World of the East. Rough Tolerance* (Philadelphia, PA).

Mackensen, M. 1998a. 'Centres of African Red Slip Ware in Tunisia from the Late 5th to the 7th Century AD, in L. Saguí (ed.), *La ceramica in Italia: VI–VII Secolo. Atti del covegno in onore di John Hayes Rome 1995* (Florence), 23–39.

Mackensen, M. 1998b. 'New Evidence for Central Tunisian Red Slip Ware with Stamped Decoration (ARS Style D)', *JRA*, 11, 355–70.

Mackensen, M. 1993. *Die spätantiken Sigillata- und Lampentöpfereien von El Mahrine (Nordtunesien): Studien zur nordafrikanischen Feinkeramik des 4. bis 7. Jahrhunderts* (Munich).

Mackensen, M. 1985. 'Prospektion einer spätantiken Sigillatatöpferei in El Mahrine/Nordtunisien', *CEDAC*, 6, 29–39.

Mackensen, Michael and Gerwulf Schneider. 2002. 'Production Centres of African Red Slip Ware (3rd–7th c.) in Northern and Central Tunisia', *JRA*, 15, 121–58.

MacMullen, Ramsay. 1965. *Soldier and Civilian in the Later Roman Empire* (Cambridge, MA).

Malaspina, Elena. 1994–5. 'L'idrovora di Unirico. Un epigramma (A.L. 387 R. = 382 Sh.B). e il suo contesto storico-culturale', *Romanobarbarica*, 13, 43–56.

Manacorda, D. 1977. 'Anfore', *Studi Miscellani*, 23, 117–254.

Mandouze, A. 1982. *Prosopographie chrétienne du bas-empire*, Vol. 1, *Prosopographie de l'Afrique chrétienne (303–533)* (Paris).

Mapwar, F. B. 1994. 'La resistance de l'Église catholique a la foi arienne en Afrique du Nord: une exemple d'une église locale inculturée?', in B. Luiselli et al. (eds.), *Cristianesimo e specificatà regionali nel Mediterraneo latino (sec IV–VI)*, Studia Ephemeridis Augustianum 46 (Rome), 189–213.

Markey, Thomas L. 1989. 'Germanic in the Mediterranean: Lombards, Vandals and Visigoths', in Frank M. Clover and R. S. Humphreys (eds.), *Tradition and Innovation in Late Antiquity* (Madison, WI), 51–71.

Markus, R. A. 1991. 'The Problem of "Donatism" in the Sixth Century', in *Gregorio Magno e il suo tempo* (Rome, 1991), 159–66; repr in his *Sacred and Secular: Studies on Augustine and Latin Christianity* (Aldershot, 1994).

Markus, R. A. 1990. *The End of Ancient Christianity* (Cambridge).

Markus, R. A. 1983. *From Augustine to Gregory the Great. History and Christianity in Late Antiquity* (London).

Markús, Gábor. 2003. 'The Vandals', in Zsolt Visy (ed.), *Hungarian Archaeology at the Turn of the Millennium* (Budapest), 271.

Marrou, H.-I. 1971. *Histoire de l'éducation dans l'antiquité*, 7th edn. (Paris).

Marsden, Jean I. 2007. *Fatal Desire: Women, Sexuality, and the English Stage, 1660–1720* (Ithaca).

Martens, Jens. 1989. 'The Vandals: Myth and Facts about a Germanic Tribe of the First Half of the 1st Millennium AD', in Stephen Shennan (ed.), *Archaeological Approaches to Cultural Identity* (London), 57–65.

Martroye, F. 1907. *Genséric. La Conquéte Vandale en Afrique et la Destruction de l'Empire d'Occident* (Paris).

Massigli, R. 1912. 'Primat de Carthage et métropolitaine de Byzacène: un conflit dans l'église aftricaine au Vie siècle', *Mélanges R. Cagnat* (Paris), 427–40.

Mastino, Attilio (ed.). 2005. *Storia della Sardegna antica* (Cagliari).

Matei, Alexandru V. and Ioan Stanciu. 2000. *Vestigii din epoca Romană (sec. II–IV P. Chr.) În Spaţiul Nord-vestic al României*, Bibliotheca Musei Porolissensis, II (Zalău, Cluj-Napoca).

Mathisen, R. W. 1997. 'Barbarian Bishops and the Churches "*in Barbaricis Gentibus*" during Late Antiquity', *Speculum*, 72, 664–95.

Mathisen, R. W. 1999. 'Sigisvult the Patrician, Maximinus the Arian and political strategems in the Western Roman Empire c.425–40', *EME*, 8, 173–96.

Matthews, John F. 1993. 'The Making of the Text', in Jill Harries and Ian Wood (eds.), *The Theodosian Code. Studies in the Imperial Law of Late Antiquity* (London), 19–44.

Matthews, John F. 1975. *Western Aristocracies and Imperial Court. AD 364–425* (Oxford).

Mattingly, D. J. 1997. *Dialogues in Roman Imperialism: Power, Discourse and Discrepant Experience in the Roman Empire* (Ann Arbor).

Mattingly, D. J. 1996. 'From One Colonialism to Another: Imperialism and the Maghreb', in J. Webster and N. J. Cooper (eds.), *Roman Imperialism: Post-Colonial Perspectives*, Leicester Archaeology Monographs, 3 (Leicester), 49–69.

Mattingly, David J. 1990. 'Appendix I: Olive Presses and Olive Production', *Ant. af.*, 26, 248–55.

Mattingly, D. J. 1989. 'Olive Cultivation and the Albertini Tablets', *L'Africa Romana*, 6, 403–15.

Mattingly, D. J. 1988. 'Oil for Export? A Comparison of Libyan, Spanish and Tunisian Olive Oil Production in the Roman Empire', *JRA*, 1, 33–56.

Mattingly, D. J. and R. B. Hitchner. 1995. 'Roman Africa: An Archaeological Review', *JRS*, 85, 165–213.

Max, G. C. 1982. 'The Emperor Majorian's Secret Embassy to the Court of the Vandal Genseric', *Byzantine Studies*, 9, 57–63.

McCormick, Michael. 2001. *The Origins of the European Economy. Communication and Commerce, AD 300–900* (Cambridge).

McCormick, Michael. 2000. 'Emperor and Court', in A. Cameron, B. Ward-Perkins and M. Whitby (eds.), *The Cambridge Ancient History, XIV. Late Antiquity: Empire and Successors, AD 425–600* (Cambridge), 135–63.

McCormick, Michael. 1998. 'Bateaux de vie, bateaux de mort: maladie, commerce, transports annonaires et le passage économique du Bas-Empire au moyen age', in *Morfologie Sociali e Culturali in Europa fra Tarda Antichità e Alto Medioevo*, SettSpol, 45 (Spoleto), 35–122.

McCormick, Michael. 1986. *Eternal Victory. Triumphal Rulership in Late Antiquity, Byzantium and the Early Medieval West* (Cambridge).

McLynn, Neil. 2005. 'Genere Hispanus: Theodosius, Spain and Nicene Orthodoxy', in Kim Bowes and Michael Kulikowski (eds.), *Hispania in Late Antiquity. Current Perspectives* (Leiden), 77–120.

Meloni, P. 1988. 'La vita monastica in Africa e in Sardinia nel VI secolo sulle orme di S. Agostino', *L'Africa Romana*, 6, 571–81.

Merlin, A. 1912. 'Découvertes à Thuburbo Majus', *CRAI*, 262–80.

Merrills, A. H. 2006. 'Comparative Histories: The Vandals, the Sueves and Isidore of Seville', in Richard Corradini, Rob Meens, Christina Pössel and Philip Shaw (eds.), *Texts and Identities in the Early Middle Ages*, Forschungen zur Geschichte des Mittelalters, 12, 35–46.

Merrills, A. H. 2005. *History and Geography in Late Antiquity* (Cambridge).

Merrills, A. H. 2004a. 'Vandals, Romans and Berbers: Understanding Late Antique North Africa', in A. H. Merrills (ed.), *Vandals, Romans and Berbers: New Perspectives on Late Antique North Africa* (London), 3–28.

Merrills, A. H. 2004b. 'The Perils of Panegyric: The Lost Poem of Dracontius and its Consequences', in A. H. Merrills (ed.), *Vandals, Romans and Berbers: New Perspectives on Late Antique North Africa* (London), 145–62.

Merrills, A. H. forthcoming a. 'The Origins of Vandalism' in *International Journal of the Classical Tradition.*

Merrills, A. H. forthcoming b. 'The Secret of My Succession: Dynasty and Crisis in Vandal Africa' in *Early Medieval Europe.*

Michel, Pierre. 1988. *Les Barbares, 1789–1848: un mythe romantique* (Paris).

Miles, R. (ed.). forthcoming. *Excavations at Bir Messaouda, Carthage: The Late Antique and Byzantine Structures* (Ghent).

Miles, R. 2006. 'British Excavations at Bir Messaouda: The Byzantine Basilica', *Babesch-Bulletin Antieke Beschaving*, 81, 199–226.

Miles, R. 2005. 'The Anthologia Latina and the Creation of Secular Space in Vandal North Africa', *Antiquité Tardive*, 13, 305–20.

Miles, R. (ed.). 1999. *Constructing Identities in Late Antiquity* (London).

Millar, Fergus. 1969. 'P, Herennius Dexippus', *JRS*, 59, 12–29.

Millar, Fergus. 1964. *A Study of Cassius Dio* (Oxford).

Mócsy, András. 1974. *Pannonia and Upper Moesia. A History of the Middle Danube Provinces of the Roman Empire*. The Provinces of the Roman Empire (London).

Modéran, Y. 2008. '"Le plus délicat des peoples et le plus malheureux". Vandales et Maures en Afrique', in Guido M. Berndt and Roland Steinacher (eds.), *Das Reich der Vandalen und seine (Vor-) Geschichten*, Österreichische Akademie der Wissenschaften, Forschungen zur Geschichte des Mittelalters, 13 (Vienna), 213–25.

Modéran, Y. 2006. 'La *Notitia provinciarum et civitatum Africae* et l'histoire de l'Afrique vandale', *Antiquité Tardive*, 14, 165–85.

Modéran, Y. 2003a. *Les Maures et l'Afrique Romaine (IVe–VIe siècle)*. Bibliothèque des Écoles françaises d'Athènes et de Rome, 314 (Rome).

Modéran, Y. 2003b. 'Une guerre de religion: les deux Églises d'Afrique à l'époque vandale', *Antiquité Tardive*, 11, 21–44.

Modéran, Y. 2002. 'L'établissement territorial des Vandales en Afrique', *Antiquité Tardive*, 10, 87–122.

Modéran, Y. 1999. 'Les frontières mouvants du royaume vandale', in C. Lepelley and X. Dupuis (eds.), *Frontières et limites géographiques de l'Afrique du Nord antique. Hommage à Pierre Salama* (Paris), 252–6.

Modéran, Y. 1998. 'L'Afrique et la persécution vandale', in L. Pietri (ed.), *Nouvelle Histoire du Christianisme, des origines à nos jours. III Les Églises d'Orient et d'Occident* (Paris), 247–78.

Modéran, Yves. 1996. 'La renaissance des cités dans l'Afrique du VIe siècle d'après une inscription récemment publiée', in *La fin de la cité antique et les débuts de la cité médiévale. Etudes réunies par Claude Lepelley* (Bari), 85–114.

Montserrat, Dominic. 2000. 'Reading Gender in the Roman World', in Janet Huskinson (ed.), *Experiencing Rome. Culture, Identity and Power in the Roman Empire* (London), 153–82.

Moorhead, John. 1992. *Theoderic in Italy* (Oxford).

Morazzani, André. 1966. 'Essai sur la puissance maritimes des Vandales', *Bulletin de l'association Guillaume Budé*, Supplément, Lettres d'Humanité. 25. 4 ser. 4, 539–61.

Morizot, P. 1991. 'Economie et société en Numidie méridionale: l'example de l'Aurès', in A. Mastino (ed.), *L'Africa Romana*, 8, 429–46.

Morizot, P. 1979. 'Vues nouvelles sur l'Aurès antique', *CRAI*, 309–37.

Morrisson, Cécile. 2003. 'L'atelier de Carthage et la diffusion de la monnaie frappée dans l'Afrique vandale et Byzantine (439–695)', *Antiquité Tardive*, 11, 65–84.

Morrisson, Cécile. 1987. 'La circulation de la monnai d'or en Afrique à l'époque vandale. Bilan des trouvailles locales', *Mélanges de Numismatique offerts à Pierre Bastien* (Wetwren), 325–34.

Morrisson, Cécile. 1983. 'The Re-use of Obsolete Coins: The Case of Roman Imperial Bronzes Revived in the Late Fifth Century', in C. N. L. Brooke, B. H. I. H. Stewart, J. G. Pollard and T. R. Volk (eds.), *Studies in Numismatic Method Presented to Philip Grierson* (Cambridge), 95–111.

Morrisson, Cécile. 1976. 'Les origines du monnayage vandale', *Actes du 8e Congrés International de Numismatique, New York–Washington 1973* (Paris), 461–72.

Morrisson, C. and J. Schwartz. 1982. 'Vandal Silver Coinage in the Name of Honorius', *ANSMN*, 27, 149–79.

Mostecky, H. 1989. 'Note sur les monnaies de cuivre frappé en Afrique du Nord après l'invasion vandale', *Bulletin de la Société Française de Numismatique*, 2, 517–18.

Moussy, Claude. 1988. *Dracontius Oeuvres, II,* Budé (Paris).

Moussy, Claude and Colette Camus (ed. and tr.). 1985. *Dracontius, De Laudibus Dei*, Budé (Paris), 2 vols.

Muhlberger, S. 1990. *The Fifth-Century Chroniclers. Prosper, Hydatius, and the Gallic Chronicler of 452* (Leeds).

Nordmann, Viktor Anton. 1934. *Die Wandalia des Albert Krantz*, Suomalaisen Tiedeakamian Toimituksia/Annales Academiae Scientiarum Fennicae, 29 (Helsinki).

O'Flynn, John Michael. 1991. 'A Greek on the Roman Throne: The Fate of Anthemius', *Historia*, 40, 122–8.

O'Flynn, John Michael. 1983. *Generalissimos of the Western Roman Empire* (Edmonton).

Oltean, Ioana, A. 2007. *Dacia. Landscape, Colonisation, Romanisation* (London).

Oost, Stewart Irvin. 1964. 'Aetius and Majorian', *CP*, 59.1, 23–9.

Ørsted, P. 1994. 'From Henchir Mettich to the Albertini Tablets. A Study in the Economic and Social Significance of the Roman Lease System (locatio conductio)', in J. Carlsen, P. Ørsted and J. E. Skydsgaard (eds.), *Landuse in the Roman Empire*, Analecta Romana Instituti Danici suppl., 22 (Rome), 115–25.

Overbeck, M. 1973. *Untersuchungen zum afrikanischen Senatsadel in der Spätantike*, Frankfurter althistorische Studien, 7 (Frankfurt).

Panella, C. 1993. 'Merci e scambi nel Mediterraneo tardantico', in A. Carandini, L. Cracco Ruggini and A. Giardina (eds.), *Storia di Roma III.2. L'età Tardoantica. I luoghi e le culture* (Turin), 613–702.

Panella, C. 1986. 'Le merci: produzioni, itinerari e destini', in A. Giardina (ed.), *Società romana e impero tardantico*, III (Bari), 431–59 and 843–5.

Papencordt, F. 1837. *Geschichte der vandalischen Herrschaft in Afrika* (Berlin).

Parvis, S. 2006. *Marcellus of Ancyra and the Lost Years of the Arian Controversy 325–345* (Oxford).

Paschoud, François. 1989. *Zosime. Histoire Nouvelle*, Budé (Paris).

Pastorino, A. 1980. 'Osservazione sulla *Historia persecutionis Africanae provinciae* di Vittore di Vita', in S. Calderone (ed.), *La Storiografia ecclesiastica nella tarda antichità* (Messina).

Peacock, D. P. S., F. Bejaoui and N. ben Lazreg 1990. 'Roman Pottery Production in Central Tunisia', *JRA*, 3, 59–84.

Peacock, D. P. S., F. Béjaoui and N. ben Lazreg. 1989. 'Roman Amphora Production in the Sahel Region of Tunisia', in *Amphores romaines et histoire économique: dix ans de recherché* (Rome), 179–222.

Peña, J. T. 1998. 'The Mobilization of State Olive Oil in Roman North Africa: The Evidence of Late 4th-c. Ostraca from Carthage', in J. T. Peña and J. J. Rossiter (eds.), *Carthage Papers* (Portsmouth, RI), 117–238.

Pergola, P. 2000. 'La christianisation du monde rural dans la Corse vandale et byzantine', *L'Africa Romana*, 12.2, 811–26.

Pergola, P. 1988. 'Economia e religione nella Sardegna vandala: nuovi dati da scavi e studi recenti', *L'Africa Romana*, 6, 553–9.

Pergola, P. 1981. 'Vandales et Lombards en Corse: sources historiques et archéologiques', *La Cultura in Italia fra Tardo Antico e Alto Medioevo*. Atti del Convegno tenuto a Roma, Consiglio Nazionale delle Ricerche, dal 12 al 16 Novembre 1979 (Rome), II. 913–17.

Pergola, Philippe and Cinzia Vismara. 1989. *Castellu (Haute Corse). Un établissement rural de l'Antiquité tardive: fouille récentes (1981–1985)*. Documents d'archéologie française, 18 (Paris).

Pingel, Volker. 2006. 'Celtic German Archaeology', in *Brill New Pauly. Classical Tradition I* (Leiden), 735–40.

Placanica, A. 1997. *Vittore da Tunnuna. Chronica. Chiesa e Impero nell'età di Giustiniano* (Florence).

Pocock, J. G. A. 2007. *Barbarism and Religion. Vol. 4. Barbarians, Savages and Empires* (Cambridge).

Pohl, Walter. 2004. 'The Vandals: Fragments of a Narrative', in A. H. Merrills (ed.), *Vandals, Romans and Berbers: New Perspectives on Late Antique North Africa* (London), 31–48.

Pohl, Walter. 2002. 'Ethnicity, Theory and Tradition: A Response', in Gillett (2002), 221–39.

Pohl, Walter. 1991. 'Concepts of Ethnicity in Early Medieval Studies', *Archaeologia Polonia*, 29, 39–49.

Pohl, W. and H. Reimitz (eds.). 1998. *Strategies of Distinction. The Construction of Ethnic Communities 300–800* (Leiden).

Poinssot, L. 1921. 'Tombeau d'Arifridos', *BCTH*, 57–8.

Potter, T. W. 1995. *Towns in Late Antiquity: Iol Caesarea and its Context* (Sheffield).

Prévot, F., P. Blaudeau, J.-L. Voisin and L. Najar. 2006. *L'Afrique Romaine, 69–439* (Neuilly).

Pringle, D. 1981. *The Defence of Byzantine Africa from Justinian to the Arab Conquest*, BAR Int. Ser. 99, 2 vols. (Oxford).

Pryor, John H. and Elizabeth M. Jeffreys. 2006. *The Age of the ΔΡΟΜΩΝ The Byzantine Navy ca. 500–1204*, The Medieval Mediterranean, Peoples, Economies and Cultures. 400–1500 (Leiden).

Raby, F. J. E. 1957. *A History of Secular Latin Poetry* (Oxford).

Rakob, E. 1991. 'Die römischen Bauperioden', in J. Holst, T. Kraus, M. Mackensen, F. Rakob, K. Rheidt, O. Teschauer, M. Vegas, I. Wiblé and A. Wolff (eds.), *Karthago I: Die Deutschen Ausgrabungen in Karthago* (Mainz), 242–51.

Raven, S. 1993. *Rome in Africa*, 3rd edn (London).

Reece, Richard. 1984. 'Coins', in H. R. Hurst and S. P. Roskams (eds.), *Excavations at Carthage: The British Mission.* Vol. I, 1, *The Avenue du President Habib Bourguiba, Salammbo. The Site and the Finds other than Pottery* (Sheffield), 171–81.

Renwick, John. 1974. *Marmontel, Voltaire, and the Bélisaire affair* (Banbury).

Reynolds, J. 2000. 'Byzantine Buildings, Justinian and Procopius in *Libya Inferior* and *Libya Superior*', *Antiquité Tardive*, 8, 169–76.

Reynolds, L. D. (ed.). 1983. *Texts and Transmission. A Survey of the Latin Classics* (Oxford).

Reynolds, Paul. 1995. *Trade in the Western Mediterranean.* AD *400–700. The Ceramic Evidence,* BAR Int. Ser. 604 (Oxford).

Rich, John. (ed.). 1992. *The City in Late Antiquity* (London).

Riché, P. 1976. *Education and Culture in the Barbarian West. Sixth through Eighth Centuries*, tr. J. J. Contreni (Columbia, SC).

Riley, John A. 1980. 'New Light on Relations between the Eastern Mediterranean and Carthage in the Vandal and Byzantine Periods: The Evidence from the University of Michigan Excavations', *Actes Colloque sur la Ceramique Antique Carthage 1* (Carthage), 111–22.

Rives, J. 1999. *Tacitus: Germania* (Oxford).

Roberts, Michael. 1992. 'Barbarians in Gaul: The Response of the Poets', in John Drinkwater and Hugh Elton (eds.), *Fifth-Century Gaul: A Crisis of Identity?* (Cambridge), 97–106.

Roncoroni, A. 1977. 'Sulla morte di re Unerico', *RomanoBarbarica*, 2, 247–57.

Rosenblum, M. 1961. *Luxorius: A Latin Poet Among the Vandals* (New York and London).

Roskams, S. 1996. 'Urban Transition in North Africa: Roman and Medieval Towns of the Maghreb', in S. T. Loseby and N. Christie (eds.), *Towns in*

Transition. Urban Evolution in Late Antiquity and the Early Middle Ages (Aldershot), 159–83.

Ruggini, Lellia Cracco. 1980. 'La Sicilia e la fine del mondo antico (IV – VI secolo)', in Emilo Gabba and Georges Vallet (eds.), *La Sicilia antica. II.2. La Sicilia Romana* (Naples), 483–524.

Ruggini, Lellia Cracco. 1961. *Economia e Società nell' 'Italia Annonaria'. Rapporti fra Agricoltura e commercio dal IV al VI secolo d.C.* (Milan).

Sakolski, A. M. 1932. *The Great American Land Bubble* (New York).

Salama, P. 1985. 'Economie monétaire de l'Afrique du Nord dans l'Antiquité Tardive', in *Histoire et Archéologie de l'Afrique du Nord. II Colloque International* (Grenoble), 183–202.

Salway, Peter. 1981. *Roman Britain* (Oxford).

Sarris, Peter. 2005. 'On Jairus Banaji Agrarian Change in Late Antiquity', *Historical Materialism* 13.1, 207–19.

Saumagne, C. 1913. 'Etude sur la propiété ecclésiastique à Carthage d'après novelles 36 et 37 de Justinien', *BZ*, 22, 77–87.

Sax, Joseph, L. 1990. 'Heritage Preservation as a Public Duty: The Abbé Grégoire and the Origins of an Idea', *Michigan Law Review*, 88.5, 1142–69.

Schmidt, L. 1953. *Histoire des Vandales* (tr. H. E. Del Medico) (Paris), orig. pub. as *Geschichte der Wandalen* (Leipzig, 1901, rev. Munich, 1942).

Schubert, O. 1875. *Quaestionum de Anthologia Codicis Salmasiani, Pars I, de Luxurio* (Weimar).

Schulze, Herman. 1859. *De Testamento Genserici. Seu de antiquissima lege successoria in Germanorum regnis* (Jena).

Schwarcz, Andreas. 2004. 'The Settlement of the Vandals in North Africa', in A. H. Merrills (ed.), *Vandals, Romans and Berbers: New Perspectives on Late Antique North Africa* (London), 49–58.

Schwarcz, Andreas. 1994. 'Bedeutung und Textüberlieferung der "*Historia persecutionis Africanae provinciae*" des Victor von Vita', in A. Scharer and G. Scheibelreiter (eds.), *Historiographie im frühen Mittelalter* (Vienna), 115–40.

Senay, P. 1992. 'Le Monument Circulaire', in *Pour Sauver Carthage* (Tunis), 105–13.

Senay, P. 1980. 'Carthage IV', *Cahiers des études anciennes*, 12, 1–220.

Shanzer, Danuta. 2004. 'Intentions and Audiences: History, Hagiography, Martyrdom and Confession in Victor of Vita's *Historia Persecutionis*', in A. H. Merrills (ed.), *Vandals, Romans and Berbers: New Perspectives on Late Antique North Africa* (London), 271–90.

Shanzer, Danuta. 1986. *A Philosophical and Literary Commentary on Martianus Capella's De nuptiis Philologiae et Mercurii, Book 1* (Berkeley, CA).

Shaw, B. D. 2005. *At the Edge of the Corrupting Sea*, The twenty-third J. L Myres Memorial Lecture (Oxford).

Shaw, B. D. 2004. 'Who Were the Circumcellions?', in A. H. Merrills (ed.), *Vandals, Romans and Berbers: New Perspectives on Late Antique North Africa* (London), 227–58.

Shaw, B. D. 1992. 'African Christianity: Disputes, Definitions and "Donatists"', in M. R. Greenshields and T. A. Robinson (eds.), *Orthodoxy and Heresy in Religious Movements: Discipline and Dissent* (Lampeter), 5–34; repr. in his *Rulers, Nomads and Christians in Roman North Africa* (Aldershot, 1995).

Sirks, B. 1991. *Food for Rome* (Amsterdam).

Sklenár, Karel. 1983. *Archaeology in Central Europe. The First 500 Years* (New York).

Slim. H, P. Trousset, R. Paskoff and A. Oueslati. 2004. *Le littoral de la Tunisie: Étude géoarchéologique et historique*, Études d'Antiquités africaines (Paris).

Smith, Rowland. 2007. 'The Imperial Court of the Late Roman Empire c. AD 300–c. AD 450', in A. J. S. Spawforth (ed.), *The Court and Court Society in Ancient Monarchies* (Cambridge), 157–232.

Sotinel, Claire. 2005. 'Emperors and Popes in the Sixth Century, The Western View', in M. Maas (ed.), *The Cambridge Companion to the Age of Justinian* (Cambridge), 267–290.

Spaul, John. 1997. 'Across the Frontier in Tingitania', in *Roman Frontier Studies 1995. Proceedings of the XVIth International Congress of Roman Frontier Studies* (Oxford), 253–8.

Stein, Ernst. 1959. *Histoire du Bas-Empire. Tome Premier. De l'État Romain à l'État Byzantine (284–476)*, tr. Jean-Remy Palanque (Paris).

Steinacher, Roland. 2008. 'Gruppen und Identitäten. Gedanken zur Bezeichnung "vandalisch" ', in Guido M. Berndt and Roland Steinacher (eds.), *Das Reich der Vandalen und seine (Vor-) Geschichten*, Österreichische Akademie der Wissenschaften. Forschungen zur Geschichte des Mittelalters, 13 (Vienna), 243–60.

Steinacher, Roland. 2006. 'Rex oder Räuberhauptmann. Ethnische und politische Identität im 5. und 6. Jahrhundert am Beispiel von Vandalen und Herulern', in Beate Burtscher-Bechter, Peter. W. Haider, Birgit Mertz-Baumgartner and Robert Rollinger (eds.), *Grenzen und Entgrenzungen. Der mediterrane Raum,* Saarbrücker Beiträge zur Vergleichenden Literatur- und Kulturwissenschaft (Würzburg), 309–30.

Steinacher, Roland. 2004. 'The So-Called *Laterculus Regum Vandalorum et Alanorum*: A Sixth-Century African Addition to Prosper Tiro's Chronicle?', in A. H. Merrills (ed.), *Vandals, Romans and Berbers: New Perspectives on Late Antique North Africa* (London), 163–80.

Steinacher, Roland and Stefan Donecker. (forthcoming). 'Der König der Schweden, Goten und Vandalen. Identität und Geschichtsbilder des 16.–18. Jahrhunderts', in Walter Pohl and Helmut Reimitz (eds.), *Vergangenheit und Vergegenwärtigung*, Forschungen zur Geschichte des Mittelalters (Vienna).

Stevens, C. E. 1957. 'Marcus, Gratian, Constantine', *Athenaeum*, 35, 316–47.

Stevens, S. T., A. V. Kalinowski, and Hans, van der Leest (eds.). 2005. *Bir Ftouha. A Pilgrimage Church Complex at Carthage*, JRA Suppl. 59 (Providence, RI).

Stevens, S. T. 2000. 'Excavations of an Early Christian Pilgrimage Complex at Bir Ftouha (Carthage)', *Dumbarton Oaks Papers*, 54, 271–4.

Stevens, S. T. 1996. 'Transitional Neighborhoods and Suburban Frontiers in Late- and Post-Roman Carthage', in R. W. Mathisen and H. S. Sivan (eds.), *Shifting Frontiers in Late Antiquity* (Aldershot), 187–200.

Stevens, S. T. 1995a. 'Sépultures tardives intra-muros', in *Monuments Funéraires. institutions autochtones. Actes du VIe Colloque International sur l'histoire el l'archéologie de l'Afrique du Nord* (Paris), 207–17.

Stevens, S. T. 1995b. 'A Late-Roman Urban Population in a Cemetery of Vandalic Date at Carthage', *Journal of Roman Archaeology*, 8, 263–70.

Stevens, S. T. 1993. 'Bir el Knissia at Carthage: A Rediscovered Cemetery Church. Report No. 1', *Journal of Roman Archaeology*, Suppl. Ser. 7 (Ann Arbor, MI)

Stevens, S. T. 1988. 'The Circus Poems in the Latin Anthology', in J. H. Humphrey (ed.), *The Circus and a Byzantine Cemetery at Carthage* (Ann Arbor, MI), Vol. 1, 153–78.

Stevens, S. T. 1982. 'The Circle of Bishop Fulgentius', *Traditio*, 38, 327–41.

Stone, D. L., D. J. Mattingly and N. ben Lazreg (eds.). (forthcoming). *Leptiminus (Lamta): A Roman Port City in Tunisia. Report 3, the Field Survey* (Ann Arbor, MI).

Thébert, Y. 2003. *Thermes romains d'Afrique du Nord et leur contexte Mediterraneen: etudes d'histoire et d'archeologie, École française de Rome* (Rome).

Theiss, Richard. 1938. *Geiserich. Der Beherricher des mittelländischen Meeres* (Leipzig).

Tilley, Maureen. 1997. *The Bible in Christian North Africa. The Donatist World* (Minneapolis, MN).

Tortorella, S. 1998. 'La sigillata Africana in Italia nel VIe nel VII secolo d.C: problemi di cronologia e di distribuzione', in L. Saguí (ed.), *La ceramica in Italia: VI–VII Secolo. Atti del covegno in onore di John Hayes Rome 1995* (Florence), 23–69.

Turcan, R. 1961. 'Trésors monétaires à Tipasa: la circulation de bronze en Afrique romaine et vandale aux Ve et VIe siècles ap. J.-C.', *Libyca: Archéologie-Epigraphie*, 9, 201–57.

Uggeri, Stella Patitucci. 1996. 'Relazioni tra Nord Africa e Sicilia in età vandalica', *L'Africa Romana*, 12, 1457–67.

Uggeri, Stella Patitucci. 1993. 'La Politica Navale di Teoderico', in *Teoderico il Grande e i Goti d'Italia. Atti del XIII Congresso internazionale di studi sull'Alto Medioevo. Milano 2–6 novembre 1992* (Spoleto), II: 771–86.

Vaday, Andrea. 2003. 'Settlements', in Zsolt Visy (ed.), *Hungarian Archaeology at the Turn of the Millennium* (Budapest), 275–8.

Vaday, Andrea. 1996. 'Roman Period Barbarian Settlement at the Site of Gyoma 133', in A. Vaday et al., *Cultural and Landscape Changes in South-East Hungary II. Prehistoric, Roman Period Barbarian and Late Avar Settlement at Gyoma 133 (Békés County Microregion)*, Archaeolingua, 5 (Budapest), 51–305.

Vaday, Andrea H., Eszter Istvánovits and Valéria Kulcsár. 1989. 'Sarmatian Costume in the Carpathian Basin', *Klio*, 71, 107–14.

Van Dam, Raymond. 1986. '"Sheep in Wolves' Clothing": The Letters of Consentius to Augustine', *Journal of Ecclesiastical History*, 37, 515–35.

Van Slyke, Daniel. 2005. 'The Devil and His Pomps in Fifth-Century Carthage: Renouncing Spectacula with Spectacular Imagery', *Dumbarton Oaks Papers*, 59, 53–72.

Van Slyke, Daniel. 2003. *Quodvultdeus of Carthage, The Apocalyptic Theology of a Roman African in Exile*, Early Christian Studies 5 (Strathfield).

Vasiliev, A. A. 1950. *Justin the First. An Introduction to the Epoch of Justinian the Great* (Cambridge, MA).

Velkov, Velizar. 1977. *Cities in Thrace and Dacia in Late Antiquity (Studies and Materials)*, Publications of the Henri Frankfort Foundation, 3 (Amsterdam).

Vera, D. 1986. 'Forma e funzione della rendita fondiaria nella tarda Antichità', in A. Giardina (ed.), *Società romana e impero tardantico*, III (Bari), 347–67.

Villedieu, Françoise. 1986. 'Les relations commerciales entre l'Afrique et la Sardaigne du IIème au Vème siècle', *L'Africa Romana*, 3, 321–32.

Villedieu, Françoise. 1984. *Turris Libisonis. Fouille d'un site romain tardif à Porto Torres, Sardaigne*. BAR Int. Ser. 224 (Oxford).

Vismara, C. 1999. '*Aetas succedit aetati.* Il riuso di elementi classici nelle città africane fino all'età islamica', in B. M. Giannattasio (ed.), *Atti X Giornata di Archeologia. Il passato riproposto. Continuità e recupero dall'antichità ad oggi* (Genova), 69–85.

Vitrone, F. 1994–5. 'Aspetti controversi e dati economico-sociali nelle Tavolette Albertini', *RomanoBarbarica*, 13, 235–58.

Volpilhac, Catherine, Dany Hadjadj and Jean-Louis Jam. 1992. 'Des Vandales au vandalisme', in Simone Bernard-Griffiths, Marie-Claude Chemin and Jean Ehrard (eds.), *Révolution française et 'vandalisme révolutionnaire' Actes du colloque international de Clermont-Ferrand. 15–17 décembre 1988* (Paris), 15–27.

von Rummel, Philipp. 2008. 'Where Have all the Vandals Gone? Migration, Ansiedlung und Identität der Vandalen im Spiegel archäologischer Quellen aus Nordafrika', in Guido M. Berndt and Roland Steinacher (eds.), *Das Reich der Vandalen und seine (Vor-) Geschichten*, Österreichische Akademie der Wissenschaften, Forschungen zur Geschichte des Mittelalters, 13 (Vienna), 151–82.

von Rummel, Philipp. 2007. *Habitus Barbarus. Kleidung und Repräsentation spätantiker Eliten im 4 und 5 Jahrhundert* (Berlin and New York).

von Rummel, Philipp. 2005. 'Les Vandales ont-ils porté en Afrique un vêtement spécifique?', in Xavier Delestre, Patrick Périn and Michel Kazanski (eds.), *La Méditerranée et le monde mérovingien: témoins archéologiques. Actes des XXIIIs Journées internationals d'archéologie mérovingienne* (Arles), 281–91.

von Rummel, Philipp. 2003. 'Zum Stand der afrikanischen Vandalenforschung nach den Kolloquien in Tunis und Paris', *Antiquité Tardive*, 11, 13–19.

von Rummel, Philipp. 2002. 'Habitas Vandalorum? Zur frage nach einer gruppenspezifischen klerdung der Vandalen in Nordafrika', *Antiquité Tardive*, 10, 131–41.

Wanner, R. 2006. 'A Gazetteer for the Kasserine Archaeological Survey (Kasserine-Thelepte Region of Tunisia)', MA dissertation, Tufts University.

Ward-Perkins, B. 1984. *From Classical Antiquity to the Middle Ages: Public Building in Northern and Central Italy, AD 300–850* (Oxford).

Ward-Perkins, B. 2000. 'Specialized Production and Exchange', in A. Cameron, B. Ward-Perkins and M. Whitby (eds.), *Cambridge Ancient History XIV. Late Antiquity: Empire and Successors AD 425–600* (Cambridge), 346–71.

Watson, Alaric. 1999. *Aurelian and the Third Century* (London).

Webster, Jane. 2001. 'Creolizing the Roman Provinces', *JRA*, 105.2, 209–25.

Wells, C. 1992. 'Le mur de Théodose et le Secteur nord est de la ville romaine', *Pour Sauver Carthage* (Tunis), 115–23.

Wenskus, Reinhard. 1961. *Stammesbildung und Verfassung* (Cologne).

Whitbread, Leslie George. 1971. *Fulgentius the Mythographer* (Columbus, OH).

Whittaker, C. R. 1994. *Frontiers of the Roman Empire: A Social and Economic Study* (London).

Wickham, Chris. 2005. *Framing the Early Middle Ages* (Oxford).

Wickham, Chris. 1988. 'Marx, Sherlock Holmes and Late Roman Commerce', *JRS*, 78, 183–93.

Wickham, Chris. 1984. 'The Other Transition: From the Ancient World to Feudalism', *Past and Present*, 103, 3–36.

Wilkes, J. J. 2005. 'The Roman Danube: An Archaeological Survey', *JRS*, 95, 124–225.

Williams, R. 2001. *Arius: Heresy and Tradition* (London).

Wilson, A. I. 2006. 'Fishy Business: Roman Exploitation of Marine Resources', *JRA*, 19.2, 525–37.

Wilson, R. J. A. 2000. 'Rural Settlement in Hellenistic and Roman Sicily: Excavations at Campanaio (AG), 1994–8', *PBSR*, 68, 337–69.

Wilson, R. J. A. 1990. *Sicily under the Roman Empire. The Archaeology of a Roman Province, 36 BC – AD 535* (London).

Wolfram, Herwig. 1997. *The Roman Empire and its Germanic Peoples*, tr. T. Dunlap (Berkeley, CA).

Wolfram, Herwig. 1988. *History of the Goths* (Berkeley, CA).

Wood, Ian. 1977. 'Kings, Kingdoms and Consent', in P. H. Sawyer and Ian Wood (eds.), *Early Medieval Kingship* (Leeds), 6–29.

Woolf, Greg. 1998. *Becoming Roman. The Origins of Provincial Civilization in Gaul* (Cambridge).

Wynn, Phillip. 1997. 'Frigeridus, the British Tyrants and the Early Fifth Century Barbarian Invasions of Gaul and Spain', *Athenaeum: Studi di letteratura e storia dell'Antichità*, 85, 69–117.

Wynn, Phillip. 1990. 'Rufinus of Aquilea's Ecclesiastical History and Victor of Vita's History of the Vandal Persecution', *Classica et Medievalia*, 41, 187–98.

Zucca, Raimondo. 1998. *Insulae Baliares. Le isole Baleari sotto il dominio romano* (Rome).

Index

CPSIA information can be obtained
at www.ICGtesting.com
Printed in the USA
BVHW01s2317160218
508174BV00019B/136/P

9 781118 785096